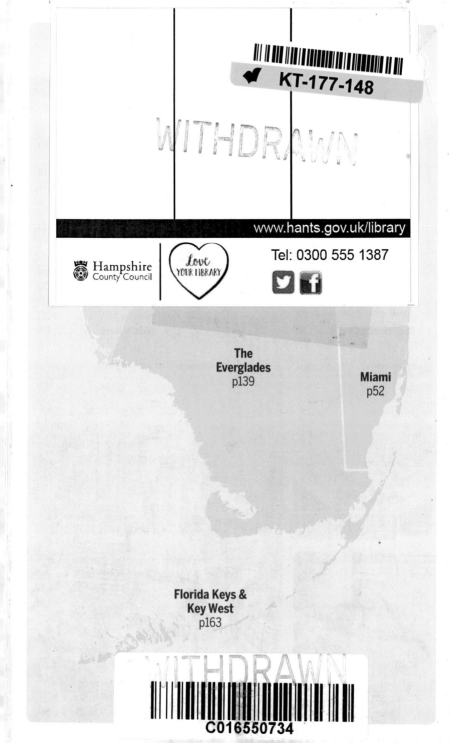

The
Everglades
p139

Miami
p52

Florida Keys &
Key West
p163

Contents

EAT & DRINK LIKE A LOCAL
P38

MUSIC P217

Contents

UNDERSTAND

SURVIVAL GUIDE

MIAMI BY NIGHT P53

HURRICANE IRMA

On September 10, 2017, one of the largest hurricanes ever recorded barrelled over the state of Florida, leaving flooding and destruction in its wake. Hurricane Irma made landfall in the Florida Keys as a category 4 storm the width of Texas, with wind speeds in excess of 130 mph. Nearly 7 million people across the state evacuated, there were widespread power outages and storm surges were seen as far north as Jacksonville. But the Florida Keys and the Everglades bore the brunt of the storm. Homes and businesses in the tiny town of Everglades City were left battered and mud-soaked after an 8-foot storm surge receded. Meanwhile, in the Keys, a FEMA survey reported that 25% of buildings had been destroyed, with another 65% damaged.

The research for this book was conducted before the storm hit and the content was sent to print soon afterward, when Irma's long-term effects were still unknown. In a state so heavily reliant on tourism, most cities were already announcing intentions to be ready for visitors soon. Still, those planning travel to Florida, especially the Florida Keys (www.fla-keys.com) or the Everglades region (www.nps.gov/ever), should check official websites for the latest information.

Welcome to Miami & the Keys

It's hard not to fall for South Florida, with its sun-kissed beaches, alluring islands and wildlife-rich wetlands.

The Magic City

South Florida is a land of dreams and Miami is known as the Magic City. Imagination and innovation are big here, manifesting in art, architecture and music. You'll see it in the extravagance of Lincoln Rd, the ephemeral neon beauty of Ocean Dr, the cloud-kissing skyline of downtown Miami and in the mid-century modern design on N Biscayne Blvd. From the pink castle walls of a Coral Gables mansion to sun-dappled marinas in Coconut Grove; from the Fabergé-egg interior of the Vizcaya Museum to cutting-edge art in Wynwood: stay in Miami long enough and you might believe magic is real.

Eat, Drink & Be Merry

In South Florida and the Keys, nothing succeeds like excess. People take indulgence to Roman Empire levels, from the music-video-like pools of Miami Beach's extravagant super hotels, to buckets of beer and fried shrimp in the Florida Keys, to expertly shaken cocktails mixed under a Little Havana moon. Even the skyscrapers are a testament to the region's push for size and extravagance. Fortunately, the best purveyors of food and fun are realizing the good times can't roll at overdrive forever, and are incorporating sustainable business practices.

Everglades Encounters

South Florida is full of natural beauty, especially the spectacular wetland ecosystem of the Everglades. A colorful cast of characters inhabits the fringes (and occasionally, the heart) of these swamps, marshes and rolling prairies. Alligator wrestlers and Bigfoot hunters share a beer at crab shacks, while panthers prowl the backyard, and environmentalists document the magic of this unique wilderness. The Everglades is nature at its most alluring; the ripple of bubbles as a gator submerges into the blackwater bayou, and the sword-billed fish dive of waterfowl hunting the sparkling sloughs.

The Keys to Quirk

America's eccentricities (and quite a few eccentrics) coalesce in the southeast corner that is South Florida. And the truly unconventional are found in the sun-dappled islands of the Florida Keys. This lovely island chain is connected by the Overseas Hwy – one of the nation's great road-trip byways. Here you'll find drag queens working day jobs as boat captains, 'No Name' islands inhabited by miniature deer, and colorful Key West: a tolerant pot of gold at the end of a rainbow flag. And all ensconced within the natural beauty of shimmering bays, serene tidal flats and emerald islands.

Why I Love Miami & the Keys

By Regis St Louis, Writer

South Florida has three world-class attractions – Miami, the Everglades and the Keys. I never tire of wandering the streets of Miami Beach, taking in deco masterpieces followed by late-afternoon strolls along the sands, when the golden light is mesmerizing. The Everglades provides that heady dose of nature, of quiet paddles over mirror-like lakes and night-time walks (on elevated boardwalks, of course) peering at gators gliding gracefully through the water. The Keys has a little of everything – peaceful mangroves for leisurely paddles, kaleidoscopic coral reefs and one zany conch capital (aka Key West) where anything goes.

For more about our writers, see p264

Above: Overseas Hwy to Key West (p166)

Miami & the Keys

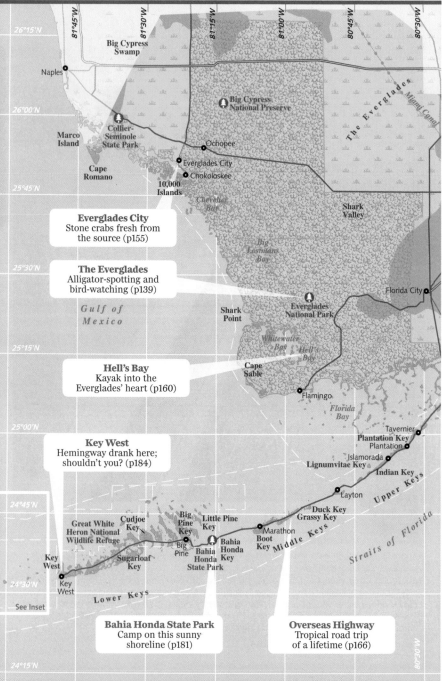

Everglades City
Stone crabs fresh from
the source (p155)

The Everglades
Alligator-spotting and
bird-watching (p139)

Hell's Bay
Kayak into the
Everglades' heart (p160)

Key West
Hemingway drank here;
shouldn't you? (p184)

Bahia Honda State Park
Camp on this sunny
shoreline (p181)

Overseas Highway
Tropical road trip
of a lifetime (p166)

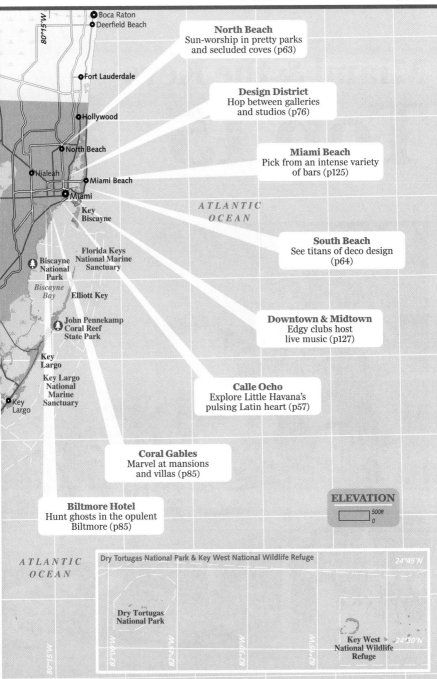

 0 ⎯⎯⎯⎯⎯⎯ 50 km
0 ⎯⎯⎯⎯⎯⎯ 30 miles

North Beach
Sun-worship in pretty parks
and secluded coves (p63)

Design District
Hop between galleries
and studios (p76)

Miami Beach
Pick from an intense variety
of bars (p125)

South Beach
See titans of deco design
(p64)

Downtown & Midtown
Edgy clubs host
live music (p127)

Calle Ocho
Explore Little Havana's
pulsing Latin heart (p57)

Coral Gables
Marvel at mansions
and villas (p85)

Biltmore Hotel
Hunt ghosts in the opulent
Biltmore (p85)

80°15'W

Boca Raton
Deerfield Beach

Fort Lauderdale

Hollywood

North Beach

Hialeah
Miami Beach

Miami

Key
Biscayne

*ATLANTIC
OCEAN*

Florida Keys
National Marine
Sanctuary

Biscayne
National
Park

*Biscayne
Bay*   Elliott Key

John Pennekamp
Coral Reef
State Park

Key
Largo

Key Largo
National
Marine
Sanctuary

Key
Largo

ELEVATION

500ft
0

*ATLANTIC
OCEAN*

Dry Tortugas National Park & Key West National Wildlife Refuge   24°45'N

Dry Tortugas
National Park

Key West
National Wildlife
Refuge   24°30'N

80°15'W   83°00'W   82°45'W   82°30'W   82°15'W

Miami & the Keys'
Top 15

Exploring Art Deco Beauties

1 Like all great cities, Miami and Miami Beach have a distinctive architectural style (p64). Actually, art deco isn't just distinctive in Miami. In places like South Beach, it's definitive. The style is an early 20th-century expression of aesthetic that embodies seemingly contradictory impulses – modernity with nostalgia for the beaux arts; streamlining coupled with fantastic embellishment; subdued colors and riots of pastel. Whatever your take on deco may be, you'll be hard-pressed to find a better concentration of it outside of Miami and Miami Beach. Below: Ocean Drive (p65), South Beach.

Alligator-Spotting in the Everglades

2 South Florida loves to embrace all the latest trends in fashion, cuisine and the arts. But look beneath the region's surface and you'll find a landscape populated by primeval inhabitants. Alligators, around since the time of the dinosaurs, are incredible survivors, having evolved into flawlessly engineered predators. You can see them all across the Everglades on boat trips, viewing platforms and boardwalk trails. One of the best places for prime gator viewing is along the Anhinga Trail (p159) at the Royal Palm Visitor Center.

LITTLENY/SHUTTERSTOCK ©

JUSTIN FOULKES/LONELY PLANET ©

MATT MUNRO/LONELY PLANET ©

ROBERTO MACHADO NOA/LIGHTROCKET VIA GETTY IMAGES ©

Partying in Key West

3 Key West is many things: counter-culture icon; southernmost tip of the continental USA; and sun-drenched haven for the gay community. But for all these things, it is also, like it or not, a floating bar. Thousands of folks come here annually to cut loose. Join 'em! Start with a sunset over Mallory Square (p184), watch a dog on a tightrope and fire-eaters, then embark on the infamous 'Duval Crawl' and get ready for the night of your life. Just don't plan much for the morning after.
Above: Mallory Square (p184)

Gallery Hopping in Wynwood & the Design District

4 Miami's hippest residents pop into South Beach clubs occasionally, but for years the loci of cool-kid activity has been Wynwood and the neighboring Design District (p76). Many buildings in these former working-class 'hoods have been transformed into galleries, studios, art warehouses and sometimes all three. Every month these art outposts open their doors on a night of art openings – a showcase for rising stars in the art world. Wine flows as the crowd hops from gallery to gallery.
Above: The Wynwood Building

Driving & Cycling the Overseas Highway

5 The Florida Keys are linked by Hwy 1, also known as the Overseas Hwy. Heading over the road's many bridges and pulling over intermittently to admire the Gulf of Mexico or Florida Bay is simply one of the great pleasures of Florida travel. If you don't feel like driving, you can cycle much of the 113-mile route; most of the way is flat, shoulder lanes are established throughout, and more than 75 miles of the Florida Keys Overseas Heritage Trail (p175) are there for cyclists to enjoy.

Feasting on Seafood

6 All across the region, you'll have the opportunity to dine on some of the best ingredients plucked straight from the ocean. For seafood lovers, the range of offerings is truly astounding. You can slurp fresh-shucked oysters at a Miami bar, chow down on conch fritters in Key West and gorge on fish sandwiches from one end of the Keys to the other. There are also delectable stone crabs available in season (mid-October to mid-May). Get them fresh from the source at old-fashioned waterfront eateries (p155) in Everglades City.

Indulging in Miami Nightlife

7 If you think Miami is all velvet ropes and phony people, you have this city all wrong. Nightlife here is as diverse as Miami's population. You'll find brassy Latin jazz joints, buzzing microbreweries, friendly neighborhood pubs, stylish rooftop lounges, creatively configured cocktail dens, open-air music jams in backyard bars and bass-heavy nightclubs where the dance party continues well into the next day. The nightlife scene has something for all, and the best way to see it is to get out and join the fray (p125). Below: Ocean Drive by night (p65)

Sun-Worshipping on North Beach

8 When people think of fun in the sun and Miami, they usually think of South Beach. And don't get us wrong! South Beach is stupendous. But if you're interested in escaping the crowds and the pressure to look fabulous, head to North Beach. Places such as Haulover Beach Park (p69) are pretty enough to serve as your screensaver, and if you really fancy a complete tan, there's a clothing-optional beach here, too. Below: Haulover Beach Park (p69)

Exploring Calle Ocho

9 One of Miami's most famous neighborhoods, Little Havana (p79) is actually populated by more than Cubans. Spanish speakers from all across Latin America mingle on Calle Ocho, otherwise known as '8th St,' one of the most colorful, culturally vibrant thoroughfares in the country. It helps to speak some Spanish, but it doesn't matter if you don't. Just don your finest *guayabera* (Cuban shirt), order a mojito (or a tall tropical fruit juice) and place your finger on Miami's multicultural pulse.

Hunting the Biltmore's Ghosts

10 Miami doesn't lack impressive buildings, and some say the grandest jewel in the city's crown is the Biltmore (p85) in Coral Gables (even the name rolls aristocratically off the tongue). Built in 1925, this hotel encapsulates the two initially disparate vibes of the Jazz Age: brilliant flashiness and elegant dignity. Today the majestic grounds are prowled by the well-to-do and the ghosts of guests past. And we don't just mean the Biltmore captures the essence of its heyday; some say spirits haunt the halls.

Marveling at Coral Gables' Mansions

11 Coral Gables (p85) is called the 'City Beautiful,' and with good reason. America in general and Miami in particular are often associated with gaudiness, but Coral Gables takes this cliché and turns it on its head. Yes, houses here are opulent, and some are admittedly over the top, but many are gorgeous executions of a Mediterranean-revival style that blends the best of Iberian villas, Moroccan *riads* and Roman pleasure domes. Coral Gables is Miami's House on the Hill; we highly recommend gawking.

Kayaking Hell's Bay

12 Good old Glades boys – who once lived in what is now one of America's most beautiful national parks – dubbed one stretch of water 'Hell's Bay.' Why? The waterway, part of a complicated capillary network of Glades streams, was 'hell to get into, hell to get out of.' But it's also heavenly once inside, shaded and shadowed by a tunnel of vegetation that cools you while water runs past your paddles. Forget fearsome titles; kayaking Hell's Bay (p160) is one of the most romantic exploratory experiences in South Florida.

Camping on Bahia Honda

13 Everyone assumes the Florida Keys are ringed with beautiful beaches, but this is actually not the case. The Keys are mangrove islands, and as such their coasts are often a tangle of bracken and vegetation – pretty, but hardly a traditional beach. Not so at Bahia Honda (p181), where a pretty smear of buttery sand is spread along the coastline. Book early and you can camp here, waking to perfect saltwater breezes and the glimmer of a new day dancing on the nearby waves.

Exploring Nightlife North of Downtown

14 There's a feast for all seasons when it comes to partying north of downtown Miami. The bars, pubs and clubs here, which stretch from the edge of artsy Wynwood to the Upper East Side, run a veritable gamut of styles: there are posh lounges draped with pretty people; gay dive bars where karaoke is often on the menu; converted studio spaces that host live-music venues. The public art project Wynwood Walls (p80) sits near the epi-center of this nightlife nexus.

Unwinding on Key Biscayne

15 Although it's an easy drive – or even a bike ride – from Downtown Miami, Key Biscayne feels like a world removed from the big-city bustle. This island has some lovely beaches, pretty nature walks and outdoor adventure aplenty, whether taking long beach walks, cycling its length or paddling out among the mangroves to look for manatees off Virginia Key. For a refreshing dose of na-ture, head to Bill Baggs Cape Florida State Park (p89) for scenic walks and frolics on untouched seashore.

Need to Know

For more information, see Survival Guide (p241)

Currency
US dollar ($)

Language
English, Spanish, Haitian Kreyol in Miami

Visas
Required for most foreign visitors unless eligible for the Visa Waiver Program.

Money
Twenty-four-hour ATMs widely available across Miami, the Keys and the towns that border the Everglades. Credit cards accepted at most businesses.

Cell Phones
Local SIM cards can be used in European or Australian phones. Europe and Asia's GSM 900/1800 standard is incompatible with the USA's cell-phone systems.

Time
Eastern Time (GMT/UTC minus five hours)

When to Go

Miami Beach
GO Jan–Apr

Miami
GO Oct–Dec

The Everglades
GO Jan–Apr

The Keys
GO Jan–Apr

Key West
GO Oct–Dec

Tropical, wet & dry seasons
Tropical climate, rain year round
Warm to hot summers, mild winters
Mild to hot summers, cold winters

High Season
(Jan–Mar)

➡ South Florida winters are dry, sunny and practically perfect.

➡ You'll need to book well in advance to reserve rooms at this time.

➡ A preponderance of festivals equals lots of fun – and crowds.

Shoulder
(Apr–May & Oct–Nov)

➡ The early end of spring resembles late winter; by May the weather gets humid.

➡ October is still hurricane season, but things dry off later in the month.

➡ Festival season gears up in late fall.

Low Season
(Jun–Sep)

➡ It's hot as hell, but sea breezes are cooling.

➡ Mosquitoes are at their worst, especially in the Everglades.

➡ Did we mention hurricanes? Fortunately there are good early-warning systems on hand.

Useful Websites

Everglades National Park (www.nps.gov/ever) Handy maps and loads of info on the park.

Visit Florida (www.visitflorida.com) Official state tourism site.

Florida State Parks (www.floridastateparks.org) Primary resource for state parks.

Miami Herald (www.herald.com) News of Miami and beyond.

Florida Keys & Key West (www.fla-keys.com) Keys visitor info.

Lonely Planet (www.lonelyplanet.com/usa/florida/south-florida-the-keys) Destinations, hotel bookings, traveler forums and more.

Important Numbers

You need to dial the area code for all calls, including domestic. The only exception is the emergency number.

Miami & the Keys/ Everglades Area Codes	☑305, ☑786/☑239
Emergency	☑911
Miami Beach Patrol	☑305-673-7714
Hurricane Hotline	☑305-468-5400
Everglades National Park	☑305-242-7700

Exchange Rates

Australia	A$1	$0.76
Canada	C$1	$0.76
Eurozone	€1	$1.12
Japan	¥100	$1.12
New Zealand	NZ$1	$0.73
UK	£1	$1.28

For current exchange rates, see www.xe.com.

Daily Costs

Budget: Less than $130

➡ Hostel dorms: $30–50

➡ Budget hotel room: $80–120

➡ Sandwich at a deli: $6–10

➡ Bicycle rental: from $15 per day

➡ Ranger-led tours in the Everglades: free

Midrange: $130–260

➡ Three-star lodging in a hotel room: $100–180

➡ Dinner at a midrange restaurant: $25–40 per person

➡ Kayak hire for the day: from $40

Top end: More than $260

➡ Double room in swanky boutique hotel: from $250

➡ Dinner at a top restaurant: $40–100 per person

➡ Cocktails: $8–14

➡ Day trip to Dry Tortugas: from $170

Opening Hours

Banks 8:30am–4:30pm Monday to Thursday, to 5:30pm Friday; sometimes 9am–12:30pm Saturday

Bars In Miami; most bars 5pm–3am (or 5am); in Key West 5pm–4am; elsewhere 5pm–2am. Some bars close earlier if business is slow

Businesses 9am–7pm Monday to Friday

Eating Breakfast 7am–10:30am Monday to Friday; brunch 9am–2pm Saturday and Sunday; lunch 11:30am–2:30pm Monday to Friday; dinner 5pm–10pm, later Friday and Saturday

Post offices 9am–5pm Monday to Friday; sometimes 9am–noon Saturday

Shopping 10am–6pm Monday to Saturday, noon–5pm Sunday; shopping malls keep extended hours

Arriving in Miami

Miami International Airport Taxis charge a flat rate for the 40-minute drive to South Beach ($35). The Miami Beach Airport Express (bus 150) costs $2.65 and makes stops all along Miami Beach. SuperShuttle runs a shared-van service, costing about $22 to South Beach.

Key West International Airport A taxi into Old Town costs about $22 and takes about 15 minutes. City Transit buses run every 80 minutes or so between 5:30am and 9pm to the Old Town (one way $2).

Getting Around

Car Most travelers in South Florida rent cars. These often come with Sun Pass transponders – devices with prepaid credit to get you through the region's many tolls.

Bus Miami has a reliable bus system, but getting around can be time-consuming; see www.miamidade.gov/transit/routes.asp for route information.

Walking & Cycling You can get around South Beach on foot or the **Citi Bike** (p252) bike-sharing program, which has numerous kiosk locations. However, many parts of Miami are not bike-friendly. Key West is very walkable and bike-friendly.

For much more on **getting around**, see p250

If You Like...

Beaches

The best beaches of South Florida are around Miami Beach, but you'll find some lovely sandy shores hidden north and south. Beaches are a rarity in the Keys.

South Beach Prime people-watching and sunrise strolls photographing those iconic lifeguard stations. (p58)

Bahia Honda State Park A windswept, serene spot that exemplifies the forested, sun-bleached beauty of the Keys. (p181)

Crandon Park A gorgeous beach that mixes nature and fun on offshore Key Biscayne. (p91)

Haulover Beach Park In North Beach, Haulover provides privacy and quiet. (p69)

Fort Zachary Taylor State Park A lovely spot for a bit of swimming, beach yoga or sunset viewing in Key West. (p185)

Nightlife

Latin American sensuality, European hipness and the raw American ability to have fun mash up in some fantastic bars and clubs in Miami. The Keys abound with fun joints that attract tourists, fisherfolk and cheerfully insane pirates.

Wynwood Miami's most innovative, interesting bars attract artists, hipsters and the creative class. (p76)

The Keys Key West gets the glory, but the other Keys have their own self-contained party scenes. (p163)

Key West This island of eccentrics at the end of the rainbow does not lack for good times. (p184)

South Beach Friendly local bars, salsa spots, creative cocktail dens and rooftop lounges are all part of the scene. (p58)

Cuisine

As a magnet for immigrants, South Florida has a wealth of eateries with roots stretching across to Latin America, Asia, Europe and other parts of the USA. Heartier home cooking can be found in small towns around the Everglades, while the Keys balance native flavor and cosmopolitan tastes.

Little Havana Miami serves up some of the best Cuban cuisine outside actual Havana. (p120)

Downtown Miami The culinary renaissance is underway downtown, with some great eateries. (p69)

Wynwood Some of Miami's most original menus are served in some of its most beautiful eating spaces. (p117)

North Beach It may not be as glamorous as South Beach, but there are great ethnic eateries up this way. (p115)

Everglades Fried gator, classic pub grub and some first-rate seafood all go down nicely with a cold beer on a steamy afternoon. (p152)

Key West For an island of this size, there's a fantastic variety of food on offer. (p192)

Scenery

South Florida's unique tropical landscape encompasses mangrove islands, hammock (forest) and the great wetland wilderness that is the Everglades. All add up to the distinctive beauty found nowhere else in America.

Everglades The 'River of Grass' has a subtle beauty that often leaves a deep impression; it can easily be the highlight of a visit to South Florida. (p139)

Crane Point Museum On the island of Marathon, this museum with lush walking trails is a great introduction to the ecology of the Florida Keys. (p177)

Oleta River State Park Drive past the condos of North Miami Beach and slip into wilderness serenity on a canoe or kayak. (p68)

Hell's Bay Canoe into the bracken heart of the marsh in this attractive series of small streams. (p160)

10,000 Islands To truly appreciate the Zen of South Florida, camp in this lovely barrier archipelago. (p154)

Music

From samba to salsa to reggaeton, the rhythms of the Caribbean, Central and South America resound in Miami alongside Euro techno, indie rock, Haitian pop and local hip-hop. There's also atmospheric local music joints throughout the Keys and a venerable live music scene down in Key West.

Cubaocho Eclectic lineup of Latin groups in an iconic spot in Little Havana. (p132)

Lagniappe Hands down one of the best little Miami bars for a bit of live music and backyard boozing. (p128)

The Anderson A buzzing, off-the-beaten-path bar with a fun crowd and weekend bands. (p129)

Green Parrot Excellent bands from all over regularly rock the scene at Key West's oldest, funkiest bar. (p197)

Churchill's If you think Miami can't rock, check out the crowd at this hard-bitten British pub. (p129)

Sounds of Little Haiti The monthly party at the Little Haiti Cultural Center is a Caribbean/Kreyol feast for the ears. (p98)

Top: Singer, Green Parrot Bar (p197), Key West

Bottom: Ahinga Trail (p159), the Everglades

Wildlife

Gaze upon reptiles that have been around for 37 million years, be awestruck at marvelous bird species and go eye-to-eye with tropical fish while swimming through coral reefs.

Anhinga Trail Stare at gators day or night while strolling this boardwalk, which also has outstanding bird-watching. (p159)

John Pennekamp Coral Reef State Park In the continental USA, diving simply doesn't get better. (p170)

Big Pine Key Tiny deer – cute as all get-out – are the inhabitants of the largest island in the Keys. (p181)

Biscayne National Park A national park that's almost entirely underwater, come to catch or spot fish. (p161)

Everglades City Head out on a cruise through the 10,000 Islands to spy dolphins and loads of birds. (p152)

Shopping

There are plenty of shopping temptations in the fashion- and art-loving city of Miami. You'll also find unique crafts and souvenirs throughout the Keys, especially in Key West.

Books & Books The best independent bookstore in Miami is a bastion of good taste and great literature. (p136)

Havana Collection Slip by this Little Havana shop and get outfitted in a classic *guayabera*, Cuba's coolest shirt. (p135)

Malaquita Creative Wynwood store of unique objects from Latin America. (p134)

Salt Island Provisions Artwork and jewelry from local artists plus gourmet salt – served up in a dapper little Key West store. (p199)

Rain Barrel Sculpture Gallery Locally made ceramics, glassworks, carvings, paintings and much more in this collection of shops in Islamorada. (p174)

Nomad Tribe Miami shop that sells attractive, well-designed clothes and accessories with sustainability in mind. (p134)

Arts

From events such as Art Basel to venues like the Adrienne Arsht Center and intimate galleries of Wynwood, the arts have paved the way for much of Miami's renaissance.

Adrienne Arsht Center for the Performing Arts Resembling a series of seashells, Miami's Arsht Center is a performance space par excellence. (p131)

New World Center Not to be outdone, Miami Beach's concert hall hosts both edgy art and mainstream productions. (p58)

Studios of Key West A one-stop gallery-gazing spot for those into the artistic output of Key West. (p185)

Cubaocho This Little Havana spot hosts visual and performing arts that showcase Miami's Cuban creativity. (p132)

Wynwood Drop by on the second Saturday of each month for an open-house peek into Miami's best galleries. (p76)

Architecture

From deco to the Design District, South Florida's architecture sets it apart as a region unlike any other in the USA.

Art Deco Historic District South Beach's heart is clustered with hotels, promenades and other prime examples of the art-deco movement. (p64)

Freedom Tower Downtown Miami is known for skyscrapers, and this classic tower was one of the first. (p74)

Coral Gables The mansions of Coral Gables run the gamut, from Mediterranean wedding cakes to neo-Arabic palaces. (p85)

Key West There's a shady joy to strolling under the eaves of Key West's French-Caribbean and Spanish-Revival homes. (p184)

Vizcaya This fairy-tale estate is the most opulent, over-the-top jewel in Miami's considerably sparkly architectural crown. (p83)

Quirky Florida

Many eccentrics are attracted to this part of the world. Be it for weather, gators or hedonism, what follows are some of our favorites from the 'Only in Florida' category.

Everglades International Hostel The backyard of this fantastic hostel resembles the trippy art of 1960s psychedelic album sleeves. (p157)

Skunk Ape Research Headquarters It's a 'reptile zoo–museum' dedicated to hunting the Everglades' Bigfoot. Why aren't you here yet? (p151)

Coral Castle A Latvian hewed this palace from coral and now it doubles as a monument to lost love. Why not? (p156)

Robbie's Marina Like an aquatic petting zoo, except the

Coral Castle (p156), built and designed by Edward Leedskalnin

pets are enormous monster tarpon fish. (p174)

Florida Keys History of Diving Museum PADI people, check out possibly the most complete collection of diving paraphernalia in the USA. (p174)

Old Florida

'Old Florida' is a bit of an invented affectation, but the term is also a byword for ecofriendly, preservation-minded attractions that are well worth your time.

Robert Is Here At this farmers market, taste the bounty of the region – sometimes shipped direct to your home. (p157)

Turtle Hospital A Keys institution, where visitors can see injured and sick sea turtles cared for by dedicated volunteers. (p178)

Smallwood Store An old trading post turned museum whose shelves are lined with the detritus of yesteryear. (p152)

Laura Quinn Wild Bird Sanctuary This sanctuary for injured avians has long been an attraction in the Keys. (p171)

No Name Key This quiet island boasts miniature deer and some of the best pizza in the Keys. (p181)

Multicultural Encounters

The Keys are a crossroads of the Caribbean, while Miami is one of the most immigrant-rich cities in the country. Diversity is more than a buzzword here – it's the cloth that the social fabric of South Florida is cut from. These sites speak to

the tropical cosmopolitan nature of this region.

Viernes Culturales Little Havana transforms into a Cuban street party on the last Friday of the month. (p101)

Goombay Festival In late October, Key West explodes into a celebration of Bahaman music, food and dance. (p190)

Little Haiti Cultural Center Pick up a beaded purse from Port-au-Prince or original art by young Haitian Americans. (p77)

Miccosukee Indian Village In the Everglades, learn about the folkways of Florida's indigenous inhabitants. (p147)

Roasters 'n Toasters Set on Arthur Godfrey Rd, this traditional deli is at the heart of Miami's sizable Jewish population. (p115)

Month by Month

January

The beginning of the new year is also the height of the tourist season. Expect fair weather, crowds, higher prices than usual and a slew of special events.

☉ Martin Luther King Jr Day Parade

This parade, held on the third Monday of January, celebrates the legacy of the USA's most iconic civil rights hero. It runs along NW 54th from NW 12th Ave to Martin Luther King Jr Memorial Park. A Caribbean twist gives it a distinctly Miami imprimatur.

☆ Key West Literary Seminar

Key West has long been a haven for writers escaping the real world, and its expat authors have turned the annual Key West Literary Seminar into one of the premier festivals of letters in the USA. (p190)

☉ Art Deco Weekend

Art deco is Miami's signature style and this weekend fair features guided tours of the city's many clusters of deco structures, concerts, classic-auto shows, sidewalk cafes, and vendors of arts and antiques. (p98)

☆ Miami Jewish Film Festival

This international film festival gets a lot of attention outside Miami. It's a great chance to cinematically *kibitz* (chat) with one of the biggest Jewish communities in the USA. (p98)

🏃 Miami Marathon

The big running event in South Florida is the Miami Marathon, which brings over 25,000 runners racing through the streets along a very scenic course. There's also a half marathon. (p98)

February

The last hurrah for northerners escaping the harsh winter, February brings arts festivals, street parties and excellent wildlife-viewing in the Everglades.

☉ Coconut Grove Arts Festival

This late-February fair features more than 300 artists from across the globe. It's one of the most prestigious festivals of its kind in a city that doesn't lack for an artistic calendar. (p98)

🔒 Original Miami Beach Antique Show

This show unearths an attic of all the world's quirky, cool stuff crossed with an archaeology dig. It attracts some 800 dealers from more than 20 countries. (p98)

🍴 South Beach Wine & Food Festival

A festival of fine dining and sipping that has become a fixture of South Florida's social calendar. Expect star-studded brunches, dinners and barbecues. This is the best time of year to brush shoulders with a celebrity chef. (p98)

March

Spring arrives, bringing warmer weather, world-class golf and tennis festivals, and St Patrick's Day. Expect to see some spring breakers behaving badly on the beach.

☆ Jazz in the Gardens

This late-March music festival (www.jazzinthegardens. com) celebrates old- and new-school R&B, soul, funk and dance music. It primarily attracts an older African American crowd, but if you have groove you are welcome. Held in Miami Gardens, a suburb just north of Miami proper.

🎊 Carnaval Miami

Miami's premier Latin festival (www.carnavalmiami. com) takes over for nine days in early March: there's a Latin drag-queen show, in-line-skate competition, domino tournament, the immense Calle Ocho Festival, Miss Carnaval Miami and more. (p98)

🎊 Spring Break

Throughout March to mid-April, American colleges unleash students for one-week spring breaks. Coeds pack Florida beaches and there is plenty of debauchery – but hey, it's all good fun. Fort Lauderdale to the north is popular, but Miami attracts its share of students too.

🎊 St Patrick's Day

Ireland's patron saint gets his due across Florida on March 17 (any excuse to drink, right?). Miami turns the greenest, with huge parties held across town; check the *New Times* for a list.

☆ Winter Music Conference

Party promoters, DJs, producers and revelers come from around the globe to hear new artists, catch up

on technology and party the nights away. If you've any interest in electronic music, it would be criminal to miss WMC (www.wmcon.com).

☆ Miami International Film Festival

The Miami International Film Festival, sponsored by Miami-Dade College, is a two-week festival showcasing documentaries and features from all over the world. Spanish-language films are an important component of the event. (p99)

🍴 Marathon Seafood Festival

One of the biggest fests in the Keys, this food-loving event takes over Marathon for a weekend in March. There's live music, an art and boat show, an arts and craft market, ample amusement for the kids and loads of stalls selling fresh-caught ocean delicacies. (p179)

April

Welcome to shoulder season: lower prices, balmier temperatures and some choice events. This is Miami's best transition period between winter crowds and summer swelter.

🎊 Wynwood Life

Held over a weekend, this newish festival is a celebration of all things Wynwood, with live music and DJs, a big arts and crafts market, fashion shows, food trucks, a culinary stage (of cooking demonstrations) and a crew of talented street artists creating live installations. (p99)

🏇 Miami Beach Polo World Cup

It may surprise you that polo is a big thing here, until you consider the sport's connections to the fashionista scene, celebrities and the European and South American upper crust. Teams come from across the world for the La Martina Trophy (www. miamipolo.com).

☆ Billboard Latin Music Awards

This prestigious awards show in late April draws top industry execs, star performers and a slew of Latin-music fans. The ceremony includes live music sets by Latin performers from across the world. (p99)

🎊 Miami Beach Gay Pride

In April, Miami Beach proudly flies the rainbow flag high in this lively weekend festival that culminates in a colorful street parade along Ocean Dr. Break out the boas, glitter and body paint! (p99)

May

Spring in South Florida can either mean pleasantly subdued heat or sweaty soup. This is when mosquito season begins in earnest in the Everglades.

🎊 Aqua Girl

Aqua Girl (www.aquagirl. org) is the biggest party of the year for Miami's lesbian population, and by any measure, is a pretty exhausting kick-ass event. DJs, jazz brunches, comedy nights, beach parties, rock concerts and art exhibitions add up to a lot of fun.

☆ Jazz in the Park

Weekend gigs are a civilized way to soak up art, culture and some chilled white wine, which tends to complement Miami's late spring swelter. There are free shows in Hialeah, at Hialeah Park Casino. (p92)

☆ MiFo LGBT Film Festival

Held late April to early May, this annual festival is screened at various South Beach theaters, as well as in Fort Lauderdale. LGBT visitors will find fun events bracketing the event, generally of a more cerebral bent than is normal for Miami's scene.

◉ Miami Museum Month

Miami Museum Month makes the entire month of May a good time to visit. It's an excellent chance to experience happy hours, special exhibitions and unique lectures in some of the best museums in the city. (p98)

☆ Sizzle

This weekend party (www. sizzlemiami.com), which celebrates gay men of color (but is open to all), brings all the boys to the yard. Structured as a multiday dusk-to-dawn party across the city, you can expect lots of debauchery at this popular circuit event.

☆ Miami Fashion Week

Vogue, darling. Models are like fish in the ocean in Miami during most of the year, but they're simply ubiquitous during Miami Fashion Week, when designers descend on the city and catwalks become disconcertingly commonplace. (p99)

June

In June the real baking heat and wet humidity begins in Miami, and the events calendar tones down a little as a result.

✯ Goombay Festival Coconut Grove

Bahamas Mama. One of a few Goombay festivals held in South Florida, this massive fest, held in the first week of June, celebrates Bahamian culture in Coconut Grove. Expect music, street food and *lots* of dancing. (p99)

July

OK – not only is it hot, but it's also hurricane season. Yay! But seriously, this is a good time to visit. There are less crowds and locals are friendlier and more accessible to tourists.

☆ Independence Day Celebration

July 4 features an excellent fireworks and laser show with live music that draws more than 100,000 people to breezy Bayfront Park. The pyrotechnics light up the sky above Biscayne Bay in an oddly romantic way. (p99)

◉ Hemingway Day Festival

One of Key West's more (in)famous annual rituals is Hemingway Days, a party that celebrates all things Hemingway (our way of saying: expect drinking, if not game hunting). The highlight is the yearly running of the Ernest-look-crowd. (p190)

August

August is sweltering and it's the deepest dip in the low tourist season. Many visitors head to the Keys, where cooling sea winds are a regular phenomenon.

✕ Miami Spice

Top restaurants around Miami participate in Miami Spice's Food Month (www.Ilovemiamispice. com), offering prix-fixe meals to lure folks out of the air-con. For most tourists, this is an easier festival to appreciate than the celebrity-focused South Beach Wine & Food Festival. (p99)

September

The weather is still steamy, and autumn brings back college students – expect lots of revelry in the university 'hoods such as Coconut Grove and Coral Gables.

☆ International Ballet Festival of Miami

While much of Miami's arts calendar is given over to modern visual art and music, the International Ballet Festival of Miami (www. internationalballetfestival. org) is the main event for the city's considerably active patrons of classical dance. (p190)

✨ Womenfest

Womenfest gives ladies the chance to seize the large LGBT spotlight in Key West. This is the premier event for the island's lesbian population, attracting thousands of visitors from all around the world. (p190)

October

As hurricane season ends and the weather gets properly pleasant again, Key West takes over the events calendar with two raucous street celebrations.

✨ Fantasy Fest

Held in late October, Fantasy Fest is by far the highlight of the Keys social calendar. The body paint, glitter, feathers and crazy floats come out, inhibitions are left at home, and a seriously decadent time is had by all. (p190)

✨ Goombay Festival Key West

In the heart of Bahama Village, one of the most vibrant Caribbean neighborhoods in the country, the Bahamanian Goombay Festival serves up music, food, singing and dancing in late October, during the same insane week as Fantasy Fest. (p190)

November

Tourist season kicks off at the end of the month, bringing more crowds and cooler days. Festival time starts in earnest with the White Party.

☆ White Party

If you're gay, and you love music, excess and naughty fun, don't miss the White Party. This week-long extravaganza draws thousands of gay men and women for nonstop partying at clubs and venues all over town. (p100)

☆ Miami Book Fair International

In mid- to late November, the Miami Book Fair International is among the most important and well-attended book fairs in the USA. Hundreds of nationally known writers join hundreds of publishers; Latin American authors form a considerably strong contingent. (p100)

December

Tourist season is in full swing. Northerners book rooms well in advance so they can bask in sunshine and be here for holiday festivities.

◉ Art Basel Miami Beach

One of the seminal international art shows in the world, Art Basel can reasonably claim responsibility for putting Miami Beach on the map of the international jet-setter crowd. Gallery showcases, public installations and parties appear throughout Miami and Miami Beach. (p100)

🏃 Orange Bowl

Hordes of football fans descend on Miami for the Super Bowl of college football: the infamous Orange Bowl. The entire city gets a youthful shot in the arm, while team rivalries simmer in sports bars. (p100)

✨ King Mango Strut

Held each year just after Christmas, this quirky Coconut Grove parade (www.kingmangostrut.org) is a politically charged, fun fair that began as a spoof on current events and the now-defunct Orange Bowl Parade. (p100)

◉ Art Miami

Held either in January or December, Art Miami is a massive fair that displays modern and contemporary works from more than 100 galleries and international artists. It may not have Art Basel's big name, but the talent is still very impressive. (p100)

Itineraries

10 DAYS Essential South Florida

On this trip you'll have a chance to explore Miami's beaches and back alleys, from white sand to classical architecture; a diverse range of neighborhoods that encapsulate the nationalities of Latin American and the Caribbean; and the unique wetland and mangrove ecosystems of the Everglades and the Florida Keys.

Start your trip in Miami's **South Beach**, which encapsulates the best of what South Florida has to offer. Exclusive hotels such as the Delano, Tides and the Shore Club capture the sheer aesthetic innovation of the South Beach experience. Enjoy people-watching on Lincoln Rd and a tour of the Art Deco Historic District.

Using South Beach as a base, spend the next four or five days exploring the neighborhoods of **Miami**, including the Latin flavor of Little Havana, the Euro-style cafes and mansions of Coral Gables, and the art galleries, excellent food and bumping nightlife around Wynwood and the Design District. Next head to the Everglades, either west along the Tamiami Trail or through Florida City and visit the **Royal Palm Visitor Center** in the Everglades. **Homestead** is the jumping-off point from Miami to the Florida Keys. Spend at least a day and a night in **Key West**.

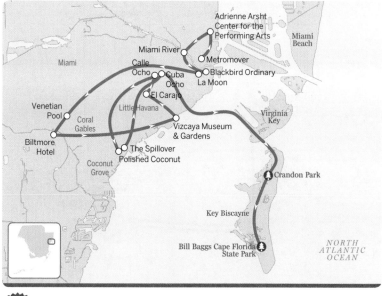

5 DAYS Downtown to South Miami

On this trip you'll experience some of the best of Miami's ethnic enclaves, hobnob in some of its wealthiest neighborhoods and witness firsthand the opulence that gives this city the nickname 'The Magic City.'

Start in Downtown, a glittering fist of steel and glass that shadows rough alleyways and cheap international flea markets. Take a long ride on the free **Metromover**, hopping on and off to see downtown sites such as the gorgeous **Adrienne Arsht Center for the Performing Arts**. Have a stroll along the **Miami River**, and stop for lunch at a waterfront spot like Casablanca. At night, catch a bit of live music over drinks at **Blackbird Ordinary** before ending the day over late-night Colombian snacks at **La Moon**.

The next day, head to Coral Gables, making sure not to miss the **Venetian Pool** (possibly the loveliest public pool in the USA), the **Biltmore Hotel** and a shopping stroll down Miracle Mile. If that isn't opulent enough, see what happens when Mediterranean Revival, Baroque stylings and money get mashed together at the **Vizcaya Museum & Gardens**. Afterward, top off a visit to these elegant manses with dinner at one of the best restaurants in Miami in – no kidding – a gas station at **El Carajo**.

On the third day, head to Little Havana and have a stroll down **Calle Ocho**, making sure to watch the dominoes at Máximo Gómez Park. Have a Cuban lunch, browse the local cigar and souvenir shops, then pop over to Coconut Grove, which retains its village-like charm amid the banyan trees. Stop in stores like **Polished Coconut**, and grab a bite and a craft brew at **The Spillover**. End the night with a live concert back in Little Havana at **Cuba Ocho**.

Spend your last day exploring Key Biscayne, enjoying beaches, sunbathing and bliss in areas such as **Bill Baggs Cape Florida State Park**. Before you leave, head to **Crandon Park** and stroll along the sand, or have an afternoon siesta. Is there a quiet, serene beach in manic Miami? You just found it.

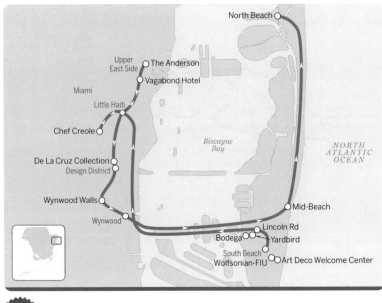

4 DAYS Miami Beach and North Miami

See some of Miami's glitziest addresses, then immerse yourself in some of the city's most fascinating ethnic enclaves, as well as hipster gentrification zones that balance art galleries with artisanal bakeries.

Start your trip in **South Beach** and use this region and its excellent hotels as your base. Make sure you visit the **Wolfsonian-FIU** design museum to get background on the surrounding art deco buildings. Head for **Lincoln Rd** to people-watch and browse the trendy shops; afterward, you'd be remiss to not take a tour with the lovely folks at the **Art Deco Welcome Center**. For a nice dinner try **Yardbird**, then take the secret entrance through a faux urinal room for late-night debaucherie at **Bodega**.

The next day, check out **Little Haiti**. This is one of the most colorful, recognizably 'foreign' neighborhoods in Miami, and it can be edgy at night, but by day you're fine to explore. Feast on ox-tail and other Haitian treats at **Chef Creole**. Next head to the Upper East Side, which is dotted with eye-catching Miami Modern architecture. Have poolside drinks at the **Vagabond**, then join the free-spirited party people at **The Anderson**.

The next morning spend the day visiting the galleries and shops of **Wynwood** and the **Design District**. Start off with a visit to the **Wynwood Walls**, an ever-changing art installation of vibrant wall-sized murals. Next explore the Margulies Collection at the Warehouse where the beautifully executed artwork is always thought-provoking. Stop for an espresso at Panther Coffee and tacos at Coyo Taco, then head up to the Design District for more art-gazing. Visit public installations like the Living Room and the Fly's Eye Dome, then stop by the **De La Cruz Collection**, one of Miami's best private collections. At night, Lagniappe is a great spot for drinks and a bit of live music in a charming backyard setting.

On your last day in town, head north along Collins Ave to **Mid-Beach** and **North Beach**. To get here you'll pass through the Condo Canyons – rows and rows of glittering residential skyscrapers, all testament to the power of real estate in Miami. In Mid-Beach, near the north end of South Beach, you'll find an excellent boardwalk where you can stroll near the sand.

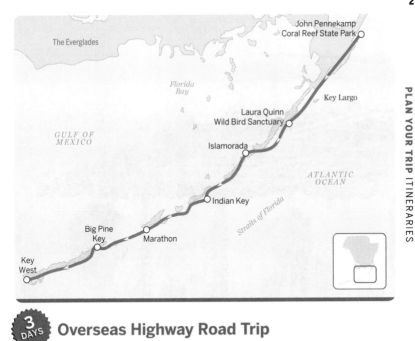

3 DAYS Overseas Highway Road Trip

The Overseas Highway (Hwy 1) runs from the tip of the Florida mainland all the way to the famed Mile 0: Key West, the end of the road and the end of America. As you tick the mile markers down, you'll be treated to some of Florida's oddest attractions and the ever-inspiring view of Florida Bay on one side and the Gulf of Mexico on the other.

Well, OK, you'll get to that view, but first you have to go through the Upper Keys: larger islands that block the view of the water via big fields of scrub pine and mangroves. On northerly Key Largo, check out the diving options at **John Pennekamp Coral Reef State Park**, then have lunch at a classic Keys waterfront shack like Shipwreck's Bar & Grill. Afterwards visit the injured birds at the **Laura Quinn Wild Bird Sanctuary**. End the day with a seafood feast and ocean views at Lazy Days in Islamorada.

Sleep in **Islamorada** on your first day in the Keys. Wake up the next morning and feed the enormous tarpon at Robbie's Marina, and if you're feeling fit, hire a kayak for a paddle through mangroves or out to **Indian Key**. Afterward, recharge over coffee at the excellent Midway Cafe.

The next stop is **Marathon**, geographic center of the Keys. If you're curious about the unique ecological background of the Keys and fancy a walk in the woods, head to the Crane Point Museum. Then learn about the Keys' best-loved endangered species at the Turtle Hospital. Eat dinner over the water at Keys Fisheries, then grab a beer at Hurricane.

Wake up and cross the Seven-Mile Bridge onto **Big Pine Key**, where tiny Key deer prance alongside the road. Stop for a meal at Square Grouper, one of the best restaurants south of Miami.

Another hour's drive south and you're in **Key West**. Truly, this island deserves its own itinerary – just make sure you don't miss the sunset show in Mallory Sq, the six-toed cats at the Hemingway House and a night out at the infamous Green Parrot, the mother of all Keys bars.

Top: Cocktail bar, Mallory Square (p184)

Bottom: Crandon Park Beach (p91), Key Biscayne

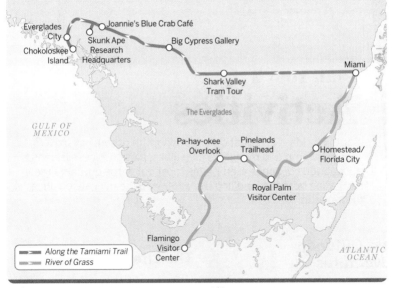

Along the Tamiami Trail
River of Grass

3 DAYS — Along the Tamiami Trail

This route takes you into the heart of the stereotypical Everglades: airboat tours through waterlogged wetlands and cypress swamps crawling with gators; with a stay in a fishing village.

From **Miami**, go west on Tamiami Trail (US 41) past the airboat tours to the Shark Valley entrance. Take the **Shark Valley Tram Tour** or rent a bicycle from the front kiosk and ride back on an asphalt path (the same one used by the tram) that curves into the swamp. You're almost guaranteed a glimpse of alligators and wading birds.

Go on to **Everglades City**, a warm hamlet and fine spot for an overnight, especially after dining on stone crabs at Camellia Street Grill. Take a morning boat tour into the 10,000 Islands, then go to **Chokoloskee Island** to visit the Smallwood Store. Lunch at Havana Cafe. Heading back northward, peek into the Museum of the Everglades.

The next day head back toward Miami. Stop in the delightfully weird **Skunk Ape Research Headquarters**, have lunch at **Joanie's Blue Crab Café**, and visit the **Big Cypress Gallery**, which contains some of the finest photos of the Glades.

2 DAYS — River of Grass

This route into the Everglades takes in vistas of long prairies and cypress domes.

Drive south from **Miami** to the adjoining towns of **Homestead** and **Florida City**, and pull over by the Coral Castle, a maudlin monument to unrequited love. You're now just outside Everglades National Park, where you'll find Robert Is Here, a fantastic farmers market and petting zoo. Continue to the Everglades Outpost, an animal hospital for exotic critters.

Push west to see the most impressive points in the park, including the **Royal Palm Visitor Center**, where walkways lead over waterways prowled by alligators; the **Pinelands Trail**, which takes you through a grove of skeleton-thin swamp pine; and **Pa-hay-okee Overlook**, with views over the Zen quiet of the greater Glades.

Spend the night back in Florida City at the fantastic Everglades International Hostel. The next morning head back into the Glades for a canoeing adventure or a slough slog – a wet walk into a Cypress dome led by park rangers. End the day with sunset views (and perhaps glimpses of manatees) at the **Flamingo Visitor Center**.

Plan Your Trip
Activities

South Florida is an aquatic wonderland with ocean, bays, rivers, marsh, swamp and mangrove coastlines, plus countless islands and glorious beaches. Getting the most out of the outdoors means navigating both the land and the water, and the delicate balance they exist in.

Best Outdoor Adventures

Paddling in the Everglades
Gliding along still waters past mangroves and over glassy lakes amid abundant bird life.

Biking Shark Valley
Spotting sunbaked gators and other Glades' residents on an easygoing 15-mile pedal in the Everglades.

Manatee spotting off Virginia Key
Looking for grazing giant giants on a kayaking or stand-up paddleboarding glide around a mangrove-lined bay.

Walking in the Everglades
Taking a sunlit stroll along the wildlife-packed Anhinga Trail then returning by night to see gators at their liveliest.

Snorkeling and diving off Key Largo
Taking in the coral reefs and colorful fish life found in John Pennekamp Coral Reef State Park.

The Life Aquatic

Likely as not you came here for the beach. Good for you! There's a lot to do on that beach and perhaps more pertinently, off it: fishing, swimming, boating, snorkeling, diving – and several different brands of boarding. Why not get under the water while you're at it? You will find the largest coral reef system in North America in Key Largo (p170), and just north of there is the nation's only national park dedicated to underwater exploration.

South Florida can give the Netherlands a run for its money in the race to the bottom of the topographic map, and as such should be traversed by the means of exploring areas that are either at or below sea level: via bicycle, or boat or scuba gear (ie really below sea level). Enjoy the land, and the water too. They exist in tandem, and are almost always experienced as such.

Get in a Hammock

All across South Florida, you'll run into displays and educational signage that ramble on about the local hammocks. You may read these and think, 'People in Florida certainly enjoy relaxing.'

While Floridians do love their hammocks, all of those signs are referring to another kind of hammock. In the southeastern USA, hammock is a term for a copse or grove of hardwood trees. What makes a hammock a hammock? In this part of the world, it comes down to elevation. Hammocks grow in patches of wetland areas that are otherwise too sodden to support them. A few extra inches of elevation gives the trees the dryness they need to grow larger and more densely; the Pineland Trail in Everglades National Park (p146) is an excellent example of a coniferous hammock. Hammocks in the Everglades typically have a distinctive teardrop shape, formed by the flow of water around the tree 'islands.'

While there are many versions of hammocks through the American southeast, the one you will most likely encounter in South Florida is the tropical hardwood hammock. Even within this category there are numerous subdivisions, including rockland hammocks (in the Big Cypress National Preserve; p150), tree island hammocks in the Everglades and coastal berm hammocks in the Florida Keys. Also in the Keys are shell mound hammocks, which grew on top of the midden shell heaps left behind by the indigenous Calusa and Tequesta Indians. The Crane Point Museum (p177) in Marathon is an excellent introduction to the many variations of hammock in South Florida in general, and the Keys in particular.

Hammocks are particularly susceptible to fire. During the long dry season, it is not unheard of to hear about (and smell) small forest fires in the Miami area down to Homestead. But the greatest threat to hammocks is development. This flora ecosystem is unique to the USA, but arguments for trees often don't hold up when placed next to arguments for hotels, condo communities, and the goods and services that accompany them.

Nature Trails & Campsites

Boardwalk paths run by still-water swamps, noodle-thin tracks lace into boonies studded with lakes and rivers, and mangrove walkways encircle white beaches. And all the while there are tents, cabins and pavilions for sleeping under the stars. Lace up your boots (or don some sandals; there are some very gentle trails here) and head into Florida's great outdoors.

South Florida swamps tend to favor 1- to 2-mile boardwalk trails; these are excellent for even out-of-shape walkers, and are almost always wheelchair accessible. You'll also find lovely short trails in many state parks. The best trails in South Florida can be found in Everglades National Park (p146) and surrounds.

Elevation & Weather

One thing Florida hikers never have to worry about is elevation gain (OK, there are some artificial slopes and hills built into certain trails, if we're going to be pedantic). But if topography is easy, the weather more than balances the negative end of the trekking scales, especially in the dry season. From November through March rain, temperature, humidity and mosquitoes decrease to tolerable levels. In summer (June to September), be sure to hike first thing in the morning, or at least before noon, to avoid the midday heat and almost daily afternoon thundershowers.

Miami

Miami is not exactly a powerhouse destination for camping. Still, two options –

TREAD LIGHTLY, EXPLORE SAFELY

It goes without saying that any wilderness, even a swamp, is a fragile place. Whether hiking, biking, paddling or snorkeling, always practice 'Leave No Trace' ethics (see www.lnt.org for comprehensive advice). In short, this boils down to staying on the trail, cleaning up your own mess, and observing nature rather than plucking or feeding it.

As you enjoy Florida's natural bounty, take care of yourself too. In particular, carry lots of water, up to a gallon per person per day, and always be prepared for rain. Line backpacks with plastic bags, and carry rain gear and extra clothes for when (not if) you get soaked. Reid Tillery's *Surviving the Wilds of Florida* will help you do just that, while Tillery's website Florida Adventuring (www.floridaadventuring.com) covers backcountry essentials.

> ### WILDERNESS WAY
> ●
> ➡ When hiking, stay on the trail and pick up your trash.
>
> ➡ Never pick wildflowers, especially orchids.
>
> ➡ Never chase or feed wild dolphins or manatees; admire but don't touch.
>
> ➡ Never feed alligators: they bite.
>
> ➡ On beaches, never approach nesting sea turtles or hatchling runs. Adhere to nighttime lights-out policies when posted (usually May to October).
>
> ➡ When snorkeling or diving, never touch coral reefs.

Oleta River State Park (p68) and Bill Baggs Cape Florida State Park (p89) – are available if you want cheap(ish) outdoor accommodation.

The Everglades & Around

The National Park Service manages both primitive and developed campgrounds and can help travelers who want to pitch in the backcountry. 'Primitive' sites lack running water and electricity, while developed sites will at least possess running water and sometimes have power hookups.

Our favorite camping option in the area is finding *chickees* (wooden platforms built above the water line) and isolated beaches and mangrove strands amid the 10,000 Islands (p154). When you're out here surrounded by the stars, dolphins, birdlife, the breeze and little else, it's backcountry bliss. Offshore islands in Biscayne National Park (p161) offer a similar experience to camping in the 10,000 Islands.

If you're into socializing with other campers and budget travelers, and aren't too interested in nights alone in the wilderness, the backyard of the Everglades International Hostel (p157) is a surreal, artsy garden, and consequently a lovely spot to pitch a tent.

The Keys

John Pennekamp Coral Reef State Park (p172) and Bahia Honda State Park (p181) both offer excellent campgrounds with a good mix of hookup sites and tent areas, but these parks are very popular, so reserve in advance. If you really want to feel like you're sleeping at the end of the earth, reserve a spot at Dry Tortugas National Park (p200). It's self-service camping, and you'll have to bring everything with you, including water. As with other popular spots, it's essential to reserve months in advance.

Canoeing & Kayaking

To really experience South Florida's swamps and rivers, its estuaries and inlets, and its lagoons and barrier islands, you need watercraft, preferably the kind you paddle. The intimate quiet of dipping among mangroves – startling alligators and ibis – stirs wonder in the soul. It's not only the Everglades that are great for paddling. Don't forget the coasts: there are some choice options for coastal kayaking and canoeing in Miami and around.

As with hiking, the winter 'dry' season is best for paddling. If it's summer, canoe near cool freshwater springs and swimming beaches, 'cause you'll be dreaming about them.

Paddler's Guide

A great all-in-one paddling guide – with everything from the state's best water trails to nitty-gritty advice about weather, equipment and supplies – is *A Paddler's Guide to the Sunshine State* (2001) by Sandy Huff.

Miami

There are many waterways in the Magic City; the trick is being able to find them, and then being able to find your way on them. We should stress that while it is easy to get into the water in Miami, a guide is crucial for getting out of it; there are strong currents in the local inlets and channels.

You'll find open waters to paddle around and mangrove tunnels to paddle through in Oleta River State Park (p68), which is next to the Haulover inlet. The other hot spot for kayaking and canoeing is Key Biscayne (p94). There's a good boat launch and seawall at Bill Baggs Cape Florida State Park (p89) that fronts No Name Harbor, while offshore paddling is a popular day-tripping task at Crandon Park (p91). Virginia Key deserves special mention; Virginia Key Outdoor Center (p94) is an top outfitter

Top: Florida Manatee
(p227)

Bottom: Kayaker,
Everglades National
Park (p146)

and leads tours. You can also hire kayaks or SUPs for DIY adventures. In the small bay there you can often spot manatees.

The Everglades

You'll likely tell your grandchildren about kayaking in Everglades National Park (p146). At times you'll feel as if there is nothing in the world but the two mirror-flat reflections of water and sky; at other moments, that the soaring sense of space is compressed into claustrophobic, capillary-esque mangrove tunnels courtesy of Hell's Bay – which, by the way, is one of the most beautiful parts of the park. Don't pass it up.

If you want an ultimate adventure, consider boating the 99-mile-long wilderness waterway along and amid the margins of the 10,000 Islands (p154). For something less involved, you can hire canoes and kayaks for scenic short- or full-day paddles from Flamingo Marina (p160) in the Southern Everglades. The national park-run Flamingo Visitor Center (p159) based there also offers free canoeing tours several times a week.

The Keys

Paddling is popular in the Keys, where the water is more teal than the sky and the sun is almost always bright overhead. On Islamorada, Anne's Beach (p174) offers offshore paddling near clumps of mangrove forest, while at John Pennekamp Coral Reef State Park (p170) you can boat over the continent's largest coral-reef formations.

Still, the ultimate in Keys kayaking and canoeing is found at Indian Key Historic State Park (p174) and Lignumvitae Key Botanical State Park (p174). Both sites are only boat accessible. They're not too difficult to paddle out to, but this added layer of inaccessibility, plus the combination of wilderness and the rotted ruins on Indian Key, makes a trip out here pretty magical.

Diving & Snorkeling

South Florida has, hands down, the best reef and wreck diving in the continental USA, and the snorkeling is just as magical. At times the clarity of the water is disconcerting, as if you were floating on air; every creature and rainbow school of fish all the way to the bottom feels just out of reach, so

that, as William Bartram once wrote, 'the trout swims by the very nose of the alligator and laughs in his face.' North America's largest coral-reef system is at your fingertips and wreck diving in Florida is equally epic.

How epic? Biscayne National Park (p161) has developed a wreck-centric maritime trail, for goodness sake. Other attractions include Dry Tortugas National Park (p200), which was named for its abundant sea turtles; the fantastic Florida Keys History of Diving Museum (p174) in Islamorada, which is awesome whether you dive or not; and of course, John Pennekamp Coral Reef State Park (p170), which offers the best diving in the lower 48 states. Barring Biscyane, all these sites are all found in the Keys.

Cycling

Florida is generally too flat for mountain biking (though there are exceptions), but there are plenty of off-road opportunities, along with hundreds of miles of paved trails for those who prefer to keep their ride clean. As with hiking, avoid cycling in summer unless you like getting hot and sweaty.

Cruiser bikes and city bikes are great here. If you're Dutch, a classic *oma* bicycle would be perfect for Miami Beach and Key West. In fact, folks from the Netherlands will find, topographically at least, the cycling conditions here are close to that of home; just throw in a *lot* more sunshine and a *lot* fewer bike lanes. Miami Beach operates a bike-share program and bikes are easy to rent in Key West, so there's really no excuse not to get on two wheels. Our favorite cycling spots in South Florida follow.

In Miami, the Promenade (p63), which fronts Ocean Dr, is an excellent ride for those who want to take in Miami Beach and get a little exercise in while they're at it. Unfortunately the Promenade does not extend all the way up the beach. Be careful riding on Collins Ave as it extends further north; that road is the only major artery running north–south, and people tend to speed on it. Oleta River State Park (p68) offers 4 miles of novice, 3 miles of paved and 10 miles of mountain-biking trails.

Cycling is a very popular means of seeing the Everglades; just make sure you wear bright clothing and measure your distances so you don't accidentally find yourself on a lonely park road after the sun sets (it

ALTERNATIVE ACTIVITIES

So you've walked the beaches, gone kayaking amid the mangroves and snorkeled the coral reefs. What next? How about heading well off the beaten path on one of South Florida's quirky adventures?

Slough slog Don your cheapest pants and lace up those (unwanted) shoes for a walk into the muck. Free ranger-led tours (p147) take you into a cypress dome in search of plant and animal life and verdant tranquility.

Moonlight paddles Virginia Key Outdoor Center (p94) leads memorable full-moon (and new moon) paddles several times a month. You'll see a sunset and with luck bioluminescent plankton in the water.

Alligator spotting by night Maybe you've seen the big piles of crocodilians by day; come back at night to the Anhinga Trail (p159) to see these primordial creatures gliding beautifully through the water. Bring a flashlight!

Eating pizza under the sea At Jules' Undersea Lodge (p172) in Key Largo, you can pay a visit – or overnight – in a former research station under the water. You'll have to scuba dive to get there; hot pizza delivered to your undersea abode is part of the deal.

Sunbathing without tan lines Join the clothing-optional crowd at Haulover Beach Park (p69) in North Beach, Miami. For ocean frolicking in the buff, this is the place.

Feeding tremendous tarpons At Robbie's Marina (p174) in Islamorada, you can feed some massive fish. The water sloshes like it's boiling when they're hungry.

---

wouldn't be dangerous, but it'd probably be pretty unnerving). An easy ride along Shark Valley's paved asphalt track (p146) takes in plenty of wildlife.

In the Keys, cycling is perhaps the most logical way of exploring Key West. Those seeking a challenging, rewarding ride should consider the Florida Keys Overseas Heritage Trail (p175), which goes from Key Largo to Key West. While not complete, new sections continue to be added, and currently 90 out of 106 miles are open for cycling.

Sailing

If you prefer the wind in your sails, Florida is your place. Miami is a sailing sweet spot, with plenty of marinas for renting or berthing your own boat – Key Biscayne is a particular gem, and marinas in swish Coconut Grove and Brickell cater to the sailing crowd. In Key West, sail on a schooner with real cannons, though tour operators are plentiful throughout the Keys.

Get On Board

South Florida is no surfing hot spot; if you want to ride waves in this state, it's generally best to head north to at least Jupiter Beach. But surfing isn't the only means of using a board to access the water. Kiteboarding and

wakeboarding are growing in popularity, and are accessible to first-timers looking to try something new.

The equipment for wake- and kiteboarding is the same: the wakeboard is a smaller version of a surfboard. In either activity you're pulled along the water – by a boat with a wakeboard and, if it wasn't already blessedly obvious, by a kite while kiteboarding. Either evolution allows you to achieve some serious speed and work some magnificent tricks, although beginners aren't going to be flipping Triple Maddog Overhang Bazooka Busters off the bat (we made that up). The flat, shallow waters around Key Biscayne are wake- and kiteboard central. Check out the following:

Miami Kiteboarding (p96) Offers a range of private lessons from $150 for one hour of one-on-one instruction. Couples get discounted rates.

Gator Bait Wakeboard School (☑305-282-5706; www.gatorbaitwakeboard.com; 3301 Rickenbacker Causeway, Key Biscayne) Half-/one-hour lessons run $90/180.

Miami Watersports Complex (MWCC; ☑305-476-9253; www.aktionparks.com; Amelia Earhart Park, 401 E 65th St, Hialeah; ⊗11am-6pm Mar-Oct, to dusk Nov-Feb) Offers lessons in cableboarding, where the rider is pulled along by an overhead cable system. That means no boat, less pollution and less noise. A 20-minute/one-hour lesson costs $25/90.

Plan Your Trip

Eat & Drink Like a Local

When South Florida sits at the table, who knows what language the menu will be written in? This region has a rich culinary identity, which is an extension of an already rich demographic identity. As a result the local culinary scene is paradoxical yet delicious: on the one hand a free-floating gastronomy for people unmoored from their homeland and detached from tradition, and on the other an attempt to connect to deeply felt roots and folkways via the immediacy of taste.

Top Food Experiences

South Beach
Plunking down at an outdoor table on Lincoln Road – Tocaya Organica (p112) is a fine choice.

Wynwood
Taste-testing your way through Miami's most creative restaurants, starting with Kyu (p119).

Little Havana
Joining Cuban expats over mouthwatering Latin fare at the iconic Versailles (p120).

Coral Gables
Enjoying haute cuisine in La Palme d'Or (p124), a culinary jewel inside the Biltmore Hotel.

The Everglades
Feasting on fresh stone crab claws at waterside spots like the Camellia Street Grill (p155).

Homestead
Enjoying smoothies and and exotic fruits at Robert Is Here (p157), one of Florida's best farm stands.

The Keys
Sampling great seafood up and down the Keys, starting with the Fish House (p173) in Key Largo.

Key West
Nibbling on conch fritters while watching the sunset from Mallory Square (p184).

A Global Palate

It's hard to isolate a 'native' South Florida cuisine (Native American dishes such as chili and fry bread found in Everglades-area restaurants are imported from the American Southwest). The first white settlers here came from all over America, and thus the American South and its food ways, which heavily influence Northern Florida, is one of many dozens of influences in Miami, although more keenly felt in the Everglades region and the Keys.

But in general, South Florida is a region defined not by any one, but by a hemisphere's-worth of cultures: Southern, Creole, Cuban, Caribbean, and Central and South American, but also Jewish, Japanese, Vietnamese, Nigerian, Thai, Chinese, Spanish and more.

Few places can boast Florida's sublime fresh bounty from land and sea, and menus playfully nick influences. Gourmets can genuflect before celebrity chefs, while gourmands hunt Florida's bizarre delicacies, such as boiled peanuts, frog's legs, snake and gator. Strip malls can contain gastronomic gems, while five-star hotel restaurants can be total duds. Smell, taste, enjoy and indulge – our advice to you, and a fitting motto for Floridians and food.

Dining Trends

South Florida in general, and Miami in particular, are obsessively trendy. If barnacles are the 'it' recipe in Manhattan, you better believe barnacle sorbet will feature on at least a dozen South Beach menus within a week. This attitude is a double-edged sword, because while you're in no danger of missing culinary trends in Miami, there's a chance you'll eat at a place where the aforementioned barnacles are prepared carelessly and sold at sky-high costs.

At the time of writing, the latest Miami trend is Hawaiian-style poke – chopped, raw, sushi-grade fish served over salads, rice and other ingredients. Meanwhile, rustic farm to table-esque cuisine – often served up in shabby chic settings (distressed wood floors, industrial fixtures) – shows no sign of going out of style. Asian and Latin fusion are also perennially popular cooking trends in Miami.

Riches of the Sea

Florida has always fed itself from the sea, which lies within arm's reach from nearly every point. If it swims or crawls in the ocean, you can bet some enterprising local has shelled or scaled it, battered it, dropped it in a fryer and put it on a menu.

Grouper is far and away the most popular fish. Grouper sandwiches are to Florida what the cheese-steak is to Philadelphia or pizza to Manhattan – a defining, iconic dish, and the standard by which many places are measured. Hunting the perfect grilled or fried grouper sandwich is an obsessive Floridian quest, as is finding the creamiest bowl of chowder.

Of course, a huge range of other fish is offered. Other popular species include snapper (with dozens of varieties), mahi-mahi and yellowfin tuna.

Florida really shines when it comes to crustaceans: try pink shrimp and rock shrimp, and don't miss soft-shell blue crab – Florida is the only place with blue-crab hatcheries, making them available fresh year-round. Winter (October to April) is the season for Florida spiny lobster and stone crab (out of season, both will be fro-zen). Florida lobster is all tail, without the large claws of its Maine cousin, and stone crab is heavenly sweet, served steamed with butter or the ubiquitous mustard sauce.

Finally, the Keys popularized conch (a giant sea snail); now fished out, most conch is from the Bahamas. For information on sustainable seafood, check out www.seafoodwatch.org.

Cuban & Latin American Cuisine

Cuban food, once considered 'exotic,' is itself a mix of Caribbean, African and Latin American influences, and in Tampa and Miami it's a staple of everyday life. Sidle up to a Cuban *lonchería* (snack bar) and order a *pan cubano:* a buttered, grilled baguette stuffed with ham, roast pork, cheese, mustard and pickles.

Integral to many Cuban dishes are *mojo* (a garlicky vinaigrette, sprinkled on sandwiches), *adobo* (a meat marinade of garlic, salt, cumin, oregano and sour orange juice) and *sofrito* (a stew-starter mix of garlic, onion and chili peppers). Main-course meats are typically accompanied by rice and beans, and fried plantains.

With its large number of Central and Latin American immigrants, the Miami area offers plenty of authentic ethnic eateries. Seek out Haitian *griots* (marinated fried pork), Jamaican jerk chicken, Brazilian barbecue, Central American *gallo pinto* (red beans and rice) and Nicaraguan *tres leches* ('three milks' cake).

In the morning, try a Cuban coffee, also known as *café cubano* or *cortadito*. This hot shot of liquid gold is essentially sweetened espresso, while *café con leche* is just *café au lait* with a different accent: equal parts coffee and hot milk.

Another Cuban treat is *guarapo* (fresh-squeezed sugarcane juice). Cuban snack bars serve the greenish liquid straight or poured over crushed ice, and it's essential to an authentic mojito (rum, sugar, mint, lemon and club soda). It also sometimes finds its way into *batidos,* a milky, refreshing Latin American fruit smoothie.

Southern Cooking

You are technically in the South down here, but much of South Florida is so south it's *sud* as opposed to Southern if you catch our drift. Basically we're saying Miami is too international to be classified as the American South. And as such, Southern cooking basically skips Miami as a city. That said, in the Everglades and the Keys the Southern influence is much more keenly felt.

Southern makes up in fat and pure tastiness what it may lack in refinement. Standard Southern fare is a main meat – such as fried chicken, catfish, barbecued ribs, chicken-fried steak or even chitlins (hog's intestines) – and three sides: perhaps some combination of hushpuppies (cornbread balls), cheese grits, cornbread, coleslaw, mashed potatoes, black-eyed peas, collard greens or buttery corn. End with pecan pie, and that's living.

In the Keys, Southern-style cooking melds with Caribbean gastronomy. In truth, there's a lot of room for overlap, as black slaves developed many of the same recipes in the USA and the Caribbean. Plus, Southern and Caribbean cooking are both unapologetically rich and heavy, and the latter may apply to you too if you're not careful when you eat in the Keys.

Cracker cooking is Florida's rough-and-tumble variation on Southern cuisine, but with more reptiles and amphibians. And you'll find a good deal of Cajun and Creole as well, which mix in spicy gumbos and bisques from Louisiana's neighboring swamps. Southern Floridian cooking is epitomized by writer Marjorie Kinnan Rawlings' famous cookbook *Cross Creek Cookery*.

Ice tea is ubiquitous in the Everglades and the Keys, but watch out for 'sweet tea,' which is an almost entirely different Southern drink – tea so sugary your eyes will cross.

Local Specialties

While South Florida has an international palate, some dishes have been here long enough to constitute something like a local cuisine.

Cuban Sandwich

The traditional Cuban sandwich is a thing of some beauty, and a possible genuine native Florida dish; that Cubans invented the thing is agreed upon, but where they did so – here or Tampa or Havana – is a subject of debate. Cuban bread is buttered or oiled and hit with mustard. Layer on thin pickles, ham, roast pork or salami, and Swiss cheese. Press the thing in a *plancha* (a smooth panino grill) and ta-da: yumminess on warm bread.

Stone Crabs

The first reusable crustacean: only one claw is taken from a stone crab – the rest is tossed back in the sea (the claw regrows in 12 to 18 months, and crabs plucked again are called 'retreads'). The claws are so perishable that they're always cooked before selling. Mid-October through mid-May is less a 'season' than

---

STONE CRAB CLAWS

Enormous stone crab claws are a staple of Floridian seafood menus, but some may have concerns with the way they are harvested. The crabs are legal to harvest from October 15 through May 15, although fishermen must toss back any ovigerous (egg-laying) female crabs.

The male crabs have a different fate. Their claws are broken off, and the crab, now a limb down, is tossed back into the water. After roughly three molts (a period when a crab regrows its shell, which usually takes a year) the claw will have grown back, only for the process to repeat itself.

Defenders of the harvest say that the act of tossing the crabs back, even with one arm, makes for a more sustainable fishery considering the alternative is simply keeping the whole crab. But the Department of Fish and Wildlife estimates some 28% of crabs die from the amputation; that number climbs to 47% for a double amputation. Those casualty numbers can be significantly reduced if a fisherman knows how to make a clean cut of the limb.

SUNSHINE STATE FOOD FESTIVALS

Many of Florida's food festivals have the tumultuous air of county fairs, with carnival rides, music, parades, beauty pageants and any number of wacky, only-in-Florida happenings.

Key West Food & Wine Festival (www.keywestfoodandwinefestival.com) Key West; three days, late January. A weekend-long party and celebration of the finest in Key West gastronomy.

Everglades Seafood Festival (www.evergladesseafoodfestival.org) Everglades City; three days, early February. Not just seafood, but gator, frog's legs and, most importantly, stone crabs.

South Beach Food & Wine Festival (www.sobefest.com) Miami; four days, late February. This Food Network–sponsored party is one of the largest food festivals in the country.

Swamp Cabbage Festival (www.swampcabbagefestival.org) La Belle; three days, late February. Armadillo races and crowning of the Miss Swamp Cabbage Queen.

Carnaval Miami (www.carnavalmiami.com) Miami; fortnight, early March. Negotiate drag queens and in-line skaters to reach the Cuban Calle Ocho food booths.

Grant Seafood Festival (www.grantseafoodfestival.com) Grant; weekend, early March. This small Space Coast town throws one of Florida's biggest seafood parties.

Florida Strawberry Festival (www.flstrawberryfestival.com) Plant City; 11 days, early March. Since 1930 over half a million folks come annually to pluck, eat and honor the mighty berry.

Island Fest (www.islamoradachamber.com) Islamorada; two days; early April. Essentially a county fair for all things Keys-related.

Taste of Key West (www.facebook.com/TasteofKeyWest) Key West; one day; mid-April. Dozens of local restaurants turn their kitchens into food carts along the Truman waterfront.

Isle of Eight Flags Shrimp Festival (www.shrimpfestival.com) Amelia Island; three days, early May. Avast, you scurvy dog! Pirates invade for shrimp and a juried art show.

Palatka Blue Crab Festival (www.bluecrabfestival.com) Palatka; four-day Memorial Day weekend (weekend before last Monday in May). Hosts the state championship for chowder and gumbo. Yes, it's that good.

Key West Lobsterfest (www.keywestlobsterfest.com) Key West; weekend, August. Celebrates the opening of spiny lobster season with seafood feasting and live music.

Florida Seafood Festival (www.floridaseafoodfestival.com) Apalachicola; two days, early November. Stand way, way back at its signature oyster shucking and eating contests.

a stone-crab frenzy. Joe Weiss of Miami Beach is credited with starting it all. For straight-out-of-the ocean freshness, try them in Everglades City.

Colombian Hot Dog

The Colombian *perro caliente* is a work of mad genius. Colombians have...a different take on hot dogs; toppings we've seen include quail eggs, plum sauce, potato chips, pineapple and 'pink sauce' (we didn't ask). These crazy creations may not be native to South Florida, but this is about the only place you'll find them in the USA, apart from a few neighborhoods in New York.

Alligator

Alligator tastes like a cross between fish and pork. The meat comes from the tail,

Top: Conch fritter stand, Mallory Square (p184)

Bottom: Traditonal Cuban sandwich (p40)

HANS GEEL/SHUTTERSTOCK ©

and is usually served as deep-fried nuggets, which overwhelms the delicate flavor and can make it chewy. Try it grilled. Alligator is healthier than chicken, with as much protein but half the fat, fewer calories and less cholesterol. Most alligator is legally harvested on farms and is often sold in grocery stores. Alligator farms have their critics, but it's worth noting said farms have no worse or better a reputation than most factory farms or slaughterhouses.

Conch

The shellfish Keys natives are named for (a 'conch' is a shellfish, while a capitalized 'Conch' is a Keys native) happen to be delicious, and are difficult to find outside of South Florida (in the USA). Conch meat is pleasantly springy and usually prepared according to Caribbean recipes: most of the time it's either curried or 'cracked' (fried). Either way it is seriously tasty. Café Solé (p197), in Key West, is famous for its conch carpaccio, oft-imitated but yet to be improved upon.

Arepas

The greatness of a city can be measured by many yardsticks. The arts. Civic involvement. Infrastructure. What you eat when you're plowed at 3am. In Miami the answer is often enough *arepas;* delicious South American corn cakes that can be stuffed (Venezuelan-style) or topped (Colombian-style) with any manner of deliciousness; generally you can't go wrong with cheese.

Frog's Legs

Those who know say the 'best' legs come from the Everglades; definitely ask, since you want to avoid imported ones from India, which are smaller and disparaged as 'flavorless.'

Key Lime Pie

Key limes are yellow, and that's the color of an authentic Key lime pie, which is a custard of Key lime juice, sweetened condensed milk and egg yolks in a cracker crust, then topped with meringue. Avoid any slice of lime that is green or stands ramrod straight. The combination of extra-tart Key lime with oversweet milk nicely captures the personality of Key West Conchs.

From Farm (& Grove) to Table

Florida has worked long and hard to become an agricultural powerhouse, and is renowned for its citrus products. The state is the nation's largest producer of oranges, grapefruits, tangerines and limes, not to mention mangoes and sugarcane. Scads of bananas, strawberries, coconuts, avocados (once called 'alligator pears') and the gamut of tropical fruits and vegetables are also grown in Florida. Homestead is a major agricultural region, with citrus groves and fields of crops extending all the way to the edge of the Everglades.

However, only relatively recently – with the advent of the USA's locavore, farm-to-table movement – has Florida started featuring vegetables in its cooking and promoting its freshness on the plate. Florida's regional highlights – its Southern and Latin American cuisines – do not usually emphasize greens or vegetarianism. But today, most restaurants with upscale or gourmet pretensions promote the local sources of their produce and offer appealing choices for vegetarians.

Inside Miami you'll find a delightful variety of vegetarian options, including a few vegan-friendly places. Funnily enough, folks here choose vegetarianism for reasons both ethical and vain; in the latter case, you'll find a lot of SUV-driving fitness nuts who don't give a fig for being green, but are obsessed with looking good. Outside Miami, dedicated vegetarian restaurants are few, and in many Keys and Everglades restaurants vegetarians can be forced to choose between iceberg-lettuce salads and pastas.

One indigenous local delicacy is heart of palm ('swamp cabbage'), which has a delicate, sweet crunch. The heart of the sabal palm, Florida's state tree, it was a mainstay for Florida pioneers. Try it if you can find it served fresh (don't bother if it's canned; it's not from Florida).

SELF-CATERING

Epicure Market (p114), a gourmet food shop just off Lincoln Rd in South Beach, has a beautiful selection of international cheeses and wines, fresh produce, baked goods and prepared dishes. Many of the more than 25 Publix supermarkets throughout Miami are quite upscale, and the Whole Foods Market (p114) is the biggest high-end grocery store around, with an excellent produce department, pretty good deli and so-so salad bar; its biggest draw is for vegetarians (not so well catered for by markets in these parts) or health nuts who are seeking a particular brand of soy milk or wheat-free pasta.

For the freshest picnic items around, hit one of the following farmers' markets:

Lincoln Road (btwn Washington and Meridian Aves; ☺9am-6:30pm Sun)

South Pointe Triangle Park (Alton Rd, btwn 1st & 2nd Sts; ☺9am-2pm Sat)

Normandy Village Fountain (7892 Rue Vendome; ☺9am-4pm Sat)

Adrienne Arsht Center for the Performing Arts (1300 Biscayne Blvd; ☺4-8:30pm Mon)

Brickell Center (btwn 7th & 8th Sts under the Metromover tracks; ☺11am-6pm Sun)

Aventura Mall (19501 Biscayne Blvd; ☺2 weekends a month mid-Feb–Oct)

Coconut Grove (3300 Grand Ave at Margaret St; ☺11am-7pm Sat)

Coral Gables City Hall (405 Biltmore Way; ☺8am-2pm Sat mid-Jan–Mar)

Floribbean Cuisine

OK, somebody worked hard to come up with 'Floribbean' – a term for Florida's tantalizing gourmet mélange of just-caught seafood, tropical fruits and eye-watering peppers, all dressed up with some combination of Nicaraguan, Salvadoran, Caribbean, Haitian, Cajun, Cuban and even Southern influences. Some call it 'Fusion,' 'Nuevo Latino,' 'New World,' 'Nouvelle Floridian' or 'Palm Tree Cuisine,' and it could refer to anything from a ceviche of lime, conch, sweet peppers and scotch bonnets to grilled grouper with mango, adobo and fried plantains.

Where to Eat

South Florida has a dazzling range of eating options. Aside from casual places, it's wise to book tables ahead of time – especially on weekends. For top-end restaurants, reserve two weeks or more in advance.

Restaurants South Florida's restaurants range from easygoing waterfront shacks to glittering, award-winning dining rooms, and cover every cuisine you can imagine.

Cafes Open from morning to early evening, cafes are good for a simple breakfast or lunch, plus coffee and snacks.

Food stands When you want a meal in a hurry, hit a taco stand, a pizza counter or a food truck.

Plan Your Trip
Travel with Children

South Florida doesn't possess the reputation that child-friendly Orlando has, but sheesh, where does? This region still knows how to care for your young ones, with a plethora of parks, nature trails, megamalls, beaches, zoos and family-friendly hotels and restaurants to keep your kids happy on holiday.

Miami & the Keys for Kids

There is a plethora of kid-themed activities in South Florida. And in Florida, every tourist town has already anticipated the needs of every age in your family. With increasing skill and refinement, nearly every Florida museum, zoo, attraction, restaurant and hotel aims to please traveling families of all stripes.

Your only real trouble is deciding what to do. Florida offers so much for kids and families that planning can be tough. Simple itineraries can suddenly become a frantic dawn-to-dusk race to pack it all in.

Children's Highlights
Beaches, Pools & Parks

South Pointe Park, South Beach (p62) Ice-cream stands, soft grass, a beach and mini waterpark.

Mid-Beach Boardwalk, North Beach (p68) Fronts a family-friendly stretch of sand.

Arch Creek Park, Miami (p92) Has nature walks and ghost walks.

Crandon Park, Key Biscayne (p91) Pretty spot with sand and nature trails.

Best Regions for Kids
Coconut Grove
Big malls, mainstream cuisine and a pedestrian-friendly center.

Everglades
Kid-friendly national park exhibits. And big alligators. Kids love alligators.

Florida Keys
Active families with older kids will adore the snorkeling, diving, fishing, boating and all-around no-worries vibe.

Key Biscayne
An enormous, central park devoted to kids and surrounded by child-friendly nature trails and public beaches.

Coral Gables
More malls, midrange restaurants that are happy to host children, and the fairy-tale Venetian Pool.

Miami Beach
Lincoln Rd, South Pointe Park, Ocean Dr neon and the sandy beach will keep your kids grinning.

Venetian Pool, Coral Gables (p94) One of the most beautiful public pools in the country.

Jacob's Aquatic Center, Key Largo (p171) Small water park and plenty of kiddie pools.

Bill Baggs Cape Florida State Park, Key Biscayne (p89) Picnic tables front a pretty sweep of beach.

Village of Key Biscayne Community Center, Key Biscayne (Map p90; ☑305-365-8900; www.activeislander.org; 10 Village Green Way, off Crandon Blvd; day pass adult/child $9/6; ☺community center 6am-10pm Mon-Fri, 10am-8pm Sat & Sun; 🚹🐾) ✦ Playgrounds, sports fields and a packed kids' activities schedule.

Barnacle Historic State Park, Coconut Grove (p85) Outdoor paths and frequent family-friendly outdoor concerts.

Fruit & Spice Park, Homestead (p156) Pretty trails wind past freshly fallen fruit.

Biscayne National Park, Homestead (p161) Glass-bottom boat tours and snorkeling over epic reefs.

John Pennekamp Coral Reef State Park, Key Largo (p170) Great coral reefs, by snorkel or glass-bottom boat tour.

Harry Harris Park, Key Largo (p171) This small park is one of the best in the Keys for kids.

Sombrero Beach Park, Marathon (p178) Sugar-soft sand lines calm water on one side; playground facilities are on the other.

Animal Encounters

Zoo Miami, Miami (p91) This extensive and wide-ranging zoo has all the big-ticket species.

Marjory Stoneman Douglas Biscayne Nature Center, Key Biscayne (p91) Kid-friendly intro to subtropical South Florida; has great hands-on programs.

Monkey Jungle, Miami (p92) The tagline at this zoo says it all: 'Where humans are caged and monkeys run wild.' Unforgettable.

Jungle Island, Miami (p75) This zoo has tropical birds and exotic species such as the liger, a tiger-and-lion crossbreed.

Everglades Outpost, Florida City (p156) This volunteer-run animal sanctuary is essentially a great small zoo.

Shark Valley, Everglades (p146) Cycle or take a tram tour along the paved road of this park. Wading birds and alligators are practically guaranteed.

Royal Palm Visitor Center, Everglades (p160) Take a boardwalk trail over some of the most beautiful wetland landscapes.

National Key Deer Refuge, Big Pine Key (p181) Kids love spotting these cute-as-a-Bambi minideer.

Laura Quinn Wild Bird Sanctuary, Tavernier (p171) Injured birdlife is sheltered along several windy paths at this refuge.

Turtle Hospital, Marathon (p178) Turtles get tender loving care from a staff of dedicated volunteers. Visitors welcome (and appreciated).

Robbie's Marina, Islamorada (p174) A sort of 'working' harbor and aquatic petting zoo.

Robert Is Here, Everglades (p157) This favorite farmers market has a petting zoo and fresh juice.

Quirky Fun

Metromover, Miami (p138) See the city from the sky via this free elevated train.

Mallory Square, Key West (p184) A carnival for the crowds that pops off as the sun sets.

Museums

Miami Children's Museum, Miami (p75) Extensive role-playing environments.

HistoryMiami, Downtown Miami (p69) Bookish kids will appreciate the thoughtful exhibitions.

Patricia and Phillip Frost Museum of Science, Downtown Miami (p71) A new museum with lots of fun and stimulating exhibits.

Gold Coast Railroad Museum, Miami (p92) Little train-spotters will get their fix here.

Florida Keys Eco-Discovery Center, Key West (p184) Fantastic and entertaining displays pull together Florida Keys ecology.

Crane Point Museum, Marathon (p177) Excellent alfresco introduction to the ecology of the Keys.

Vizcaya Museum & Gardens, Coconut Grove (p83) Older children will appreciate the whimsy of this fairy-tale mansion.

Coral Castle, Homestead (p156) Kids may not appreciate the kitsch, but they still love the weirdness of this odd structure.

Miami-Dade Public Library, Downtown Miami (p76) Flagship library for Miami.

Miccosukee Village, Everglades (p147) On Tamiami Trail, this Native American village has culture shows and alligator wrestling.

Top: Miccosukee Indian man carves cooking utensils, Miccosukee Indian Village (p147)

Bottom: Zoo Miami (p91)

ROMRODPHOTO/SHUTTERSTOCK ©

Planning

If you're a parent, you already know that fortune favors the prepared. But in Florida's crazy-crowded, overbooked high-season tourist spots, planning can make all the difference. Before you come, plot your trip like a four-star general: make reservations for every place you might go. Then, arrive, relax and go with the flow.

For all-round information and advice, check out Lonely Planet's *Travel with Children*.

What to Bring

If you forget something, don't sweat it. Just bring yourself, your kids and any of their can't-sleep-without items. Florida can supply the rest, from diapers to clothes to sunscreen to boogie boards.

That said, consider the following:

➡ For sleeping, a pack-and-play/portacot for infants and/or an inflatable mattress for older kids can be handy, especially if you're road-tripping or sticking to amenity-poor, budget-range motels.

➡ Bring light rain gear and umbrellas; it *will* rain at some point.

➡ Bring water sandals for the beach, water parks and play fountains.

➡ Bring sunscreen (a daily necessity) and mosquito repellent.

➡ Prepare a simple first-aid kit; the moment an unexpected cut or fever strikes is not the time to run to the drugstore.

Accommodations

The vast majority of Florida hotels stand ready to aid families with cribs (often pack-and-plays), rollaway beds (some charge extra), refrigerators, microwaves, adjoining rooms and suites. Ask about facilities when you book. Large hotels and resorts can go toe-to-toe with condos for amenities: including partial or full kitchens, laundry facilities, pools and barbecues, and activities.

While some high-end boutique hotels in Miami Beach and adult-oriented B&Bs in the Keys may discourage young kids, they aren't allowed to discriminate and ban them. If you're unsure, ask about their minimum age preference. In general, the best Miami neighborhoods to stay with kids are South Beach (despite the mad party scene, it has the best hotels in town), North Beach, Coconut Grove and Coral Gables. Children should be fine at most of these places, except for South Beach's priciest hotels – these hotels generally attract a celebrity-party crowd rather than families. Good family-style motels and B&Bs can be found in the Keys, Marathon, Islamorada and Key Largo.

Dining

Most midrange restaurants have a dedicated kids' menu, along with high chairs, crayons for coloring, and changing tables in restrooms. Even cheap ethnic eateries – a delicious, ubiquitous constant in the South Florida dining scene – are good at accommodating kids. Most restaurants, even high-end ones, are happy to make a kids' meal by request. As a rule, families with infants or toddlers will get better service earlier in the dinner hour (by 6pm). Some high-end restaurants may look askance at young diners; simply ask when making reservations.

Our favorite restaurants for kids:

Big Pink (p114)

Boater's Grill (p89)

11th St Diner (p113)

Steve's Pizza (p125)

Shuckers (p116)

Blue Heaven (p196)

Keys Fisheries (p179)

Camellia Street Grill (p155)

Robert Is Here (p157)

Animal Parks

Some visitors expect Disney World and Universal Studios to be just outside Miami

---

RULES OF THE ROAD

Florida car-seat laws require children aged under three to be in a car seat, and children under five in at least a booster seat (unless they are over 80lb and 4ft 9in tall, allowing seat belts to be positioned properly). Rental-car companies are legally required to provide child seats, but only if you reserve them in advance; they typically charge upwards of $10 a day extra. You can also rent them from baby-gear-rental companies.

(they're actually a few hours away). South Florida isn't a theme-park contender, but what it does possess, in oddly high numbers, are animal parks. Some are grassroots volunteer outfits that rescue injured beasts, such as the Turtle Hospital (p178) and Laura Quinn Wild Bird Sanctuary (p171) in the Keys. Others more closely resemble hybrid zoo-theme parks, such as Monkey Jungle (p92) and Jungle Island (p75) in Miami. These locations are a hit with kids, although you can expect more child-oriented infrastructure and exhibits in the Miami examples. There's also easy wildlife access at Royal Palm Visitor Center (p160) in the Everglades.

Beaches

The prototypical Florida family beach is fronted by – or near – very active, crowded commercial centers with lots of water sports and activities, tourist shops, grocery stores, and midrange eats and sleeps. Admittedly the region's most popular beach, South Beach, is a bit more sophisticated and snooty. But c'mon – this is still Florida. Lots of families hang out on the southern end of South Beach. Mid-Beach and North Beach are also more traditionally family-oriented, as are the beaches on Key Biscayne.

The Keys have only a few small beaches, despite being islands. However, Bahia Honda State Park (p181) on Bahia Honda Key is safe, reasonably nature-focused while still fun in a beachy way, and has a small, kid-oriented science center on-site. Sombrero Beach (p178) on Marathon is near a playground and has good food options.

Museums & Attractions

South Florida and the Keys holds its own in the 'Stuff Kids Love' stakes. In addition to all the animal life in the Everglades National Park (p146) and outside of it, there is decades worth of only-in-America kitsch. Hard to define 'sites' such as the Coral Castle (p156) in Homestead wow kids if only for their unique weirdness. The visitor centers of the area's many parks all have child-friendly interactive exhibits.

Some of the art museums may not jive with your kids (although the more cerebral ones will appreciate the trip), but institutions such as the Bass (p59) directly and indirectly sneak learning right into a child's day.

DATE NIGHT

Traveling with kids doesn't necessarily mean doing *everything* as a family. Want a romantic night on the town? Several child-care services offer in-hotel babysitting by certified sitters; a few run their own drop-off centers. Rates vary based on the number of children, and typically they require a four-hour minimum (plus a $10 travel surcharge). Hourly rates cost $14 to $25. These services generally apply to Miami; in the Keys you may have to ask the folks at your hotel front desk about local babysitting options, although larger resorts should have sitter staff in-house.

Kid's Nite Out (www.kidsniteout.com)

Sittercity (www.sittercity.com)

Sunshine Babysitting (www.sunshinebabysitting.com) Statewide.

Getting into Nature

Much of your time here is spent in air-conditioning, but don't overlook unpackaged nature. Florida is exceedingly flat, so rivers and trails are ideal for short legs. Raised boardwalks through alligator-filled swamps make perfect pint-sized adventures. Placid rivers and intercoastal bays are custom-made for first-time paddlers, adult or child. Never snorkeled a coral reef or surfed? Florida has gentle places to learn. Book a sea-life cruise, a manatee swim, a nesting-sea-turtle watch or a glass-bottom boat tour. At Oleta River State Park (p68) and almost every state park we review in the Keys, there's family-accessible kayaking and boating.

Travel Advice & Baby Gear

If you prefer to pack light, several services offer baby-gear rental (high chairs, strollers, car seats etc), while others sell infant supplies (diapers, wipes, formula, baby food etc), all delivered to your hotel; book one to two weeks in advance.

These websites provide family-centered travel advice and services:

Baby's Away (http://babysaway.com)

Babies Travel Lite (www.babiestravellite.com)

Jet Set Babies (http://jetsetbabies.com)

Regions at a Glance

Miami

**Food
Nightlife
Architecture**

Edible Exploration
Be it Venezuelan *arepas* stuffed with plantains or Thai-Japanese fusion cafes, the shabbiest Central American shack or Italian *osterias* prepping truffles and pasta, this city has a taste for cheap ethnic eateries and their budgetary evolution into high-end, four-star restaurants.

Party People
With a large Latin population, warm tropical evenings and money to burn, Miami doesn't like to stay at home. Bump shoulders with students in Coconut Grove or dance to EDM and trip-hop in the clubs that adjoin Wynwood and Downtown.

Deco Decor
In North Beach, the Miami Modern movement is felt in the shadows of enormous condos. In South Beach, deco rules the day. Take a few hours to wander the Art Deco Historic District, one of the most distinctive pockets of architectural preservation in the USA.

p52

The Everglades

**Wildlife
Quirkiness
Outdoor
Adventures**

Gator-Gawking
Wildlife-viewing is good in the Glades any time, but during the winter dry season, you'll see a *Jurassic Park*-style landscape of prehistoric reptiles plus an avian rainbow of wading birds.

Only in Florida
From a blue-crab shack across the street from the USA's smallest post office, to a giant Coral Castle located next to a sanctuary housing hyenas, timber wolves and tigers, the Everglades attracts America's eccentrics.

Early-Morning Kayaking
There is something magical about paddling over sheets of sunrise-dappled water, be it a slow marsh trickle or the wide teal expanses of Florida Bay. It's how mornings were made to be spent.

p139

Florida Keys & Key West

**Scenery
Arts
Food**

Mangroves & Hammocks
The Keys are an ecological anomaly in the USA: a series of mangrove islands that hide hammocks or groves of palm, pine and hardwoods found nowhere else in the country (and in some cases, the world).

Authors & Artists
Thanks to its open-mindedness and free-spirited allure, the Keys have long been an artist colony. Authors, from Hemingway to Frost, have been attracted to the island and its piratical, creative cast as well.

Fish & Mango Salsa
Folks here are mad for fishing and the culinary accompaniment to said hobby. Land food exists as well, accompanied by tropical garnishes and the famous Key lime pie.

p163

On the Road

South Beach (p58), Miami

Miami

POP 509,000 / ☎ 305, 786

Best Places to Eat

➡ Kyu (p119)

➡ 27 Restaurant (p115)

➡ Yardbird (p114)

➡ El Carajo (p121)

Best Places to Sleep

➡ Biltmore Hotel (p111)

➡ Washington Park Hotel (p103)

➡ Langford Hotel (p110)

➡ Betsy Hotel (p103)

➡ Freehand Miami (p108)

➡ EAST, Miami (p110)

Why Go?

Miami has so many different facets to its diverse neighborhoods that it's hard to believe it all fits in one place. By day you can admire incredible photorealistic murals in Wynwood, then spend the evening immersed in Afro Cuban jazz in Little Havana, followed perhaps by rooftop drinks atop the city's latest skyscraper. Crossing town you can't help feeling like you've passed into another city. Over in Miami Beach, you can wander the streets amid a veritable gallery of deco masterpieces, each one bursting with personality, best followed by late-afternoon strolls along the sands, when the golden light is mesmerizing.

When to Go
Miami

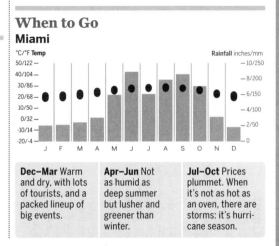

Dec–Mar Warm and dry, with lots of tourists, and a packed lineup of big events.

Apr–Jun Not as humid as deep summer but lusher and greener than winter.

Jul–Oct Prices plummet. When it's not as hot as an oven, there are storms: it's hurricane season.

Miami Highlights

1 Taking a stroll along Ocean Dr, seeing South Beach's **art-deco beauties** (p64).

2 Checking out a show and wandering the sculpture garden in the **Pérez Art Museum Miami** (p69).

3 Checking out the stunning collection of colorful outdoor murals at the epicenter of **Wynwood** (p80).

4 Sitting on the sands of **South Beach** (p58) and taking in the blend of peoples and cultures.

5 Marveling at the art and antiquities of **Vizcaya Museum & Gardens** (p83), followed by a stroll through its European gardens.

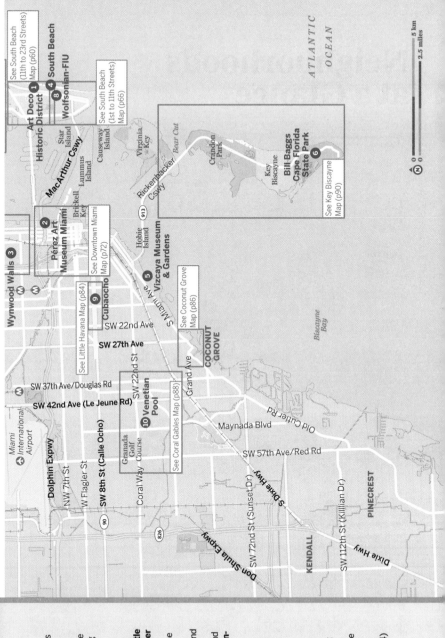

6 Walking the boardwalks and trails of **Bill Baggs Cape Florida State Park** (p89), basking on the beach, and snapping the Cape Florida Lighthouse.

7 Catching an exhibition at the **Little Haiti Cultural Center** (p77) especially on the third Friday of the month.

8 Browsing 19th- and 20th-century works of decorative arts and design at **Wolfsonian-FIU** (p58).

9 Catching a live performance from top artists from Cuba and beyond at the intimate and atmospheric **Cubaocho** (p132).

10 Splashing about the faux grottoes and coral cliffs of the whimsical aquatic masterpiece that is **Venetian Pool** (p94).

Neighborhoods at a Glance

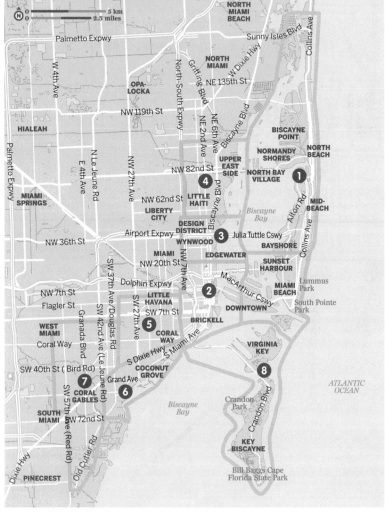

❶ North Beach (p63)

The long strip of beach and condo-studded landscape of North Beach offers a slightly different version of Miami Beach decadence. Instead of art deco, you'll find the so-called MiMo (Miami Modernist) style, of grand buildings constructed in the post-WWII boom days. Although it has a lower population density (and fewer restaurants, bars and shops), there's plenty of allure to North Beach – chief of all the beautiful shoreline, which the locals swear is covered in whiter sands.

② Downtown Miami (p69)

Downtown Miami, the city's international financial and banking center, is split between tatty indoor shopping arcades on the one hand, and new condos and high-rise luxury hotels in the area known as Brickell on the other. The lazy, gritty Miami River divides Downtown into north and south. Miami is defined by an often frenetic pace of growth, with construction a near constant as new luxury towers arrive with each passing month.

③ Wynwood & the Design District (p76)

Wynwood and the Design District are two of Miami's most creative neighborhoods, and are justly famed for a burgeoning arts scene. Wynwood is packed with galleries, as well as large-format street art covering once industrial spaces. It's also the place for great nightlife, and an emerging restaurant scene. The smaller Design District also has galleries, plus high-end shopping and a mixed bag of bars and eateries.

④ Little Haiti & the Upper East Side (p77)

Well north of Wynwood and the Design District, these two big neighborhoods see relatively few visitors. Little Haiti still feels derelict in parts, though it has a vibrant Haitian expat community, with much activity revolving around the colorful Little Haiti Cultural Center. Further east, the Upper East Side is best known for its striking modernist buildings lining Biscayne Blvd. It's something of Miami's great new frontier, with new restaurants, hotels and galleries setting up shop here in the last few years.

⑤ Little Havana (p79)

Little Havana's main thoroughfare, Calle Ocho (SW 8th St), doesn't just cut through the heart of the neighborhood; it *is* the heart of the neighborhood. In a lot of ways, this is every immigrant enclave in the USA – full of restaurants, mom-and-pop convenience shops and phonecard kiosks. Admittedly the Cubaness of Little Havana is slightly exaggerated for visitors, though it's still an atmospheric place to explore, with the crack of dominoes, the scent of wafting cigars, and Latin jazz spilling out of colorful storefronts.

⑥ Coconut Grove (p83)

Coconut Grove was once a hippie colony, but these days its demographic is middle-class, mall-going Miamians and college students. It's a pleasant place to explore with intriguing shops and cafes, and a walkable village-like vibe. It's particularly appealing in the evenings, when residents fill the outdoor tables of its bars and restaurants. Coconut Grove backs onto the waterfront, with a pretty marina and some pleasant green spaces.

⑦ Coral Gables (p85)

The lovely city of Coral Gables, filled with Mediterranean-style buildings, feels like a world removed from other parts of Miami. Here you'll find pretty banyan-lined streets, and a walkable village-like center, dotted with shops, cafes and restaurants. The big draws are the striking Biltmore Hotel, a lush tropical garden and one of America's loveliest swimming pools.

⑧ Key Biscayne (p87)

Key Biscayne and neighboring Virginia Key are a quick and easy getaway from Downtown Miami. But once you've passed across those scenic causeways, you'll feel like you've been transported to a far-off tropical realm, with magnificent beaches, lush nature trails in state parks, and aquatic adventures aplenty. The stunning skyline views of Miami alone are worth the trip out.

◉ Sights

◉ South Beach

The typical South Beach (Map p60; Ocean Dr; ☺ 5am-midnight) experience is anything but. You'll find plenty of early risers who head out for runs along the beach, followed by breakfast at a favorite vegan spot, yoga at a sun-drenched studio in the afternoon, a healthy meal and then perhaps an evening concert at the New World Center.

For others, the day starts about noon, with coffee and bloody Marys at a rock-blaring spot on Ocean Dr, then a lounge on the beach, a bit of strolling and window shopping on Lincoln Rd, dinner at a new hot spot in Sunset Harbour, followed by a late night of carousing at assorted lounges, rooftop bars and hidden dance clubs all over town.

Though you might have a fixed idea of what South Beach is all about, the stereotypes often fall short. South Beach is both chaotic and hedonistic (Ocean Dr around 9th St) and local and sedate (SoFi – or the blocks South of 5th St). In short, this burgeoning neighborhood is very much what you make of it – whether your interests are architecture, shopping, dining, drinking or just watching it all unfold as a dynamic jumble of peoples and cultures intersect in one very captivating tropical setting.

★ **Wolfsonian-FIU**   MUSEUM
(Map p66; ☑ 305-531-1001; www.wolfsonian.org; 1001 Washington Ave; adult/child $10/5, 6-9pm Fri free; ☺ 10am-6pm Mon, Tue, Thu & Sat, to 9pm Fri, noon-6pm Sun, closed Wed) Visit this top design museum early in your stay to put the aesthetics of Miami Beach into context. It's one thing to see how wealth, leisure and the pursuit of beauty manifest in Miami Beach, but it's another to understand the roots and shadings of local artistic movements. By chronicling the interior evolution of everyday life, the Wolfsonian reveals how these trends manifested architecturally in SoBe's exterior deco.

Art Deco Museum   MUSEUM
(Map p66; www.mdpl.org/welcome-center/art-deco-museum; 1001 Ocean Dr; $5; ☺ 10am-5pm Tue-Sun, to 7pm Thu) This small museum is one of the best places in town for an enlightening overview of the art-deco district. Through videos, photography, models and other displays, you'll learn about the pioneering work of Barbara Capitman, who helped save these buildings from certain destruction back in the 1970s, and her collaboration with Leonard Horowitz, the talented artist who designed the pastel color palette that become an integral part of the design visible today.

The museum also touches on other key architectural styles in Miami, including Mediterranean Revival (typefied by the Villa Casa Casuarina; p107) and the post-deco boom of MiMo (Miami Modern), which emerged after World War II, and is particularly prevalent in North Miami Beach.

New World Center   NOTABLE BUILDING
(Map p60; ☑ 305-673-3330, tours 305-673-3331; www.newworldcenter.com; 500 17th St; tours $5; ☺ tours 4pm Tue & Thu, 1pm Fri & Sat) Designed by Frank Gehry, this performance hall rises majestically out of a manicured lawn just above Lincoln Rd. Not unlike the ethereal power of the music within, the glass-and-steel facade encases characteristically Gehry-esque sail-like shapes within that help shape the magnificent acoustics and add to the futuristic quality of the concert hall. The grounds form a 2½-acre public park aptly known as SoundScape Park.

Some performances inside the center are projected outside via a 7000-sq-ft projection wall (the so-called 'Wallcast'), which might make you feel like you're in the classiest open-air theater on the planet. Reserve ahead for a 35-minute guided tour.

SoundScape Park   PARK
(Map p60; www.nws.edu; 500 17th St) Outside of the New World Center, this park is one of the best places for open-air screenings in Miami Beach. During some New World Symphony performances, the outside wall of the Frank Gehry–designed concert hall features a 7000-sq-ft projection of the concert within.

In addition from October through May, you can watch movies, with weekly film screenings (currently Wednesdays) at 8pm. Bring a picnic and enjoy the free show.

Holocaust Memorial   MEMORIAL
(Map p60; www.holocaustmmb.org; cnr Meridian Ave & Dade Blvd; ☺ 9:30am-10pm) Even for a Holocaust piece, this memorial is particularly powerful. With over 100 sculptures, its centerpiece is the *Sculpture of Love and Anguish,* an enormous, oxidized bronze arm with an artistic patina that bears an Auschwitz tattoo number – chosen because it was never issued at the camp, in order to represent all prisoners. Terrified families scale the sides of the arm, trying to pass their loved ones, including children, to safety only to see them later

massacred, while below lie figures of all ages in various poses of suffering.

Around the perimeter of the memorial are dozens of panels, which detail the grim history that led to the greatest genocide of the 20th century. This is followed by names of many who perished. The memorial doesn't gloss over the past. The light from a Star of David is blotted by the racist label of *Jude* (the German word for 'Jew'); representative of the yellow star that Jews in ghettos were forced to wear, and two Menora sculptures, flanking the Dome of Contemplation descent to the center, show the transformation from life to death in a rather lurid fashion. It's impossible to spend time here and not be moved.

The memorial was completed in 1990 through the efforts of Miami Beach Holocaust survivors, local business leaders and sculptor Kenneth Treister. Download the excellent free app (Holocaust Memorial Miami Beach) for iPhone or Android to learn more about the sculpture as well as hear testimonials from survivors, peruse slideshows and view interactive maps and additional audio and video.

The Bass MUSEUM
(Map p60; ☑ 305-673-7530; www.thebass.org; 2121 Park Ave; adult/child $8/6; ☉ noon-5pm Wed & Thu, Sat & Sun, to 9pm Fri) The best art museum in Miami Beach has a playfully futuristic facade, a crisp interplay of lines and a bright, white-walled space – like an Orthodox church on a space-age Greek isle. All designed, by the way, in 1930 by Russell Pancoast (grandson of John A Collins, who lent his name to Collins Ave). The collection isn't shabby either: permanent highlights range from 16th-century European religious works to northern European and Renaissance paintings.

The Bass recently underwent a $12 million renovation that added 50% more space to its layout. There are three new galleries, a Creativity Center, a new museum store and a cafe. The Bass also rebranded itself – officially adopting the informal name locals always used rather than the more formal 'Bass Museum of Art.' The museum forms one point of the Collins Park Cultural Center triangle, which also includes the three-story Miami City Ballet (p131) and the lovingly inviting Miami Beach Regional Library, which is a great place for free wi-fi.

Jewish Museum of Florida-FIU MUSEUM
(Map p66; ☑ 305-672-5044; www.jmof.fiu.edu; 301 Washington Ave; adult/student & senior $6/5, Sat free; ☉ 10am-5pm Tue-Sun, closed Jewish holi-days) Housed in a 1936 Orthodox synagogue that served Miami's first congregation, this small museum chronicles the rather large contribution Jews have made to the state of Florida. After all, it could be said that while Cubans made Miami, Jews made Miami Beach, both physically and culturally. Yet there were times when Jews were barred from the American Riviera they carved out of the sand, and this museum tells that story, along with some amusing anecdotes (like seashell Purim dresses).

ArtCenter/South Florida GALLERY
(Map p60; ☑ 305-674-8278; www.artcentersf.org; 924 Lincoln Rd, 2nd fl; ☉ 11am-7pm Mon-Fri, noon-8pm Sat & Sun) Established in 1984 by a small but forward-thinking group of artists, this compound is the creative heart of South Beach. In addition to some 52 artists' studios (many of which are open to the public), ArtCenter offers an exciting lineup of classes and lectures.

Post Office ARCHITECTURE
(Map p60; 1300 Washington Ave; ☉ 8am-5pm Mon-Fri, 8:30am-2pm Sat) Make it a point to mail a postcard from this 1937 deco gem of a post office, the very first South Beach renovation project tackled by preservationists in the '70s. This Depression moderne building in the 'stripped classic' style was constructed under President Roosevelt's administration and funded by the Works Progress Administration (WPA) initiative, which supported artists who were out of work during the Great Depression.

On the exterior, note the bald eagle and the turret with iron railings and, inside, a large wall mural of the Seminole's Florida invasion.

World Erotic Art Museum MUSEUM
(Map p60; ☑ 305-532-9336; www.weam.com; 1205 Washington Ave; over 18yr $15; ☉ 11am-10pm Mon-Thu, to midnight Fri-Sun) In a neighborhood where no behavior is too shocking, the World Erotic Art Museum celebrates its staggering but artful pornography, including pieces by Rembrandt and Picasso. Back in 2005, 70-year-old Naomi Wilzig turned her 5000-piece erotica collection into a South Beach attraction.

WEAM takes itself seriously, which is part of the charm of this fascinating collection spanning the ages, from ancient sex manuals to Victorian peep-show photos to an elaborate four-poster (four-phallus rather) Kama Sutra bed, with carvings in wood depicting

South Beach (11th to 23rd Streets)

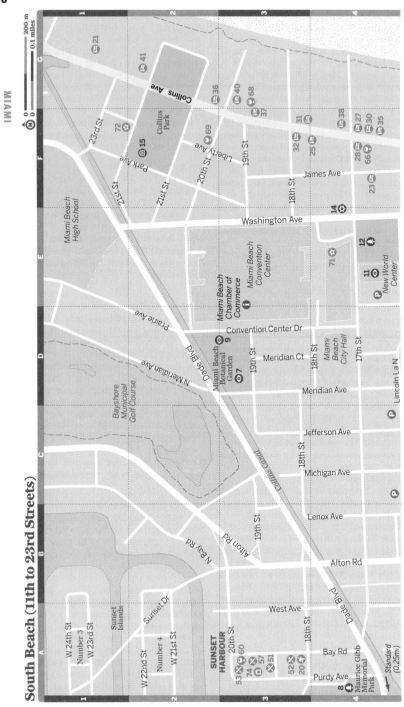

MIAMI

N
0 — 200 m
0 — 0.1 miles

1 ... **2** ... **3** ... **4**

W 24th St
Number 3
W 23rd St
23rd St
21st St
Miami Beach High School
Collins Ave
21
41
Collins Park
72
15
Park Ave
21st St
20th St
Liberty Ave
19th St
18th St
36
40
68
37
31
32
25
38
27
30
35
28
66
James Ave
23
Washington Ave
14

Sunset Islands
Number 4
W 22nd St
W 21st St
Sunset Dr
Sunset Dr
W 20th St
Bayshore Municipal Golf Course
Prairie Ave
N Meridian Ave
Dade Blvd
Miami Beach Botanical Garden
9
7
19th St
Convention Center Dr
Miami Beach Convention Center
Miami Beach Chamber of Commerce
71
Meridian Ct
Miami Beach City Hall
18th St
17th St
New World Center
12
11
Meridian Ave
Lincoln La N

SUNSET HARBOUR
53
74
60
57
51
52
20
20th St
19th Rd
N Bay Rd
Alton Rd
18th St
Collins Canal
West Ave
Bay Rd
Purdy Ave
Maurice Gibb Memorial Park
8
Alton Rd
Dade Blvd
Standard (0.25mi)

Jefferson Ave
18th St
Michigan Ave
Lenox Ave
Meridian Ave

ATLANTIC OCEAN

South Beach

13

Lincoln Rd

16th St

15th St

14th La

Ocean Dr

34

45

Promenade

Lummus Park

5 42 24 4 2

16 39

12th St

Ocean Ct

33

Collins Ave

22 29 55

62

63 64

67

48 65

49 6

26

54 50

17

Collins Ct

Washington Ave

18

Drexel Ave

14th St

Drexel Ave

12th St

Old City Hall

11th St

10

Pennsylvania Ave

Espanola Way

Euclid Ave

46

Lincoln Rd Mall

16th St

15th St

14th Pl

Meridian Ave

Meridian Ave

Jefferson Ave

Flamingo Park

Jefferson Ave

Courtyard

73

3 56

Michigan Ave

MIAMI BEACH

Lincoln La S

70

Lenox Ave

14th St

13th St

12th St

11th St

59 58

19

Sun Trust Bank

1 47

907

44

61

Alton Rd

14th Ct

Alton Ct

13th St

Alton Ct

15th Tce

15th St

Flamingo Way

14th Tce

13th Tce

West Ave

Lincoln Rd

Bay Rd

See South Beach (1st to 11th Streets) Map (p66)

MIAMI SIGHTS

South Beach (11th to 23rd Streets)

various ways (138 in fact) to get intimate. Other curiosities include the phallus bone of a whale with hand-carved wolf faces and the oversized sculpted genitals used as a murder weapon in *A Clockwork Orange*.

South Pointe Park   PARK
(Map p66; ☏305-673-7779; 1 Washington Ave; ☉sunrise-10pm; 🚼🐾) The very southern tip of Miami Beach has been converted into a lovely park, replete with manicured grass for lounging; a beach; views over a remarkably teal and fresh ocean; a restaurant; a refreshment stand; a tiny waterpark for kids; warm, scrubbed-stone walkways; and lots of folks who want to enjoy the great weather and views sans the South Beach strutting.

Española Way Promenade   AREA
(Map p60; btwn 14th & 15th Sts) Española Way is an 'authentic' Spanish promenade...in the Florida theme-park spirit of authenticity. Oh, whatever; it's a lovely terracotta and cobbled arcade of rose-pink and Spanish-cream architecture, perfect for an alfresco meal with

a side of people-watching at one of the many restaurants lining the strip.

Promenade
WATERFRONT

(Map p66; Ocean Dr) This beach promenade, a wavy ribbon sandwiched between the beach and Ocean Dr, extends from 5th St to 15th St. A popular location for photo shoots, especially during crowd-free early mornings, it's also a breezy, palm-tree-lined conduit for inline skaters, cyclists, volleyball players (there's a net at 11th St), dog walkers, yahoos, locals and tourists.

The beach that it edges, Lummus Park, sports six floridly colored lifeguard stands. There's a public bathroom at 11th St; the sinks are a popular place for homeless bathing.

1111 Lincoln Rd
ARCHITECTURE

(Map p60; www.1111lincolnroad.com; Ⓟ) The west side of Lincoln Rd is anchored by a most impressive parking garage: a geometric pastiche of sharp angles, winding corridors and incongruous corners that looks like a lucid fantasy dreamed up by Pythagoras after a long night out.

In fact, the building was designed by Swiss architecture firm Herzog & de Meuron, who describe the structure as 'all muscle without cloth.' Besides parking, 1111 Lincoln is filled with retail shops and residential units.

A1A
BRIDGE

'Beachfront Avenue!' The A1A causeway, coupled with the Rickenbacker Causeway in Key Biscayne, is one of the great bridges in America, linking Miami and Miami Beach via the glittering turquoise of Biscayne Bay.

To drive this road in a convertible or with the windows down, with a setting sun behind you, enormous cruise ships to the side, the palms swaying in the ocean breeze, and let's just say 'Royals' by Lorde on the radio, is basically the essence of Miami.

Miami Beach Community Church
CHURCH

(Map p60; www.miamibeachcommunitychurch. com; 1620 Drexel Ave; ◎8am-4pm Tue-Fri, service 10:30am Sun) In rather sharp and refreshing contrast to all the ubermodern structures muscling their way into the art-deco design of South Beach, this church puts one in mind of an old Spanish mission – humble, modest and elegantly understated in an area where overstatement is the general philosophy.

Temple Emanu-El
SYNAGOGUE

(Map p60; www.tesobe.org; Washington Ave at 17th St) An art-deco temple? Not exactly, but the smooth, bubbly dome and sleek, almost aerodynamic profile of this Conservative synagogue, established in 1938, fits right in on SoBe's deco parade of moderne this and streamline that. Shabbat services are on Friday at 7pm and on Saturday at 10am.

Miami Beach Botanical Garden
GARDENS

(Map p60; www.mbgarden.org; 2000 Convention Center Dr; suggested donation $2; ◎9am-5pm Tue-Sat) This lush but little-known 2.6 acres of plantings is operated by the Miami Beach Garden Conservancy, and is a veritable secret garden in the midst of the urban jungle – an oasis of palm trees, flowering hibiscus trees and glassy ponds. It's a great spot for a picnic.

◉ North Beach

For many folks who come to North Miami Beach, the draw is the shoreline, plain and simple. Of course, given the undulating coastline and diverse layout of the land, coming to the shore can mean many different things. It can mean holing up in one of the area's new five-star hotels, taking a long stroll along a pretty boardwalk or exploring one of the many protected reserves further north – kayaking and mountain biking in the Oleta River State Park or simply frolicking in the waves of photogenic Haulover Beach Park.

Beaches aside, there's a first-rate assortment of dining and nightlife here, which if anything feels a little classier than (and just as pricey as) options down on South Beach.

Faena Forum
CULTURAL CENTER

(Map p70; www.faena.com; Collins Ave & 33rd St) Part of the ambitious new $1 billion Faena District, this new cultural center has been

---

KEEPING IT KOSHER IN MIAMI BEACH

They're no shtetls, but Arthur Godfrey Rd (41st St) and Harding Ave between 91st and 96th Sts in Surfside are popular thoroughfares for the Jewish population of Miami Beach. Just as the Jewish population have shaped Miami Beach, so has the beach shaped them: you can eat lox *y arroz con moros* (salmon with rice and beans) and while the Orthodox men don yarmulkes and the women wear headscarves, many have nice tans and drive flashy SUVs.

TOP SIGHT
ART DECO HISTORIC DISTRICT

The world-famous Art Deco Historic District of Miami Beach is pure exuberance: architecture of bold lines, whimsical tropical motifs and a color palette that evokes all the beauty of the Miami landscape. Among the 800 deco buildings listed on the National Register of Historic Buildings, each design is different, and it's hard not to be captivated when strolling among these restored beauties from a bygone era.

Background

For much of its history, Miami Beach was little more than an empty landscape of swaying palm trees, scrubland and sandy shoreline. It wasn't until the early 20th century that a few entrepreneurs began to envision transforming the island into a resort. Beginning in the 1920s, a few hotels rose up, catering to an elite crowd of wealthy industrialists vacationing from the north. And then disaster struck. In 1926 a hurricane left a devastating swath across the island and much of South Florida.

When it was time to rebuild, Miami Beach would undergo a dramatic rebirth. This is where art deco enters from stage left. As luck would have it, at exactly that moment, a bold new style of architecture was all the talk in America, having burst onto the scene at a renowned fair known as the Exposition Internationale des Arts Décoratifs et Industriels Modernes held in Paris in 1925.

Over the next few years developers arrived in droves, and the building boom was on. Miami Beach would become the epicenter of this ground-breaking new design (which incidentally was not called 'art deco' in those days, but simply 'art moderne' or 'modernistic'). Hundreds of new hotels were built during the 1930s to accommodate the influx of middle-class tourists flooding into Miami Beach for a slice of sand and sun. And the golden era of deco architecture continued until it all came to an end during WWII.

DON'T MISS
➡ Eyebrow-like window ledges on the Congress Hotel

➡ Hidden seahorses on the facade of the Cavalier Hotel

➡ Nautical motifs in the Tides Hotel

PRACTICALITIES
➡ Map p60

➡ Ocean Dr

Deco Style

The art-deco building style was very much rooted in the times. The late 1920s and 1930s was an era of invention – of new automobiles, streamlined machines, radio antennae and cruise ships. Architects manifested these elements in the strong vertical and horizontal lines, at times coupled with zig-zigs or sleek curves, all of which created the illusion of movement, of the bold forward march into the future.

In Miami Beach architects also incorporated more local motifs such as palm trees, flamingos and tropical plants. Nautical themes also appeared, with playful representations of ocean waves, sea horses, starfish and lighthouses. The style later became known as tropical deco.

Architects also came up with unique solutions to the challenges of building design in a hot, sun-drenched climate. Eyebrow-like ledges jutted over the windows, providing shade (and cooler inside temperatures), without obstructing the views. And thick glass blocks were incorporated into some building facades. These let in light while keeping out the heat – essential design elements in those days before air-conditioning.

The Best of Ocean Drive

One stretch of Ocean Dr has a collection of some of the most striking art-deco buildings in Miami Beach. Between 11th and 14th Sts, you'll see many of the classic deco elements at play in beautifully designed works – each bursting with individual personality. Close to 11th St, the Congress Hotel (Map p66; 1052 Ocean Dr) shows perfect symmetry in its three-story facade, with window-shading 'eyebrows' and a long marquee down the middle that's reminiscent of the grand movie palaces of the 1930s. About a block north, the Tides (Map p60; ☑305-250-0784; www.tidessouthbeach.com; 1220 Ocean Dr; r from $340; P❋☎☀) is one of the finest of the nautical themed hotels, with porthole windows over the entryway, a reception desk of Key limestone (itself imprinted with fossilized sea creatures), and curious arrows on the floor, meant to denote the ebb and flow of the tide. Near 13th St, the Cavalier (p102) plays with the seahorse theme, in stylized depictions of the sea creature and also has palm-tree-like iconography.

TOP TIPS

➡ Go early in the day when the crowds are thinnest, and the light is best for taking pictures.

➡ For deeper insight into the architecture, take a guided walking tour offered daily by the Miami Design Preservation League (p96).

➡ Complete the deco experience by checking out the excellent exhibitions at the Art Deco Museum (p58) or the Wolfsonian-FIU (p58), both nearby.

➡ Stop in for sandwiches, gelato and excellent espresso at Pinocchio (p127).

➡ Complete the journey into the past with a meal in the 11th St Diner (p113), set in a 1940s train car.

South Beach (1st to 11th Streets)

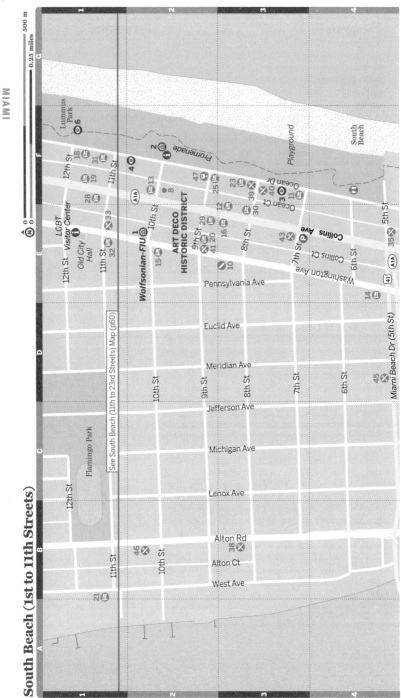

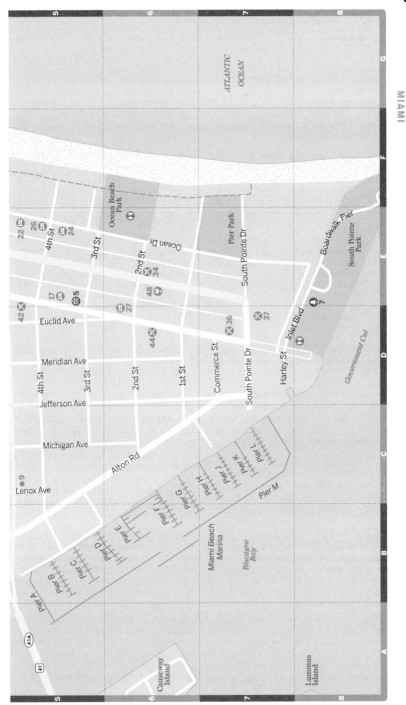

MIAMI

ATLANTIC OCEAN

Ocean Beach Park

Pier Park

South Pointe Dr

Boardwalk Pier

South Pointe Park

Government Cut

4th St
3rd St
Ocean Dr
2nd St
Euclid Ave
Meridian Ave
4th St
3rd St
Jefferson Ave
Michigan Ave
Alton Rd
Lenox Ave
2nd St
1st St
Commerce St
South Pointe Dr
Harley St
Inlet Blvd

22
26
24
17
5
42
48
27
44
34
36
37
9
7

A1A
41

Pier A
Pier B
Pier C
Pier D
Pier E
Pier F
Pier G
Pier H
Pier J
Pier K
Pier L
Pier M

Miami Beach Marina

Biscayne Bay

Causeway Island

Lummus Island

South Beach (1st to 11th Streets)

turning heads ever since its opening in late 2016. The circular Rem Koolhaas–designed building features rooms for performances, exhibitions, lectures and other events. Check the website to see what's coming up.

Oleta River State Park   STATE PARK
(☎305-919-1844; www.floridastateparks.org/oletariver; 3400 NE 163rd St; vehicle/pedestrian & bicycle $6/2; ⊙8am-sunset; P⊕) Tequesta people were boating the Oleta River estuary as early as 500 BC, so you're just following in a long tradition if you paddle in this park. At almost 1000 acres, this is the largest urban park in the state and one of the best places in Miami to escape the madding crowd. Boat out to the local mangrove island, watch the eagles fly by, or just chill on the pretension-free beach.

On-site BG Oleta River Outdoor Center (p93) rents out kayaks, canoes, stand-up paddleboards and mountain bikes. It also offers paddling tours, yoga classes on stand-up paddleboards and other activities. The park is off 163rd St NE/FL 826 in Sunny Isles, about 8 miles north of North Miami Beach.

Fontainebleau   HISTORIC BUILDING
(Map p70; www.fontainebleau.com; 4441 Collins Ave) As you proceed north on Collins, the condos and apartment buildings grow in grandeur and embellishment until you enter an area nicknamed Millionaire's Row. The most fantastic jewel in this glittering crown is the Fontainebleau hotel (p109). The hotel – mainly the pool, which has since been renovated – features in Brian de Palma's classic *Scarface*.

Eden Roc Renaissance   HISTORIC BUILDING
(Map p70; www.nobuedenroc.com; 4525 Collins Ave) The Eden Roc was the second groundbreaking resort from Morris Lapidus, and it's a fine example of the architecture known as MiMo (Miami Modern). It was the hangout for the 1960s Rat Pack – Sammy Davis Jr, Dean Martin, Frank Sinatra and crew. Extensive renovation has eclipsed some of Lapidus' style, but with that said, the building is still an iconic piece of Miami Beach architecture, and an exemplar of the brash beauty of Millionaire's Row.

Boardwalk   BEACH
(Map p70; www.miamibeachboardwalk.com; 21st St-46th St) What's trendy in beachwear this season? Seventeenth-century Polish gabardine coats, apparently. There are plenty of skimpily dressed hotties on the Mid-Beach boardwalk, but there are also Orthodox Jews going about their business in the midst of gay joggers, strolling tourists and sunbathers. Nearby are numerous condo buildings occupied by middle-class Latinos and Jews, who walk their dogs and play with their kids here, giving the entire place a laid-back, real-world vibe that contrasts with the nonstop glamour of South Beach.

Haulover Beach Park   PARK
(☑ 305-947-3525; www.miamidade.gov/parks/haulover.asp; 10800 Collins Ave; per car Mon-Fri $5, Sat-Sun $7; ☺ sunrise-sunset; Ⓟ) Where are all those tanned men in gold chains and Speedos going? That would be the clothing-optional beach in this 40-acre park hidden from condos, highways and prying eyes by vegetation. There's more to do here than get in the buff, though; most of the beach is 'normal' (there's even a dog park) and is one of the nicer spots for sand in the area. The park is on Collins Ave about 4.5 miles north of 71st St.

◎ Downtown Miami

Once a fairly barren area as far as sights go, Downtown has gone through a remarkable renaissance in recent years, with new projects planned on the horizon. While the neighborhood spreads across a lot of ground, this is one part of Miami where you don't need a car. Free public transport can whisk you from place to place, and parts of Downtown are quite walkable, and well worth exploring on foot (such as Bayfront Park and the riverside).

You could easily spend a few days taking in Downtown attractions, visiting the excellent museums here, taking in pretty views and catching a show at one of its fine performing arts venues. Downtown is very much a local hangout, with rooftop bars, plush nightclubs and creative eateries catering to both city workers and well-heeled condo dwellers who've been lured into the neighborhood in the last few years.

★ Pérez Art Museum Miami   MUSEUM
(PAMM; Map p72; ☑ 305-375-3000; www.pamm.org; 1103 Biscayne Blvd; adult/seniors & students $16/12, 1st Thu & 2nd Sat of month free; ☺ 10am-6pm Fri-Tue, to 9pm Thu, closed Wed; Ⓟ) The Pérez can claim fine rotating exhibits that concentrate on post-WWII international art, but just as impressive are its location and exterior. This art institution inaugurated Museum Park, a patch of land that overseas the broad blue swath of Biscayne Bay. Swiss architects Herzog & de Meuron designed the structure, which integrates tropical foliage, glass and metal – a melding of tropical vitality and fresh modernism that is a nice architectural analogy for Miami itself.

PAMM stages some of the best contemporary exhibitions in Miami. The permanent collection rotates through unique pieces every few months drawing from a treasure trove of work spanning the last 80 years, which is assembled in exhibitions that are always thought-provoking. The temporary shows and retrospectives bring major crowds (past exhibitions have included the works of famed Chinese artist Ai Weiwei and kinetic artist Julio Le Parc). Meanwhile the outdoor space also functions as an open-air sculpture garden.

If you need a little breather amid all this contemporary culture, PAMM has a first-rate cafe, or you can simply hang out in the grassy park or lounge on a deck chair enjoying the views over the water.

★ HistoryMiami   MUSEUM
(Map p72; ☑ 305-375-1492; www.historymiami.org; 101 W Flagler St; adult/child $10/5; ☺ 10am-5pm Mon-Sat, from noon Sun; ♿) South Florida – a land of escaped slaves, guerilla Native Americans, gangsters, land grabbers, pirates, tourists, drug dealers and alligators – has a special history, and it takes a special kind of museum to capture that narrative. This highly recommended place, located in the Miami-Dade Cultural Center, does just that, weaving together the stories of the region's successive waves of population, from Native Americans to Nicaraguans.

The collection is spread between two buildings. Start off in the permanent collection, which has interactive exhibits showing life among the Seminoles, early Florida industries like sponge diving, and wealth made from 'wreckers' (those who salvaged treasure lost on the reefs). More recent-era exhibits touch on the WWII period (when troops were stationed in Miami Beach), African American history and Cuban refugees (with a rustic homemade boat that managed

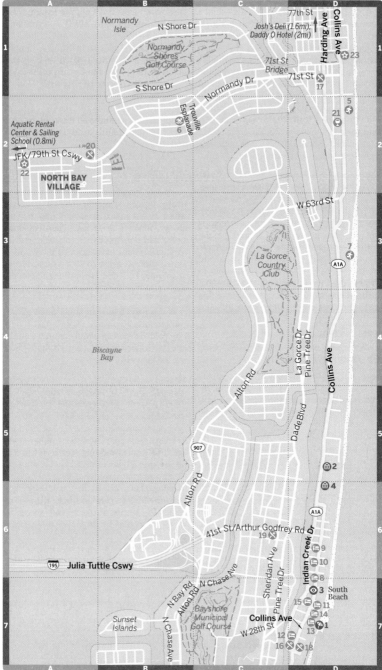

North Beach

N 0 ——————— 1 km
0 ——————— 0.5 miles

Normandy Isle

N Shore Dr

Normandy Shores Golf Course

S Shore Dr

Normandy Dr

77th St

Josh's Deli (1.6mi);
Daddy O Hotel (2mi)

Harding Ave

Collins Ave

71st St Bridge

71st St

Aquatic Rental Center & Sailing School (0.8mi)

JFK/79th St Cswy

NORTH BAY VILLAGE

Trouville Esplanade

W 63rd St

La Gorce Country Club

Biscayne Bay

Alton Rd

La Gorce Dr
Pine Tree Dr

Collins Ave

Dade Blvd

Alton Rd

907

A1A

Julia Tuttle Cswy

195

41st St/Arthur Godfrey Rd

Indian Creek Dr

South Beach

Sheridan Ave

Pine Tree Dr

N Bay Rd
N Chase Ave
Alton Rd

Bayshore Municipal Golf Course

N Chase Ave

Sunset Islands

N Chase Ave

Collins Ave

W 28th St

North Beach

to survive the treacherous crossing to Florida). Get off the Metromover at the Government Center stop.

★ **Bayfront Park** PARK
(Map p72; ☎ 305-358-7550; www.bayfrontpark miami.com; 301 N Biscayne Blvd) Few American parks can claim to front such a lovely stretch of turquoise (Biscayne Bay), but Miamians are lucky like that. Notable park features are two performance venues: the Klipsch Amphitheater (p131), which boasts excellent views over Biscayne Bay and is a good spot for live-music shows, while the smaller 200-seat (lawn seating can accommodate 800 more) **Tina Hills Pavilion** hosts free springtime performances.

Look north for the **JFK Torch of Friendship**, and a fountain recognizing the accomplishments of longtime US congressman Claude Pepper. There's a huge variety of activities here, including flying trapeze classes and free yoga classes (p94), plus a great playground for the kids.

Noted artist and landscape architect Isamu Noguchi redesigned much of Bayfront Park in the 1980s and dotted the grounds with three sculptures. In the southwest corner is the **Challenger Memorial**, a monument designed for the astronauts killed in the 1986 space-shuttle explosion, built to resemble both the twisting helix of a human DNA chain and the shuttle itself. The **Light Tower** is a 40ft, somewhat abstract allusion to Japanese lanterns and moonlight over Miami. Our favorite is the **Slide Mantra**, a twisting spiral of marble that doubles as a playground piece for the kids.

Patricia & Phillip Frost Museum of Science MUSEUM
(Map p72; ☎ 305-434-9600; www.frost science.org; 1101 Biscayne Blvd; adult/child $28/20; ☺ 9am-6pm; ⓟ ⓱) This sprawling new Downtown museum spreads across 250,000 sq ft that includes a three-level aquarium, a 250-seat, state-of-the-art planetarium and two distinct wings that delve into the wonders of science and nature. Exhibitions range from weather phenomena to creepy crawlies, feathered dinosaurs and vital-microbe displays, while Florida's fascinating Everglades and biologically rich coral reefs play starring roles.

The new facility, which cost a staggering $305 million to complete, was built with sustainability in mind. It opened in 2017.

Brickell City Centre AREA
(Map p72; www.brickellcitycentre.com; 701 S Miami Ave; ☺ 10am-9:30pm Mon-Sat, noon-7pm Sun) One of the hottest new developments in Miami finally opened its doors in late 2016, after four long years of construction. The massive billion-dollar complex spreads across three city blocks, and it encompasses glittering residential towers, modernist office blocks and a soaring five-star hotel (the EAST, Miami; p110). There's much to entice both Miami residents and visitors to the center, with restaurants, bars, a cinema

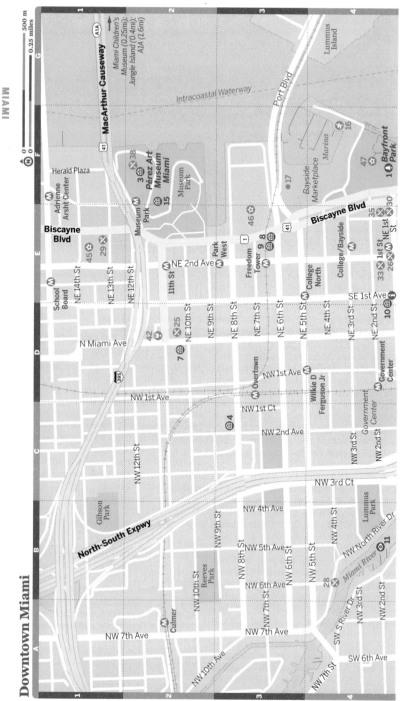

MIAMI

Downtown Miami

500 m
0.25 miles

Miami Children's
Museum (0.25mi);
Jungle Island (0.4mi);
A1A (1.6mi)

MacArthur Causeway

A1A

41

Intracoastal Waterway

Port Blvd

Lummus
Island

Herald Plaza

Pérez Art
Museum
Miami

3 ❌ 38
15

Museum Park

Museum
Park

16

Bayfront
Park

47

Bayside
Marketplace

Marina

17

Adrienne
Arsht Center

Biscayne Blvd

Biscayne
Blvd

45 ❌ 29

41

46

Freedom
Tower

1

9 8

35
30

Biscayne Blvd

College/Bayside

NE 14th St
NE 13th St
NE 12th St

11th St

NE 2nd Ave

Park
West

College
North

1st St ❌ 33
26 ❌
NE 1st
St

School
Board

Museum
Park

N Miami Ave

42

❌ 25

NE 10th St

NE 9th St

NE 8th St

NE 7th St

NE 6th St

NE 5th St

NE 4th St

NE 3rd St

SE 1st Ave

NE 2nd St

10

7

395

Overtown

NW 1st Ave

NW 1st Ave

NW 1st Ct

Wilkie D
Ferguson Jr

Government
Center

4

NW 2nd Ave

NW 3rd St

NW 2nd St

Government
Center

NW 12th St

NW 3rd Ct

Gibson
Park

NW 4th Ave

Lummus
Park

North-South Expwy

NW 10th St
Reeves
Park

NW 9th St

NW 8th St

NW 5th Ave

NW 6th St

NW 5th St

NW 4th St

NW North River Dr

11

28

Miami River

NW 6th Ave

SW S River Dr

NW 3rd St

NW 2nd St

Culmer

NW 7th Ave

NW 7th St

NW 7th Ave

NW 7th Ave

NW 10th Ave

SW 6th Ave

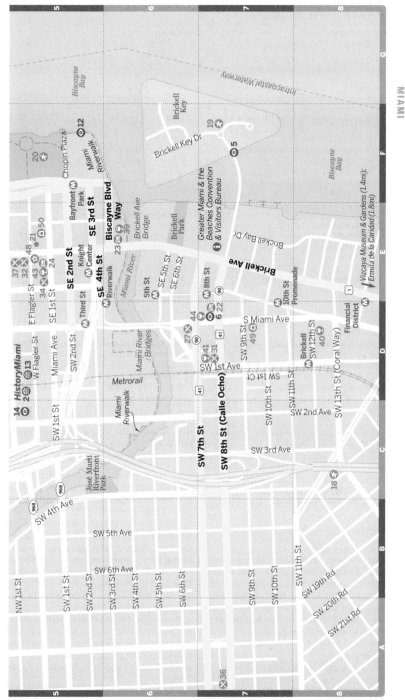

MIAMI

Biscayne Bay

Intracoastal Waterway

Brickell Key

Brickell Key Dr

19

5

Biscayne Bay

Chopin Plaza

20

12

Miami Riverwalk

Bayfront Park

Brickell Blvd Way

SE 3rd St

Brickell Ave Bridge

39

Brickell Park

Greater Miami & the Beaches Convention & Visitors Bureau

Brickell Bay Dr

Vizcaya Museum & Gardens (1.4mi);
Ermita de la Caridad (1.8mi)

50

21

48

Knight Center

24

37

32

SE 2nd St

E Flagler St

SE 1st St

43

34

Third St

Riverwalk

SE 4th St

Miami River

5th St

SE 5th St

SE 6th St

Brickell Ave

8th St

90

10th St Promenade

1

Financial District

SW 2nd St

Miami Ave

SW 1st St

W Flagler St

HistoryMiami

13

14

2

SW 1st St

Miami River Bridges

SW 1st Ave

44

27

90

6 22

41

31

S Miami Ave

SW 9th St

49

Brickell

SW 12th St

40

SW 13th St (Coral Way)

Metrorail

Miami Riverwalk

SW 1st Ct

SW 1st St

SW 10th St

SW 11th St

SW 2nd Ave

SW 7th St

SW 8th St (Calle Ocho)

41

SW 3rd Ave

José Martí Riverfront Park

968

SW 4th Ave

968

NW 1st St

SW 1st St

SW 2nd St

SW 3rd St

SW 4th St

SW 5th St

SW 6th St

SW 5th Ave

SW 6th Ave

SW 9th St

SW 10th St

SW 11th St

SW 19th Rd

SW 20th Rd

SW 21st Rd

18

36

Downtown Miami

and loads of high-end retailers (Ted Baker, All Saints, Kendra Scott).

You'll find shops scattered across both sides of S Miami Ave between 7th and 8th Sts, including a massive Saks Fifth Ave. Still in the works was a three-story Italian food emporium, with restaurants, cafes, a bakery, an enoteca and a culinary school. It was slated to open by early 2018.

Miami Riverwalk
WATERFRONT

(Map p72) This pedestrian walkway follows along the northern edge of the river as it bisects Downtown, and offers some peaceful vantage points of bridges and skyscrapers dotting the urban landscape. You can start the walk at the south end of Bayfront Park and follow it under bridges and along the waterline till it ends just west of the SW 2nd Ave Bridge.

The Riverwalk is one small section of the ambitious Miami River Greenway project, which aims to extend a green path along both banks of the river all the way to the river's intersection with the Dolphin Expressway.

Freedom Tower
HISTORIC BUILDING

(Map p72; 600 Biscayne Blvd; ⊙10am-5pm) An iconic slice of Miami's old skyline, the richly ornamented Freedom Tower is one of two surviving towers modeled after the Giralda bell tower in Spain's Cathedral of Seville. As the 'Ellis Island of the South,' it served as an immigration processing center for almost half a million Cuban refugees in the 1960s. Placed on the National Register of Historic Places in 1979, it was also home to the *Miami Daily News* for 32 years.

In the beautifully restored lobby, above the elevators and stretching toward the coffered ceiling, you can see reliefs of men at work on the printing presses. The tower also houses the MDC Museum of Art & Design.

Black Archives Historic Lyric Theater

HISTORIC BUILDING

(Map p72; ☑786-708-4610; www.bahlt.org; 819 NW 2nd Ave; ☺museum 10am-6pm Mon-Sat, noon-5pm Sun) Duke Ellington and Ella Fitzgerald once walked across the stage of the Lyric, a major stop on the 'Chitlin' Circuit' – the black live-entertainment trail of preintegration USA. As years passed both the theater and the neighborhood it served, Overtown, fell into disuse. Then the Black Archives History & Research Foundation of South Florida took over the building. Today the theater hosts occasional shows, while the Archives hosts excellent exhibitions exploring African American heritage both in Miami and beyond.

Brickell Avenue Bridge & Brickell Key

ISLAND

(Map p72) Crossing the Miami River, the lovely Brickell Avenue Bridge between SE 4th St and SE 5th St was made wider and higher several years ago, which was convenient for the speedboat-driving drug runners being chased by Drug Enforcement Administration agents on the day of the bridge's grand reopening! Note the 17ft bronze statue by Cuban-born sculptor Manuel Carbonell of a Tequesta warrior and his family, which sits atop the towering Pillar of History column.

MDC Museum of Art & Design

MUSEUM

(Freedom Tower; Map p72; ☑305-237-7700; www. mdcmoad.org; 600 Biscayne Blvd) Miami-Dade College operates a small but well-curated art museum in Downtown; the permanent collection includes works by Matisse, Picasso and Chagall and focuses on minimalism, pop art and contemporary Latin American art. The museum's home building is art itself: it's set in the soaring 255ft (78m) Freedom Tower, a masterpiece of Mediterranean Revival, built in 1925.

Miami City Cemetery

CEMETERY

(Map p78; 1800 NE 2nd Ave; ☺7am-3:30pm Mon-Fri, 8am-4:30pm Sat & Sun) This quiet graveyard, the final resting place of some of Miami-Dade's most important citizens, is a sort of narrative of the history of the city cast in bone, dirt and stone. The dichotomy of the past and modernity gets a nice visual representation in the form of looming condos shadowing the last abode of the Magic City's late, great ones.

More than 9000 graves are divided into separate white, black and Jewish sections. Buried here are mayors, veterans (including about 90 Confederate soldiers) and the godmother of South Florida, Julia Tuttle, who purchased the first orange groves that attracted settlers to the area.

Miami Center for Architecture & Design

MUSEUM

(Old US Post Office; Map p72; ☑305-448-7488; www.miamicad.org; 100 NE 1st Ave; ☺10am-5pm Mon-Fri) **FREE** It makes sense that the Miami branch of the American Institute of Architects would pick the Old US Post Office as headquarters of their Center for Architecture & Design. Built in 1912, this was the first federal building in Miami. It features a low-pitched roof, elaborate doors and carved entryways, and was purchased in 1937 to serve as the country's first savings and loan association.

Today it houses lectures and events related to architecture, design and urban planning, and hosts a small but vibrant exhibition on all of the above subjects. Two-hour walking tours on alternate Saturdays depart from here (at 10am), and take in some of the historic buildings of Downtown. Visit the website for upcoming times and reservations.

Miami River

RIVER

(Map p72) For a taste of old Florida, take a stroll along the Miami River. A shoreline promenade leads past a mix of glittering high-rise condos and battered warehouses tinged with graffiti, with a few small tugboats putting along the glassy surface. Fisherfolk float in with their daily catch – en route to places like Casablanca (p116) – while fancy yachts make their way in and out of the bay.

There are some photogenic vantage points over the river from the bridges – particularly the Brickell Ave bridge at dusk, when the city lights glow against the darkening night sky.

Miami Children's Museum

MUSEUM

(☑305-373-5437; www.miamichildrensmuseum. org; 980 MacArthur Causeway; $20; ☺10am-6pm; ⓐ) This museum, located between South Beach and Downtown Miami, isn't exactly a museum. It feels more like an uberplayhouse, with areas for kids to practice all sorts of adult activities – banking and food shopping, caring for pets, and acting as a local cop or firefighter.

Other imaginative areas let kids make music, go on undersea adventures, make wall sketches, explore a little castle made of colored glass or play on outdoor playgrounds.

Jungle Island
ZOO

(☑305-400-7000; www.jungleisland.com; 1111 Parrot Jungle Trail, off MacArthur Causeway; adult/child/senior $40/33/38; ☺10am-5pm; P♿) Jungle Island, packed with tropical birds, alligators, orangutans, chimps, lemurs, a (wait for it *Napoleon Dynamite* fans) liger (a cross between a lion and a tiger) and a Noah's Ark of other animals, is a ton of fun. It's one of those places kids (justifiably) beg to go, so just give up and prepare for some bright-feathered, bird-poop-scented fun in this artificial, self-contained jungle.

Cisneros Fontanal
Arts Foundation
MUSEUM

(CIFO; Map p72; ☑305-455-3380; www.cifo.org; 1018 N Miami Ave; ☺noon-6pm Thu & Fri, 10am-4pm Sat & Sun) This arts foundation displays the work of contemporary Latin American artists, and has an impressive showroom to boot. Even the exterior blends postindustrial rawness with a lurking, natural ambience, offset by the extensive use of Bisazza tiles to create an overarching tropical motif. The opening hours only apply during exhibition showings, although informal tours can be arranged if you call ahead.

Miami-Dade Public Library
LIBRARY

(Map p72; ☑305-375-2665; www.mdpls.org; 101 W Flagler St; ☺10am-6pm Mon-Sat) To learn more about Florida (especially South Florida), take a browse through the extensive Florida Collection, or ask about the Romer Photograph Collection, an archive of some 17,500 photos and prints that chronicles the history of the city from its early years to 1945. At the library, ask for John Shipley, head of the Florida Collection, for more details.

Miami-Dade
County Courthouse
HISTORIC BUILDING

(Map p72; 73 W Flagler St) If you end up on trial here, at least you'll get a free tour of one of the most imposing courthouses in the USA. Built between 1925 and 1929, this a very... appropriate building: if structures were people, the 28-story neoclassical courthouse would definitely be a judge. Some trivia: back in the day, the top nine floors served as a 'secure' prison, from which more than 70 prisoners escaped.

◉ Wynwood &
the Design District

Wynwood has become quite the celebrity in recent years. First came the Wynwood Walls (p80) – a collection of vibrant building-sized murals painted by top internationtal street artists. Then came the trickle of galleries, bars and restaurants, which was shortly thereafter followed by explosive growth. Today Wynwood has some of the city's best cafes, bakeries, taco stalls and fusion eateries, as well as creative boutiques, microbreweries and cocktail dens. That said, you could spend a few days just exploring the neighborhood. Come in the daytime for gallery-hopping, window shopping and snacking, but return at night when the neighborhood is at its liveliest. That's when the creative set mingles in its candlelit brewpubs and backyard music joints.

Just north of Wynwood, the Design District has a more refined (ie expensive) feel. Its main shopping strip is filled with lovely if stratospherically priced objects: Italian-designed chairs, Russian Romanov-era cabinets, Dale Chihuly–esque chandeliers – that sort of thing. Shopping aside, several excellent galleries are here, as well as public sculptures, and some appealing eating and drinking spots orbiting on the perimeter.

Between Wynwood and the Design District is Midtown, essentially one giant upscale outdoor mall sprinkled with boutiques, restaurants and bars catering to new condo residents. It feels decidedly less bohemian than Wynwood, but is worth a look when visiting these two 'hoods.

★ Margulies Collection
at the Warehouse
GALLERY

(Map p78; ☑305-576-1051; www.marguglieswarehouse.com; 591 NW 27th St; adult/student $10/5; ☺11am-4pm Tue-Sat mid-Oct–Apr) Encompassing 45,000 sq ft, this vast not-for-profit exhibition space houses one of the best collections in Wynwood. Thought-provoking, large-format installations are the focus at the Warehouse, and you'll see works by some leading 21st-century artists here.

Rotating exhibitions pull from Martin Margulies' awe-inspiring 4000-piece collection, which includes sculptures by Isamu Noguchi, George Segal, Richard Serra and Olafur Eliasson – among many others luminaries in the art world – plus sound installations by Susan Philipsz and jaw-dropping room-sized works by Anselm Kiefer.

Bakehouse Art Complex
GALLERY

(BAC; Map p78; ☑305-576-2828; www.bacfl.org; 561 NW 32nd St; ☺noon-5pm; P) FREE One of the pivotal art destinations in Wynwood, the

Bakehouse has been an arts incubator since well before the creation of the Wynwood Walls. Today this former bakery houses galleries and some 60 studios, and the range of works you can find here is quite impressive. Check the schedule for upcoming artist talks and other events.

De La Cruz Collection   GALLERY
(Map p78; ☑ 305-576-6112; www.delacruzcollection. org; 23 NE 41st St; ☉10am-4pm Tue-Sat) FREE Housing one of Miami's finest private collections, this 30,000-sq-ft gallery has a treasure trove of contemporary works scattered across three floors, which you can roam freely. Rosa and Carlos de la Cruz, who originally hail from Cuba, have particularly strong holdings in postwar German paintings, as well as fascinating works by Jim Hodges, Ana Mendieta and Felix Gonzalez-Torres.

Fly's Eye Dome   SCULPTURE
(Map p78; 140 NE 39th St, Palm Court) Installed during Art Basel (p100) in 2014, Buckminster Fuller's striking geodesic dome looks otherworldly as it appears to float in a small reflecting pool surrounded by slender, gently swaying palm trees. The 24ft-tall sculpture was dubbed an 'autonomous dwelling machine' by Fuller when he conceived it back in 1965.

Palm Court   COURTYARD
(Map p78; 140 NE 39th St) At the epicenter of the Design District is this pretty courtyard, which opened just before Art Basel back in 2014. It's set with tall palm trees, two floors of high-end retailers and one eye-catching sculpture, namely the Fly's Eye Dome.

Locust Projects   GALLERY
(Map p78; ☑ 305-576-8570; www.locustprojects. org; 3852 N Miami Ave; ☉10am-6pm Tue-Sat) FREE Locust Projects has become a major name for emerging artists in the contemporary art scene. Run by artists as a nonprofit collective since 1998, LP has exhibited work by more than 250 local, national and international artists over the years. The gallery often hosts site-specific installations by artists willing to take a few more risks than those in more commercial venues.

Art Fusion   GALLERY
(Map p78; www.artfusionartists.com; 3550 N Miami Ave; ☉11am-6pm Mon-Sat) FREE This sprawling gallery in Midtown carries a hugely varied collection, with artists from around the globe. You'll find sculpture, portraiture, landscapes

and mixed media spread across two floors of the 8000-sq-ft space.

Living Room   PUBLIC ART
(Map p78; cnr NW 40th St & N Miami Ave) Just to remind you that you're entering the Design District is a big, surreal public art installation of, yep, a living room – just the sort of thing you're supposed to shop for while you're here. Actually the *Living Room,* by Argentine husband-and-wife team Roberto Behar and Rosario Marquardt, is an 'urban intervention' meant to be a criticism of the disappearance of public space.

Bacardi Building   ARCHITECTURE
(Map p78; 2100 Biscayne Blvd) FREE You don't need to be a rum-lover to appreciate the former Miami headquarters of the world's largest family-owned spirits company, Bacardi. The main event is a beautifully decorated jewelbox-like building built in 1973 that seems to hover over the ground from a central pillar supporting the entire structure. One-inch thick pieces of hammered glass cover the exterior in a wild Mesoamerican-style pattern modeled after a mosaic designed by German artist Johannes M Dietz.

⊙ Little Haiti & the Upper East Side

Traditional sights are fairly thin on the ground here. Most locals tend to time their visit to when a special exhibition or event is underway at one of the galleries and cultural spaces in the area. Architecture fans, on the other hand, won't want to miss the so-called MiMo on Bibo, a historic district that stands for Miami Modern on Biscayne Blvd – encompassing a spread of photogenic buildings running from 50th St to 77th St.

By day the options for neighborhood explorations feel limited, but by night the district springs to life. You'll find some vibrant nightlife in the Upper East Side (poolside drinks, indie rock bands etc) and crafty experimentation on the dining scene – all of which remains little known to the Miami Beach gang. For neighborhood exploring off the beaten path, this is a great place to start.

Be aware that Little Haiti still has a serious crime problem, and it's best not to wander around this area after dark.

Little Haiti Cultural Center   GALLERY
(Map p82; ☑ 305-960-2969; www.littlehaiti culturalcenter.com; 212 NE 59th Tce; ☉10am-9pm Tue-Fri, 9am-4pm Sat, 11am-7pm Sun) FREE This

Wynwood & Design District

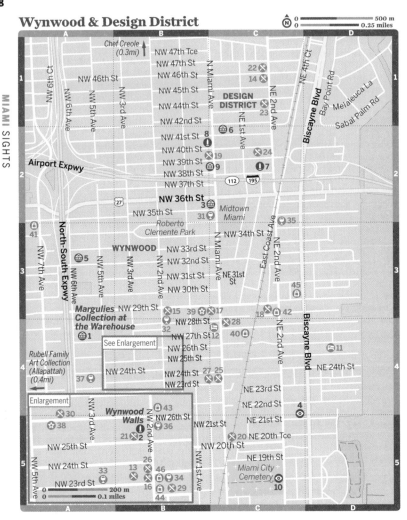

cultural center hosts an art gallery with often thought-provoking exhibitions from Haitian painters, sculptors and multimedia artists. You can also find dance classes, drama productions and a Caribbean-themed market during special events. The building itself is quite a confection of bold tropical colors, steep A-framed roofs and lacy decorative elements. Don't miss the mural in the palm-filled courtyard.

The best time to visit is for the Sounds of Little Haiti (p98), a music- and food-filled fête held on the third Friday of every month from 6pm to 10pm.

Miami Ironside ARTS CENTER
(Map p82; www.miamiironside.com; 7610 NE 4th Ct) 🍃 A new hub of creativity in Miami is this urban oasis in an otherwise industrial 'hood known as Little River. Here you'll find art and design studios, showrooms and galleries as well as a few eating and drinking spaces. It's a lushly landscaped property, with some intriguing public art.

Morningside Park PARK
(Map p82; 750 NE 55 Tce) On the waterfront, this aptly named park is a great spot to be in the morning, when the golden light is just right for getting a bit of fresh air. There's lots

Wynwood & Design District

going on in the park, with walking paths, basketball courts, tennis courts, sports fields, a playground for kids and a swimming pool (admission $3).

If you come on Saturday, you can hire kayaks (from $12 per hour) and stand-up paddleboards (from $20 per hour).

PanAmerican Art Projects GALLERY
(PAAP; ☑ 305-573-2400; www.panamericanart. com; 6300 NW 2nd Ave; ☺10am-6pm Tue-Fri, noon-6pm Sat) Despite the name, PanAmerican also showcases work from the occasional European artist. But much of what is on display comes from fine artists representing Latin America, the Caribbean and the USA.

Formerly located in Wynwood, PAAP made the move up to Little Haiti back in 2016 – a growing trend as gallerists get priced out of the neighborhood they helped popularize.

⊙ Little Havana

Little Havana makes a fine destination for a leisurely morning or afternoon's wander. The district is most vibrant during the day (and preferably on a weekend), when you can see wise-cracking old timers chattering away over fast-moving games of dominoes in Máximo Gómez Park and get an eyeful of modern art at the galleries around town. You can cap the day with a bit of souvenir and cigar shopping in the stores dotting 8th St, stopping for strong coffee and/or mojitos along the way. While you can see everything in a few hours on an easygoing stroll, it's worth coming back at night. You can book in for dinner (there's great Cuban fare, but much more besides) then catch some live bands at one of two key music venues in Little Havana.

★ Máximo Gómez Park PARK
(Map p84; cnr SW 8th St & SW 15th Ave; ☺9am-6pm) Little Havana's most evocative reminder of Old Cuba is Máximo Gómez Park, or 'Domino Park,' where the sound of elderly men trash-talking over games of chess is harmonized with the quick clack-clack of slapping dominoes. The jarring backtrack, plus the heavy smell of cigars and a sunrise-bright

TOP SIGHT
WYNWOOD WALLS

The launch of the Wynwood Walls was like a meteor soaring through the upper atmosphere of the art world. It came in the form of eye-popping, color-saturated murals blanketing the walls of a former warehouse district. Artists from around the world have added their touch to this ever-changing open-air gallery, transforming Wynwood into a mecca for art lovers.

Back Story

During the early 2000s, there wasn't much happening in Wynwood. Ever since the 1970s, Wynwood had been known as little more than a district of sprawling warehouses. And then Tony Goldman arrived.

Goldman, who's credited with the revitalization of South Beach (as well as New York's SoHo district), saw enormous potential in the blighted neighborhood. Although artists were already living in the area, it remained barren and forbidding at night. Goldman began buying up properties. Once assembled, he unleashed his master plan. He would invite artists from around the world to create the biggest and boldest collection of street art ever assembled in Miami. Around the corner, he also opened the first restaurant in the neighborhood – Joeys, a pioneering Italian restaurant, which is still around today.

Goldman started with the warehouse complex of six buildings on 25th to 26th Sts. Using the buildings (perfectly configured as they lacked windows) as blank canvases, his roster of artists set to work. Art-world superstar Jeffrey Deitch helped co-curate the first year's project in 2009. Artists were offered free airfare, hotel accommodation and all the supplies they needed, then given free rein to paint Goldman's 18 walls. The plan was a smash success. That year at Art Basel (p100), thousands of visitors came to see the street murals, and the new Wynwood Walls were the talk of the town.

DID YOU KNOW?

Here Comes the Neighborhood is a documentary about the creation of the walls, the artists behind the work, and the people who made it happen. Watch it online at www.hctn.tv.

PRACTICALITIES

➜ Map p78

➜ www.thewynwoodwalls. com

➜ NW 2nd Ave btwn 25th & 26th Sts

The Art

One of the most extraordinary features of the Wynwood Walls is that nothing here remains the same – which is perhaps an appropriate metaphor for the ephemeral nature of street art in general. The average lifespan for a mural here is less than one year before it's painted over by another artist – surprising given the stunning quality of work on display.

Since the founding of the project, over 50 artists from 16 different countries have painted on the walls. Among the first crop of talented artists was Shepard Fairey, whose 'Obey' street tags (depicting the mug of Andre the Giant) and 'Hope' posters (with Obama's portrait) helped garner him wide-reaching acclaim. Other famous artists who've installed their work include Os Gemeos (twin brothers who hail from Brazil), French painter Invader, the Japanese artist Aiko and the Portuguese Alexandre Farto (aka Vhils), who 'carves' rather than paints – at times even using a jack-hammer to create realistic portraits on concrete walls.

Unlike in many gallery paintings, the street art contains a visceral edge that explores topics like homelessness, police brutality, disenfranchisement, rampant materialism and the ever-widening chasm of inequality between the haves and the have-nots. There are also fantastical science-fiction scenes, dynamic color swaths swirling with abstract patterns and beautiful portraits of positive people. The Dali Lama, Aung San Suu Kyi, Martin Luther King Jr, Bob Marley and uh, Yoda, have all graced the walls at one time or another.

Museum of the Streets

The Wynwood Walls is the heart of Wynwood's open-air gallery, but it is no longer the only game in town. After Goldman's success, other property owners decided to follow suit, inviting artists to paint the walls of their buildings. Within a few years, the whole neighborhood became one giant street museum – one that presents constant surprises at every turn, and endless opportunities to capture great street photography.

TOP TIPS

➡ Go early in the day to beat the crowds.

➡ Wynwood Walls offers private walking tours ($25 per person) led by street artists. Book online.

➡ You can learn more about the neighborhood's street art and its gallery scene on a walking tour offered by Wynwood Art Walk (p97).

➡ Grab some delicious Mexican-style street food at Coyo Taco (p118).

➡ Stay caffeinated at Panther Coffee (p118), serving the best pour-overs in Miami.

Little Haiti & the Upper East Side

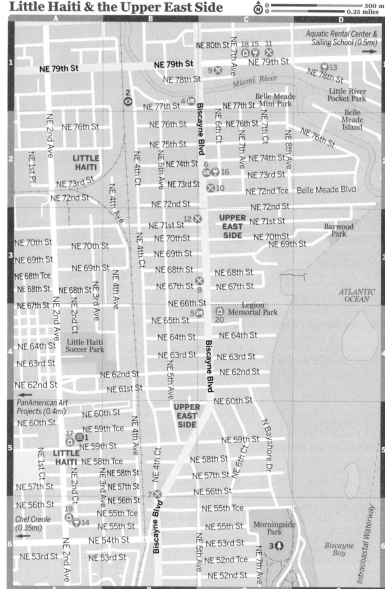

mural of the 1994 Summit of the Americas, combine to make Máximo Gómez one of the most sensory sites in Miami (although it is admittedly one of the most tourist-heavy ones as well).

Cuban Memorial Park　　　　MONUMENT
(Map p84; SW 13th Ave, btwn 8th & 11th Sts) Stretching along SW 13th Ave south of Calle Ocho (SW 8th St), Cuban Memorial Park contains a series of monuments to Cuban and Cuban American icons. The memorials include the

Little Haiti & the Upper East Side

Eternal Torch in Honor of the 2506th Brigade, for the exiles who died during the Bay of Pigs Invasion; a José Martí memorial; and a Madonna statue, supposedly illuminated by a shaft of holy light every afternoon.

There's also a map of Cuba, with a quote by José Martí. At the center of the map is a massive ceiba tree, still revered by followers of Santeria (a syncretic religion that evolved in Cuba among African slaves in the 18th century).

⊙ Coconut Grove

Coconut Grove itself is compact, and can be easily explored on foot. An afternoon's stroll down along its tree-lined streets, followed by dinner and drinks, is a great way to experience the 'hood. If more time allows, you can visit the small Barnacle Historic State Park (p85) and take in a bit of the waterfront (another good spot for a meal).

Several key sites in this neighborhood lie a fair bit beyond the boundaries of its walkable centre. Located 2.5 miles north of Coconut Grove on the bayside, the Vizcaya Museum & Gardens is best reached by car or bicycle. Go in the early morning to beat the crowds. South of the Grove, the verdant tropical gardens of the Kampong are well worth the effort of getting there (and you'll need to call ahead to visit), though again you'll need to get there by car or bicycle.

★ **Vizcaya Museum & Gardens**   HISTORIC BUILDING
(☑ 305-250-9133; www.vizcayamuseum.org; 3251 S Miami Ave; adult/6-12yr/student & senior $18/6/12; ⊙ 9:30am-4:30pm Wed-Mon; P) They call Miami the Magic City, and if it is, this Italian villa, the housing equivalent of a Fabergé egg, is its most fairy-tale residence. In 1916 industrialist James Deering started a Miami tradition by making a ton of money and building ridiculously grandiose digs. He employed 1000 people (then 10% of the local population) and stuffed his home with 15th- to 19th-century furniture, tapestries, paintings and decorative arts; today the grounds are used for rotating contemporary-art exhibitions.

The Renaissance-inspired mansion is a classic of Miami's Mediterranean Revival stye. The largest room in the house is the informal living room, sometimes dubbed 'the Renaissance Hall' for its works dating from the 14th to the 17th centuries. The music room is intriguing for its beautiful wall canvases, which come from Northern Italy, while the banquet hall evokes all the grandeur of

EVA MUNROE'S GRAVE

Tucked into a small gated area near the Coconut Grove Library (Map p86; 2875 McFarlane Rd; ⊙ 10am-6pm Mon, Wed, Thu & Sat, to 8pm Tue, closed Fri & Sun), you'll find the humble headstone of one Ms Eva Amelia Hewitt Munroe. Eva, who was born in New Jersey in 1856 and died in Miami in 1882, lies in the oldest American grave in Miami-Dade County (a sad addendum: local African American settlers died before Eva, but their deaths were never officially recorded).

Eva's husband Ralph entered a deep depression, which he tried to alleviate by building the Barnacle (p85), now one of the oldest historic homes in the area.

Little Havana

Little Havana

imperial dining rooms of Europe, with its regal furnishings.

On the south side of the house stretch a series of lovely gardens that are just as impressive as the interior of Vizcaya. Modeled on formal Italian gardens of the 17th and 18th centuries, these manicured spaces form a counterpoint to the wild mangroves beyond. Sculptures, fountains and vine-draped surfaces give an antiquarian look to the grounds, and an elevated terrace (the Garden Mound) provides a fine vantage point over the greenery.

The on-site Vizcaya Cafe has decent light snacks and coffee to keep energy levels up while perusing the lavish collections.

Kampong GARDENS
(✆305-442-7169; www.ntbg.org/tours/kampong; 4013 Douglas Rd; adult/child $15/5; ⊙tours by appointment only 10am-3pm Mon-Sat) David Fairchild, the Indiana Jones of the botanical world and founder of Fairchild Tropical

Garden, would rest at the Kampong (Malay/Indonesian for 'village') in between journeys in search of beautiful and economically viable plant life. Today this lush garden is listed on the National Register of Historic Places and the lovely grounds serve as a classroom for the National Tropical Botanical Garden. Self-guided tours (allow at least an hour) are available by appointment, as are $20 one-hour guided tours.

Peacock Park PARK
(Map p86; 2820 McFarlane Rd) Extending down to the edge of the waterfront, Peacock Park serves as the great open backyard of Coconut Grove. Young families stop by the playground and join the action on the ball fields, while power walkers take in the view on a scenic stroll along the bayfront.

Ermita de la Caridad MONUMENT
(✆305-854-2404; www.ermitadelacaridad.org; 3609 S Miami Ave) The Catholic diocese purchased

some of the bayfront land from Deering's Villa Vizcaya estate and built a shrine here for its displaced Cuban parishioners. Symbolizing a beacon, it faces the homeland, exactly 290 miles due south. There is also a mural that depicts Cuban history. Just outside the church is a grassy stretch of waterfront that makes a fine spot for a picnic.

Barnacle Historic State Park   STATE PARK

(Map p86; 🕿 305-442-6866; www.florida stateparks.org/thebarnacle; 3485 Main Hwy; admission $2, house tours adult/child $3/1; 🕙 9am-5pm Fri-Mon; 👪) In the center of Coconut Grove village is the 1891, 5-acre pioneer residence of Ralph Monroe, Miami's first honorable snowbird. The house is open for guided tours (every 90 minutes between 10am and 2:30pm), and the park it's located in is a shady oasis for strolling. Barnacle hosts frequent (and lovely) moonlight concerts, from jazz to classical.

◉ Coral Gables

Coral Gables has a unique design and feel, more reminiscent of an old Mediterranean village-town than a city in greater Miami.

The center of town is walkable, with a string of boutiques, cafes and upscale eateries scattered along (and just off) the so-called Miracle Mile – a pretty boulevard that runs through the heart of town. The big attractions though are outside of the center, namely the soaring architectural masterpiece of the Biltmore Hotel, the pretty Venetian pool and the lush Fairchild Tropical Garden. It's best to have a car to visit these sights, as well as some of the more intriguing restaurants in the area.

★ Fairchild Tropical Garden   GARDENS

(🕿 305-667-1651; www.fairchildgarden.org; 10901 Old Cutler Rd; adult/child/senior $25/12/18; 🕙 9:30am-4:30pm; P 👪) If you need to escape Miami's madness, consider a green day in the country's largest tropical botanical garden. A butterfly grove, tropical plant conservatory and gentle vistas of marsh and keys habitats, plus frequent art installations from artists like Roy Lichtenstein, are all stunning. In addition to easy-to-follow, self-guided walking tours, a free 45-minute tram tours the entire park on the hour from 10am to 3pm (till 4pm weekends).

A favorite among the garden's youngest visitors is the Wings of the Tropics exhibition. Inside of an indoor gallery, hundreds of butterflies flutter freely through the air, the sheen of their wings glinting in the light. There are some 40 different species represented, including exotics from Central and South America, like blue morphos and owl butterflies. Visitors can also watch in real time as chrysalises emerge as butterflies at Vollmer Metamorphosis Lab.

The lushly lined pathways of the Tropical Plant Conservatory and the Rare Plant House contain rare philodendrons, orchids, begonias, rare palms, rhododendrons, ferns and moss, while the Richard H Simons Rainforest, though small in size, provides a splendid taste of the tropics, with a little stream and waterfalls amid orchids, plus towering trees with lianas (long woody vines) and epiphytes up in the rainforest canopy.

There's a couple of on-site cafes serving simple light fare or you can bring your own picnic and eat on the grounds.

Fairchild Tropical Garden lies about 6 miles south of Coral Gables downtown. It's easiest to get here by car or taxi. Another option is to take metrorail to South Miami, then transfer to bus 57.

★ Biltmore Hotel   HISTORIC BUILDING

(Map p88; 🕿 855-311-6903; www.biltmorehotel. com; 1200 Anastasia Ave; 🕙 tours 1:30 & 2:30pm Sun; P) In the most opulent neighborhood of one of the showiest cities in the world, the Biltmore peers down her nose and says, 'hrmph.' It's one of the greatest of the grand hotels of the American Jazz Age, and if this joint were a fictional character from a novel, it'd be, without question, Jay Gatsby. Al Capone had a speakeasy on site, and the Capone Suite is said to be haunted by the spirit of Fats Walsh, who was murdered here.

MIAMI SIGHTS

Coconut Grove

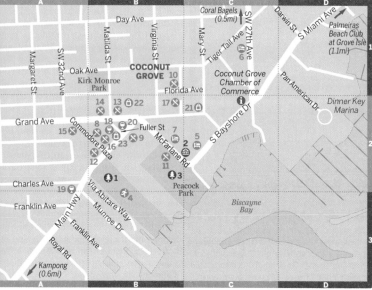

Coconut Grove

Back in the day, imported gondolas transported celebrity guests like Judy Garland and the Vanderbilts around because, of course, there was a private canal system out the back. It's gone now, but the largest hotel pool in the continental USA, which resembles a sultan's water garden from *One Thousand & One Nights*, is still here. If you'd like to sidestroke across it without the price tag of an overnight stay, visitors can use the pool and fitness center by purchasing a $35 day pass.

Lowe Art Museum   MUSEUM

(☎ 305-284-3535; www.miami.edu/lowe; 1301 Stanford Dr; adult/student/child $13/8/free; ⊙ 10am-4pm Tue-Sat, noon-4pm Sun) Your love of the Lowe, on the campus of the University of Miami, depends on your taste in art. If you're into modern and contemporary works, it's good. If you're into the art and archaeology of cultures from Asia, Africa and the South Pacific, it's great. And if you're into pre-Columbian and Mesoamerican art, it's fantastic.

That isn't to discount the lovely permanent collection of Renaissance and Baroque art, Western sculpture from the 18th to 20th centuries, and paintings by Gauguin, Picasso and Monet.

Coral Gables City Hall   HISTORIC BUILDING

(Map p88; 405 Biltmore Way; ◷8am-5pm Mon-Fri) This grand building has housed boring city-commission meetings since it opened in 1928. It's impressive from any angle, certainly befitting its importance as a central government building. Check out Denman Fink's *Four Seasons* ceiling painting in the tower, as well as his framed, untitled painting of the underwater world on the 2nd-floor landing.

There's a small farmers market on site from 8am to 2pm on Saturdays from mid-January to March.

Coral Gables Congregational Church   CHURCH

(Map p88; ☑305-448-7421; www.gablesucc.org; 3010 De Soto Blvd; ◷hours vary) Developer George Merrick's father was a New England Congregational minister, so perhaps that accounts for him donating the land for the city's first church. Built in 1924 as a replica of a church in Costa Rica, the yellow-walled, red-roofed exterior is as far removed from New England as...well, Miami. The interior is graced with a beautiful sanctuary and the grounds are landscaped with stately palms.

It isn't open much, though you can stop in for a look during Sunday services at 9am and 11am.

Merrick House   HISTORIC BUILDING

(Map p88; ☑305-460-5361; 907 Coral Way; adult/child/senior $5/1/3) It's fun to imagine this simple homestead, with its little hints of Med-style, as the core of what would eventually become the gaudy Gables. When George Merrick's father purchased this plot, site unseen, for $1100, it was all dirt, rock and guavas. The property is now used for meetings and receptions, and you can tour both the house and its pretty organic garden. The modest family residence looks as it did in 1925, outfitted with family photos, furniture and artwork.

Call ahead for the latest tour times. The house was closed for renovations at research time.

GATES TO THE CITY BEAUTIFUL

Designer George Merrick planned a series of elaborate entry gates to Coral Gables, the City Beautiful, but the real-estate bust meant that many projects went unfinished. Among the completed gates worth seeing, many of which resemble the entrance pavilions to grand Andalucian estates, is the Country Club Prado (Map p88; Country Club Prado), the Alhambra Entrance (Map p88; cnr Alhambra Circle & Douglas Rd), the Granada Entrance (Map p88; cnr Alhambra Circle & Granada Blvd) and the Coral Way Entrance (Map p88; cnr Red Rd & Coral Way). Also notable is the Alhambra Watertower (Map p88; Alhambra Circle), where Greenway Ct and Ferdinand St meet Alhambra Circle, which resembles a Moorish lighthouse.

Coral Gables Museum   MUSEUM

(Map p88; ☑305-603-8067; www.coralgablesmuseum.org; 285 Aragon Ave; adult/child/student $10/3/8; ◷noon-6pm Tue-Fri, 11am-5pm Sat, noon-5pm Sun) This museum is a well-plotted introduction to the oddball narrative of the founding and growth of the City Beautiful (Coral Gables). The collection includes historical artifacts and mementos from succeeding generations in this tight-knit, eccentric little village. The main building is the old Gables police and fire station (note the deco-style firemen faces jutting out of the facade); it's a lovely architectural blend of Gables' Mediterranean Revival and Miami Beach's muscular, Depression-moderne style.

Matheson Hammock Park   PARK

(☑305-665-5475; www.miamidade.gov/parks/matheson-hammock.asp; 9610 Old Cutler Rd; per car weekday/weekend $5/7; ◷sunrise-sunset; P⊞) This 630-acre county park is the city's oldest and one of its most scenic. It offers good swimming for children in an enclosed tidal pool, lots of hungry raccoons, dense mangrove swamps and (pretty rare) alligator-spotting. It's just south of Coral Gables.

⊙ Key Biscayne

Start early in the day for the drive or bike ride out to these picturesque keys, roughly 5 miles southeast of Downtown Miami (a 10-minute drive). Heading out along the

Coral Gables

Coral Gables

Rickenbacker Causeway leads first to small Virginia Key, which has a few worthwhile sites – tiny beaches, a small mountain-bike park and pretty spots for kayaking.

The road continues to Key Biscayne, an island that's just 7 miles long with unrivaled views of the Miami skyline. As you pass over the causeway, note the small public beaches, picnic areas and fishing spots arranged on its margins. Keep heading all the way to the south to reach the Bill Baggs Cape Florida State Park, a wonderful spot for a day's outing with beaches, nature trails, a photogenic lighthouse and outdoor gear (including kayaks) available for hire.

★ **Bill Baggs Cape Florida State Park** STATE PARK
(Map p90; ☎305-361-5811; www.florida stateparks.org/capeflorida; 1200 S Crandon Blvd; per car/person $8/2; ☺8am-sunset, lighthouse 9am-5pm; ℗🚻🐾) 🏖 If you don't make it to the

Florida Keys, come to this park for a taste of their unique island ecosystems. The 494-acre space is a tangled clot of tropical fauna and dark mangroves – look for the 'snorkel' roots that provide air for half-submerged mangrove trees – all interconnected by sandy trails and wooden boardwalks, and surrounded by miles of pale ocean. A concession shack rents out kayaks, bikes, in-line skates, beach chairs and umbrellas.

At the state recreation area's southernmost tip, the 1845 brick **Cape Florida Lighthouse** is the oldest structure in Florida (it replaced another lighthouse that was severely damaged in 1836 during the Second Seminole War). Free tours run at 10am and 1pm Thursday to Monday. If you're not packing a picnic, there are several good places to dine in the park, including **Boater's Grill** (Map p90; ☎305-361-0080; mains $14-32, burgers $7-10; ☺9am-8pm Sun-Thu, to 10pm Fri & Sat) and **Lighthouse Cafe** (Map p90; ☎305-361-8487; ☺9am-5:30pm).

Virginia Key Beach North Point Park STATE PARK
(Map p90; 3801 Rickenbacker Causeway, Virginia Key; per vehicle weekday/weekend $6/8; ☺7am-6pm) This lovely green space has several small but pleasing beaches, and some short nature trails. Pretty waterfront views aside, there are two big reasons to come here. The first is to get out on the water by hiring kayaks or stand-up paddleboards at Virginia Key Outdoor Center (p94). The second is to go mountain biking in a gated-off section known as the **Virginia Key North Point Trails** FREE, with a series of trails ranging from beginner to advanced.

The mountain-bike trails, which are tucked away at the northern tip of the park, are free, but you'll need your own bike (and helmet), which you can hire from the nearby Virginia Key Outdoor Center. Coming from Miami, this is the first park entrance (the second leads to the smaller Historic Virginia Key Beach Park).

Historic Virginia Key Park STATE PARK
(Map p90; www.virginiakeybeachpark.net; 4020 Virginia Beach Dr, Virginia Key; vehicle weekday/weekend $5/8, bike & pedestrian free; ☺7am-sunset; 🚻) A short drive (or bike ride) from Downtown Miami, the Historic Virginia Key Park is a fine place for a dose of nature, with a small but pretty beachfront and playgrounds for the kids (as well as a carousel). From time to time there are concerts, ecology-minded family picnics and other events. Coming from Downtown Miami, this is the second park

Key Biscayne

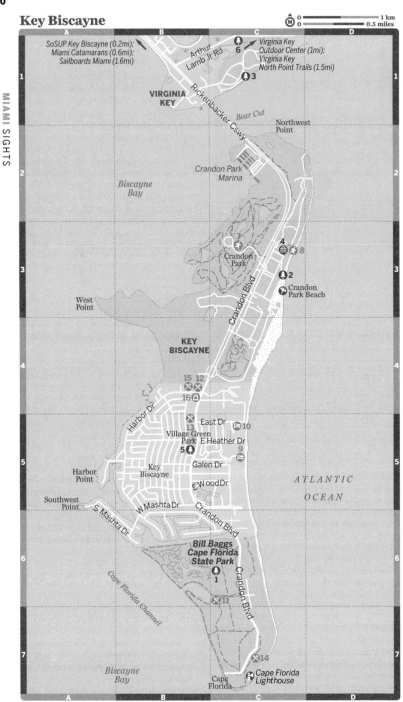

SoSUP Key Biscayne (0.2mi);
Miami Catamarans (0.6mi);
Sailboards Miami (1.6mi)

Arthur
Lamb Jr Rd

Virginia Key
Outdoor Center (1mi);
Virginia Key
North Point Trails (1.5mi)

VIRGINIA
KEY

Rickenbacker Cswy

Bear Cut

Northwest
Point

Biscayne
Bay

Crandon Park
Marina

West
Point

Crandon
Park

Crandon
Park Beach

KEY
BISCAYNE

Crandon Blvd

East Dr

Village Green
Park E Heather Dr

Galen Dr

Harbor
Point

E Wood Dr

Key
Biscayne

Harbor Dr

Southwest
Point

S Mashta Dr

W Mashta Dr

Crandon Blvd

ATLANTIC

OCEAN

Bill Baggs
Cape Florida
State Park

Crandon Blvd

Cape Florida Channel

Biscayne
Bay

Cape
Florida

Cape Florida
Lighthouse

Key Biscayne

entrance on the left (just past the entrance to the Virginia Key Beach North Point Park).

In the dark days of segregation, this beachfront, initially accessible only by boat, was an official 'colored only' recreation site (African Americans were not allowed on other beaches). Opened in 1945, it remained a major destination for African American communities (as well as Cubans, Haitians and many others from Latin America) seeking to enjoy a bit of the Miami coastline. It was popular until the early 1960s when the city's beaches were finally desegregated.

Marjory Stoneman Douglas Biscayne Nature Center   MUSEUM
(Map p90; ☎305-361-6767; www.biscayne naturecenter.org; 6767 Crandon Blvd, Crandon Park; ⊗10am-4pm; ⓟ☒) ✐[FREE] Marjory Stoneman Douglas was a beloved environmental crusader and worthy namesake of this child-friendly nature center. It's a great introduction to South Florida's unique ecosystems, with hands-on exhibits as well as aquariums in back full of parrot fish, conch, urchins, tulip snails and a fearsome-looking green moray eel. You can also stroll a nature

trail through coastal hammock or enjoy the beach in front.

Once a month, the center hosts naturalist-led walks ($14 per person) through seagrass in search of marine life. It's always a big hit with families. Reserve ahead.

Crandon Park   PARK
(Map p90; ☎305-361-5421; www.miamidade.gov/parks/parks/crandon_beach.asp; 6747 Crandon Blvd; per car weekday/weekend $5/7; ⊗sunrise-sunset; ⓟ☒☒) This 1200-acre park boasts Crandon Park Beach, a glorious stretch of sand that spreads for 2 miles. Much of the park consists of a dense coastal hammock (hardwood forest) and mangrove swamps. The beach here is clean and uncluttered by tourists, faces a lovely sweep of teal goodness and is regularly named one of the best beaches in the USA. Pretty cabanas at the south end of the park can be rented by the day ($40).

◉ **Greater Miami**

Deering Estate at Cutler   LANDMARK
(☎305-235-1668; www.deeringestate.org; 16701 SW 72nd Ave; adult/child under 14yr $12/7; ⊗10am-5pm; ⓟ☒) The Deering estate is sort of 'Vizcaya lite,' which makes sense as it was built by Charles, brother of James Deering (of Vizcaya mansion (p83) fame). The 150-acre grounds are awash with tropical growth, an animal-fossil pit of bones dating back 50,000 years and the remains of Native Americans who lived here 2000 years ago. There's a free tour of the grounds at 3pm included in admission, and the estate often hosts jazz evenings.

Zoo Miami   ZOO
(Metrozoo; ☎305-251-0400; www.zoomiami.org; 12400 SW 152nd St; adult/child $22/18; ⊗10am-5pm) Miami's tropical weather makes strolling around the Metrozoo almost feel like a day in the wild. Look for Asian and African elephants, rare and regal Bengal tigers prowling an evocative Hindu temple, pygmy hippos, Andean condors, a pack of hyenas, cute koalas, colobus monkeys, black rhinoceroses and a pair of Komodo dragons from Indonesia. For a quick overview (and because the zoo is so big), hop on the Safari Monorail; it departs every 20 minutes.

Rubell Family Art Collection (Allapattah)   GALLERY
(1100 NW 23rd St) One of the major icons in Miami's art world moves to a new space in Allapattah in late 2018 (in time for Art Basel (p100), which happens in December). The

museum will feature a greatly expanded space (some 100,000 sq ft) from its former digs in Wynwood. The 2.5-acre campus will house 40 exhibition galleries, a sculpture garden, research library and a restaurant.

Arch Creek Park   PARK

(☏ 305-944-6111; www.miamidade.gov/parks/arch-creek.asp; 1855 NE 135th St; ⊘ 9am-5pm Wed-Sun; ▣ ♿) This compact and cute park, located near Oleta River, encompasses a cozy habitat of tropical hardwood species that surrounds a pretty, natural limestone bridge. Naturalists can lead you on kid-friendly ecotours of the area, which include a lovely butterfly garden, or visitors can peruse a small but well-stocked museum of Native American and pioneer artifacts. The excellent Miami EcoAdventures (p97) is based here. The park is just off North Biscayne Blvd, 7 miles north of the Design District.

Ancient Spanish Monastery   CHURCH

(☏ 305-945-1461; www.spanishmonastery.com; 16711 W Dixie Hwy; adult/child $10/5; ⊘ 10am-4:30pm Mon-Sat, from 11am Sun; ▣) Finding a fully intact medieval monastery in North Miami Beach is yet another reason why the moniker 'Magic City' seems so fitting. Constructed in 1141 in Segovia, Spain, the Monastery of St Bernard de Clairvaux is a striking early-Gothic and Romanesque building that rather improbably found its way to South Florida. The property – today a church that's part of the Episcopal diocese – gets busy for weddings, so call before making the long trip out here. It's roughly 15 miles north of Downtown Miami.

Pinecrest Gardens   PARK

(☏ 305-669-6990; www.pinecrest-fl.gov/gardens; 11000 SW 57th Ave; adult/senior/child $5/3/5; ⊘ 10am-6pm Apr-Sep, to 5pm Oct-Mar; ▣ ♿) When Parrot Jungle – now Jungle Island (p75) – flew the coop for the big city, the village of Pinecrest purchased the property in order to keep it as a municipal park. It's now a quiet oasis with some of the best tropical gardens this side of the Gulf of Mexico, topped off by a gorgeous centerpiece banyan tree. Outdoor movies and jazz concerts are held here, and all in all this is a total gem that is utterly off the tourism trail.

Monkey Jungle   ZOO

(☏ 305-235-1611; www.monkeyjungle.com; 14805 SW 216th St; adult/child/senior $30/24/28; ⊘ 9:30am-5pm, last entry 4pm; ▣ ♿) At the Monkey Jungle, the zoo experience gets flipped on its head: visitors step into the cage while monkeys run wild and free. Indeed, you'll be walking through screened-in trails, with primates swinging, screeching and chattering all around you. It's incredibly fun, and just a bit odorous. The big show of the day takes place at feeding time, when crab-eating monkeys and Southeast Asian macaques dive into the pool for fruit and other treats.

Museum of Contemporary Art North Miami   MUSEUM

(MoCA; ☏ 305-893-6211; www.mocanomi.org; 770 NE 125th St; adult/student/child $5/3/free; ⊘ 11am-5pm Tue-Fri & Sun, 1-9pm Sat; ▣) The Museum of Contemporary Art has long been a reason to hike up to the far reaches of North Miami. Its galleries feature excellent rotating exhibitions of contemporary art by local, national and international artists.

Gold Coast Railroad Museum   MUSEUM

(☏ 305-253-0063; www.gcrm.org; 12450 SW 152nd St; adult/child 3-11yr $8/6; ⊘ 10am-4pm Mon-Fri, from 11am Sat & Sun; ▣) Primarily of interest to train buffs, this museum displays more than 30 antique railway cars, including the Ferdinand Magellan presidential car, where President Harry Truman famously brandished a newspaper with the erroneous headline 'Dewey Defeats Truman.'

On weekends the museum offers 25-minute rides on old cabooses ($6) and standard gauge cabs ($12). It's advised you call ahead to book rides.

Hialeah Park Casino   CASINO

(www.hialeahparkcasino.com; 2200 E 4th Ave; ⊘ casino 9am-3am; ▣) Hialeah is more Havanan than Little Havana (more than 90% of the population speak Spanish as a first language), and the symbol and center of this working-class Cuban community is this grand former racetrack. In 2013 the track was converted into a casino, which also shows other races (that you can gamble on) via simulcast.

🏃 Activities

Miami doesn't lack for ways to keep yourself busy. From sailing the teal waters to hiking through tropical undergrowth, yoga in the parks and (why not?) trapeze artistry above the city's head, the Magic City rewards those who want an active holiday.

🏃 South Beach

Fritz's Skate, Bike & Surf   SKATING

(Map p60; ☏ 305-532-1954; www.fritzsmiami beach.com; 1620 Washington Ave; bike & skate rental

STILTSVILLE

Head to the southern shore of Bill Baggs Cape Florida State Park and you'll see, way out in the distance, a collection of seven houses that stands on pilings in Biscayne Bay. The buildings, known as Stiltsville, have been around since the early 1930s, ever since 'Crawfish Eddie Walker' built a shack on the waves. More buildings were added over the years, and the 'village' was, at times, a gambling den, smuggling haven and, during the 1960s, a bikini club where women drank for free if they wore a two piece, and anything could famously go.

At its peak in 1960, there were 27 'homes' in Stiltsville, but as one might guess, hurricanes and erosion took their toll. No one lives in Stiltsville today, but it is possible to take a boat tour (p97) out here with the illustrious historian Dr Paul George.

In 2003 the nonprofit Stiltsville Trust was set up by the National Parks Service to rehabilitate the buildings into as-yet-unknown facilities; proposals include a National Parks Service visitor center, artist-in-residence colony or community center. Many years down the track, not much work seems to have progressed toward this idea, but if you'd like more information, check out www.stiltsvilletrust.org.

per hour/day/5 days $10/24/69; ⊙10am-9pm Mon-Sat, to 8pm Sun) Rent your wheels from Fritz's, which offers skateboards, longboards, in-line skates, roller skates, razor scooters and bicycles (cruisers, mountain bikes, kids bikes). Protective gear is included with skate rentals, and bikes come with locks.

Spa at the Setai SPA

(Map p60; ☑855-923-7908; www.thesetai hotel.com; 101 20th St, Setai Hotel; 1hr massage from $180; ⊙9am-9pm) A silky Balinese haven in one of South Beach's most beautiful hotels (p106).

SoBe Surf SURFING

(☑786-216-7703; www.sobesurf.com; group/private lesson from $70/120) Offers surf lessons both in Miami Beach and in Coca Beach, where there tends to be better waves. Instruction on Miami Beach usually happens around South Point. All bookings are done by phone or email.

Green Monkey Yoga YOGA

(Map p60; ☑305-397-8566; www.greenmonkey.net; 1800 Bay Rd; drop-in class $25) This yoga studio has a beautiful setting with huge windows on the top floor of a building in Sunset Harbour. There's a wide range of classes throughout the day, including Vinyasa, power yoga, hip-hop flow and meditation. If you're around for a while ask about the new student special ($69 for one month of unlimited classes).

Glow Hot Yoga YOGA

(Map p60; ☑305-534-2727; www.glowhotyoga miami.com; 1560 Lenox Ave; drop-in class/weekly unlimited rate $27/59) Offers excellent hot yoga classes in a big, inviting studio that's kept

sparkling clean. There's also an outdoor patio where you can unwind after an intense Bikram class. It's just south of Lincoln Rd.

🏃 North Beach

Russian & Turkish Baths MASSAGE

(Map p70; ☑305-867-8316; www.russianand turkishbaths.com; 5445 Collins Ave; treatments from $40; ⊙noon-midnight) Just because you enjoy a good back rub doesn't mean you need to go to some glitzy spa where they constantly play soft house music on a repetitive loop. Right? Why not head to a favorite 'hot' spot among folks who want a spa experience without the glamour. Enter this little labyrinth of *banyas* (steam rooms) for a plethora of spa choices.

Carillon Miami Wellness Resort SPA

(Map p70; ☑866-276-2226; www.carillonhotel.com; 6801 Collins Ave, Carillon Hotel; treatments $165-300; ⊙8am-9pm) For pure pampering, the Carillon's 70,000-sq-ft spa and wellness center is hard to knock. It has an excellent range of treatments and fitness classes (spinning, power yoga, meditation, core workouts) plus pretty views of the crashing waves.

BG Oleta River Outdoor Center WATER SPORTS

(☑786-274-7945; www.bgoletariveroutdoor.com; 3400 NE 163rd St; kayak/canoe hire per 90min $25/30; ⊙8am-1 hour before sunset; 🖈) Located in the Oleta River State Park, this outfitter hires out loads of water-sports gear; for a two-hour rental, options include single/tandem kayaks ($30/60), canoes ($35), stand-up paddleboards ($40) and bikes (from $25).

It also organizes group tours: weekend morning paddles (at 10am, from $45), sunset

CYCLING IN MIAMI

The Miami-Dade County Parks and Recreation Department maintains a list of traffic-free cycling paths as well as downloadable maps on its website (www.miamidade.gov/parks masterplan/bike-trails-map.asp). For less strenuous rides, try the side roads of South Beach or the shady streets of Coral Gables and Coconut Grove. Some good trails include the Old Cutler Bike Path, which starts at the end of Sunset Dr in Coral Gables and leads through Coconut Grove to Matheson Hammock Park and Fairchild Tropical Garden. The Rickenbacker Causeway takes you up and over the bridge to Key Biscayne for an excellent workout combined with gorgeous water views. A bit further out, the Oleta River State Park (p68) has a challenging dirt trail with hills for off-road adventures. Need to rent a bike? Try Bike & Roll (p97) or Brickell Bikes (p138); there's also the Citi Bike (p138) bike-sharing program for shorter hops.

paddles (on Fridays, from $35), once-a-month full-moon paddles, stand-up paddleboard classes, and stand-up paddleboard yoga classes (Sundays at 9am, $30).

Normandy Isle Park & Pool   SWIMMING
(Map p70; ☑305-673-7750; 7030 Trouville Esplanade; adult/child $10/6; ⊙6:30am-8:30pm; ⚐) For a fun day out, head to this family-friendly four-lane pool. It's lap swimming only at various times of day (before 9am and after 7pm), but otherwise it's open to all. There's also an outdoor splash-play area for the kids, with cascades to keep things interesting.

🏃 Downtown Miami

Tina Hills Pavilion   YOGA
(Map p72; Biscayne Blvd, Bayfront Park) FREE
This small open-air pavilion hosts free events, including free 75-minute yoga sessions, suitable for all levels. These take place Mondays and Wednesdays at 6pm, and 9am Saturday morning.

Spa at Mandarin Oriental Miami   SPA
(Map p72; ☑305-913-8332; www.mandarin oriental.com/miami/luxury-spa; 500 Brickell Key Dr, Mandarin Oriental Miami; manicures $75, spa treatments $175-425; ⊙8:30am-9:30pm) Calling this spa over the top is an understatement. Treatments utilize materials like bamboo and rice paper, and services include Ayurvedic herbal baths, aromatherapy, oiled massages and plenty more decadence.

Miami Yoga   YOGA
(Map p72; ☑305-856-1387; www.miami yoga.com; 301 SW 17th Rd, Brickell; 1-/5-/10-class pass $22/95/180) Yoga fans need not leave their practice behind on a trip to Miami. The style here is a bit eclectic: it's hot power Vinyasa yoga, offering a little bit of everything

(strengthening, stretching, meditation) in a studio that's heated but not unbearably so.

Blue Waters II   FISHING
(Map p72; ☑305-373-5016; www.fishingmiami. net; 401 Biscayne Blvd, Bayside Marketplace, Pier 5) For an action-filled day on the water, book a fishing charter with this top-notch outfit. Captain John Barker has more than 30 years of experience fishing these waters and can take you out on four-, six- or eight-hour private charters around Miami and Key Biscayne.

🏃 Coral Gables

★Venetian Pool   SWIMMING
(Map p88; ☑305-460-5306; www.coralgables venetianpool.com; 2701 De Soto Blvd; adult/child Sep-May $15/10, Jun-Aug $20/15; ⊙11am-5:30pm Tue-Fri, 10am-4:30pm Sat & Sun, closed Dec-Feb; ⚐) Imagine: it's 1923, tons of rock were quarried for one of the most beautiful neighborhoods in Miami, but now an ugly gash sits in the middle of the village. What to do? How about pump the hole full of water, mosaic and tile up the whole affair, and make it look like a Roman emperor's aquatic playground?

Result: one of the few pools listed on the National Register of Historic Places, a wonderland of coral rock caves, cascading waterfalls, a palm-fringed island and Venetian-style moorings. Take a swim and follow in the footsteps (fin-steps?) of stars like Esther Williams and Johnny 'Tarzan' Weissmuller.

🏃 Key Biscayne

★Virginia Key Outdoor Center   OUTDOORS
(VKOC; www.vkoc.net; 3801 Rickenbacker Causeway, Virginia Key; kayak or bike hire 1st hour $25, each additional hour $10; ⊙9am-4:30pm Mon-Fri, from 8am Sat & Sun) This highly recommended outfitter

Walking Tour
Art-Deco Miami Beach

START ART DECO MUSEUM
END OCEAN'S TEN
LENGTH 1.2 MILES; TWO TO THREE HOURS

Start at the **1 Art Deco Museum** (p58), at the corner of Ocean Dr and 10th St (named Barbara Capitman Way here, after the Miami Design Preservation League's founder). Step in for an exhibit on art-deco style, then head out and north along Ocean Dr; between 12th and 14th Sts you'll see three examples of deco hotels: the **2 Leslie**, a boxy shape with eyebrows (cantilevered sunshades) wrapped around the side of the building; the **3 Carlyle** (1250 Ocean Dr) featured in the film *The Birdcage* and boasting modernistic styling; and the graceful **4 Cardozo Hotel** (1300 Ocean Dr), built by Henry Hohauser, owned by Gloria Estefan and featuring sleek, rounded edges. At 14th St peek inside the **5 Winter Haven Hotel** (p108) to see its terrazzo floors, made of stone chips set in mortar that's polished when dry. Turn left and down 14th St to Washington Ave and the **6 US Post Office** (p59), at 13th St. It's a curvy block of white deco in the stripped classical style. Step inside to admire the wall mural, domed ceiling and marble stamp tables. Lunch at **7 11th St Diner** (p113), a gleaming aluminum Pullman car that was imported in 1992 from Wilkes-Barre, Pennsylvania. Get a window seat and gaze across the avenue to the corner of 10th St and the restored **8 Hotel Astor** (p102), designed in 1936 by T Hunter Henderson. Next, walk half a block east to the imposing **9 Wolfsonian-FIU** (p58), a top design museum, formerly the Washington Storage Company. Wealthy snowbirds of the '30s stashed their belongings here before heading back up north. Continue walking Washington Ave, turn left on 7th St and go north along Collins Ave to the **10 Hotel of South Beach** (p108), featuring an interior and roof deck by Todd Oldham. L Murray Dixon designed the hotel as the Tiffany Hotel, with a deco spire, in 1939. Turn right on 9th St and go two blocks to Ocean Dr, where you'll spy nonstop deco beauties; at 960 Ocean Dr (the middling **11 Ocean's Ten restaurant**) you'll see an exterior designed in 1935 by deco legend Henry Hohauser.

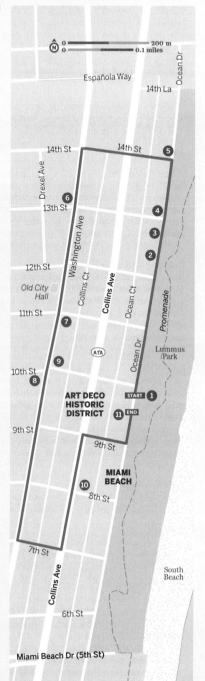

will get you out on the water in a hurry with kayaks and stand-up paddleboards, which you can put in the water just across from their office. The small mangrove-lined bay (known as Lamar Lake) has manatees, and makes for a great start to the paddle before you venture further out.

One of the highlights is partaking in one of VKOC's guided sunset and full moon paddles, which happen several times a month.

You can also hire mountain bikes for the Virginia Key North Point Trails (p89) located nearby.

Miami Catamarans   BOATING
(☑ 305-345-4104; www.facebook.com/miami catamarans; 3300 Rickenbacker Causeway, Virginia Key; per hour from $64; ☺11am-6pm Mon-Fri, from 10am Sat & Sun) Head out on the water on a small Hobie Cat catamaran. If you've never sailed before, take a one-hour lesson for $120.

Crandon Golf Course   GOLF
(Map p90; ☑ 305-361-9129; www.golfcrandon.com; 6700 Crandon Blvd; 18 holes $200, after 2pm/3:30pm $70/35) Out on Key Biscayne, this course has great views over the water. Avid golfers consider it one of the loveliest and most challenging par-72 courses in Florida.

SoSUP Key Biscayne   WATER SPORTS
(☑ 786-301-3557; www.sosupkeybiscayne.com; 3979 Rickenbacker Causeway, Virginia Key; bike/ kayak/stand-up paddleboard per hour $10/20/25; ☺10am-5pm) A good outfitter for all sorts of outdoor adventures, SoSUP rents out stand-up paddleboards, kayaks, pedal boats and bikes from a stall on the beach. Despite the name, it's located on Virginia Key.

YOGA WITH A SIDE OF SALT BREEZE

The beach is definitely not the only place to salute the sun in Miami. There are lovely **Yoga by the Sea** (Map p86; www. thebarnacle.org; class $15; ☺6:30-7:45pm Mon & Wed) lessons offered at the Barnacle Historic State Park (p85) in Coconut Grove. If you don't feel like breaking out your wallet, try the free yoga classes at Bayfront Park (p71), held outdoors at Tina Hills Pavilion, at the south end of the park, three times a week.

Studios offer a large range of classes; bring your own mat (though some places hire out mats as well for around $2 a class).

Miami Kiteboarding   WATER SPORTS
(Map p90; ☑ 305-345-9974; www.miamikite boarding.com; 6747 Crandon Blvd, Crandon Park; ☺10am-6pm Apr-Sep, 9am-5pm Oct-Mar) Offers a range of private lessons starting from $150 for one hour of one-on-one instruction. Couples get discounted rates.

Sailboards Miami   WATER SPORTS
(☑ 305-892-8992; www.sailboardsmiami.com; 1 Rickenbacker Causeway; windsurf lesson $85, wind-surf/kayak/SUP hire per hour from $30/20/30; ☺10am-6pm Fri-Tue) A good one-stop spot for getting out on the water. It offers two-hour intro windsurfing lessons, or if you already have the know-how you can simply rent the gear. You can also hire kayaks and stand-up paddleboards.

🌊 Courses & Tours

If you're a bona-fide seaworthy sailor, the **Aquatic Rental Center & Sailing School** (☑ 305-751-7514; www.arcmiami.com; 1275 NE 79th St; sailboats per 2hr/3hr/4hr/day $90/130/160/225; ☺9am-9pm) will rent you a sailboat. If you're not, it can teach you how to operate one (sailing courses $450, $600 for two people).

👉 South Beach

Miami Design Preservation League   WALKING
(MDPL; ☏ 305-672-2014; www.mdpl.org; 1001 Ocean Dr; guided tours adult/student $25/20; ☺10:30am daily & 6:30pm Thu) Tells the stories and history behind the art-deco buildings in South Beach, with a lively guide from the Miami Design Preservation League. Tours last 90 minutes. Also offers tours of Jewish Miami Beach, Gay & Lesbian Miami Beach and a once-monthly tour (first Saturday at 9:30am) of the MiMo district in the North Beach area. Check website for details.

Miami Food Tours   FOOD & DRINK
(Map p66; ☑ 786-361-0991; www.miamifood tours.com; 429 Lenox Ave; South Beach tour adult/ child $58/35, Wynwood tour $75/55; ☺tours South Beach 11am & 4:30pm daily, Wynwood 10:30am Mon-Sat) This highly rated tour explores various facets of the city – culture, history, art and of course cuisine – while making stops at restaurants and cafes along the way. It's a walking tour, though distances aren't great, and happens in South Beach and Wynwood.

Bike & Roll CYCLING
(Map p66; 305-604-0001; www.bikemiami. com; 210 10th St; hire per 2hr/4hr/day from $10/18/24, tours $40; 9am-7pm) This well-run outfit offers a good selection of bikes, including single-speed cruisers, geared hybrids and speedy road bikes. Staff move things along quickly, so you won't have to waste time waiting to get out and riding. Bike tours are also available (daily at 10am).

Downtown Miami

History Miami Tours TOURS
(www.historymiami.org/city-tour; tours $30-60) Historian extraordinaire Dr Paul George leads fascinating walking tours, including culturally rich strolls through Little Haiti, Little Havana, Downtown and Coral Gables at twilight, plus the occasional boat trip to Stiltsville and Key Biscayne. Tours happen once a week or so. Get the full menu and sign up online.

Urban Tour Host WALKING
(Map p72; 305-416-6868; www.miamicultural tours.com; 25 SE 2nd Ave, Ste 1048; tours from $20) Urban Tour Host runs a program of custom tours that provide face-to-face interaction in all of Miami's neighborhoods. For something different, sign up for a Miami cultural community tour that includes Little Haiti and Little Havana, with opportunities to visit Overtown, Liberty City and Allpattah.

Island Queen BOATING
(Map p72; 305-379-5119; www.islandqueen cruises.com; 401 Biscayne Blvd; adult/child $28/20) This outfit runs 90-minute boat tours that take in Millionaire's Row, the Miami River and Fisher Island. There are frequent daily departures (hourly between 11am and 6pm).

Wynwood & the Design District

Wynwood Art Walk WALKING
(305-814-9290; www.wynwoodartwalk.com; tours from $29) Not to be confused with the monthly art celebration of the same name, this Wynwood Art Walk is actually a 90-minute guided tour taking you to some of the best gallery shows of the day, plus a look at some of the top street art around the 'hood.

Coral Gables

Coral Gables Tours OUTDOORS
(Map p88; 305-603-8067; www.coralgables museum.org/tours; 285 Aragon Ave) The Coral

DON'T MISS

DON'T MISS: MIAMI ECOADVENTURES

The Dade County parks system leads a variety of tours under the rubric of Miami EcoAdventures (305-666-5885; www.miamidade.gov/ecoadventures; bike tours $45, canoeing $30-70), including excellent bike tours on Key Biscayne and out in the Everglades. You can also go on one of six different canoe trips, out on the Oleta River, on the Matheson Mangrove trek or paddling to Indian Key down in the Keys. There's also kayaking, snorkeling trips, walking tours and birdwatching. Trips depart from different locations; call or go online for details.

Gables Museum runs various tours throughout the month, including downtown walking tours (Saturdays at 11am, $10), exhibition tours at the museum (Sundays at 1pm, free with admission) and bike tours (third Sunday of the month at 10am, $10).

Best of all are the two-hour paddling tours on the Coral Gables Waterway (last Sunday of the month at 9:30am, $40) – a scenic series of constructed canals that provide the chance to take in a bit of nature and history. Call ahead to reserve a spot on a tour.

Key Biscayne

Stiltsville Boat Tour BOATING
(305-379-5119; www.islandqueencruises.com/ stiltsville.htm; tours $60) Island Queen Cruises based out of the Bayside Marketplace, offers infrequent trips to Stiltsville (approximately once a month), on three-hour tours narrated by Dr Paul George. Check www.historymiami.org/city-tour for the latest schedule.

Festivals & Events

Wynwood Art Walk ART
(www.artcircuits.com; 7-10pm 2nd Sat of the month) One of the best ways to take in the burgeoning Miami art scene is to join in the Wynwood Art Walk. Despite the name, these events aren't really about walking but more about celebration. Many of the galleries around Wynwood host special events and art openings, with ever-flowing drinks (not always free), live music around the 'hood, food trucks and special markets.

Sounds of Little Haiti
CULTURAL

(www.rhythmfoundation.com/series/big-night-in-little-haiti; 212 NE 59 Terrace, Little Haiti Cultural Center; ⊘6-10pm 3rd Fri of month) **FREE** For a taste of Caribbean culture, head to this family-friendly fest held on the third Friday of every month. The celebration is rife with music, Caribbean food and kids' activities.

January

Miami Marathon
SPORTS

(www.themiamimarathon.com; ⊘late-Jan) The big running event in South Florida is the Miami Marathon, which brings over 25,000 runners racing through the streets along a very scenic course. There's also a half marathon.

Art Deco Weekend
CULTURAL

(www.artdecoweekend.com; Ocean Dr, btwn 1st St & 23rd St; hmid-Jan) This weekend fair features guided tours, concerts, classic-auto shows, sidewalk cafes, arts and antiques.

Miami Jewish Film Festival
FILM

(www.miamijewishfilmfestival.com; 4200 Biscayne Blvd; ⊘Jan) A great chance to cinematically *kvetch* with one of the biggest Jewish communities in the USA.

February

Art Wynwood
ART

(www.artwynwood.com; ⊘mid-Feb) The dozens of galleries spread throughout Wynwood strut their artistic stuff during this festival, which showcases the best of Miami's burgeoning arts scene. There's a palpable commercial bent to this artistic event; big wallet buyers are wooed and marketed to. Expect murals and installations to appear throughout the area. Typically held on the third weekend in February.

Coconut Grove Arts Festival
CULTURAL

(www.coconutgroveartsfest.com; Bayshore Dr, Coconut Grove; ⊘late Feb) One of the most prestigious arts festivals in the country, this three-day fair features works by more than 350 visual artists. There are also concerts, dance and theater troupes, a culinary arts component (with cooking demos) and a global village with foods from around the world.

South Beach Wine & Food Festival
FOOD & DRINK

(www.sobefest.com; ⊘late-Feb) A five-day festival of fine dining and sipping to promote South Florida's culinary image. Expect cooking demonstrations, star-studded brunches, dinners and barbecues, plus wine tastings, happy-hour munching and cocktail sipping.

Original Miami Beach Antiques Show
FAIR

(www.originalmiamibeachantiquesshow.com; Miami Beach Convention Center; ⊘Feb) One of the largest events of its kind in the USA, with more than 800 dealers from 20 countries. It happens over four days in February.

March

Carnaval Miami
CARNIVAL

(Calle Ocho Festival; www.carnavalmiami.com; ⊘Mar) One of the biggest events in Little Havana's yearly calendar is this premier Latin festival, which takes over the area for nine days in early March: there's a Latin drag-queen show, in-line-skate competition, domino tournament, the immense Calle Ocho street festival, Miss Carnaval Miami and more.

Ultra Music Festival
MUSIC

(www.ultramusicfestival.com; Bayfront Park, 301 N Biscayne Blvd) In late March, huge

---

HIBISCUS, PALM & STAR ISLANDS

Floating off the edge of the A1A, in the heart of Biscayne Bay (and posh exclusivity), Hibiscus Island, Palm Island and Star Island are little floating Primrose Hills. There aren't many famous people living here – just wealthy ones – although Star Island is home to Gloria Estefan and for a short time Al Capone lived (and died) on Palm Island. In the 1970s and '80s a mansion on Star Island was the headquarters of the Ethiopian Zion Coptic Church, a Rastafarian sect eventually convicted of smuggling large amounts of marijuana into the USA. That incident prompted a media circus that focused on both the indictments and neighborly disputes between the long-haired, bearded white Rastas and their aristocratic Star Island neighbors, who complained about the fog of cannabis smoke constantly emanating from the EZCC's compound.

Today the drives for the islands are guarded by a security booth, but the roads are public, so if you ask politely, you can get in. Star Island is little more than one elliptical road lined with royal palms, sculpted ficus hedges and fancy gates guarding houses you can't see.

LOCAL KNOWLEDGE: MIAMI CRITICAL MASS

If you're in Miami at the beginning of the weekend late in any given month, you may spot hordes of cyclists and, less frequently, some skateboarders, roller-skaters and other self-propelled individuals. So what's it all about?

It's Miami Critical Mass. The event, put on by the Miami Bike Scene (www.themiamibikescene.com) is meant to raise awareness of cycling and indirectly advocate for increased bicycle infrastructure in the city. Anyone is welcome to join; the mass ride gathers at Government Center by HistoryMiami (p69) at 6:30pm on the last Friday of each month.

The whole shebang departs on the 12-to-18-mile trek at 7:15pm. The average speed of the ride is a not-too-taxing 12mph, and you will be expected to keep up (at the same time, you're not to go faster than the pace setters). All in all, it's a fun experience, and a good way to meet members of the local cycling community.

dance-loving crowds gather at Bayfront Park for three days of revelry. Top DJs from around the globe jet in to spin electronica on eight different stages scattered about the park. There are light shows, wild costumes and mega-decibel sound systems that spill bass far across the city.

Book tickets early. Over 150,000 attend, and the event always sells out.

Miami International Film Festival FILM
(www.miamifilmfestival.com; ⊙ Mar) This event, sponsored by Miami-Dade College, is an intensive 10-day festival showcasing documentaries and features from all over the world. Over half-a-dozen cinemas participate across the city.

Calle Ocho Festival CULTURAL
(Carnaval Miami; www.carnavalmiami.com; ⊙ Mar) This massive street party in March is the culmination of Carnaval Miami (p98), a 10-day celebration of Latin culture.

April

Miami Beach Gay Pride PARADE
(www.miamibeachgaypride.com; ⊙ Apr) In April Miami Beach proudly flies the rainbow flag high in this lively weekend festival that culminates in a colorful street parade along Ocean Dr. Break out the boas, glitter and body paint!

Outshine Film Festival FILM
(www.mifofilm.com; ⊙ Apr) Held over 10 days in late April, this annual event screens shorts, feature films and documentaries with a LGBT focus shown at various South Beach theaters. Over 65 films are screened, including many world premieres.

Billboard Latin Music Awards MUSIC
(www.billboardevents.com; ⊙ late-Apr) This prestigious awards show draws top industry execs, star performers and Latin-music fans.

Wynwood Life MUSIC
(www.wynwoodlife.com; ⊙ Apr) Held over one weekend in April, this newish festival is a celebration of all things Wynwood, with live music and DJs, a big market of arts and crafts, fashion shows, food trucks, a culinary stage (of cooking demonstrations) and a crew of talented street artists creating live installations throughout the fest.

May, June & July

Miami Museum Month CULTURAL
(www.miamimuseummonth.com; ⊙ May) Held through the month of May, this is an an excellent chance to see and hang out in some of the best museums in the city in the midst of happy hours, special exhibitions and lectures.

Miami Fashion Week CULTURAL
(www.miamifashionweek.com; Miami Beach Convention Center; ⊙ May or Jun) Models are as abundant as fish in the ocean as designers descend on the city and catwalks become ubiquitous.

Goombay Festival CULTURAL
(www.goombayfestivalcoconutgrove.com; ⊙ Jun/Jul) A massive festival, held in June or July, which celebrates Bahamian culture.

Independence Day Celebration CULTURAL
(Bayfront Park; ⊙ July 4) July 4 is marked with excellent fireworks, a laser show and live music that draw more than 100,000 people to breezy Bayfront Park (p71).

August & September
**Miami Spice
Restaurant Month** FOOD & DRINK
(www.facebook.com/ilovemiamispice; ⊙ Aug-Sep) Top restaurants around Miami offer three-course lunches and dinners to try to lure folks out during the heat wave. Prices hover

MIAMI'S TOP EVENTS

Art Basel Miami Beach (p100), December

Art Deco Weekend (p98), January

Coconut Grove Arts Festival (p98), February

Carnaval Miami (p98), March

Ultra Music Festival (p98), March

around $25 for lunch and $40 for dinner. Reservations essential.

International Ballet Festival DANCE

(www.internationalballetfestival.org; ☺ Aug-Sep) Some of the most important dance talent in the world performs at venues across the city. Performances happen over various weekends from August to September.

November

Miami Book Fair International CULTURAL

(www.miamibookfair.com; 401 NE 2nd Ave; ☺ Nov) Occurring in mid- to late-November, this is among the most important and well-attended book fairs in the USA. Hundreds of nationally known writers join hundreds of publishers and hundreds of thousands of visitors.

White Party MUSIC

(www.whiteparty.org; ☺ Nov) If you're gay and not here, there's a problem. This weeklong extravaganza draws more than 15,000 gay men and women for nonstop partying at clubs and venues all over town.

December

Design Miami ART

(www.designmiami.com; ☺ early Dec) Held in conjunction with Art Basel (p100), Design Miami is a high-profile party hosting some of the world's top design professionals and assorted entourages. Design-inspired lectures and showcases center on the Miami Beach Convention Center.

Art Basel Miami Beach ART

(www.artbasel.com/miami-beach; ☺ early Dec) One of the most important international art shows in the world, with works from more than 250 galleries and a slew of trendy parties. Even if you're not a billionaire collector, there's much to enjoy at this four-day fest, with open-air art installations around town, special exhibitions at many Miami galleries and outdoor film screenings, among other goings-on.

King Mango Strut PARADE

(www.kingmangostrut.org; Main Ave & Grand Ave, Coconut Grove; ☺ Dec) Held each year just after Christmas since 1982, this quirky Coconut Grove parade is a politically charged, fun freak that began as a spoof on current events and the now-defunct Orange Bowl Parade.

Art Miami ART

(www.art-miami.com; ☺ Dec) This massive fair displays modern and contemporary works from more than 100 galleries and international artists.

Orange Bowl SPORTS

(www.orangebowl.org; Hard Rock Stadium, 347 Don Shula Dr, Miami Gardens) Hordes of football fans descend on Miami for the Super Bowl of college football. The game happens either at the end of December (typically December 30 or 31) or the first few days of January.

🛏 Sleeping

Miami has some alluring lodging options – and for some travelers, it's a big draw to the city. South Beach has all the name recognition with boutique hotels set in lovely art-deco buildings, but there are plenty of other options in Miami – from Downtown high-rises with sweeping views and endless amenities to historic charmers in Coral Gables, Coconut Grove and other less touristy neighborhoods.

🛏 South Beach

SoBe Hostel HOSTEL $

(Map p66; ☏ 305-534-6669; www.sobe-hostel. com; 235 Washington Ave; dm $22-52; ❄ @ 🛜) On a quiet end of SoFi (the area south of 5th St, South Beach), this massive multilingual hostel has a happening common area and spartan rooms. The staff are friendly and the on-site bar (open to 5am) is a great spot to meet other travelers. Free breakfasts and dinners are included in the rates.

There are loads of activities on offer – from volleyball games to mojito-making nights, screenings of big games and bar crawls.

HI Miami Beach HOSTEL $

(Map p60; ☏ 305-787-3122; www.hi-miamibeach. com/contact; 1506 Collins Ave; dm $30-50; 🛜) This reliable budget spot from Hostelling International has friendly staff, well-maintained rooms and loads of activities on offer – particularly when it comes to nightlife. There's a kitchen and a terrace, plus some of Miami's best tacos just downstairs. Great location just a short stroll to the beach.

Rock Hostel
HOSTEL $

(Map p60; ☎ 305-763-8146; www.miamirock hostel.com; 1351 Collins Ave; dm $30-50; ✱ 🛜) Party people need only apply at this lively, well-run hostel a few minutes from the beach. Fairly simple six- to 10-bed dorms (including all-female) are enhanced by myriad activities on offer, including nights out to bars and clubs. Located on site, SoCal Cantina doles out tasty tacos and tropical cocktails, plus there's a small front deck overlooking the sidewalk.

Bed & Drinks
HOSTEL $

(Map p60; ☎ 786-230-1234; http://bedsn drinks.com; 1676 James Ave; dm/d from $29/154) This hostel pretty shamelessly plays to the sex-appeal-seeking crowd – check the name – but hey, it's a few blocks from the beach, so the placement works. The rooms range from average to slightly below average, but the young party-minded crowd (mostly) doesn't mind. Friendly staff, a lively on-site bar and nightlife outings to clubs around town make up for the minuses.

Aqua Hotel
BOUTIQUE HOTEL $

(Map p60; ☎ 305-538-4361; www.aquamiami.com; 1530 Collins Ave; r $110-200; P ✱ 🛜) On the outside this hotel stays true to name and embraces marine-like hues, while the rooms within have a crisp white paint job, with wood floors and a few touches of artwork. Although there's no pool, you can escape the noise of Collins Ave in the small backyard.

Miami Beach
International Hostel
HOSTEL $

(Map p66; ☎ 305-534-0268; www.hostel miamibeach.com; 236 9th St; dm/r from $34/150; ✱ @ 🛜) An extensive makeover has turned this reliable old hostel into something like a boutique club with dorm rooms. Bright plaster, marble accents, deco-and-neon decor and hip, clean rooms all make for a good base in South Beach. Wallflowers need not apply: there's a party-friendly social vibe throughout.

Townhouse Hotel
BOUTIQUE HOTEL $$

(Map p60; ☎ 305-534-3800; www.townhouse hotel.com; 150 20th St at Collins Ave; r $200-400; ✱ 🛜) The Townhouse embraces stylish minimalism with a cool white lobby and igloo-like rooms with random scarlet accents. The whole place has a welcoming and somewhat whimsical vibe (who needs mints on pillows when the Townhouse provides beach balls?).

There's a festive rooftop lounge (open 6pm to midnight), a lively ramen and burger bar downstairs (open till 4am) and a pastry and coffee counter (from 7am to 1pm) in the lobby. There's no pool, but guests can swim at the nearby Raleigh Hotel (p108).

Fashion Boutique Hotel
BOUTIQUE HOTEL $$

(Map p66; ☎ 786-398-4408; www.fashionhaus hotel.com; 534 Washington Ave; r from $179; P ✱ ✱ 🛜) There's a theatrical flair to this budget-friendly hotel in a quieter part of South Beach. The 48 well-equipped rooms have ruby red blankets and throws, light gray walls and thick accordian-like curtains. The signature statement piece though is the massive photo mural over the bed ,– which depicts a model preening for the camera, and looking somewhat voyeuristic in these quiet rooms.

Catalina Hotel
BOUTIQUE HOTEL $$

(Map p60; ☎ 305-674-1160; www.catalinahotel. com; 1732 Collins Ave; r from $220; P ✱ 🛜 ✱) The Catalina is a lovely example of mid-range deco style. Most appealing, besides the playfully minimalist rooms, is the vibe – the Catalina doesn't take itself too seriously, and staff and guests all seem to be having fun as a result. The back pool, concealed behind the main building's crisp white facade, is particularly attractive and fringed by a whispery grove of bamboo trees.

Clay Hotel
HOTEL $$

(Map p60; ☎ 305-250-0759; www.clayhotel.com; 1438 Washington Ave; r $140-250; ✱ 🛜) Hotels are always nicer when they come packaged in a 100-year-old Spanish-style villa. The Clay has clean and comfortable rooms, not too flashy but hardly spartan, located in a medinalike maze of adjacent buildings. If you're on a budget but don't want dorm-y hostel atmosphere, head here. This is yet another Miami place where Al Capone got some shut-eye.

> ### CULTURAL FRIDAYS
>
> The Little Havana Arts District may not be Wynwood, but it constitutes an energetic strip of galleries and studios (concentrated on 8th St between SW 15th Ave & SW 17th Ave), and there's no better time to visit than on **Viernes Culturales** (Cultural Fridays; www.viernesculturales.org; ⊙7-11pm last Fri of month). No wine-sipping art walk this: Cultural Fridays in Little Havana are like little carnival seasons, with music, old men in *guayaberas* (Cuban dress shirts) crooning to the stars and Little Havana galleries opening their doors for special exhibitions.

Chesterfield Hotel
BOUTIQUE HOTEL $$

(Map p66; ☑877-762-3477; www.thechester fieldhotel.com; 855 Collins Ave; r from $215; P ❋ 🕾) Hip-hop gets funky with zebra-stripe curtains and cushions in the small lobby, which hosts a chill happy hour at the in-house Safari Bar when the sun goes down. Rooms mix up dark-wood furniture overlaid with bright-white beds and vaguely tropical colors swathed throughout. Be sure to enjoy the view from the roof deck.

Stiles Hotel
BOUTIQUE HOTEL $$

(Map p66; ☑844-289-8145; www.thestiles hotel.com; 1120 Collins Ave; r $170-340; P ❋ 🕾 🕾) This Stiles gets positive reviews for its (relatively) fair prices, friendly staff and attractive chambers. Guest rooms are set in sandy earth tones, with natural fiber carpeting, modular bedside lamps and black-out curtains. The courtyard, with three small spa pools, is a fine spot to unwind.

Room Mate Lord Balfour
BOUTIQUE HOTEL $$

(Map p66; ☑305-673-0401; www.lordbalfour miami.com; 350 Ocean Dr; r $150-340; P ❋ 🕾) Why not name a hotel for a minor, generally ill-regarded British prime minister? Name choice aside, the Lord Balfour features the usual minimalist-plus-pop-art rooms Miami Beach is famous for, along with wood floors, big windows and rain showers – plus a massive mural of a boldly tattooed lass with luxuriant hair behind the bed.

The lobby/bar area is a gem, mixing retro accoutrements with pop art and sweeping lines leading to the terrace out front – a fine spot for taking in this peaceful stretch of Ocean Dr.

Cavalier South Beach
BOUTIQUE HOTEL $$

(☑305-673-1199; www.cavaliersouthbeach.com; 1320 Ocean Dr; r from $240) The exterior plays a bit with tropical and marine themes (seahorse-like etchings on the center of the facade, with a palm trunk racing down each side). Inside, a 2015 renovation showcases unique design features uncommon in these parts – namely warm wood hues and exposed-brick walls, plus marble bathrooms, whimsical color-saturated paintings and all the high-tech finishes (including 50-inch-screen smart TVs).

Hotel Astor
BOUTIQUE HOTEL $$

(Map p66; ☑305-531-8081; www.hotelastor. com; 956 Washington Ave; r/ste from $220/375; P ❋ 🕾 🕾) The Astor aims for retro chic, without being too over-the-top. The lobby is all class, with potted palms, straight lines and geometric marble floors, which flow past a convivial bar and out to the tiny pool, shaded by a single artfully placed palm tree. The pink-toned rooms are relaxing and well appointed.

There are appealing spots for cocktails including a lively downstairs drinking den of throwback 1920s glam, complete with leopard-print loungers.

Kent Hotel
BOUTIQUE HOTEL $$

(Map p66; ☑305-604-5068; www.thekenthotel. com; 1131 Collins Ave; r $120-290; P ❋ 🕾 🕾) Built in 1936, the Kent has a classic art-deco facade, with striking vertical and horizontal lines that seem to beckon passers to come hither for a closer look. The rooms themselves are small and fairly boxy, with a modern gray-and-white color scheme, and can be noisy on weekend nights.

The terrace restaurant (the Limetree Lounge) is a fine feature, with outdoor seating backed by a small thatch-roof bar.

Hotel St Augustine
BOUTIQUE HOTEL $$

(Map p66; ☑305-532-0570; www.hotelst augustine.com; 347 Washington Ave; r $210-345; P ❋ 🕾) Wood that's blonder than Barbie, a soft color palette, and a crisp-and-clean deco theme combine to create one of SoFi's better-value sleeps. The familiar, warm service adds to the value, as do the glass showers that turn into personal steam rooms at the flick of a switch.

On the downside, the hotel is starting to show its age, and some rooms could use an update.

Hotel Shelley
BOUTIQUE HOTEL $$

(Map p66; ☑305-531-3341; www.hotelshelley.com; 844 Collins Ave; r from $170; ❋ 🕾) This deco beauty isn't a wallflower. The white and lavender color scheme on the facade screams 'look at me!' and the lively lobby-lounge is pure eye candy with its terracotta tile floors, spider-like chandeliers and distressed walls hung with old photos. The rooms are affordably stylish, but can be on the small side.

Free evening drinks (from 7pm to 8pm) is a nice extra.

Room Mate
Waldorf Towers
BOUTIQUE HOTEL $$

(Map p66; ☑786-439-1600; www.room-matehotels. com; 860 Ocean Dr; r $190-440; 🕾) An immaculate white lobby and stylish rooms comparable to most boutiques on the strip – light colours, high-design furnishings and sea views (in some rooms) – feature in this place, but the real thing to look for is the streamlined facade and rooftop cupola. Designed by deco godfather L Murray Dixon, it's meant to resemble a lighthouse shining out from its corner on Ocean Dr.

Ocean Five Hotel — BOUTIQUE HOTEL $$
(Map p66; ☏ 305-532-7093; www.oceanfive.com; 436 Ocean Dr; r/ste from $210/270; P ❀ 🛜) This boutique hotel is a cheerfully painted deco building with cozy, quiet rooms that reveal a sleek cabin-like aesthetic. Think whites and light yellows with Italian travertine marble floors and soothing photos of seascapes on the walls. It's not fussy, and overall is good value for South Beach.

⭐1 Hotel — HOTEL $$$
(Map p60; ☏ 866-615-1111; www.1hotels.com/southbeach; 2341 Collins Ave; r from $400; ❀ 🛜 ≋) 🏊 One of the top hotels in the USA, the 1 Hotel has 400-plus gorgeous rooms that embrace both luxurious and eco-friendly features – including tree-trunk coffee tables/desks, custom hemp-blend mattresses and salvaged driftwood feature walls, plus in-room water filtration (no need for plastic bottles). The common areas are impressive, with four pools, including an adults-only rooftop infinity pool.

The restaurant serves locally sourced farm-to-table fare (under the helm of award-winning chef Tom Colicchio), and the list of amenities is long, with a lavish spa, a 14,000-sq-ft gym (with many classes), watersports activities, a kids club and, of course, direct access to the fine sands of South Beach.

⭐Washington Park Hotel — BOUTIQUE HOTEL $$$
(Map p66; ☏ 305-421-6265; www.wphsouthbeach.com; 1050 Washington Ave; r $250-500; ❀ 🛜 ≋) In a great location two blocks from the beach, the Washington Park is spread among five beautifully restored art-deco buildings fronted by a pool and a palm-fringed courtyard. The rooms are all class, with muted color schemes, distressed laminate wood flooring and elegant design touches like bedside globe lamps and wood and cast-iron work desks.

The vibe is welcoming and fun, with bocce in the courtyard, cocktails at Employees Only (a NYC bar that opened on site in 2017) and stylish green Martone bikes for zipping about town.

⭐Surfcomber — HOTEL $$$
(Map p60; ☏ 305-532-7715; www.surfcomber.com; 1717 Collins Ave; r $250-480; P ❀ 🛜 ≋ ❀) The

Surfcomber has a classic deco exterior with strong lines and shade-providing 'eyebrows' that zigzag across the facade. But the interior is what takes most people aback. Rooms have undeniable appeal, with elegant lines in keeping with the deco aesthetic, while bursts of color keep things contemporary.

The lobby and adjoining restaurant are awash with bold colors, decorative wood elements, playful tropical themes and skylights, while a terrace overlooking Collins Ave connects indoor and outdoor spaces. Head around back for a dazzling view: a massive sun-drenched pool, fringed by palm trees and backed by lovely oceanfront, the beach just steps away.

⭐Pelican Hotel — BOUTIQUE HOTEL $$$
(Map p66; ☏ 305-673-3373; www.pelicanhotel.com; 826 Ocean Dr; r $260-420; ❀ 🛜) When the owners of Diesel jeans purchased the Pelican in 1999, they started scouring garage sales for just the right ingredients to fuel a mad experiment: 29 themed rooms that come off like a fantasy-suite hotel dipped in hip.

From the cowboy-hipster chic of 'High Corral, OK Chaparral' to the jungly electric tiger stripes of 'Me Tarzan, You Vain,' all the rooms are completely different, though all set for good times (including quality sound systems and high-end fixtures).

⭐Betsy Hotel — BOUTIQUE HOTEL $$$
(Map p66; ☏ 844-862-3157; www.thebetsyhotel.com; 1440 Ocean Dr; r from $310; P ❀ 🛜 ≋) One of South Beach's finest hotels, the Betsy has a classy vibe with excellent service and first-rate amenities. The historic gem has two wings, with rooms set in either a colonial style or an art-deco aesthetic – don't miss the view from the outside of the Dali-esque 'Orb' that joins the two buildings.

Thoughtful touches include orchids in the rooms, a 24-hour fitness center, two swimming pools and rather curious bathroom mirrors with inbuilt LCD TVs.

Gale South Beach — HOTEL $$$
(Map p60; ☏ 305-673-0199; www.galehotel.com; 1690 Collins Ave; r $220-410; P ❀ 🛜 ≋) The Gale's exterior is an admirable re-creation of classic boxy deco aesthetic expanded to the grand dimensions of a modern SoBe super resort. This blend of classic and haute South Beach carries on indoors, where you'll find bright rooms with a handsome color scheme, sharp lines and a retro chic vibe inspired by the Mid-Century Modern movement.

LAZY DAYS

There are many ways to spend an easygoing day in Miami, from basking on an island beach to taking a meandering stroll through the city's most captivating neighborhoods.

SHOPPING SOUTH BEACH

The pedestrian-only strip of **Lincoln Road** is a great spot for an easygoing amble. Dotted with palm trees and fountains, the promenade is packed with eye candy of all sorts: colorful stores, outdoor eateries and a wide cross section of Miami society.

A DAY AT THE POOL

When the surf is too rough or you need a break from the beach, make your way to one of Miami's lovely swimming pools. Coral Gables' **Venetian Pool** (p94) is an aquatic wonderland, complete with tiny waterfalls and a mini island. You can also spend the day at the **Biltmore Hotel** (p85), with it's enormous pool, plus various on-site restaurants.

WANDERING WYNWOOD

Head to **Wynwood** (p76) for a leisurely afternoon stroll, checking out Miami's most creative side. You'll find art galleries, indie shops and plenty of cafes and restaurants around the neighborhood, particularly along NW 2nd Ave near the **Wynwood Walls** (p80).

ISLAND ESCAPE

Just a short drive from Miami, **Key Biscayne** (p87) has fine beaches, a hands-on nature center for kids, and an excellent park at the southern tip. It's hard to match **Bill Baggs Cape Florida State Park** (p89), where you can stroll scenic nature trails, check out a lighthouse, then unwind on a lovely beach.

1. Lincoln Road 2. Venetian Pool 3. Wynwood
4. Cape Florida Lighthouse, Bill Baggs State Park

The elegant rooftop pool is rather narrow but gets sun all day, and the bar and restaurant are a major draw, even for those not staying in the hotel.

Royal Palm
HOTEL $$$

(Map p60; ☑305-604-5700; www.royalpalmsouthbeach.com; 1545 Collins Ave; r/ste from $260/510; P✳☎☆☀) Even the tropical fish tank with its elegant curves and chrome accents has a touch of deco flair, to say nothing of the streamlined bar with mint-green accents – all of which adds up to South Beach's most striking example of building-as-cruise-liner deco theme. The shipboard theme carries into the plush rooms, which are also offset by bright whites and minty subtle marine-like hues.

As with other big properties anchored between the beach and Collins Ave, the Royal Palm has extensive amenities, including two pools and good drinking and dining spaces, including Byblos, a recommended Greek restaurant.

Standard
BOUTIQUE HOTEL $$$

(☑305-673-1717; www.standardhotels.com/miami; 40 Island Ave; r/ste from $240/510; P✳☎☆☀) Look for the upside-down 'Standard' sign on the old Lido building on Belle Island (between South Beach and Downtown Miami) and you'll find the Standard – which is anything but. This boutique blends a bevy of spa services, hipster funk and South Beach sexiness, and the result is a '50s motel gone glam.

There are raised white beds, spa rain showers and gossamer curtains that open onto a courtyard of earthly delights, including a heated *hammam* (Turkish bath).

The Franklin
BOUTIQUE HOTEL $$$

(Map p66; ☑305-432-7061; www.franklinsouthbeach.com; 860 Collins Ave; r $240-490; ✳☎) A classic from 1934, the Franklin is a beautifully restored art-deco hotel with modern loftlike rooms. Think polished-concrete floors, sleek modular white surfaces, touches of pop art on the walls and good natural light. The rooms are spacious, and the mini kitchen (with coffeemakers) in each is a nice touch.

Friendly service and a great location around the corner from the beach (but not amid the madness of Ocean Dr) add to the value.

Redbury South Beach
BOUTIQUE HOTEL $$$

(Map p60; ☑855-220-1776; www.theredbury.com/southbeach; 1776 Collins Ave; r $250-700; ✳☎☆) What sets the Redbury apart is its refusal to toe the line of identikit South Beach minimalist rooms. Rather, the interior here references art across the 20th century, with fun but easygoing comfort in mind (striped carpets, Italian linens and in-room record players – and albums! – available on request).

A rooftop pool makes for some chilled-out lounging, while the lobby channels East Asian exoticism, plus there's a giant ornamental cage just outside the entrance.

W Hotel
RESORT $$$

(Map p60; ☑305-938-3000; www.wsouthbeach.com; 2201 Collins Ave; r from $440; P✳☎☆☀) There's an astounding variety of rooms available at the South Beach outpost of the W chain, which touts the whole W-brand mix of luxury and style in a big way. The 'spectacular studios' balance long panels of reflective glass with cool tablets of cipollino marble, while the Oasis suite lets in so much light you'd think the sun had risen in your room.

The attendant bars, restaurants, clubs and pool built into this complex are some of the best-regarded on the beach.

Setai
BOUTIQUE HOTEL $$$

(Map p60; ☑305-520-6000; www.thesetaihotel.com; 2001 Collins Ave; r from $745; P✳☎☆☀) Inside a deco building, the Setai has a stunning interior that mixes elements of Southeast Asian temple architecture and contemporary luxury. The spacious rooms are decked out in chocolate teak wood, with clean lines and Chinese and Khmer embellishments. The amenities are exquisite, with

---

MIAMI'S TOP HOTEL POOLS

Miami has some of the most beautiful hotel pools around, and they're more about seeing and being seen than swimming. Most of these pools double as bars, lounges or even clubs. Some hotels have a guests-only policy when it comes to hanging out at the pool, but if you buy a drink at the poolside bar you should be fine.

➡ Delano Hotel (p107)

➡ Shore Club (p108)

➡ Kimpton EPIC Hotel (p110)

➡ Biltmore Hotel (p111)

➡ Raleigh Hotel (p108)

➡ Fontainebleau (p109)

a heavenly spa, three palm-fringed swimming pools, a top restaurant and a great beach location.

Sagamore BOUTIQUE HOTEL **$$$**

(Map p60; ☑ 305-535-8088; www.sagamorehotel. com; 1671 Collins Ave; r $270-455; P ✳ 🛜 ☒) This hotel-cum-exhibition-hall likes to blur the boundaries between interior decor, art and conventional hotel aesthetics. Almost every space within this hotel, from the lobbies to the rooms, doubles as an art gallery thanks to a talented curator and an impressive roster of contributing artists. Rooms? Soft whites and creams, accented by artsy photography and sleek designer accents.

The Villa Casa Casuarina RESORT **$$$**

(Map p66; ☑ 786-485-2200; www.vmmiamibeach. com; 1116 Ocean Dr; r $750-1400; P ✳ 🛜 ☒) Formerly the home of fashion legend Gianni Versace, this jaw-dropping mansion has been turned into one of South Beach's most upscale resorts. You can't help but feel like royalty lodging here. It has a mosaic-lined pool plucked from Ancient Rome, marble-lined corridors and lavishly decorated rooms with antique furnishings and vibrantly painted murals on the walls.

Sense South Beach BOUTIQUE HOTEL **$$$**

(Map p66; ☑ 305-538-5529; www.sense beachhouse.com; 400 Ocean Dr; r from $280; P ✳ ☒) The 18-room Sense is fantastically atmospheric – smooth white walls disappearing behind melting blue views of South Beach, wooden paneling arranged around lovely sharp angles that feel inviting rather than imposing, and rooms that contrast two tones (white with either blue-gray or sandy tones). Geometric lamps and slender furnishings round out the MacBook-esque air.

Essex House Hotel BOUTIQUE HOTEL **$$$**

(Map p66; ☑ 305-534-2700; www.clevelander. com; 1001 Collins Ave; r $246-600; ✳ 🛜 ☒) When you gaze at this lobby, one of the best-preserved interiors in the deco district, you're getting a glimpse of South Beach's gangster heyday. Beyond that the Essex has helpful staff, rooms furnished with subdued colors and a side verandah filled with rattan furnishings that's a particularly pleasant people-watching perch.

Though close to the beach, the Essex is a quieter option than South Beach hotels on the strip. The pool here is small, but guests can take a dip at the larger, livelier Clevelander around the corner door.

Inn at the Fisher Island Club RESORT **$$$**

(☑ 305-535-6000; www.fisherislandclub.com; r $700-4050; P ✳ 🛜 ☒) One of Florida's most exclusive residences, this luxury island resort has beautiful accommodations, which don't quite measure up to the price tag. The amenities, however, are world class: a top-rated spa, plus golf, tennis (clay, grass and hard courts), a fitness center with classes (yoga, crossfit, spinning etc) and half-a-dozen restaurants (from fine dining in a restored 1930s mansion to open-air seaside dining).

And don't forget the lovely beach (with white sand imported from the Bahamas, of course) and a salt-water pool.

National Hotel HOTEL **$$$**

(Map p60; ☑ 305-532-2311; www.nationalhotel. com; 1677 Collins Ave; r $280-490, ste from $600; P ✳ 🛜 ☒) The National is an old-school deco icon, with its bell-tower-like cap and slim yet muscular facade. Inside the hotel itself you'll find elegant rooms with mahogany furnishings offering a timeless look. The lobby and halls are covered in artwork, with the dynamic chords of Rachmaninoff playing overhead, while outside a lovely infinity pool beckons guests.

The decadent cabana suites are exercises in luxury, offering unfettered access to the pool, private terraces and on-site tropical gardens.

Delano BOUTIQUE HOTEL **$$$**

(Map p60; ☑ 305-672-2000; www.delano-hotel. com; 1685 Collins Ave; r from $360; P ✳ 🛜 ☒) The Delano opened in the 1990s and immediately started ruling the South Beach roost. If there's a quintessential I'm-too-sexy-for-this...South Beach moment, it's when you walk into the Delano's lobby, which has all the excess of an overbudgeted theater set. Rooms are almost painfully white and bright: all long, smooth lines, reflective surfaces and modern, luxurious amenities.

The pool area resembles the courtyard of a Disney princess's palace and includes a giant chess set.

Mondrian South Beach RESORT **$$$**

(Map p66; ☑ 305-514-1500; www.mondrian-miami.com; 1100 West Ave; r/ste from $350/475; P ✳ 🛜 ☒) Morgan Hotel Group hired Dutch design star Marcel Wanders to basically crank it up to 11 at the Mondrian. The theme's inspired by Sleeping Beauty's castle – columns carved like giant table legs, a 'floating' staircase and spectacular bay views from the floor-to-ceiling windows. Upstairs the design whimsy continues with plush rooms sporting Delft tiles with beach scenes instead of windmills, and chandelier-like rainfall showers.

Winter Haven Hotel　BOUTIQUE HOTEL **$$**
(Map p60; ☎305-531-5571; www.winterhaven hotelsobe.com; 1400 Ocean Dr; r $265-390; P❄🕾🌊) Al Capone used to stay here; maybe he liked the deco ceiling lamps in the lobby, with their sharp, retro sci-fi lines and grand-Gothic proportions, and the intriguing Eastern-themed mirrors. The rooms, with their creams, whites and neutral tones coupled with wood accents, have a soothing if fairly conventional aesthetic.

There's a good Italian restaurant, with outdoor seating, on the ground floor.

Raleigh Hotel　BOUTIQUE HOTEL **$$$**
(Map p60; ☎305-534-6300; www.raleigh hotel.com; 1775 Collins Ave; r/ste from $335/520; P❄🕾🌊) While everyone else was trying to get all modern, the Raleigh painstakingly tried to restore itself to prewar glory. It succeeded in a big way. Celebrity hotelier André Balazs has managed to capture a to-bacco-and-dark-wood men's club ambience and old-school elegance while sneaking in modern design and amenities. Have a swim in the stunning pool: Hollywood actress Esther Williams used to.

Shore Club　BOUTIQUE HOTEL **$$$**
(Map p60; ☎305-695-3100; www.shoreclub.com; 1901 Collins Ave; r from $250; P❄@🌊) In a highly coveted location in South Beach (backing onto lovely beachfront), the Shore Club has airy but rather simply furnished rooms with a few color splashes amid the otherwise white design scheme. There are some appealing areas for amusement, including the Sky-bar (Map p60; 4pm-2am Mon-Wed, to 3am Thu-Sat), which is a fine garden-like spot for a drink (though located rather surprisingly at ground level).

Hotel Victor　BOUTIQUE HOTEL **$$$**
(Map p66; ☎305-779-8700; www.hotelvictor southbeach.com; 1144 Ocean Dr; r $260-700; P❄🕾🌊) Overlooking Ocean Dr, the Hotel Victor has an easygoing style, its lobby full of elegant art-deco fixtures, plus a vintage mural of flamingos and striking ink-on-newsprint portraits of famous faces by Gregory Auerbach. The rooms are comfortable and classically appointed (the best of which have

terraces facing the sea), and the pool is a great retreat on hot days.

The Hotel of South Beach　BOUTIQUE HOTEL **$$$**
(Map p66; ☎305-531-2222; www.thehotelof southbeach.com; 801 Collins Ave; r $265-440; P❄🕾🌊) This place has style. Which is not surprising since Todd Oldham designed the boldly beautiful rooms. The themed palette of 'sand, sea and sky' adds a dash of eye candy to the furnishings, as do the custom-made mosaic handles and brushed-steel sinks. The Hotel boasts a fine rooftop pool, overshadowed only by a lovely deco spire.

🛏 North Beach

⭐**Croydon Hotel**　BOUTIQUE HOTEL **$$**
(Map p70; ☎305-938-1145; www.hotelcroydon miamibeach.com; 3720 Collins Ave; r from $190; ❄🕾🌊) The Croydon earns high marks for its bright, classically appointed rooms with dark-wood floors, luxurious beds and modern bathrooms with CO Bigelow products. Head to the ground-floor restaurant with its elaborately patterned ceramic floors for good meals. Fringed by palms, the terrace around the pool has a crisp modern design.

There's also beach service – though the hotel is a block away from the sands.

⭐**Freehand Miami**　BOUTIQUE HOTEL **$$**
(Map p70; ☎305-531-2727; www.thefreehand. com; 2727 Indian Creek Dr; dm $35-55, r $160-250; ❄🕾🌊) The Freehand is the brilliant re-imagining of the old Indian Creek Hotel, a classic of the Miami Beach scene. Rooms are sunny and attractively designed, with local artwork and wooden details. The vintage-filled common areas are the reason to stay here though – especially the lovely pool area and backyard that transforms into one of the best bars in town.

Dorms serve the hostel crowd, while private rooms are quite appealing.

Daddy O Hotel　BOUTIQUE HOTEL **$$**
(☎305-868-4141; www.daddyohotel.com; 9660 E Bay Harbor Dr; r $170-290; P❄🕾) The Daddy O is a cheerful, hip option that looks, from the outside, like a large B&B that's been fashioned for MTV and Apple employees. This vibe continues in the lobby and the rooms: cool, clean lines offset by bright, bouncy colors, plus a nice list of amenities: flat-screen TVs, in-room Keurig coffeemakers, custom wardrobes, gym access and the rest.

Circa 39   BOUTIQUE HOTEL **$$**

(Map p70; ☑ 305-538-4900; www.circa39.com; 3900 Collins Ave; r $180-290; P❄🛜♿🐾) If you love South Beach style but loathe South Beach attitude, Circa has got your back. The lobby has molded furniture and wacky embellishments, and staff go out of their way to make guests feel welcome. Chic (but tiny) rooms, bursting with tropical lime green and subtle earth tones, are attractive enough for the most design-minded visitors.

Red South Beach   BOUTIQUE HOTEL **$$**

(Map p70;   ☑ 305-531-7742;   www.redsouth beach.com; 3010 Collins Ave; r $165-400; ❄🛜♿) Red is indeed the name of the game, from the cushions on the sleek chairs in the lobby to the flashes dancing around the marble pool to deep, blood-crimson headboards and walls wrapping you in warm sexiness in the small but beautiful guest rooms. Come evening, the pool-bar complex is a great place to unwind and meet fellow guests.

Faena Hotel Miami Beach   HOTEL **$$$**

(Map p70; ☑ 305-534-8800; www.faena.com/miami -beach; 3201 Collins Ave; r from $525; ❄🛜♿) One of Miami Beach's most talked about new hotels, the Faena has lavish, artfully designed spaces both inside and out. The rooms, set with a royal red and teal color scheme, are full of beauty and whimsy: animal-print fabrics, coral and seashell decorative touches, custom-designed carpets and window seats (or terraces) for taking in the views. Each room also has butler service.

Gilded columns and exquisite tropical murals line the lobby, with a pretty pool in back – a few paces away from a fully intact gold-covered woolly mammoth skeleton created by British artist Damien Hirst. Two great restaurants are on hand (and another by the pool), as is a massive spa that takes up one whole floor of the hotel, plus lavish drinking dens and a 150-seat theater inspired by Europe's grand old theaters.

Miami Beach Edition   HOTEL **$$$**

(Map p70; ☑ 786-257-4500; www.editionhotels. com/miami-beach; 2901 Collins Ave; d from $420; ❄🛜♿) Design guru Ian Schrager's latest Miami venture is a gorgeous retooling of a 1950s Mid-Beach classic. The 294-room property (including 28 bungalows) has deep luxury imprint, while its artfully designed lobby and minimalist rooms stay true to mid-century style.

The best features are the pool with its hanging gardens, the plush spa, a top res-

taurant (Matador by Jean-Georges), a Studio 54–esque nightclub (called Basement Miami) and an indoor skating rink.

Fontainebleau   RESORT **$$$**

(Map p70; ☑ 305-535-3283; www.fontainebleau. com; 4441 Collins Ave; r from $360; P❄🛜♿🐾) The grand Fontainebleau opened in 1954, when it became a celeb-sunning spot. Numerous renovations have added beachside cabanas, a shopping mall, a fabulous swimming pool and one of Miami's best nightclubs. The rooms are surprisingly bright and cheerful – we expected more hard-edged attempts to be cool, but the sunny disposition of these chambers is a welcome surprise.

Eden Roc Renaissance   RESORT **$$$**

(Map p70; ☑ 305-531-0000; www.nobuedenroc. com; 4525 Collins Ave; r from $360; P❄🛜♿🐾) The Roc's immense inner lobby draws inspiration from the Rat Pack glory days of Miami Beach cool, and rooms in the Ocean Tower boast lovely views over the Intracoastal Waterway. All the digs here have smooth, modern embellishments and a beautiful ethereal design. The location backing onto a pristine stretch of Mid-Beach is a big draw.

The amenities are staggering: three swimming pools, two Jacuzzis, an extensive spa, 24-hour fitness center and access to some excellent restaurants.

Casa Faena   HOTEL **$$$**

(Map p70; ☑ 305-604-8485; www.faena.com/ casa-faena; 3500 Collins Ave; r from $275; ❄) Part of the growing Faena empire in Mid-Beach, this 1928 Mediterranean-style palace feels like an (Americanized) Tuscan villa, with a honey-stone courtyard, frescoed walls and gleaming stone floors. The sunny rooms have abundant old-world charm, and some rooms have private terraces. Staff are eager to please.

Palms Hotel   HOTEL **$$$**

(Map p70; ☑ 305-534-0505; www.thepalms hotel.com; 3025 Collins Ave; r/ste from $270/460; P❄@🛜♿) The Palms' lobby manages to be imposing and comfortable all at once; the soaring ceiling, cooled by giant, slow-spinning rattan fans, makes for a colonial-villa-on-convention-center-steroids vibe. Upstairs the rooms are perfectly fine, though a touch on the masculine side with tobacco-brown hues and orange-and-brown carpeting. Thoughtful touches include comfy high-end mattresses, iPod docking stations, in-room coffeemakers and Aveda bath products.

🛏 Downtown Miami

Langford Hotel　　　　　HERITAGE HOTEL **$$**
(Map p72; 🕿 305-250-0782; www.langfordhotel
miami.com; 121 SE 1st St; r from $180; ✳🛜) Set
in a beautifully restored 1925 Beaux-Arts
high-rise, the Langford opened to much
fanfare in 2016. Its 126 rooms blend com-
fort and nostalgia, with elegant fixtures and
vintage details, including white oak flooring
and glass-encased rain showers. Thoughtful
design touches abound, and there's a rooftop
bar and an excellent ground-floor restaurant
on site.

EAST, Miami　　　　　　　　HOTEL **$$$**
(Map p72; 🕿 305-712-7000; www.east-miami.com;
788 Brickell Plaza; r from $260; ✳🛜🏊) Part of
the burgeoning Brickell City Centre development, this cosmopolitan hotel has loads
of style in its 352 spacious, attractively furnished rooms and suites. Apart from the
beach (a 20-minute drive away), you've got
everything at your fingertips, with swimming pools, a state-of-the-art fitness center,
an excellent Uruguayan-style grillhouse, and
a tropically inspired rooftop bar.

Kimpton EPIC Hotel　　　　HOTEL **$$$**
(Map p72; 🕿 305-424-5226; www.epichotel.com;
270 Biscayne Blvd Way; r $285-550, ste from $605;
🅿✳🛜🏊) Epic indeed! This massive Kimp-
ton hotel is one of the more attractive op-
tions Downtown and it possesses a coolness
cred that could match any spot on Miami
Beach. Of particular note is the outdoor pool
and sun deck, which overlook a gorgeous
sweep of Brickell and the surrounding con-
do canyons.

The rooms are outfitted in designer-chic
furnishings and some have similarly beau-
tiful views of greater Miami-Dade. There's a
youthful energy throughout that's lacking in
other corporate-style Downtown hotels.

🛏 Wynwood & the Design District

Real Living Residence　　　APARTMENT **$$$**
(Map p78; 🕿 877-707-0461; www.rlmiami.com;
2700 N Miami Ave, entrance on N 28th St; apt $250-
350; 🅿✳🛜🏊) A short stroll to the galleries
and restaurants of Wynwood, this modern
place has 11 studio apartments, with a min-
imal design of polished-concrete floors, tall
ceilings and high-end furnishings. The best
(and priciest) studios are rather spacious
with a living-room and dining area (though

still within the one-room space). All have
small kitchen units, washer/dryer, satellite
TV and free parking.

Fortuna House　　　　　　　APARTMENT **$**
(Map p78; 🕿 954-232-4705; www.fortunahouse.
com; 432 NE 26th St; $90-190; ✳🛜) With
sparse lodging options near Wynwood, the
Fortuna House is an affordable base for
exploring the neighborhood's galleries and
bars – though it's still a good 20-minute (1
mile) walk to Wynwood's epicenter. It's set in
an attractive but aging three-story building
on a quiet street. The accommodations are
small and minimally furnished but not a bad
option for short stays.

🛏 Little Haiti & the Upper East Side

New Yorker　　　　　　　　　　HOTEL **$**
(Map p82; 🕿 305-759-5823; www.hotelnewyorke
rmiami.com; 6500 Biscayne Blvd; r from $105;
🅿✳🛜🏊) Dating back to the 1950s, the
New Yorker has an eye-catching design
that's right at home in the architecturally
rich MiMo district. Renovated in 2009, the
New Yorker has comfortable rooms done up
with pop art, geometric designs and solid
colors; it's not fancy, but the prices are fair.

There's also a small courtyard and a pool.
On the downside, the street out front is
quite noisy, though thankfully staff provide
free earplugs.

Motel Blu　　　　　　　　　　　MOTEL **$**
(Map p82; 🕿 305-757-8451; www.motelblu.com;
7700 Biscayne Blvd; r $85-190; 🅿✳🛜🏊) Situ-
ated above Miami's Little River, the Blu may
not look like much from the outside, but inside you'll find simple motel rooms with all
the modern amenities. Rooms are comfortable and have a pastel-hued interior.

Vagabond Hotel　　　　BOUTIQUE HOTEL **$$**
(Map p82; 🕿 305-400-8420; www.thevagabond
hotel.com; 7301 Biscayne Blvd; r $170-275;
🅿✳🛜🏊) An icon in the MiMo district, the
Vagabond is a 1953 motel and restaurant
where Frank Sinatra and other Rat Packers
used to hang out. Today it's been reborn as
a boutique hotel, though its lost none of its
allure, with plush retro-inspired rooms, a
photogenic restaurant (mains $18 to $25)
and a lushly landscaped pool, complete with
gurgling fountain.

There's also a great bar (p129) fronting
the pool – well worth visiting even if you're
not lodging here.

📑 Coconut Grove

Sonesta Hotel & Suites

Coconut Grove   HOTEL $$

(Map p86; ☑305-529-2828; www.sonesta.com/
coconutgrove; 2889 McFarlane Rd; r $230-420,
ste $305-680; P❄🛜🏊) The Coco Grove
outpost of this luxury chain of hotels has
decked out its rooms in almost all white
with a splash of color (South Beach style).
The amenities, from flat-screen TVs to mi-
ni-kitchenettes, add a layer of luxury to this
surprisingly hip big-box. Make your way to
the top of the building to enjoy a wonderful
outdoor deck pool.

There's also a fitness center and two
squash courts.

Mutiny Hotel   HOTEL $$

(Map p86; ☑305-441-2100; www.provident
resorts.com/mutiny-hotel; 2951 S Bayshore Dr;
1-bedroom ste $170-320, 2-bedroom ste $400-600;
P❄🛜🏊) This small, luxury bayfront hotel,
with one- and two-bedroom suites featuring
balconies, boasts indulgent staff, high-end
bedding, gracious appointments, fine amenities and a small heated pool and Jacuzzi.
Although it's on a busy street, you won't hear
the traffic once inside. The property has fine
views over the water.

Palmeiras Beach

Club at Grove Isle   RESORT $$$

(☑305-858-8300; www.groveisle.com; 4 Grove Isle
Dr; r $232-520; P❄🛜🏊) One of those 'I've got
my own little island' type places, Grove Isle is
off the coast of Coconut Grove. This stunning
boutique hotel has colonial elegance, lush
tropical gardens, a lovely spa, decadent pool,
sunset views over Biscayne Bay, amenities
galore and the cachet of staying in your own
water-fringed temple of exclusivity.

Ritz-Carlton Coconut Grove   RESORT $$$

(Map p86; ☑305-644-4680; www.ritzcarlton.com;
3300 SW 27th Ave; r $310-440; P❄🛜🏊)
Another member of the Ritz-Carlton organization in Miami, this one overlooks the bay,
has immaculate rooms and offers butlers for
every need, from shopping to dog-walking.
You can while away time beside the heated
pool (or swim laps), and find your inner bliss
at the massive spa.

📑 Coral Gables

Hotel St Michel   HOTEL $$

(Map p88; ☑305-444-1666; www.hotelstmichel.
com; 162 Alcazar Ave; r $162-282; P❄🛜) Built

MIMO ON BIBO

That cute little phrase means 'Miami
Modern on Biscayne Boulevard,' and
refers to the architectural style of buildings on North Biscayne Blvd past 55th
St. Specifically, there are some great
roadside motels here with lovely, Rat
Pack–era '50s neon beckoning visitors in.
This area was neglected for a long time,
and some of these spots are seedy. But
north BiBo is also one of Miami's rapidly
gentrifying areas, and savvy motel owners are cleaning up their act and looking
to attract the hipsters, artists and gay
population flocking to the area. There's
already exciting food here. Now the lodg-
ings are getting stimulating too. All these
hotels provide South Beach comfort at
half the price:

➡ Vagabond Hotel (p110)

➡ New Yorker (p110)

➡ Motel Blu (p110)

---

in 1926, this building exudes class, with an
elegant sense of style that feels more Old Europe than South Florida. Recent renovations
have added more light and a refined look to
the rooms, while still maintaining the historical charm beneath.

You won't have to go far for a meal. An excellent new Italian restaurant opened on the
property in 2017 – though the hotel's location
puts you within walking distance of other
appealing spots in downtown Coral Gables.

Extended Stay   HOTEL $

(Map p88; ☑305-443-7444; www.extended
stayamerica.com; 3640 22nd St; r from $125;
P❄🛜🏊) Sure it's a chain hotel, but this
place has spacious, modern rooms that are
decent value for the price, and the good location puts you within walking distance of
Coral Gables' attractions and eateries.

Rooms get plenty of light and are well
equipped with small kitchens.

⭐ Biltmore Hotel   HISTORIC HOTEL $$$

(Map p88; ☑855-311-6903; www.biltmorehotel.
com; 1200 Anastasia Ave; r/ste from $409/560;
P❄🛜🏊) Though the Biltmore's standard
rooms can be small, a stay here is a chance
to sleep in one of the great laps of US luxury.
The grounds are so palatial it would take a
solid week to explore everything the Biltmore

has to offer – we highly recommend reading a book in the Romanesque/Arabian Nights opulent lobby, sunning underneath enormous columns and taking a dip in the largest hotel pool in continental USA.

Key Biscayne

Silver Sands Beach Resort RESORT $$
(Map p90; 305-361-5441; www.silversands keybiscayne.net; 301 Ocean Dr; r $169-189, cottages $329-349; P❄️🛜🏊) Silver Sands: aren't you cute, with your one-story, stucco tropical tweeness? How this little, Old Florida–style independent resort has survived amid the corporate competition is beyond us, but it's definitely a warm, homey spot for those seeking some intimate, individual attention – to say nothing of the sunny courtyard, garden area and outdoor pool.

Ritz-Carlton Key Biscayne RESORT $$$
(Map p90; 305-365-4500; www.ritzcarlton. com; 455 Grand Bay Dr; r/ste from $391/625; P❄️🛜🏊) Many Ritz-Carlton outposts feel a little cookie-cutter, but the Key Biscayne outpost of the empire is pretty impressive. There's the magnificent lobby, vaulted by four giant columns lifted from a Cecil B De-Mille set. Tinkling fountains, the view of the bay and the marble grandeur speak less of a chain hotel and more of early-20th-century glamour. Rooms and amenities are predictably excellent.

Eating

Miami is a major immigrant entrepôt and a sucker for food trends. Thus you get a good mix of cheap ethnic eateries and high-quality top-end cuisine here, alongside some good-value dross in touristy zones like Miami Beach. The best new areas for dining are in Downtown, Wynwood and the Upper East Side; Coral Gables has great classic options.

South Beach

Dirt CAFE $
(Map p66; www.dirteatclean.com; 232 5th St; mains $12-15; 9am-9pm) This stylish, sunlit cafe on busy 5th St draws a chatty cross-section of South Beach folk, who come for good coffee and deliciously healthy food options. Among the hits: roasted mushroom and raw-beet vegan wraps, white-bean hummus, and 'bowls' full of sautéed kale, chickpeas and other goodies.

Soups, smashed-avocado toast and craft beer and wine round out the menu. Outdoor dining in front.

Panther Coffee CAFE $
(Map p60; www.panthercoffee.com; 1875 Purdy Ave, Sunset Harbour; coffees $3-6; 7am-9pm) Panther has the best coffee in Miami Beach, though the location is not all that convenient if you're on the beach. It has the same elegant vintage-chic vibe as its Wynwood branch and outdoor seating, though this one serves up pastries from nearby True Loaf.

Taquiza MEXICAN $
(Map p60; 305-748-6099; www.taquizamiami. com; 1506 Collins Ave; tacos $3.50-5; 8am-midnight Sun-Thu, to 2am Fri & Sat) Taquiza has acquired a stellar reputation among Miami's street-food lovers. The take-out stand with a few outdoor tables serves up delicious perfection in its steak, pork, shrimp or veggie tacos (but no fish options) served on handmade blue-corn tortillas. They're small, so order a few.

For something a little different, throw in an order of *chapulines* (grasshoppers), and wash it all down with a craft brew.

Tocaya Organica MEXICAN $
(Map p60; 305-909-0799; www.tocayaorganica. com; 920 Lincoln Rd; mains $11-16; 11am-midnight Mon-Thu, to 2am Fri-Sun; 🌱) Next to a gurgling fountain on Lincoln Rd, Tocaya whips up delicious modern Mexican fare with ample healthy and vegetarian options. The menu is a choose-your-own-adventure culinary style: pick from salads, tacos, burritos or veggie-based bowls, top with a protein (like mahi mahi, veggie sausage or grilled steak) and cheese of choice, and enjoy.

Creative drink options (like the tequila- and blackberry-based Adios Felisha, served with a popsicle), a good kids' menu and tasty appetizers add to the overall appeal.

True Loaf BAKERY $
(Map p60; 786-216-7207; 1894 Bay Rd, Sunset Harbour; pastries $3-5; 7am-6pm Mon-Sat, from 8am Sun) The best bakery in South Beach is True Loaf, a small space where you can pick up heavenly croissants, berry tarts and *kouign amman* (a Breton-style butter cake). With nowhere to eat these goodies, you'll have to take them around the corner to the waterfront **Maurice Gibb Memorial Park** (Map p60; 18th St & Purdy Ave, Sunset Harbour) – stopping for Panther Coffee (p112) on the way of course.

Pizzarium
PIZZA $

(Map p66; ☑786-452-7261; www.pizzarium.us; 540 Washington Ave; slices around $4; ☺11am-10pm Sun-Thu, to 11pm Fri & Sat) An excellent place for a quick slice, this Roman-style pizza shop whips up delicious square decadence, piled high with tasty toppings. Grab a seat at a sidewalk table in front and watch the city stroll past.

Paradigm Kitchen
MODERN AMERICAN $

(Map p60; ☑786-453-2488; www.paradigmkitchen.com; 1834 Bay Rd; mains $9-17; ☺8am-9pm Mon-Thu, to 5pm Fri, 9am-3pm Sat & Sun; ☎) Part of a growing array of restaurants in Sunset Harbour, Paradigm Kitchen has earned a loyal local following for its delectable and nutritious breakfast and lunch offerings – most of which are plant-based. Smashed-avocado toast, roast vegetable dosas, spicy lamb wraps and savory bowls of market greens topped with goodness are among the many hits.

It's a well-designed but laid-back space (order at the counter), and a fine spot to start the day (or end the afternoon).

Moshi Moshi
JAPANESE $

(Map p60; ☑305-531-4674; www.moshimoshi.us; 1448 Washington Ave; mains $10-15, sushi rolls from $4; ☺noon-5am; ☎) The best-known name in South Beach when it comes to sushi, Moshi Moshi serves up mouthwatering perfection in its tender rolls, daikon salads and steaming noodle soups. Prices are fair and it's open late, meaning you can join the party crowd when sushi cravings strike at 3am.

Puerto Sagua
CUBAN $

(Map p66; ☑305-673-1115; 700 Collins Ave; mains $8-18; ☺7:30am-2am) There's a secret colony of older working-class Cubans and construction workers hidden among South Beach's sex-and-flash, and evidently they eat here. Puerto Sagua challenges the US diner with this reminder: Cubans can greasy-spoon with the best of them. Portions of favorites such as *picadillo* (spiced ground beef with rice, beans and plantains) are enormous.

The Cuban coffee here is not for the faint of heart – strong stuff.

La Sandwicherie
SANDWICHES $

(Map p60; ☑305-532-8934; www.lasandwicherie.com; 229 14th St; mains $6-11; ☺8am-5am Sun-Thu, to 6am Fri & Sat; ☑) Closed just a few hours each day, this boxcar long eatery does a roaring trade in filling baguette sandwiches sold at rock-bottom prices. Ingredients are fairly classic: roast beef, smoked salmon, avocado or combos like prosciutto with mozzarella, though you can load up with toppings for a deliciously satisfying meal.

Seating is limited to stools lining the restaurant's outside counter, but you can always get it to go and head to the beach.

11th St Diner
DINER $

(Map p66; ☑305-534-6373; www.eleventhstreetdiner.com; 1065 Washington Ave; mains $10-20; ☺7am-midnight Sun-Wed, 24hr Thu-Sat) You've seen the art-deco landmarks. Now eat in one: a Pullman-car diner trucked down from Wilkes-Barre, Pennsylvania – as sure a slice of Americana as a *Leave It to Beaver* marathon. The food is as classic as the architecture, with oven-roasted turkey, baby back ribs and mac 'n' cheese among the hits – plus breakfast at all hours.

If there's a diner where you can replicate Edward Hopper's *Nighthawks,* it's here.

A La Folie
FRENCH $

(Map p60; ☑305-538-4484; www.alafoliecafe.com; 516 Española Way; mains $10-17; ☺9am-midnight; ☑) It's easy to fall for this charming French cafe on the edge of picturesque Española Way. You can enjoy duck confit salad, a decadent onion soup and savory galettes (buckwheat crepes) before satisfying your sweet tooth with dessert crepes – try the Normande (with caramelized apples and Calvados cream sauce).

Vine-trimmed outdoor seating makes for a peaceful setting – and a fine break from the mayhem of Ocean Dr.

Gelateria 4D
ICE CREAM $

(Map p60; ☑305-538-5755; 670 Lincoln Rd; 2-/3-scoops $6/8; ☺9am-midnight Sun-Thu, to 1:30am Fri & Sat) It's hot. You've been walking all day. You need ice cream, stat. Why hello, 4D! This is an excellent spot for creamy, pillowy waves of European-style frozen goodness, and based on the crowds it's the favorite ice cream on South Beach.

News Cafe
AMERICAN $

(Map p66; www.newscafe.com; 800 Ocean Dr; mains $11-19; ☺24hr; ☎) News Cafe is an Ocean Dr landmark that attracts thousands of travelers. We find the food to be pretty uninspiring, but the people-watching is good, so take a perch, eat some over-the-average but not-too-special food and enjoy the anthropological study that is South Beach as it skates, salsas and otherwise shambles by.

SELF-CATERING

If you can tear yourself away from the Cuban sandwiches, celebrity hot spots and farm-to-table gems, Miami has a decent selection of options for self-caterers offering fresh produce and obscure ingredients aplenty.

Epicure Market (Map p60; 305-672-1861; www.epicuremarket.com; 1656 Alton Rd; mains $8-18; 9am-8pm), a gourmet food shop just off Lincoln Rd in South Beach, has a beautiful selection of international cheeses and wines, fresh produce, baked goods and prepared dishes. Many of the more than 25 Publix supermarkets throughout Miami are quite upscale, and the Whole Foods Market (Map p66; 305-938-2800; www.wholefoodsmarket.com; 1020 Alton Rd; 8am-11pm) is the biggest high-end grocery store around, with an excellent produce department, pretty good deli and so-so salad bar; its biggest draw is for vegetarians (not so well catered for by markets in these parts) or health nuts who are seeking a particular brand of soy milk or wheat-free pasta.

Pizza Rustica   PIZZA $

(Map p66; 305-674-8244; www.pizza-rustica. com; 863 Washington Ave; slices $4-6, mains $9-20; 11am-6am) One of South Beach's favorite pizzerias has several locations to satisfy the demand for crusty Roman-style slices topped with an array of exotic offerings. A slice is a meal unto itself and sure hits the spot after a night of drinking (hence the late hours).

★ Yardbird   SOUTHERN US $$

(Map p60; 305-538-5220; www.runchickenrun.com/miami; 1600 Lenox Ave; mains $18-38; 11am-midnight Mon-Fri, from 8:30am Sat & Sun;) Yardbird has earned a die-hard following for its delicious haute Southern comfort food. The kitchen churns out some nice shrimp and grits, St Louis–style pork ribs, charred okra, and biscuits with smoked brisket, but it's most famous for its supremely good plate of fried chicken, spiced watermelon and waffles with bourbon maple syrup.

The setting is all charm, with a shabby-chic interior of distressed wood, painted white brick columns, wicker basket-type lamps and big windows for taking in the passing street scene.

★ Pubbelly   FUSION $$

(Map p60; 305-532-7555; www.pubbellyboys. com/miami/pubbelly; 1418 20th St; sharing plates $11-24, mains $19-30; 6pm-midnight Tue-Thu & Sun, to 1am Fri & Sat;) Pubbelly's dining genre is hard to pinpoint, besides delicious. It skews between Asian, North American and Latin American, gleaning the best from all cuisines. Examples? Try black-truffle risotto, pork-belly dumplings or the mouthwatering kimchi fried rice with seafood. Hand-crafted cocktails wash down the dishes a treat.

Lilikoi   CAFE $$

(Map p66; 305-763-8692; www.lilikoiorganicliving.com; 500 S Pointe Dr; mains $12-20; 8am-7pm Mon-Wed, to 8:30pm Thu-Sun;) Head to the quieter, southern end of South Beach for healthy, mostly organic and veg-friendly dishes at this laid-back, indoor-outdoor spot. Start the morning off with big bowls of açai and granola or bagels with lox (and eggs Benedict on weekends); or linger over kale Caesar salads, mushroom risotto and falafel wraps at lunch.

Rosella's Kitchen   ITALIAN $$

(Map p66; 305-397-8852; www.rossellassobe. com; 110 Washington Ave; mains lunch $12-18, dinner $16-29; 8am-11pm Tue-Fri, from 9am Sat & Sun;) Rosella's well-executed Italian fare served in SoFi ('south of Fifth St') makes this a favorite haunt morning, noon and night. The outdoor tables on the sidewalk feel like the perfect spot for good Italian cooking made with care, including crispy prosciutto and mozzarella panini, crabmeat and feta salads and spaghetti with clams, plus grilled branzino or filet mignon by evening.

Big Pink   DINER $$

(Map p66; 305-532-4700; 157 Collins Ave; mains $13-26; 8am-midnight Sun-Wed, to 2am Thu, to 5am Fri & Sat) Big Pink does American comfort food with joie de vivre and a dash of whimsy. The Americana menu is consistently good throughout the day; pulled Carolina pork holds the table next to a nicely done Reuben. The interior is somewhere between a '50s sock hop and a South Beach club; expect to be seated at a long communal table.

Spiga   ITALIAN $$

(Map p60; 305-534-0079; www.spigarestaurant.com; 1228 Collins Ave; mains $16-32;

6pm-midnight) This romantic nook is a perfect place to bring your partner and gaze longingly at one another over candlelight, before you both snap out of it and start digging into excellent traditional Italian such as baby clams over linguine or red snapper with kalamata olives, tomatoes and capers.

Front Porch Cafe AMERICAN $$

(Map p60; ✆ 305-531-8300; www.frontporch oceandrive.com; 1458 Ocean Dr; mains $10-25; ⊙ 7am-11pm; ✐) An open-sided perch just above the madness of the cruising scene, the Porch has been serving excellent salads, sandwiches and the like since 1990 (eons by South Beach standards). Breakfast is justifiably popular; the challah French toast is delicious, as are fluffy omelets, eggs Benedict and strong coffees.

Tap Tap HAITIAN $$

(Map p66; ✆ 305-672-2898; www.taptapmiami beach.com; 819 5th St; mains $15-35; ⊙ noon-11pm) In Haiti tap-taps are brightly colored pickup trucks turned public taxis, and their tropi-psychedelic paint schemes inspire the decor at this popular Haitian eatery. Meals are a happy marriage of West African, French and Caribbean: spicy pumpkin soup, snapper in a scotch-bonnet lime sauce, stewed beef and okra, and Turks and Caicos conch.

Macchialina ITALIAN $$$

(Map p66; ✆ 305-534-2124; www.macchialina. com; 820 Alton Rd; mains $23-32) This buzzing Italian trattoria has all the right ingredients for a terrific night out; namely great service and beautifully turned-out cooking, served in a warm rustic-chic interior of exposed brick and chunky wood tables (plus outdoor tables in front).

Joe's Stone Crab Restaurant AMERICAN $$$

(Map p66; ✆ 305-673-0365; www.joesstonecrab. com; 11 Washington Ave; mains lunch $14-30, dinner $19-60; ⊙ 11:30am-2:30pm Tue-Sat, 5-10pm daily) The wait is long and the prices for iconic dishes can be high. But if those aren't deal-breakers, queue up to don a bib in Miami's most famous restaurant (around since 1913!) and enjoy deliciously fresh-stone crab claws.

Juvia FUSION $$$

(Map p60; ✆ 305-763-8272; www.juviamiami.com; 1111 Lincoln Rd, access via Lenox Ave elevator; mains $27-46; ⊙ 6-11pm daily & noon-3pm Sat & Sun) Juvia blends the trendsetters that have staying power in Miami's culinary world: France, Latin America and Japan. Chilean sea bass comes with maple-glazed eggplant, while sea scallops are dressed with okra and oyster mushrooms. The big, bold, beautiful dining room and open-air terrace, which sit on the high floors of 1111 Lincoln Rd (p63), is quintessential South Beach glam.

Osteria del Teatro ITALIAN $$$

(Map p60; ✆ 305-538-7850; www.osteriadel teatro.miami; 1200 Collins Ave; mains $28-40; ⊙ 6-11pm Sun-Thu, to midnight Fri & Sat) There are few things to swear by, but the Northern Italian cooking at Osteria, one of the best Italian restaurants in Greater Miami, ought to be one. When you get here, let the gracious Italian waiters seat you, coddle you and guide you along the first-rate menu, with temptations like polenta with wild mushrooms, black squid-ink linguine and locally caught red snapper.

✖ North Beach

Roasters 'n Toasters DELI $

(Map p70; ✆ 305-531-7691; www.roastersn toasters.com; 525 Arthur Godfrey Rd; mains $10-18; ⊙ 6:30am-3:30pm) Given the crowds and the satisfied smiles of customers, Roasters 'n Toasters meets the demanding standards of Miami Beach's large Jewish demographic, thanks to juicy deli meat, fresh bread, crispy bagels and warm latkes. Sliders (mini-sandwiches) are served on challah bread, an innovation that's as charming as it is tasty.

Josh's Deli DELI $

(✆ 305-397-8494; www.joshsdeli.com; 9517 Harding Ave; sandwiches $14-16; ⊙ 8:30am-3:30pm) Josh's is simplicity itself. Here in the heart of Jewish Miami, you can nosh on thick cuts of house-cured pastrami sandwiches and matzo-ball soup for lunch or challah French toast, eggs and house-cured salmon for breakfast. It's a deliciously authentic slice of Mid-Beach culture.

★ 27 Restaurant FUSION $$

(Map p70; ✆ 786-476-7020; www.freehand hotels.com/miami/27-restaurant; 2727 Indian Creek Dr; mains $17-28; ⊙ 6:30pm-2am Mon-Sat, 11am-4pm & 6:30pm-2am Sun; ✐) This new spot sits on the grounds of the very popular Broken Shaker (p126), one of Miami Beach's best-loved cocktail bars. Like the bar, the setting is amazing – akin to dining in an old tropical cottage, with worn wood floorboards, candlelit tables, and various rooms slung with artwork and curious knickknacks, plus a lovely terrace. The cooking is exceptional, and incorporates flavors from around the globe.

Cafe Prima Pasta
ITALIAN $$

(Map p70; ☑305-867-0106; www.cafeprimapasta.com; 414 71st St; mains $17-26; ⊙5-11:30pm Mon-Sat, 4-11pm Sun) We're not sure what's better at this Argentine-Italian place: the much-touted pasta, which deserves every one of the accolades heaped on it, or the atmosphere, which captures the dignified sultriness of Buenos Aires. You can't go wrong with the small, well-curated menu, with standouts including gnocchi formaggi, baked branzino, and squid-ink linguine with seafood in a lobster sauce.

Indomania
INDONESIAN $$

(Map p70; ☑305-535-6332; www.indomaniarestaurant.com; 131 26th St; mains $18-32; ⊙5:30-10:30pm Mon-Sun, plus noon-4pm Sat & Sun) There's a lot of watered-down Asian cuisine in Miami; Indomania bucks this trend with an authentic execution of dishes from Southeast Asia's largest nation. Dishes reflect Indonesia's diversity, ranging from braised beef in spicy coconut sauce to gut-busting *rijsttafel*, a sort of buffet of small, tapas-style dishes that reflects the culinary character of particular Indonesian regions.

Shuckers
AMERICAN $$

(Map p70; ☑305-866-1570; www.shuckersbarandgrill.com; 1819 79th St Causeway; mains $12-27; ⊙11am-1am; 🕾) With excellent views overlooking the waters from the 79th St Causeway, Shuckers has to be one of the best-positioned restaurants around. The food is pub grub: burgers, fried fish and the like. The chicken wings, basted in several mouthwatering sauces, deep-fried and grilled again, are famous.

✖ Downtown Miami

Manna Life Food
VEGAN $

(Map p72; ☑786-717-5060; www.mannalifefood.com; 80 NE 2nd Ave; mains $8-12; ⊙10am-7pm Mon-Fri, 11am-4pm Sat) This airy, stylish eatery has wowed diners with its plant-based menu loaded with superfoods. Filling 'life bowls,' *arepas* (corn cakes) and noritos (like a burrito but wrapped with seaweed rather than a tortilla) are packed with flavorful ingredients such as red quinoa, baked tofu, roasted veggies, coconut brown rice and raw falafel.

All Day
CAFE $

(Map p72; www.alldaymia.com; 1035 N Miami Ave; coffee $3.50, breakfast $10-14; ⊙7am-7pm Mon-Fri, from 9am Sat & Sun; 🕾) All Day is one of the best places in the Downtown area to linger over coffee or breakfast – no matter the hour. Slender Scandinavian-style chairs, wood-and-marble tables and the Françoise Hardy soundtrack lend an easygoing vibe to the place.

Bali Cafe
INDONESIAN $

(Map p72; ☑305-358-5751; 109 NE 2nd Ave; mains $10-16; ⊙11am-4pm daily, 6-10pm Mon-Fri; 🖋) It's odd to think of the clean flavors of sushi and the bright richness of Indonesian cuisine coming together in harmony, but they're happily married in this tropical hole in the wall. Have some spicy tuna rolls for an appetizer, then follow up with *soto betawi* – beef soup cooked with coconut milk, ginger and shallots.

La Moon
COLOMBIAN $

(Map p72; ☑305-860-6209; www.lamoonrestaurant.com; 97 SW 8th St; mains $7-17; ⊙10am-midnight Sun & Tue-Thu, to 6am Fri & Sat) Nothing hits the spot after a late night of partying quite like a Colombian hot dog topped with eggs and potato sticks. Or an *arepa* (corn cake) stuffed with steak and cheese. These street-food delicacies are available well into the wee hours on weekend nights, plus La Moon is conveniently located within stumbling distance of bars including Blackbird Ordinary (p127).

★ Casablanca
SEAFOOD $$

(Map p72; www.casablancaseafood.com; 400 N River Dr; mains $15-34; ⊙11am-10pm Sun-Thu, to 11pm Fri & Sat) Perched over the Miami River, Casablanca serves up some of the best seafood in town. The setting is a big draw – with tables on a long wooden deck just above the water, and the odd seagull winging past. But the fresh fish is the real star here.

Verde
AMERICAN $$

(Map p72; ☑786-345-5697; www.pamm.org/dining; 1103 Biscayne Blvd, Pérez Art Museum Miami; mains $13-19; ⊙Fri-Tue 11am-5pm, to 9pm Thu, closed Wed; 🖋) Inside the Pérez Art Museum Miami (p69), Verde is a local favorite for its tasty market-fresh dishes and great setting – with outdoor seating on a terrace overlooking the bay. Crispy mahimahi tacos, pizza with squash blossoms and goat cheese, and grilled endive salads are among the temptations.

MIAMI EATING

River Oyster Bar SEAFOOD **$$**
(Map p72; ☑305-530-1915; www.therivermiami.
com; 650 S Miami Ave; mains $16-32; ⊙noon-
10:30pm Mon-Thu, to midnight Fri, 4:30pm-midnight
Sat, to 9:30pm Sun) A few paces from the Miami
River, this buzzing little spot with a classy
vibe whips up excellent plates of seafood.
Start off with their fresh showcase oysters
and ceviche before moving on to grilled red
snapper or yellowfin tuna. For a decadent
meal, go for a grand seafood platter ($125),
piled high with Neptune's culinary treasures.

NIU Kitchen SPANISH **$$**
(Map p72; ☑786-542-5070; www.niukitchen.
com; 134 NE 2nd Ave; sharing plates $14-25;
⊙noon-3:30pm & 6-10pm Mon-Fri, 1-4pm & 6-11pm
Sat, 6-10pm Sun; ☑) NIU is a stylish living-
room-sized restaurant serving up delectable
contemporary Spanish cuisine. It's a showcase of culinary pyrotechnics, with complex
sharing plates with clipped Catalan names
like Ous (poached eggs, truffled potato foam,
jamon iberico and black truffle) or Tonin-
ya (smoked tuna, green guindillas and pine
nuts). Wash it all down with good wine.

PB Station MODERN AMERICAN **$$**
(Map p72; ☑305-420-2205; http://pbstation.
com; 121 SE 1st St, Langford Hotel; mains $20-57;
⊙11:30am-3pm & 6-11pm Mon-Sat) The creative
team behind the popular Pubbelly (p114) in
Sunset Harbour brought their award-win-
ning formula to Downtown in 2016. Set
on the ground floor of the Langford Hotel
(p110), the dining room channels a classy,
old-fashioned elegance with its arched ceil-
ings, globe lights and well-dressed servers.
Culinary highlights include bistro classics
such as grilled bone marrow, French onion
soup and grilled octopus.

CVI.CHE 105 PERUVIAN **$$**
(Map p72; ☑305-577-3454; www.ceviche105.com;
105 NE 3rd Ave; ⊙noon-10pm Sun-Thu, to 11pm Fri
& Sat) White is the design element of choice
in Juan Chipoco's ever-popular Peruvian
Downtown eatery. Beautifully presented ce-
viches, *lomo saltado* (marinated steak) and
arroz con mariscos (seafood rice) are ideal
for sharing and go down nicely with a round
of Pisco Fuegos (made with jalapeño-infused
pisco) and other specialty Peruvian cocktails.

Soya e Pomodoro ITALIAN **$$**
(Map p72; ☑305-381-9511; www.soyaepomodoro.
com; 120 NE 1st St; lunch $11-18, dinner $16-26;
⊙11:30am-4:30pm Mon-Fri, 7-11:30pm Wed-Sat)
This spot feels like a bohemian retreat for
Italian artists and filmmakers, who can dine
on bowls of fresh pasta under vintage posters,
rainbow paintings and curious wall-hangings.
Adding to the vibe is live Latin jazz (on Thurs-
day nights from 9pm to midnight), plus read-
ings and other arts events that take place here
on select evenings.

Bonding FUSION **$$**
(Map p72; ☑786-409-4796; www.bondingmiami.
com; 638 S Miami Ave; mains $16-30; ⊙noon-
11pm Mon-Fri, to midnight Sat, 5pm-midnight Sun;
☑) Multiple Asian cuisines, including Thai,
Japanese and Korean, come together into an
excellent whole at Bonding. Chicken is expertly tossed with chilies and basil, red curry
is deliciously fiery and sushi rolls are given
a South Florida splash with ingredients like
mango salsa and spicy mayo. The bar here
keeps some excellent sake under the counter.

Pollos & Jarras PERUVIAN **$**
(Map p72; www.pollosyjarras.com; 115 NE 3rd Ave;
⊙noon-10pm Sun-Thu, to 11pm Fri & Sat) The
same celebrated team behind CVI.CHE105
next door also operate this festive spot with
outdoor patio. The focus is less on seafood
and more on meat: namely outstanding barbecued chicken, though of course signature
dishes (including ceviche) are also available.

✕ Wynwood & the Design District

Wynwood Yard FOOD TRUCKS **$**
(Map p78; www.thewynwoodyard.com; 56 NW 29th
St; mains $7-14; ⊙noon-11pm Tue-Thu, to 1am Fri-
Sun; ☑☑) ✐ On a once vacant lot, the Wynwood Yard is something of an urban oasis
for those who want to enjoy a bit of casual
open-air eating and drinking. Around a doz-
en different food trucks park here, offering
gourmet mac 'n' cheese, cruelty-free salads,
meaty schnitzel plates, zesty tacos, desserts
and more. There's also a bar, and often live
music.

One of the Yard anchors is the **Della Test
Kitchen** (Map p78; ☑305-351-2961; www.della
bowls.com; 56 NW 29th St, Wynwood Yard; mains
$11-14; ⊙noon-10pm Tue-Sun; ☑), which serves
tasty vegan fare, and even grows some vegetables on site. Live music typically happens
on Wednesday to Saturday nights from
9pm, and from 2pm on Sundays. Check the
website for other one-off events, including
food tastings, pilates and yoga sessions and
hands-on art workshops for kids.

Coyo Taco
MEXICAN $

(Map p78; ☎305-573-8228; www.coyo-taco.com; 2300 NW 2nd Ave; mains $7-12; ⊗11am-2am Mon-Sat, to 11pm Sun; ☑) If you're in Wynwood and craving tacos, this is the place to be. You'll have to contend with lines day or night, but those beautifully turned-out tacos are well worth the wait – and come in creative varieties such as chargrilled octopus, marinated mushrooms or crispy duck, along with the usual array of steak, grilled fish and roasted pork.

Kush
AMERICAN $

(Map p78; ☎305-576-4500; www.kushwynwood. com; 2003 N Miami Ave; mains $13-15; ⊗noon-11pm Sun-Tue, to midnight Wed-Sat; ☑) Gourmet burgers plus craft brews is the simple but winning formula at this lively eatery and drinking den on the southern fringe of Wynwood. Juicy burgers topped with hot pastrami, Florida avocados and other decadent options go down nicely with drafts from Sixpoint and Funky Buddha. There are great vegetarian options too, including a house-made black-bean burger and vegan jambalaya.

SuViche
FUSION $

(Map p78; ☎305-501-5010; www.suviche.com; 2751 N Miami Ave; ceviche $8-14; ⊗noon-11pm) SuViche is a great place to start off the night, with a buzzing open-sided setting of garrulous couples chatting over swinging chairs, graffiti-esque murals and party beats. The menu is a blend of Peruvian dishes (including half a dozen varieties of ceviche) and sushi, which goes down nicely with the creative *macerados* (pisco-infused cocktails).

Salty Donut
DOUGHNUTS $

(Map p78; ☎305-925-8126; www.saltydonut.com; 50 NW 23rd St; doughnuts $3-6; ⊗8am-6pm Tue-Sun; ☎) Although 'artisanal doughnuts' sounds pretentious, no one can deny the merits of these artfully designed creations featuring seasonal ingredients – probably the best in South Florida. Maple and bacon, guava and cheese, and brown butter and salt are a few classics, joined by changing hits such as pistachio and white chocolate or strawberry and lemon cream.

Panther Coffee
CAFE $

(Map p78; ☎305-677-3952; www.panther coffee.com; 2390 NW 2nd Ave; coffees $3-6; ⊗7am-9pm Mon-Sat, from 8am Sun; ☎) Miami's best independent coffee shop specializes in single-origin, small-batch roasts, fired up to perfection. Aside from sipping on a zesty brewed-to-order Chemex-made coffee (or a latte), you can enjoy microbrews, wines and sweet treats. The front patio is a great spot for people-watching.

Buena Vista Deli
CAFE $

(Map p78; ☎305-576-3945; www.buenavista deli.com; 4590 NE 2nd Ave; mains $8-15; ⊗7am-9pm) Never mind the uninspiring name: French-owned Buena Vista Deli is a charming Parisian-style cafe that warrants a visit no matter the time of day. Come in the morning for fresh croissants and other bakery temptations, and later in the day for thick slices of quiche, big salads and hearty sandwiches – plus there's wine, beer and good coffees.

Enriqueta's
LATIN AMERICAN $

(Map p78; ☎305-573-4681; 186 NE 29th St; mains $6-9; ⊗6am-3:45pm Mon-Fri, to 2pm Sat) Back in the day, Puerto Ricans, not installation artists, ruled Wynwood. Have a taste of those times in this perpetually packed roadhouse, where the Latin-diner ambience is as strong as the steaming shots of *cortadito* (half espresso and half milk) served at the counter. Balance the local gallery fluff with a juicy Cuban sandwich.

Ono Poke
HAWAIIAN $

(Map p78; ☎786-618-5366; www.onopokeshop. com; 2320 N Miami Ave; mains $10-16; ⊗noon-8pm Mon-Sat, to 6pm Sun) This popular little eatery has been all the rage since its 2016 debut. The key to success is all in the execution: diners build their own *poke* bowl, featuring mouthwateringly fresh sushi-grade fish, then place atop greens or rice, and add toppings (ginger, cucumber, scallion), creative extras (wasabi peas), sauce of choice and enjoy – a delicious, nutritious, but refreshingly uncomplicated meal.

Lemoni Café
CAFE $

(Map p78; ☎305-571-5080; www.mylemonicafe. com; 4600 NE 2nd Ave; mains $10-18; ⊗11am-10:30pm Mon-Sat, to 6pm Sun; ☑) Lemoni is a small and dimly lit cafe with a creative Mediterranean-inspired menu in its panini, salads and appetizers (including hummus, bruschetta and spicy Moroccan eggplant). Weekend brunch (till 2pm Saturday, till 5pm Sunday) features beautifully turned-out French toast and blueberry pancakes. Located in the pretty Buena Vista neighborhood, this is a fine place to grab a sidewalk alfresco lunch or dinner.

★**Kyu** FUSION **$$**
(Map p78; ☑786-577-0150; www.kyumiami.com;
251 NW 25th St; sharing plates $17-38; ☺noon-
11:30pm Mon-Sat, 11am-10:30pm Sun, bar till 1am
Fri & Sat; ☑) ✐ One of the best new restau-
rants in Wynwood, Kyu has been dazzling
locals and food critics alike with its creative,
Asian-inspired dishes, most of which are
cooked up over the open flames of a wood-
fired grill. The buzzing, industrial space is
warmed up via artful lighting and wood ac-
cents (tables and chairs, plus shelves of fire-
wood for the grill).

Cake Thai THAI **$$**
(Map p78; ☑305-573-5082; www.cakethai
miami.com; 180 NW 29th St; mains $16-25;
☺noon-midnight Tue-Sun; ☑) When cravings
for Thai food strike, Wynwooders no longer
need to make the trek up to 79th St and Biscayne (Cake Thai's tiny original location).
Now they've got expertly prepared Thai
cooking right in their backyard, with all of
the same culinary wizardry of chef Phuket
Thongsodchaveondee (who goes by the
name 'Cake').

Michael's Genuine MODERN AMERICAN **$$**
(Map p78; ☑305-573-5550; www.michaels
genuine.com; 130 NE 40th St; mains lunch $16-
26, dinner $19-44; ☺11:30am-11pm Mon-Sat, to
10pm Sun) The liveliest place in the Design
District is this long-running upscale tav-
ern that combines excellent service with a
well-executed menu of wood-fired dishes,
bountiful salads and raw bar temptations
(including oysters and stone crabs). Mi-
chael's tends to draw a well-dressed crowd,
and the place gets packed most days.
There's also outdoor dining on the plant-
lined pedestrian strip out front.

Zak the Baker DELI **$$**
(Map p78; ☑786-347-7100; www.zakthebaker.com;
405 NW 26th St; sandwiches $14-18; ☺8am-5pm
Sun-Fri) Miami's best-loved kosher deli is
admired by all for its delicious (but pricey)
sandwiches: try the braised, handcut corned
beef or a satisfying gravlax sandwich. You can
also come early for potato latkes and eggs.

Butcher Shop AMERICAN **$$**
(Map p78; ☑305-846-9120; www.butchershop
miami.com/tbs; 165 NW 23rd St; mains $13-34;
☺11am-11pm Sun-Thu, to 2am Fri & Sat) This Wyn-
wood joint is called the Butcher Shop for a
reason, and that's because it's unashamedly
aimed at carnivores. From bone-in rib eyes
to smoked sausages to full charcuterie, meat

MONDAY MARKET DINING
On Monday nights, you can feast on a
delicious five-course vegetarian meal,
served family-style at outdoor tables
in front of the Arsht Center. It's an
excellent value, with a creative menu
inspired by the farmers market held on
the same day. **Chef Allen's Farm-to-
Table Dinner** (Map p72; ☑786-405-1745;
1300 Biscayne Blvd; dinner $25, with wine
pairing $40; ☺6:30pm Mon; ☑) is a local
favorite, especially among vegetarians.
Call ahead to reserve a spot.

lovers have reason to rejoice. Beer lovers too:
this butcher doubles as a beer garden, which
gets lively as the sun goes down.

Harry's Pizzeria PIZZA **$$**
(Map p78; ☑786-275-4963; www.harryspizzeria.
com; 3918 N Miami Ave; pizzas $13-17, mains $16-
21; ☺11:30am-10pm Sun-Thu, to midnight Fri & Sat;
☑) A stripped-down yet sumptuous dining
experience awaits (pizza) pie lovers in the
Design District. Harry's tiny kitchen and
dining room dishes out deceptively simple
wood-fired pizzas topped with creative ingredients (like slow-roasted pork or kale and
caramelized onion). Add in some not-to-be
missed appetizers like polenta fries and you
have a great, budget-friendly meal.
There are also non-pizza hits like pan-
seared mahimahi and oven-roasted chicken
with fennel salad.

Mandolin GREEK **$$**
(Map p78; ☑305-749-9140; www.mandolin
miami.com; 4312 NE 2nd Ave; mains $18-34;
☺noon-11pm; ☑) For a quick trip across
the Aegean, book a table at Mandolin. The
Greek cooking doesn't disappoint, whether
you're dining on sea bass grilled in lemon
and olive oil, lamb kebabs with spicy yogurt
or satisfying mezes such as smoked eggplant
and grilled octopus.

★**Alter** MODERN AMERICAN **$$$**
(Map p78; ☑305-573-5996; www.altermiami.
com; 223 NW 23rd St; set menu 5/7 courses
$69/89; ☺7-11pm Tue-Sun) This new spot,
which has garnered much praise from food
critics, brings creative high-end cooking to
Wynwood courtesy of its award-winning
young chef Brad Kilgore. The changing
menu showcases Florida's high-quality ingredients from sea and land in seasonally

inspired dishes with Asian and European accents. Reserve ahead.

✖ Little Haiti & the Upper East Side

★ Phuc Yea
VIETNAMESE $

(Map p82; ☑305-602-3710; www.phucyea.com; 7100 Biscayne Blvd; ☺6pm-midnight Tue-Sat, 11:30am-3:30pm & 6-9pm Sun) Not unlike its cheeky name, Phuc Yea pushes boundaries with its bold and deliciously executed Vietnamese cooking – served up in a graffiti-smeared and hip-hop loving setting. You too can heed the call to get 'Phuc'd up!' (undoubtedly a good thing since 'phuc' means 'blessings and prosperity') by indulging in lobster summer rolls, fish curry, spicy chicken wings and other great sharing plates.

The raw bar in front doles out sushi, fresh oysters and creative cocktails (happy hour runs from 5pm to 7pm). There's also outdoor dining in a paper-lantern-filled garden.

Chef Creole
HAITIAN $

(☑305-754-2223; www.chefcreole.com; 200 NW 54th St; mains $7-20; ☺11am-10pm Mon-Sat) When you need Caribbean food on the cheap, head to the edge of Little Haiti and this excellent take-out shack. Order up fried conch, oxtail or fish, ladle rice and beans on the side, and you'll be full for a week. Enjoy the food on nearby picnic benches while Haitian music blasts out of tinny speakers – as island an experience as they come.

Service can be slow: you're on island time at Chef Creole.

Jimmy's East Side Diner
DINER $

(Map p82; ☑305-754-3692; 7201 Biscayne Blvd; mains $7-13; ☺6:30am-4pm) Come to Jimmy's, a classic greasy spoon (that happens to be very gay-friendly; note the rainbow flag out front), for big cheap breakfasts of omelets, French toast or pancakes, and turkey clubs and burgers later in the day.

As an aside, the diner played a starring role in the final scene of Barry Jenkins' powerful film *Moonlight,* which won the Oscar for Best Picture in 2017.

Choices
VEGETARIAN $

(Map p82; ☑786-408-9122; www.choicescafemiami-ues.com; 646 NE 79th St; mains $10-17; ☺8am-9pm Mon-Fri, 9am-9pm Sat, to 8pm Sun; ☑♿) ✔ The description everyone writes when vegan food tastes good is that you're not missing the meat. This trope actually holds true at Choices. With clever ingredient

combinations like walnut 'meat' and daiya cheese, this restaurant lives up to its name, offering burgers, tacos and pizza – all 100% vegan, and all delicious.

★ Mina's
MEDITERRANEAN $$

(Map p82; ☑786-391-0300; www.minasmiami.com; 749 NE 79th St; mains $16-30, sharing plates $6-16; ☺5-10pm Tue-Thu, to 11pm Fri, noon-11pm Sat, 11am-9pm Sun; ☑) Soaring ceilings, vintage travel posters and a friendly vibe set the stage for a memorable meal at Mina's. The Mediterranean menu is great for sharing, with creamy hummus, refreshing dolmas, spanakopita (spinach-filled pastries) and toothsome fried calamari among the great starters.

Andiamo
PIZZA $$

(Map p82; ☑305-762-5751; www.andiamopizzamiami.com; 5600 Biscayne Blvd; pizzas $12-20; ☺11am-11pm Sun-Thu, to midnight Fri & Sat; ☑) In a converted industrial space (once a tire shop), Andiamo fires up some of Miami's best thin-crust pizzas from its brick oven at center stage. With over 30 varieties, Andiamo does not lack for options. It's a lively setting to start off the night, with flickering tiki torches scattered around the outdoor tables and large screens showing sports on big-game nights.

Blue Collar
AMERICAN $$

(Map p82; ☑305-756-0366; www.bluecollarmiami.com; 6730 Biscayne Blvd; mains $16-27; ☺11:30am-3:30pm daily, 6-10pm Sun-Thu, to 11pm Fri & Sat; ☑☑♿) ✔ True to name, Blue Collar tosses pretension aside and fires up American comfort food done to perfection in a classic 1960s coffee-shop-style interior. Start off with shrimp and grits or the four-cheese Mac(aroni) before moving on to seared rainbow trout, a smoky plate of ribs or lip-smacking jambalaya. A well-curated veg board keeps non-carnivores happy.

✖ Little Havana

★ Versailles
CUBAN $

(☑305-444-0240; www.versaillesrestaurant.com; 3555 SW 8th St; mains $6-21; ☺8am-1am Mon-Thu, to 2:30am Fri & Sat, 9am-1am Sun) Versailles (ver-*sigh*-yay) is an institution – one of the mainstays of Miami's Cuban gastronomic scene. Try the excellent black-bean soup or the fried yucca before moving onto heartier meat and seafood plates. Older Cubans and Miami's Latin political elite still love coming here, so you've got a real chance to rub elbows with Miami's most prominent Latin citizens.

Lung Yai Thai Tapas
THAI $

(Map p84; ☑786-334-6262; 1731 SW 8th St; mains $10-15; ☉noon-3pm & 5pm-midnight) A sure sign of the changing times is this tiny gem in Little Havana, whipping up some truly mouthwatering Thai cooking. Chef Bas performs culinary wizardry with a menu ideal for sharing. You can't go wrong – whether it's perfectly spiced fried chicken wings, tender duck salad or a much-revered Kaho Soi Gai (a rich noodle curry).

El Nuevo Siglo
LATIN AMERICAN $

(Map p84; 1305 SW 8th St; mains $8-12; ☉7am-8pm) Hidden inside a supermarket of the same name, El Nuevo Siglo draws foodie-minded locals who come for delicious cooking at excellent prices – never mind the unfussy ambience. Grab a seat at the shiny black countertop and nibble on roast meats, fried yucca, tangy Cuban sandwiches, grilled snapper with rice, beans and plantains, and other daily specials.

Viva Mexico
MEXICAN $

(Map p84; ☑786-350-6360; 502 SW 12th Ave; tacos $2; ☉11am-9pm Tue-Thu, to 11pm Fri & Sat, to 6pm Sun) Head up busy 12th Ave for some of the best tacos in Little Havana. From a take-out window, smiling Latin ladies dole out heavenly tacos topped with steak, tripe, sausage and other meats. There are a few outdoor tables – or get it to go.

On the downside, there's nothing here for vegetarians.

Yambo
LATIN AMERICAN $

(1643 SW 1st St; mains $5-12; ☉24hr) If you're a bit drunk in the middle of the night and can find a cab or a friend willing to drive all the way out to Little Havana, direct them to Yambo. At night Yambo does a roaring trade selling trays and take-away boxes about to burst with juicy slices of *carne asada* (grilled beef), piles of rice and beans, and sweet fried plantains.

San Pocho
COLOMBIAN $

(Map p72; ☑305-854-5954; www.sanpocho.com; 901 SW 8th St; mains $9-15; ☉7am-8pm Mon-Thu, to 9pm Fri-Sun) For a quick journey to Colombia, head to friendly, always hopping San Pocho. The meat-centric menu features hearty platters like *bandeja paisa* (with grilled steak, rice, beans, fried plantains, an egg, an *arepa* and fried pork skin). There's also *mondongo*

(tripe soup) as well as Colombian-style tamales and requisite sides like *arepas* (corn cakes).

Azucar
ICE CREAM $

(Map p84; ☑305-381-0369; www.azucaricecream.com; 1503 SW 8th St; ice cream $4-6; ☉11am-9pm Mon-Wed, to 11pm Thu-Sat, to 10pm Sun) One of Little Havana's most recognizable snack spots (thanks to the giant ice-cream cone on the facade) serves delicious ice cream just like *abuela* (grandmother) used to make. Deciding isn't easy with dozens of tempting flavors, including rum raisin, dulce de leche, guava, mango, cinnamon, jackfruit and lemon basil.

Exquisito Restaurant
CUBAN $

(Map p84; ☑305-643-0227; www.elexquisitomiami.com; 1510 SW 8th St; mains $9-13; ☉7am-11pm) For great Cuban cuisine in the heart of Little Havana, this place is exquisite (ha ha). The roast pork has a tangy citrus kick and the *ropa vieja* (spiced shredded beef) is wonderfully rich and filling. Even standard sides like beans and rice and roasted plantains are executed with a little more care and tastiness. Prices are a steal, too.

★ El Carajo
SPANISH $$

(☑305-856-2424; www.el-carajo.com; 2465 SW 17th Avenue; tapas $5-15; ☉noon-10pm Mon-Wed, to 11pm Thu-Sat, 11am-10pm Sun; ☑) Pass the Pennzoil please. We know it is cool to tuck restaurants into unassuming spots, but the Citgo station on SW 17th Ave? Really? Really. Walk past the motor oil into a Granadan wine cellar and try not to act too fazed. And now the food, which is absolutely incredible.

Bacon-wrapped stuffed dates are pure decadence on a plate, while fluffy tortillas (thick Spanish omelets) have just the right bite. And don't miss the sardines – cooked with a bit of salt and olive oil till they're dizzyingly delicious.

Doce Provisions
MODERN AMERICAN $$

(Map p84; ☑786-452-0161; www.doceprovisions.com; 541 SW 12th Ave; mains $11-25; ☉noon-3:30pm & 5-10pm Mon-Thu, noon-3:30pm & 5-11pm Fri, noon-11pm Sat, 11am-9pm Sun) For a break from old-school Latin eateries, stop in at Doce Provisions, which has more of a Wynwood vibe than a Little Havana one. The stylish industrial interior sets the stage for dining on creative American fare – rock shrimp mac 'n' cheese, fried chicken with sweet plantain waffle, short-rib burgers and truffle fries – plus local microbrews.

Brunch is justifiably popular on Sunday (11am to 3pm).

Xixón
SPANISH $$
(☑ 305-854-9350; www.xixonspanishrestaurant.com; 2101 SW 22nd St; tapas $7-16; ☺ 11am-10pm Mon-Thu, to 11pm Fri & Sat, noon-5pm Sun; ☑) It takes a lot to stand out in Miami's crowded tapas-spot stakes. Bread that has a crackling crust and a soft center, delicate explosions of *bacalao* (cod) fritters and sizzling shrimp and baby eel cooked in garlic secures Xixón's status as a top tapas contender. The *bocatas* (sandwiches), with lavish Serrano ham and salty Manchego cheese, are great picnic fare.

✖ Coconut Grove

Bianco Gelato
ICE CREAM $
(Map p86; ☑ 786-717-5315; 3137 Commodore Plaza; ice cream $3.50-7) A much-loved spot in the neighborhood, particularly among Coconut Grove's youngest residents, Bianco whips up amazing gelato. It's made from organic milk and all-natural ingredients. Flavors change regularly, but a few recent hits are guava and cheese, avocado with carmelized nuts, hazelnut, and vegan chocolate.

Last Carrot
VEGETARIAN $
(Map p86; ☑ 305-445-0805; 3133 Grand Ave; mains $6-8; ☺ 10:30am-6pm Mon-Sat, 11am-4:30pm Sun; ☑ ⊞) Going strong since the 1970s, the Last Carrot serves up fresh juices, delicious pita sandwiches, avocado melts, veggie burgers and rather famous spinach pies, all amid old-Grove neighborliness. The Carrot's endurance next to massive CocoWalk is testament to the quality of its good-for-your-body food served in a good-for-your-soul setting.

Coral Bagels
DELI $
(☑ 305-854-0336; 2750 SW 26th Ave; mains $7-11; ☺ 6:30am-3pm Mon-Fri, 7am-4pm Sat & Sun; ℗ ☑) Although it's out of the way (one mile north of Coconut Grove's epicenter), this is a great place to start the day. The buzzing little deli serves proper bagels, rich omelets and decadent potato pancakes with apple sauce and sour cream. You'll be hard pressed to spend double digits, and you'll leave satisfied.

LoKal
AMERICAN $
(Map p86; ☑ 305-442-3377; 3190 Commodore Plaza; burgers $14-16; ☺ noon-10pm Sun-Tue, to 11pm Wed-Sat; ⊞ ☑ ⊞) ✔ This little Coconut Grove joint does two things very well: burgers and craft beer. The former come in several variations, all utilizing excellent beef (bar the oat

and brown-rice version). When in doubt, go for the frita, which adds in guava sauce, plus melted gruyere and crispy bacon.

Spillover
MODERN AMERICAN $$
(Map p86; ☑ 305-456-5723; www.spillover miami.com; 2911 Grand Ave; mains $13-25; ☺ 11:30am-10pm Sun-Tue, to 11pm Wed-Sat; ☎ ☑) Tucked down a pedestrian strip near the CocoWalk, the Spillover serves up locally sourced seafood and creative bistro fare in an enticing vintage setting (cast-iron stools and recycled doors around the bar, suspenders-wearing staff, brassy jazz playing overhead). Come for crab cakes, buffalo shrimp tacos, spear-caught fish and chips, or a melt-in-your-mouth lobster Reuben.

Boho
MEDITERRANEAN $$
(Map p86; ☑ 305-549-8614; 3433 Main Hwy; mains $19-26, pizzas $12-17; ☺ noon-11pm Mon-Fri, from 10am Sat & Sun) This Greek-run charmer is helping to lead the culinary renaissance in Coconut Grove, serving up fantastic Mediterranean dishes, including tender marinated octopus, creamy risotto, thin-crust pizzas drizzled with truffle oil and zesty quinoa and beet salads. The setting invites long, leisurely meals with its jungle-like wallpaper, big picture windows and easygoing vibe.

There's also outdoor tables on the sidewalk in front – a fine spot to take in the passing street scene.

Glass & Vine
MODERN AMERICAN $$
(Map p86; www.glassandvine.com; 2820 McFarlane Rd; mains lunch $9-14, dinner $17-32; ☺ 11:30am-3:30pm & 5:30-10pm Sun-Thu, to 11pm Fri & Sat) It's hard to beat the open-air setting of this wine-loving eatery on the edge of Peacock Park. Stop by for tabbouleh and shrimp sandwiches at lunch, or charred cauliflower and sea scallops at dinner. All of which go nicely with the extensive wine and cocktail menu. Excellent weekend brunches too.

Bombay Darbar
INDIAN $$
(Map p86; ☑ 305-444-7272; 2901 Florida Ave; mains $15-23; ☺ noon-3pm Thu-Sun, 6-10pm Wed-Mon, closed Tue; ☑) Indian food is a rarity in Latin-loving Miami and all the more so in Coconut Grove – which makes Bombay Darbar even more of a culinary gem. Run by a couple from Mumbai, this upscale but friendly place hits all the right notes, with its beautifully executed tandooris and tikkas, best accompanied by piping-hot naan and flavor-bursting samosas.

Lulu
MODERN AMERICAN $$

(Map p86; ☑ 305-447-5858; 3105 Commodore Plaza; mains lunch $12-19, dinner $15-29; ⊙ 11:30am-10:30pm Sun-Thu, to 11:30pm Fri & Sat; ☑) Lulu is the Grove's exemplar of using local, organic ingredients in its carefully prepared bistro dishes, all of which are best enjoyed at the outdoor tables. You can make a meal of tasty appetizers like roasted dates, Tuscan hummus or ahi tuna tartare, or go for more filling plates of slow-braised pork tacos and seared diver scallops.

GreenStreet Cafe
AMERICAN $$

(Map p86; ☑ 305-567-0662; www.greenstreet cafe.net; 3468 Main Hwy; mains $15-29; ⊙ 7:30am-1am Sun-Tue, to 3am Wed-Sat) Sidewalk spots don't get more popular (and many say more delicious) than GreenStreet, where the Grove's young and gregarious congregate at sunset. The menu of high-end pub fare ranges from roast vegetable and goat cheese lasagna and mesclun endive salad to blackened mahimahi and braised short ribs with polenta.

Jaguar
LATIN AMERICAN $$

(Map p86; ☑ 305-444-0216; www.jaguarhg.com; 3067 Grand Ave; mains lunch $15, dinner $22-33; ⊙ 11:30am-11pm Mon-Sat, 11am-10pm Sun) The menu spans the Latin world, but really everyone's here for the ceviche 'spoon bar.' The idea: pick from six styles of ceviche (raw, marinated seafood), ranging from tuna with ginger to corvina in lime juice, and pull a culinary version of DIY. It's novel and fun, and the ceviche varieties are outstanding.

✖ Coral Gables

Threefold
CAFE $$

(Map p88; ☑ 305-704-8007; 141 Giralda Ave; mains $13-19; ⊙ 8am-4:30pm; 🛜☑) Coral Gables' most talked-about cafe is a buzzing, Aussie-run charmer that serves up perfectly pulled espressos (and a good flat white), along with creative breakfast and lunch fare. Start the morning with waffles and berry compote, smashed avocado toast topped with feta, or a slow-roasted leg of lamb with fried eggs.

Bulla Gastrobar
SPANISH $$

(Map p88; ☑ 305-441-0107; www.bullagastro bar.com; 2500 Ponce de Leon Blvd; small plates $7-19; ⊙ noon-10pm Sun-Thu, to midnight Fri & Sat; ☑) With a festive crowd chattering away over delicious bites of tapas, this stylish spot has great ambience that evokes the lively eating and drinking dens of Madrid. *Patatas bravas* (spicy potatoes), *huevos* 'bulla' (eggs, serrano ham and truffle oil) and Iberian ham croquettes keep the crowds coming throughout the night.

Frenchie's Diner
FRENCH $$

(Map p88; ☑ 305-442-4554; www.frenchiesdiner. com; 2618 Galiano St; mains lunch $14-24, dinner $24-34; ⊙ 11am-3pm & 6-10pm Tue-Sat) Tucked down a side street, it's easy to miss this place. Inside, Frenchie's channels an old-time American diner vibe, with black-and-white checkered floors, a big chalkboard menu, and a smattering of old prints and mirrors on the wall. The cooking, on the other hand, is a showcase for French bistro classics.

Matsuri
JAPANESE $$

(Map p88; ☑ 305-663-1615; 5759 Bird Rd; mains $12-19, lunch specials $10; ⊙ 11:30am-2:30pm Tue-Fri, 5:30-10:30pm Tue-Sat) Matsuri, tucked into a nondescript shopping center, is consistently packed with Japanese customers. They don't want scene; they want a taste of home, although many of the diners are actually South American Japanese who order *unagi* (eel) in Spanish. Spicy *toro* (fatty tuna) and scallions, grilled mackerel with natural salt, and an ocean of raw fish are all *oishii* (delicious).

Swine
SOUTHERN US $$$

(Map p88; ☑ 786-360-6433; 2415 Ponce de Leon Blvd; mains $20-38, sharing plates $10-25; ⊙ 10am-10pm Sun-Thu, to midnight Fri & Sat) Rustic smoked pork and craft cocktails come to Coral Gables at this stylish spot near the Miracle Mile. Amid exposed-brick walls, a cascade of hanging light bulbs and reclaimed wood elements, you'd be forgiven for thinking you took a wrong turn on the way to Brooklyn.

Pascal's on Ponce
FRENCH $$$

(Map p88; ☑ 305-444-2024; www.pascalmiami. com; 2611 Ponce de Leon Blvd; mains lunch $22-31, dinner $31-45; ⊙ 11:30am-2pm Mon-Fri, 6-10pm Mon-Thu, to 11pm Fri & Sat) They're fighting the good fight here: sea scallops with beef short rib, crispy duck confit with wild mushroom fricasée and other French fine-dining classics set the stage for a night of high-end feasting. Pascal's is a favorite among Coral Gables foodies who appreciate time-tested standards.

The menu and the atmosphere rarely change, and frankly that's not a bad thing. After all, if it ain't broke…

La Palme d'Or
FRENCH $$$

(Map p88; 305-913-3200; 1200 Anastasia Ave, Biltmore Hotel; 6-course tasting menu $115; 6:30-10:30pm Tue-Sat) The acclaimed Palme d'Or is the culinary match for the Jazz Age opulence that ensconces it. With its white-gloved, old-world class and US attention to service, unmuddled by pretensions of hipness, this place captures, in one elegant stroke, all the refinement a dozen South Beach restaurants could never grasp.

Caffe Abbracci
ITALIAN $$$

(Map p88; 305-441-0700; www.caffe abbracci.com; 318 Aragon Ave; mains $19-45; 11:30am-3:30pm Mon-Fri, 6-11pm daily) Perfect moments in Coral Gables come easy. Here's a simple formula: you, a loved one, a muggy Miami evening, some delicious pasta and a glass of red at a sidewalk table at Abbracci – one of the finest Italian restaurants in the Gables.

✖ Key Biscayne

Oasis
CUBAN $

(Map p90; 305-361-9009; 19 Harbor Dr; mains $8-12; 8am-9pm) This excellent Cuban cafe has a customer base that ranges from the working poor to city players, and the socio-economic barriers come tumbling down fast as folks sip high-octane Cuban coffee. Come for decadent, meaty Cuban sandwiches or the homestyle cooking of platters of pork, rice and beans and deep-fried plantains, then finish with super-strong coffee.

La Boulangerie Boul'Mich
CAFE $

(Map p90; www.laboulangerieusa.com; 328 Crandon Blvd; mains $12-15, pastries $3-6; 7:30am-8pm Mon-Sat, 8am-3pm Sun;) This delightful French-style bakery whips up delicious quiches, satisfying veggie- or meat-filled empanadas, heavenly pastries and, of course, perfectly buttery croissants. It's also a fine place for breakfast (fruit platters, omelets, eggs Benedict) or lunch (prosciutto and mozzarella sandwiches, four-cheese gnocchi, quinoa salads).

It's in a shopping complex, but has a classy vintage vibe, with a few outdoor tables in front.

Golden Hog Gourmet
SUPERMARKET $

(Map p90; 91 Harbor Dr; mains $8-15; 8am-8pm Mon-Sat, to 6:30pm Sun) Tucked into a small shopping complex, this is the best place in Key Biscayne to grab picnic fare before hitting the beach or state parks. Aside from good cheeses, bakery items, tasty spreads and fresh fruits, there are various counters where you can order take-away sandwiches, soups of the day and ready-made dishes (oven-roasted salmon, paella, green beans).

✖ Greater Miami

Fritanga Montelimar
NICARAGUAN $

(305-388-8841; 15722 SW 72nd St; mains $8-14; 9am-11pm) A *fritanga* is a Nicaraguan cafe, and if you've never eaten at one, here's a warning: Nicaraguans are not scared of big portions. This beloved spot, located deep in Kendall, serves up grilled pork, chicken stew, meltingly soft beef and other goodies on Styrofoam plates collapsing under the weight of beans and rice.

KEEP ON TRUCKIN'

Food trucks are a huge deal in Miami. There's far too many to list here, but if you want a taste of what's good on four wheels, head to the Wynwood Yard (p117), which has some excellent options, plus a bar, live music and plenty of outdoor seating.

If you're around on the last Friday of the month and have a car, head down to the Food Truck Invasion. Like a herd of gastronomic wildebeests, the city's food trucks gather on the last Friday of the month from 6pm to 11pm at Tropical Park (7900 SW 40th St), which is located a few miles southwest of Coral Gables. Otherwise, here are some favorite purveyors of mobile cuisine; check their Twitter handles to find their locations:

Purple People Eatery (www.purpleppleatery.com; mains $6-12) Battered mahimahi, herb-crusted mac 'n' cheese and gourmet bison burgers.

Della Test Kitchen (p117) In Wynwood Yard, this is one veg-lovers shouldn't miss.

MsCheezious (www.twitter.com/MsCheezious; sandwiches $7-10;) Unusual cheeses (like goat cheese, blue cheese and gouda) are paired with prosciutto, pulled pork and pesto to great effect.

Lots of Lox
DELI $$

(☑ 305-252-2010; www.originallotsoflox.com; 14995 S Dixie Hwy; mains breakfast $7-16, lunch $12-16, dinner $15-19; ⊘ 7am-9pm Mon-Fri, to 4pm Sat & Sun) In a city with no shortage of delis, especially in mid–Miami Beach, who would have thought some of the best chopped liver on rye could be found in this unassuming place all the way down in Palmetto Bay? It is bustling, friendly and a great slice of old-school Miami.

Steve's Pizza
PIZZA $$

(☑ 305-891-0202; www.facebook.com/steves pizzanorthmiami; 12101 Biscayne Blvd; slices $4, pizzas $12-23; ⊘ 11am-3am Mon-Thu, to 4am Fri & Sat, to 2am Sun) So many pizza chains compete for the attention of tourists in South Beach, but ask a Miami Beach local where to get the best pizza and they'll tell you about Steve's. This is New York–style pizza: thin crust and handmade with care and good ingredients.

New branches of Steve's are opening elsewhere in Miami, all in decidedly nontouristy areas, which preserves that feeling of authenticity. Steve's flagship is in South Miami; the closer North Miami outpost listed here caters to nighthawks, and is located about 6 miles (15 minutes' drive) north of the Design District.

🍸 Drinking & Nightlife

Too many people assume Miami's nightlife is all about being wealthy and attractive and/or phony. Disavow yourself of this notion, which only describes a small slice of the scene in South Beach. Miami has an intense variety of bars to pick from that range from grotty dives to beautiful – but still laid-back – lounges and nightclubs.

🍸 South Beach

★ Sweet Liberty
BAR

(Map p60; www.mysweetliberty.com; 237 20th St; ⊘ 4pm-5am Mon-Sat, from noon Sun) A much-loved local haunt near Collins Park, Sweet Liberty has all the right ingredients for a fun night out: friendly, easygoing bartenders who whip up excellent cocktails (try a mint julep), great happy-hour specials (including 75¢ oysters) and a relaxed, pretension-free crowd. The space is huge, with flickering candles, a long wooden bar and the odd band adding to the cheer.

There's also decent food ($6 to $31) on hand, from crab toast and cauliflower nachos right through to brisket sandwiches and beet and farro risotto.

★ Bodega
COCKTAIL BAR

(Map p60; ☑ 305-704-2145; www.bodegasouth beach.com; 1220 16th St; ⊘ noon-5am) Bodega looks like your average hipster Mexican joint – serving up delicious tacos ($3 to $5) from a converted Airstream trailer to a party-minded crowd. But there's actually a bar hidden behind that blue porta-potty door on the right. Head inside (or join the long line on weekends) to take in a bit of old-school glam in a sprawling drinking den.

Tarnished mirrors, leather sofas, graffiti-smeared walls, antler chandeliers and curious portraits of famous figures (but with eyepatches) – plus great cocktails and a fun crowd – set the scene for a memorable night out. Go early to avoid the lines.

★ Mango's Tropical Café
BAR

(Map p66; ☑ 305-673-4422; www.mangos tropicalcafe.com; 900 Ocean Dr; $10; ⊘ 11:45am-5am) A mix of Latin-loving locals and visitors from far-flung corners of the globe mix things up at this famous bar on Ocean Dr. Every night feels like a celebration, with a riotously fun vibe, and plenty of entertainment: namely minimally dressed staff dancing on the bar, doing Michael Jackson impersonations, shimmying in feather headdresses or showing off some amazing salsa moves.

It's a kitschy good time, which doesn't even take into consideration the small dance floor and stage in the back, where brassy Latin bands get everyone moving. As with other spots on Ocean Dr, the drinks are ridiculously overpriced (around $10 for a beer and $20 for a cocktail).

Bay Club
COCKTAIL BAR

(Map p60; ☑ 305-695-4441; 1930 Bay Rd; ⊘ 5pm-2am) A great little nightspot in Sunset Harbour, Bay Club has an enticing low-lit vintage vibe with red banquettes, antique wallpaper, wood paneling and old chandeliers. It's a good date spot with craft cocktails and occasional live music (jazz guitar and other subdued sounds).

Kill Your Idol
BAR

(Map p60; ☑ 305-672-1852; www.killyouridol.com; 222 Española Way; ⊘ 8pm-5am) Kill Your Idol is a bit of a dive, but it has plenty of appeal, with graffiti and shelves full of retro bric-a-brac covering the walls, drag shows on Monday and DJs spinning danceable old-school grooves. The crowd is a fairly laid-back mix

MIAMI DRINKING & NIGHTLIFE

of locals and out-of-towners. The bar is tiny, so prepare for the crowds on weekends.

Rose Bar at the Delano
BAR

(Map p60; ☑ 305-674-5752; www.delano-hotel.com; 1685 Collins Ave, Delano Hotel; ☉ noon-2am) The ultrachic Rose Bar at this elegant Ian Schrager original is a watering hole for beautiful creatures (or at least those with a healthy ego). Get ready to pay up for the privilege – but also prepare to enjoy it.

The pool bar in the back of the Delano (p107) is another winner; wait for staff to set out a wrought-iron table in the shallow end of the pool and you'll start rethinking your definition of opulence.

Campton Yard
BEER GARDEN

(Map p60; 1500 Collins Ave, Hall Hotel; ☉ 5pm-midnight Mon-Fri, from noon Sat & Sun) Spread beneath a towering banyan tree, this pebble-strewn backyard draws a youthful crowd who come for a night of laid-back merriment beneath the faerie lights. There are games (giant Jenga and Connect 4, ping pong, beanbag tossing), craft beer, picnic tables and a welcome lack of pretension. Enter through the Hall Hotel, and make your way to the backyard oasis.

Story
CLUB

(Map p66; ☑ 305-479-4426; www.storymiami.com; 136 Collins Ave; ☉ 11pm-5am Thu-Sun) For the big megaclub experience, Story is a top destination. Some of the best DJs (mostly EDM) from around the globe spin at this club, with parties lasting late into the night. It has a fairly roomy dance floor, but gets packed on weekend nights. Be good looking and dress to impress, as getting in can be a pain.

Score
GAY

(Map p60; ☑ 305-535-1111; www.scorebar.net; 1437 Washington Ave; ☉ 10pm-5am Thu-Sun) Muscle boys with mustaches, glistening six-packs gyrating on stage, and a crowd of men who've decided shirts really aren't their thing: do we need to spell out the orientation of Score's customer base? It's still one of the best dedicated – and decadent – gay bars in South Beach.

Lost Weekend
BAR

(Map p60; ☑ 305-672-1707; www.sub-culture.org/lost-weekend-miami; 218 Española Way; ☉ noon-5am) The Weekend is a grimy, sweaty, slovenly dive, filled with pool tables, cheap domestics and – hell yeah – *Golden Tee* and *Big Buck Hunter* arcade games. God bless

it. Popular with local waiters, kitchen staff and bartenders.

Abbey Brewery
MICROBREWERY

(Map p60; www.abbeybrewinginc.com; 1115 16th St; ☉ 1pm-5am) The oldest brew-pub in South Beach is on the untouristed end of South Beach (near Alton Rd). It's friendly and packed with folks listening to throwback hits (grunge, '80s new wave) and slinging back some excellent homebrew: give Father Theo's stout or the Immaculate IPA a try.

Mac's Club Deuce Bar
BAR

(Map p60; ☑ 305-531-6200; www.macsclubdeuce.com; 222 14th St; ☉ 8am-5am) The oldest bar in Miami Beach (established in 1926), the Deuce is a real neighborhood bar and hype-free zone. It's just straight-up seediness, which depending on your outlook can be quite refreshing. Plan to see everyone from transgendered ladies to construction workers – some hooking up, some talking rough, all having a good time.

North Beach

★ Broken Shaker
BAR

(Map p70; ☑ 305-531-2727; www.freehandhotels.com/miami/broken-shaker; 2727 Indian Creek Dr, Freehand Miami Hotel; ☉ 6pm-3am Mon-Fri, 2pm-3am Sat & Sun) Craft cocktails are having their moment in Miami, and if mixology is in the spotlight, you can bet Broken Shaker is sharing the glare. Expert bartenders run this spot, located in the back of the Freehand Miami hotel (p108), which takes up one closet-sized indoor niche and a sprawling plant-filled courtyard of excellent drinks and beautiful people.

Sandbar Lounge
BAR

(Map p70; ☑ 305-865-1752; 6752 Collins Ave; ☉ 4pm-5am) True to its name this dive bar has sand – lots and lots of it covering the floor. Never mind that the beach is a block away, Sandbar's a local institution, and a fine antidote to the high-end drinking spots covering Miami Beach. It has a welcoming vibe, sports on TV, a fun jukebox and great happy-hour specials. Come on in and join the gang.

WunderBar
LOUNGE

(Map p70; ☑ 305-503-1120; www.circa39.com/wunderbar; 3900 Collins Ave, Circa39; ☉ 11am-11pm Sun-Thu, to midnight Fri & Sat) Tucked off to the back of Circa 39's (p109) moody front lobby, this designer dream bar has a warm, welcoming feel to it. Definitely stop in for a drink if you're up this way, before sauntering across the street and checking out the lapping waves on the beach.

🍷 Downtown Miami

⭐ Blackbird Ordinary BAR
(Map p72; ☎305-671-3307; www.blackbird ordinary.com; 729 SW 1st Ave; ⊙3pm-5am Mon-Fri, 5pm-5am Sat & Sun) Far from ordinary, the Blackbird is an excellent bar, with great cocktails (the London Sparrow, with gin, cayenne, lemon juice and passion fruit, goes down well) and an enormous courtyard. The only thing 'ordinary' about the place is the sense that all are welcome for a fun and pretension-free night out.

You can often catch great bands playing here, and on quiet nights there's always the pool table. Tuesday nights are a wonderful thing for the gals: it's ladies night, and women drink free until 1:30am.

Eleven Miami CLUB
(E11EVEN; Map p72; ☎305-570-4803; www.11 miami.com; 29 NE 11th St; ⊙24hr) Since its opening back in 2014, Eleven Miami has remained one of the top Downtown clubs. There's much eye candy here (and we're not talking just about the attractive club-goers): go-go dancers, aerialists and racy (strip-tease-esque) performances, amid a state-of-the-art sound system, laser lights and video walls, with top DJs working the crowd into a frenzy.

Sugar LOUNGE
(Map p72; 788 Brickell Plaza, EAST, Miami Hotel, 40th fl; ⊙4pm-1am Mon-Thu, to 3am Fri & Sat, to midnight Sun) One of Miami's hottest bars of the moment sits on the 40th floor of the EAST, Miami Hotel (p110). Calling it a rooftop bar doesn't quite do the place justice. Verdant oasis is more like it, with a spacious open-air deck full of plants and trees – and sweeping views over the city and Key Biscayne.

Batch Gastropub BAR
(Map p72; www.batchmiami.com; 30 SW 12th St; ⊙noon-3am Sun-Thu, to 4am Fri & Sat) This gastropub in Brickell draws a fairly straight-laced crowd. But if you don't mind the slacks and the sports on TV, Batch has appeal: namely a first-rate selection of microbrews and fizzes (carbonated cocktails) on tap, plus creative cocktails and lots of great snacks (truffle fries, grouper tacos, brisket burgers, wild-mushroom pizzas).

There are good food and drink deals during happy hour (weekdays 5pm to 8pm).

Area 31 ROOFTOP BAR
(Map p72; www.area31restaurant.com; 270 Biscayne Blvd Way, Klimpton Epic Hotel; ⊙5-11pm Sun-Thu, to midnight Fri & Sat) On the rooftop of the Kimpton EPIC Hotel (p110), this buzzing open-air bar draws in the after-work happy-hour crowd, which morphs into a more party-minded gathering as the evening progresses. The view – overlooking the river and the high-rises of Downtown – is stunning.

Pawnbroker ROOFTOP BAR
(Map p72; ☎305-420-2200; www.pawn brokermiami.com; 121 SE 1st St, Langford Hotel;

5pm-midnight Mon-Thu, to 2am Fri & Sat, 4-10pm Sun) Head up to the top (penthouse) floor of the Langford Hotel (p110) for sweeping views of Downtown, first-rate cocktails and a welcoming, snooty-free vibe. It's a lively spot at happy hour (5pm to 7pm weekdays), when you can catch the sunset, though you won't be alone (go early to beat the crowds).

Wynwood & the Design District

★ Lagniappe   BAR
(Map p78; ☑ 305-576-0108; www.lagniappe house.com; 3425 NE 2nd Ave; ⊙ 7pm-2am Sun-Thu, to 3am Fri & Sat) A touch of New Orleans in Miami, Lagniappe has an old-fashioned front room bar, packed with art, faded vintage furnishings and weathered walls. The vibe is just right: with great live music (nightly from 9pm to midnight) and an easygoing crowd, plus there's a sprawling back garden with palm trees and fairy lights.

Bardot   CLUB
(Map p78; ☑ 305-576-5570; www.bardotmiami. com; 3456 N Miami Ave; ⊙ 8pm-3am Tue & Wed, to 5am Thu-Sat) You really should see the interior of Bardot before you leave the city. It's all sexy French vintage posters and furniture (plus a pool table) seemingly plucked from a private club that serves millionaires by day, and becomes a scene of decadent excess by night. The entrance looks to be on N Miami Ave, but it's actually in a parking lot behind the building.

Boxelder   BAR
(Map p78; ☑ 305-942-7769; www.bxldr.com; 2817 NW 2nd Ave; ⊙ 4pm-midnight Mon, 1pm-

midnight Tue-Thu, to 2am Fri & Sat, to 10pm Sun) This long, narrow space is a beer-lover's Valhalla, with a brilliantly curated menu of brews from near and far, though its 20 rotating beer taps leave pride of place for South Florida beers. There's also more than 100 different varieties by the bottle. What keeps the place humming is Boxelder's friendly, down-to-earth vibe.

Wynwood Brewing Company   MICROBREWERY
(Map p78; ☑ 305-982-8732; www.wynwood brewing.com; 565 NW 24th St; ⊙ noon-10pm Sun & Mon, to midnight Tue-Sat) The beer scene has grown in leaps and bounds in Miami, but this warmly lit spot, which was the first craft brewery in Wynwood, is still the best. The family-owned 15-barrel brewhouse has friendly and knowledgeable staff, excellent year-round brews (including a blonde ale, a robust porter and a top-notch IPA) and seasonal beers, and there's always a food truck parked outside.

Wood Tavern   BAR
(Map p78; ☑ 305-748-2828; www.woodtavern miami.com; 2531 NW 2nd Ave; ⊙ 5pm-3am Tue-Sat, 3pm-midnight Sun) So many new bars in Miami want to be casual but cool; Wood is one of the few locales achieving this Golden Mean of atmosphere and aesthetic. Food specials are cheap, the beer selection is excellent and the crowd is friendly – this Wood's got the right grain.

Gramps   BAR
(Map p78; ☑ 786-752-6693; www.gramps.com; 176 NW 24th St; ⊙ 11am-1am Sun-Wed, to 3am Thu-Sat) Friendly and unpretentious (just like some grandpas), Gramps always has something

---

MICROBREWERIES & BEER BARS

The microbrew renaissance is underway in Miami with a growing number of craft brewers arriving on the scene. At these Miami spots, you'll find creative brews and a strong neighborhood vibe. Some stock other beers on rotating taps (with a focus on South Florida brewers) as well as their own. Most microbreweries also have food available, or work with food trucks who park outside.

Wynwood is the epicenter of the beer scene, with a handful of brewers, plus beer-focused bars and eateries. With soaring real estate prices in the neighborhood however, more brewers are choosing to open in the western reaches of Miami.

A few good beer-loving places include the following:

➡ Boxelder

➡ Concrete Beach Brewery (p129)

➡ Wynwood Brewing Company

➡ Abbey Brewery (p126)

afoot whether it's live music and DJs (Fridays and Saturdays), trivia and bingo nights (Tuesdays and Wednesdays) or straight-up karaoke (Thursdays). The big draw though is really just the sizable backyard that's perfect for alfresco drinking and socializing.

Coyo Taco BAR

(Map p78; www.coyo-taco.com; 2300 NW 2nd Ave; ☉5pm-midnight Sun-Wed, to 3am Thu-Sat) Secret bars hidden behind taco stands are all the rage in Miami these days. To find this one, head inside Coyo Taco, down the corridor past the bathrooms and enter the unmarked door. Inside you'll find a classy low-lit spot with elaborate ceramic tile floors, a long wooden bar and a DJ booth, with brassy Latin rhythms and Afro Cuban funk filling the space.

Concrete Beach Brewery BREWERY

(Map p78; ☎305-796-2727; www.concrete beachbrewery.com; 325 NW 24th St; ☉5-11pm Mon-Thu, to 1am Fri, from 1pm Sat & Sun) Concrete Beach is a great little neighborhood brewery, with a gated courtyard where you can linger over hoppy IPAs, wheat beers with a hint of citrus, and easy-drinking pilsners, plus seasonal brews (like a juniper saison called Miami Gras, which typically launches in February). It's not always the liveliest spot, but a fine stop for beer connoisseurs.

⬤ Little Haiti & the Upper East Side

Vagabond Pool Bar BAR

(Map p82; ☎305-400-8420; www.vagabond kitchenandbar.com; 7301 Biscayne Blvd; ☉5-11pm Sun-Thu, to midnight Fri & Sat) Tucked behind the Vagabond Hotel, this is a great spot to start off the evening, with perfectly mixed cocktails, courtesy of pro bartenders (the kind who will shake your hand and introduce themselves). The outdoor setting overlooking the palm-fringed pool and eclectic crowd pairs nicely with elixirs like the Lost in Smoke (mezcal, amaro, amaretto and orange bitters).

The Anderson BAR

(Map p82; www.theandersonmiami.com; 709 NE 79th St; ☉5pm-2am Sun-Thu, to 4am Fri & Sat) The Anderson is a great neighborhood bar with a dimly lit interior sprinkled with red couches, animal-print fabrics, wild wallpaper and a glittering jukebox. Head to the back patio for more of a tropical-themed setting where you can dip your toes in the sand (never mind the absent oceanfront).

Churchill's BAR

(Map p82; ☎305-757-1807; www.churchillspub.com; 5501 NE 2nd Ave; ☉3pm-3am Sun-Thu, to 5am Fri & Sat) A Miami icon that's been around since 1979, Churchill's is a Brit-owned pub in the midst of what could be Port-au-Prince. There's a lot of live music here, mainly punk, indie and more punk. Not insipid modern punk either: think the Ramones meets the Sex Pistols.

Boteco BAR

(Map p82; ☎305-757-7735; www.botecomiami.com; 916 NE 79th St; ☉noon-midnight) If you're missing the *cidade maravilhosa* (aka Rio de Janeiro), come to Boteco on Friday evening to see the biggest Brazilian expat reunion in Miami. *Cariocas* (Rio natives) and their countrymen flock here to listen to samba and bossa nova, and chat each other up over the best caipirinhas in town.

⬤ Little Havana

Ball & Chain BAR

(Map p84; www.ballandchainmiami.com; 1513 SW 8th Street; ☉noon-midnight Mon-Wed, to 3am Thu-Sat, 2-10pm Sun) The Ball & Chain has survived several incarnations over the years. Back in 1935, when 8th St was more Jewish than Latino, it was the sort of jazz joint Billie Holiday would croon in. That iteration closed in 1957, but the new Ball & Chain is still dedicated to music and good times – specifically, Latin music and tropical cocktails.

Los Pinareños Frutería JUICE BAR

(Map p84; 1334 SW 8th St; snacks & drinks $3-6; ☉7am-6pm Mon-Sat, to 3pm Sun) Nothing says refreshment on a sultry Miami afternoon like a cool glass of fresh juice (or smoothie) at this popular fruit and veggie stand. Try a combination like the 'abuelo' (sugarcane juice, pineapple and lemon) for something particularly satisfying. The produce is also quite flavorful.

⬤ Coconut Grove

Barracuda BAR

(Map p86; ☎305-918-9013; 3035 Fuller St; ☉noon-3am Tue-Sun, from 6pm Mon) Coconut Grove has its share of divey, pretension-free bars, and Barracuda is one of the best of the bunch, with a fine jukebox, pool table, darts and sports playing on the various TV

ROOFTOP BARS

Miami's high rises are put to fine use in the many rooftop bars you'll find scattered around the city. These are usually located in high-end hotels found in Miami Beach and in Downtown. The view is of course the big reason to come – and it can be sublime, with the sweep of Biscayne Bay or sparkling beachfront in the background. Despite being in hotels, some spots are a draw for locals, and it can be quite a scene, with DJs, a dressy crowd and a discriminating door policy at prime time on weekend nights. If you're here for the view and not the party, come early. Happy hour is fabulous – as you can catch a fine sunset, and getting in is usually not a problem. The following are some of our favorite spots:

➡ Townhouse Hotel (p101)

➡ Pawnbroker (p127)

➡ Sugar (p127)

➡ Area 31 (p127)

---

screens. It's a fine retreat from CG's shiny shopping surfaces – the inside is decorated with wood salvaged from an old Florida shrimp boat.

Taurus BAR
(Map p86; ☑ 305-529-6523; 3540 Main Hwy; ☺ 4pm-3am Mon-Fri, from 1pm Sat & Sun) The oldest bar in Coconut Grove is a cool mix of wood paneling, smoky leather chairs, about 100 beers to choose from and a convivial vibe – as neighborhood bars go in Miami, this is one of the best.

Tavern in the Grove BAR
(Map p86; ☑ 305-447-3884; 3416 Main Hwy; ☺ 3pm-3am Mon-Sat, from noon Sun) To say this sweatbox is popular with University of Miami students is like saying it rains sometimes in England. More of a neighborhood dive on weekdays.

⬤ Coral Gables

Seven Seas BAR
(Map p88; ☑ 305-266-6071; 2200 SW 57th Ave; ☺ noon-1am Sun-Wed, to 2am Thu-Sat) Seven Seas is a genuine Miami neighborhood dive, decorated on the inside like a nautical theme park and filled with University of Miami students, Cuban workers, gays, straights, lesbians and folks from around the way. Come for the best karaoke in Miami on Tuesday, Thursday and Saturday, and for trivia on Monday.

Titanic Brewing Company MICROBREWERY
(☑ 305-668-1742; www.titanicbrewery.com; 5813 Ponce de Leon Blvd; ☺ 11:30am-1am Sun-Thu, to 2am Fri & Sat) During the day Titanic is an all-American-type brewpub, but at night it turns into a popular University of Miami watering hole. Titanic's signature brews are quite refreshing – particularly the White Star IPA. Lots of good pub grub on hand, including Sriracha wings, and corn and crawfish fritters.

☆ Entertainment

Miami's artistic merits are obvious, even from a distance. Could there be a better creative base? There's Southern homegrown talent, migratory snowbirds bringing the funding and attention of northeastern galleries, and immigrants from across the Americas. All that adds up to some great live music, theater and dance – with plenty of room for experimentation.

☆ South Beach

New World Symphony CLASSICAL MUSIC
(NWS; Map p60; ☑ 305-673-3330; www.nws.edu; 500 17th St) Housed in the New World Center (p58) – a funky explosion of cubist lines and geometric curves, fresh white against the blue Miami sky – the acclaimed New World Symphony holds performances from October to May. The deservedly heralded NWS serves as a three- to four-year preparatory program for talented musicians from prestigious music schools.

Colony Theater PERFORMING ARTS
(Map p60; ☑ 305-674-1040, box office 800-211-1414; www.colonymb.org; 1040 Lincoln Rd) The Colony is an absolute art-deco gem, with a classic marquee and Inca-style crenellations, which looks like the sort of place gangsters would go to watch *Hamlet*. This treasure now serves as a major venue for

performing arts – from comedy and occasional musicals to theatrical dramas, off-Broadway productions and ballet – as well as hosting movie screenings and small film festivals.

Miami City Ballet DANCE
(Map p60; ☑305-929-7000; www.miamicity ballet.org; 2200 Liberty Ave) Formed in 1985, this troupe is based out of a lovely three-story headquarters designed by famed local architectural firm Arquitectonica. The facade allows passers-by to watch the dancers rehearsing through big picture windows, which makes you feel like you're in a scene from *Fame,* except the weather is better and people don't spontaneously break into song.

Fillmore Miami Beach PERFORMING ARTS
(Map p60; ☑305-673-7300; www.fillmoremb. com; 1700 Washington Ave) Built in 1951, South Beach's premier showcase for touring Broadway shows, orchestras and other big musical productions has 2700 seats and excellent acoustics. Jackie Gleason chose to make the theater his home for the long-running 1960s TV show, but now you'll find an eclectic lineup: Catalan pop or indie rock one night, the comedian Bill Maher or an over-the-top vaudeville group the next.

☆ North Beach

North Beach Bandshell LIVE MUSIC
(Map p70; www.northbeachbandshell.com; 7275 Collins Ave) This outdoor venue features an excellent lineup of concerts, dance, theater, opera and spoken word throughout the year. Some events are free. It's run by the nonprofit Rhythm Foundation, and the wide-ranging repertoire features sounds from around the globe, with many family-friendly events. Check online to see what's on the roster.

**Chopin Foundation
of the United States** CLASSICAL MUSIC
(Map p70; ☑305-868-0624; www.chopin.org; 1440 JFK/79th St Causeway) This national organization hosts a treasure trove of performances for Chopin fans – the Chopin Festival, a series of free monthly concerts and the less-frequent National Chopin Piano Competition, an international contest held in Miami every five years.

☆ Downtown Miami

**★ Adrienne Arsht Center
for the Performing Arts** PERFORMING ARTS
(Map p72; ☑305-949-6722; www.arshtcenter.org; 1300 Biscayne Blvd; ⊘box office 10am-6pm Mon-Fri, and 2 hr before performances) This magnificent venue manages to both humble and enthrall visitors. Today the Arsht is where the biggest cultural acts in Miami come to perform; a show here is a must-see on any Miami trip. There's an Adrienne Arsht Center stop on the Metromover.

This performing-arts center is Miami's beautiful, beloved baby. It is also a major component of Downtown's urban equivalent of a facelift and several regimens of Botox. Designed by César Pelli (the man who brought you Kuala Lumpur's Petronas Towers), the center has two main components, connected by a thin pedestrian bridge.

Inside the theaters there's a sense of ocean and land sculpted by wind; the rounded balconies rise up in spirals that resemble a sliced-open seashell. Hidden behind these impressive structures are highly engineered, state-of-the-art acoustics ensuring that no outside sounds can penetrate, creating the perfect conditions to enjoy one of the 300 performances staged at the center each year.

Klipsch Amphitheater LIVE MUSIC
(Map p72; www.klipsch.com/klipsch-amphi theater-at-bayfront-park; 301 N Biscayne Blvd, Bayfront Park) In Bayfront Park in Downtown Miami, the Klipsch Amphitheater stages a wide range of concerts throughout the year. The open-air setting beside Biscayne Bay is hard to top.

American Airlines Arena STADIUM
(Map p72; ☑786-777-1000; www.aaarena.com; 601 N Biscayne Blvd) Resembling a massive spaceship that perpetually hovers at the edge of Biscayne Bay, this arena has been the home of the city's NBA franchise, the Miami Heat, since 2000. The Waterfront Theater, Florida's largest, is housed inside; throughout the year it hosts concerts, Broadway performances and the like.

Olympia Theater PERFORMING ARTS
(Map p72; ☑305-374-2444; www.olympiatheater. org; 174 E Flagler St) This elegantly renovated 1920s movie palace services a huge variety of performing arts including film festivals,

symphonies, ballets and touring shows. The acoustics are excellent.

Miami loves modern, but the Olympia Theater at the Gusman Center for the Performing Arts is vintage-classic beautiful. The ceiling, which features 246 twinkling stars and clouds cast over an indigo-deep night, frosted with classical Greek sculpture and Vienna Opera House–style embellishment, will melt your heart. The theater first opened in 1925.

☆ Wynwood & the Design District

O Cinema Wynwood   CINEMA
(Map p78; ☑ 305-571-9970; www.o-cinema.org; 90 NW 29th St) This much-loved nonprofit cinema in Wynwood screens indie films, foreign films and documentaries. You'll find thought-provoking works you won't see elsewhere.

Light Box at Goldman Warehouse   PERFORMING ARTS
(Map p78; ☑ 305-576-4350; www.miamilight project.com; 404 NW 26th St) The Miami Light Project, a nonprofit cultural foundation, stages a wide range of innovative theater, dance, music and film performances at this intimate theater. It's in Wynwood, and a great place to discover cutting-edge works by artists you might not have heard of.

ART WALKS: NIGHTLIFE MEETS ART

Ever-flowing (not always free) wine and beer, great art, a fun crowd and no cover charge (or velvet rope): welcome to the wondrous world where art and nightlife collide. The Wynwood and Design District Art Walks are among the best ways to experience an alternative slice of Miami culture. Just be careful, as a lot of galleries in Wynwood are separated by short drives (the Design District is more walkable). Art Walks (p97) take place on the second Saturday of each month, from 7pm to 10pm (some galleries stretch to 11pm); when it's all over, lots of folks repair to Wood Tavern (p128) or Bardot (p128). Visit www.artofmiami.com/maps/art-walks for information on participating galleries.

They're particularly supportive of troupes from South Florida.

☆ Little Havana

★ Cubaocho   LIVE PERFORMANCE
(Map p84; ☑ 305-285-5880; www.cubaocho. com; 1465 SW 8th St; ☉ 11am-10pm Tue-Thu, to 3am Fri & Sat) Jewel of the Little Havana Art District, Cubaocho is renowned for its concerts, with excellent bands from across the Spanish-speaking world. It's also a community center, art gallery and research outpost for all things Cuban. The interior resembles an old Havana cigar bar, yet the walls are decked out in artwork that references both the classical past of Cuban art and its avant-garde future.

Aside from the busy concert schedule, Cubaocho also has film screenings, drama performances, readings and other events.

Tower Theater   CINEMA
(Map p84; ☑ 305-237-2463; www.towertheater miami.com; 1508 SW 8th St) This renovated 1926 landmark theater has a proud deco facade and a handsomely renovated interior, thanks to support from the Miami-Dade Community College. In its heyday, it was the center of Little Havana social life, and via the films it showed served as a bridge between immigrant society and American pop culture. Today it frequently shows independent and Spanish-language films (sometimes both).

Hoy Como Ayer   LIVE MUSIC
(Map p84; ☑ 305-541-2631; www.hoycomoayer. us; 2212 SW 8th St; ☉ 8:30pm-4am Thu-Sat) This Cuban hot spot – with authentic music, unstylish wood paneling and a small dance floor – is enhanced by first-rate mojitos and Havana transplants. Stop in nightly for *son* (a salsalike dance that originated in Oriente, Cuba), *boleros* (a Spanish dance in triple meter) and modern Cuban beats.

☆ Coral Gables

Coral Gables Art Cinema   CINEMA
(Map p88; ☑ 786-385-9689; www.gables cinema.com; 260 Aragon Ave) In the epicenter of Coral Gables' downtown, you'll find one of Miami's best art-house cinemas. It screens indie and foreign films in a modern 144-seat screening room. Check out cult favorites shown in the original 35mm format at Saturday midnight screenings (part of the After Hours series).

GableStage
THEATER

(Map p88; ☎305-445-1119; www.gablestage.org; 1200 Anastasia Ave; tickets $48-65) Founded as the Florida Shakespeare Theatre in 1979 and now housed on the property of the Biltmore Hotel in Coral Gables, this company still performs an occasional Shakespeare play, but mostly presents contemporary and classical pieces.

☆ Greater Miami

Miami Symphony Orchestra
CLASSICAL MUSIC

(☎305-275-5666; www.themiso.org; tickets $20-50) Miami's well-loved hometown symphony has many fans. Its yearly series features world-renowned soloists performing at either the Adrienne Arsht Center for the Performing Arts (p131) or the Fillmore Miami Beach (p131). Performances run from November to May.

Ifé-Ilé Afro-Cuban Dance
DANCE

(☎786-704-8609; www.ife-ile.org) Ifé-Ilé is a non-profit organization that promotes cultural understanding through dance and performs in a range of styles – traditional Afro Cuban, mambo, rumba, conga, *chancleta, son,* salsa and ritual pieces. Their big event is an Afro Cuban dance festival they headline in August.

Hard Rock Stadium
FOOTBALL

(☎305-943-8000; www.hardrockstadium.com; 347 Don Shula Dr, Miami Gardens; tickets from $35) The newly renovated (and renamed) Hard Rock Stadium (formerly known as Sun Life Stadium) is the home turf of the Miami Dolphins. 'Dol-fans' are respectably crazy about their team, even if a Super Bowl showing has evaded them since 1985. Games are wildly popular and the team is painfully successful, in that they always raise fans' hopes but never quite fulfill them.

University of Miami Hurricanes
SPECTATOR SPORT

(☎800-462-2637; www.hurricanesports.com; tickets $25-70) The Hurricanes were once undisputed titans of university football, but have experienced a slow decline since 2004. Regardless, attending a game surrounded by UM's pack of fanatics is lots of fun. Their season runs from August to December.

🔒 Shopping

Temptation comes in many forms in Miami. For shoppers, this means high-end fashion, designer sunglasses, vintage clothing, books, records, Latin American crafts, artwork,

MIAMI SHOPPING

gourmet goodies and much more. You'll also find sprawling air-conditioned malls where you can retreat when the weather sours. No matter where you shop, you'll find good restaurant options along the way, as dining is an important part of the whole shopping experience.

🔒 South Beach

Taschen
BOOKS

(Map p60; ☎305-538-6185; www.taschen.com; 1111 Lincoln Rd; ⊙11am-9pm Mon-Thu, to 10pm Fri & Sat, noon-9pm Sun) An inviting well-stocked collection of art, photography, design and coffee-table books to make your home look that much smarter. A few volumes worth browsing include David Hockney's color-rich art books, the *New Erotic Photography* (always a great conversation starter) and Sebastião Salgado's lushly photographed human-filled landscapes.

Books & Books
BOOKS

(Map p60; ☎305-532-3222; www.booksandbooks.com; 927 Lincoln Rd; ⊙10am-11pm Sun-Thu, to midnight Fri & Sat) Stop in this fantastic indie bookstore for an excellent selection of new fiction, beautiful art and photography books, award-winning children's titles and more. The layout – a series of elegantly furnished rooms – invites endless browsing, and there's a good restaurant and cafe in front of the store.

Sunset Clothing Co
FASHION & ACCESSORIES

(Map p60; www.facebook.com/SunsetClothing Co; 1895 Purdy Ave; ⊙10am-8pm Mon-Sat, 11am-6pm Sun) A great little men's and women's fashion boutique in Sunset Harbour for stylish gear that won't cost a fortune (though the merchandise isn't cheap either). You'll find well-made long-sleeved shirts, soft cotton

T-shirts, lace-up canvas shoes, nicely fitting denim (including vintage Levi's), warm pullover sweaters and other casual gear. Helpful, friendly service too.

Alchemist FASHION & ACCESSORIES
(Map p60; ☑ 305-531-4653; 1111 Lincoln Rd; ⊙10am-10pm) Inside one of Lincoln Rd's most striking buildings, this high-end boutique has a wild collection of artful objects, including Warhol-style soup-can candles, heavy gilded corkscrews, Beats headphones by Dr Dre, and mirrored circular sunglasses that are essential for the beach. The clothing here tends to be fairly avant-garde (straight from the runway it seems).

🏠 Downtown Miami

Mary Brickell Village SHOPPING CENTER
(Map p72; ☑ 305-381-6130; www.marybrickell village.com; 901 S Miami Ave; ⊙10am-9pm Mon-Sat, noon-6pm Sun) This outdoor shopping and dining complex has helped revitalize the Brickell neighborhood, with a range of boutiques, outdoor restaurants, cafes and bars. It's a magnet for new condo residents in the area, with a central location in the heart of the financial district.

Supply & Advise CLOTHING
(Map p72; www.supplyandadvise.com; 223 SE 1st St; ⊙11am-7pm Mon-Sat) Supply & Advise brings a heavy dose of men's fashion to Downtown Miami, with rugged, well-made and handsomely tailored clothing plus shoes and accessories, set in a historic 1920s building. Most merchandise here is made in the USA. There's also a barbershop, complete with vintage chairs and that impeccable look of bygone days.

🏠 Wynwood & the Design District

Nomad Tribe CLOTHING
(Map p78; ☑ 305-364-5193; www.nomadtribe shop.com; 2301 NW 2nd Ave; ⊙noon-8pm) 🍃 This boutique earns high marks for carrying only ethically and sustainably produced merchandise. You'll find cleverly designed jewelry from Miami-based Kathe Cuervo, Osom brand socks (made of upcycled thread), ecologically produced graphic T-shirts from Thinking MU, and THX coffee and candles (which donates 100% of profits to nonprofit organizations) among much else.

Brooklyn Vintage & Vinyl MUSIC
(Map p78; www.facebook.com/brooklynvintage andvinyl; 3454 NW 7th Ave; ⊙noon-9pm Tue-Sat) Although it opened in late 2016, this record store on the edge of Wynwood has already attracted a following. It's mostly vinyl (as well as some cassettes and a few T-shirts), with around 5000 records in the inventory. Staff can give good tips for exploring new music.

Shinola FASHION & ACCESSORIES
(Map p78; ☑ 786-374-2994; www.shinola.com; 2399 NW 2nd Ave; ⊙11am-7pm Mon-Sat, noon-6pm Sun; ☎) This dapper little store by the Detroit-based Shinola proves that American manufacturing is far from dead. Shinola makes beautifully crafted watches, wallets, journals, pens, bicycles and even limited-edition turntables. The prices can be rather staggering, but you can rest assured that the build is of the highest quality.

Art by God GIFTS & SOUVENIRS
(Map p78; ☑ 305-573-3011; www.artbygod.com; 60 NE 27th St; ⊙10am-5pm Mon-Fri, 11am-4pm Sat) Take a walk on the wild side at this sprawling warehouse full of relics of days past. Fossils, minerals and semiprecious stones play supporting roles to the more eye-catching draws: full-size giraffes, lions, bears and zebras in all their taxidermied glory.

You'll also find rhino heads, dinosaur bones (even a triceratops horn!) and organic parts closer to home – namely skulls with trephination (a primitive surgical practice) from pre-Columbian peoples.

Out of the Closet THRIFT STORE
(Map p78; ☑ 305-764-3773; www.outofthe closet.org; 2900 Biscayne Blvd; ⊙10am-7pm Mon-Sat, to 6pm Sun) You'll find all manner of treasure-trash at this sizable thrift store on busy Biscayne Blvd: men's and women's clothing, accessories, books, CDs, records, housewares and more. Friendly staff can help guide you on the search.

The store benefits the AIDS Healthcare Foundation and offers free HIV testing.

Malaquita ARTS & CRAFTS
(Map p78; www.malaquitadesign.com; 2613 NW 2nd Ave; ⊙11am-7pm) This artfully designed store has merchandise you won't find elsewhere, including lovely handblown vases, embroidered clothing, Mesoamerican tapestries, vibrantly painted bowls, handwoven palm baskets and other fair-trade objects – some

of which are made by indigenous artisans in Mexico.

Genius Jones   TOYS
(Map p78; ☑ 305-571-2000; www.geniusjones.com; 2800 NE 2nd Ave; ⊙ 10am-7pm Mon-Sat, noon-6pm Sun) High-end toys, dolls and gear for babies and toddlers and their parents. Fatboy 'beanbag' chairs, ride-on racing cars and Bugaboo strollers: there are loads of covet-worthy gear for the little ones.

🏠 Little Haiti & the Upper East Side

Sweat Records   MUSIC
(Map p82; ☑ 786-693-9309; www.sweatrecordsmiami.com; 5505 NE 2nd Ave; ⊙ noon-10pm Mon-Sat, to 5pm Sun) Sweat's almost a stereotypical indie record store – there's funky art and graffiti on the walls, it sells weird Japanese toys, there are tattooed staff with thick glasses arguing over LPs and EPs you've never heard of and, of course, there's coffee and vegan snacks.

Marky's Gourmet   FOOD & DRINKS
(Map p82; ☑ 305-758-9288; www.markys.com; 687 NE 79th St; ⊙ 9am-7pm Mon-Fri, 10am-6pm Sat, to 5pm Sun) A Miami institution among Russians, Russophiles and those that simply love to explore global cuisine, Marky's has been going strong since 1983. In-the-know foodies from afar flock here to load up on gourmet cheeses, olives, European-style sausages, wines, cakes, teas, jams, chocolates, caviar and much more. As in the good old days of the Soviet Union, service does not come with a smile.

Upper East Side Farmers Market   MARKET
(Map p82; cnr Biscayne Blvd & 66th St, Legion Park; ⊙ 9am-2pm Sat) For a taste of local culture, stop by this small farmers market held each Saturday in the Upper East Side's Legion Park. Here you can meet some of the farmers producing delectable fresh fruits and veggies, plus stock up on breads and crackers, pastries, cheeses, jams, honeys and fresh juices. In short, everything you need for a great picnic. It's open year-round.

Libreri Mapou   BOOKS
(Map p82; ☑ 305-757-9922; www.librerimapou.com; 5919 NE 2nd Ave; ⊙ noon-7pm Fri, Sat & Mon-Wed, to 5pm Sun, closed Thu) Haitian bookshop that specializes in English, French and Creole titles and periodicals.

🏠 Little Havana

Guantanamera   CIGARS
(Map p84; www.guantanameracigars.com; 1465 SW 8th St; ⊙ 10:30am-8pm Sun-Thu, to midnight Fri & Sat) In a central location in Little Havana, Guantanamera sells high-quality hand-rolled cigars, plus strong Cuban coffee. It's an atmospheric shop, where you can stop for a smoke, a drink (there's a bar here) and some friendly banter. There's also live music here most nights. The rocking chairs in front are a fine perch for people-watching.

Havana Collection   CLOTHING
(Map p84; ☑ 786-717-7474; 1421 SW 8th St; ⊙ 10am-6pm) One of the best and most striking collections of *guayaberas* (Cuban dress shirts) in Miami can be found in this shop. Prices are high (plan on spending about $85

LITTLE HAITI'S BOTANICAS

If you pay a visit to Little Haiti, you might notice a few storefronts emblazoned with 'botanica' signs. Not to be confused with a plant store, a *botanica* is a *vodou* shop. *Botanicas* are perhaps the most 'foreign' sight in Little Haiti. Storefronts promise to help in matters of love, work and sometimes 'immigration services,' but trust us, there are no marriage counselors or INS guys in here. As you enter you'll probably get a funny look, but be courteous, curious and respectful and you should be welcomed.

Before you browse, forget stereotypes about pins and dolls. Like many traditional religions, *vodou* recognizes supernatural forces in everyday objects, and powers that are both distinct from and part of one overarching deity. Ergo you'll see shrines to Jesus next to altars to traditional *vodou* deities. Notice the large statues of what look like people; these actually represent *loa* (pronounced lwa), intermediary spirits that form a pantheon below God in the *vodou* religious hierarchy. Drop a coin into a *loa* offering bowl before you leave, especially to Papa Legba, spirit of crossroads and, by our reckoning, travelers.

for shirt), but so is the quality, so you can be assured of a long-lasting product.

Cuba Tobacco Cigar Co CIGARS
(Map p84; www.cubatobaccocigarco.com; 1528 SW 8th St; ⊙10am-5pm) The Bellos family has been making high-quality cigars for over a century. Stop in this tiny welcoming shop to see the hand-rolling in action, and pick up a few smokable souvenirs for that cigar-loving uncle of yours.

🅰 Coconut Grove

Polished Coconut FASHION & ACCESSORIES
(Map p86; 3444 Main Hwy; ⊙11am-6pm Mon-Sat, noon-5pm Sun) 🖉 Colorful textiles from Central and South America are transformed into lovely accessories and home decor at this eye-catching store in the heart of Coconut Grove. You'll find handbags, satchels, belts, sun hats, pillows, bedspreads and table runners made by artisans inspired by traditional indigenous designs.

First Flight Out FASHION & ACCESSORIES
(Map p86; www.thefirstflightout.com; 3015 Grand Ave, CocoWalk; ⊙11am-10pm Mon-Thu, to 11pm Fri-Sun) Inside the CocoWalk shopping gallery, this place sells vintage Pan Am gear – leather satchels, luggage tags, T-shirts and passport covers with that iconic logo from a bygone era of travel. You'll also find swimwear, button-down shirts, summer dresses and other men's and women's clothing, which would pack nicely for today's traveler.

Bookstore in the Grove BOOKS
(Map p86; ☑305-483-2855; www.thebook storeinthegrove.com; 3390 Mary St; ⊙7am-8pm Mon-Thu, to 9pm Fri & Sat, 8am-8pm Sun) Coconut Grove's independent bookstore is a good spot for all kinds of lit, and has a great cafe (including all-day breakfast and some excellent empanadas), and even happy-hour drink specials.

🅰 Coral Gables

Retro City Collectibles MUSIC
(Map p88; ☑786-879-4407; 277 Miracle Mile, 2nd fl; ⊙5-9pm Mon-Thu, noon-7pm Sat & Sun) This cluttered little upstairs store is a fun place to browse, with all manner of eye-catching and collectible Americana. You'll find comic books, records, baseball cards, Pez dispensers, old film posters and action figures (Star Wars, Star Trek, Dr Who etc).

Books & Books BOOKS
(Map p88; ☑305-442-4408; 265 Aragon Ave; ⊙9am-11pm Sun-Thu, to midnight Fri & Sat) The best indie bookstore in South Florida is a massive emporium of all things literary. B&B hosts frequent readings and is generally just a fantastic place to hang out; there's also a good restaurant, with dining on a Mediterranean-like terrace fronting the shop.

Books & Books has other outposts on Lincoln Rd and at the Bal Harbour shops.

Boy Meets Girl CHILDREN'S CLOTHING
(Map p88; ☑305-445-9668; www.bmgkids. com; 358 San Lorenzo Ave, Village of Merrick Park; ⊙10am-9pm Mon-Sat, noon-7pm Sun) Fantastically upscale and frankly expensive clothing for wee ones – if the kids are getting past puberty, look elsewhere, but otherwise they'll be fashionable far before they realize it.

🅰 Key Biscayne

Metta Boutique GIFTS & SOUVENIRS
(Map p90; ☑305-763-8230; 200 Crandon Blvd; ⊙10am-6pm Mon-Sat) 🖉 A cute store that brings some sustainability to Miami. All of the goodies – clothes, journals, accessories, gifts and tchotchkes – are decidedly green/ organic/sustainable/fair trade.

❶ Information

Art Deco Welcome Center (Map p66; ☑305-672-2014; www.mdpl.org; 1001 Ocean Dr, South Beach; ⊙9:30am-5pm Fri-Wed, to 7pm Thu) Run by the Miami Design Preservation League (MDPL), it has tons of art-deco district information and organizes excellent walking tours. There's a **museum** (p58) attached to the center that provides a great overview of the art-deco district.

Greater Miami & the Beaches Convention & Visitors Bureau (Map p72; ☑305-539-3000; www.miamiandbeaches.com; 701 Brickell Ave, 27th fl; ⊙8:30am-6pm Mon-Fri) Offers loads of info on Miami and keeps up-to-date with the latest events and cultural offerings. Located in an oddly intimidating high-rise building.

LGBT Visitor Center (Map p66; ☑305-397-8914; www.gogaymiami.com; 1130 Washington Ave; ⊙9am-6pm Mon-Fri, 11am-4pm Sat & Sun) An excellent source for all LGBT info on Miami, this friendly welcome center has loads of recommendations on sights, restaurants, nightlife and cultural goings-on. Also has meetings and other events.

Check the website for Pink Flamingo–certified hotels, ie hotels that are most welcoming to the LGBT crowd.

Mount Sinai Medical Center (☎ 305-674-2121, emergency room 305-674-2200; www.msmc.com; 4300 Alton Rd; ☺ 24hr) The area's best emergency room. Be aware that you must eventually pay, and fees are high.

ⓘ Getting There & Away

The majority of travelers come to Miami by air, although it's feasible to arrive by car, bus or even train. Miami is a major international airline hub, with flights to many cities across the USA, Latin America and Europe. Most flights come into Miami International Airport (MIA), although many are also directed to Fort Lauderdale-Hollywood International Airport (FLL). Figure 3½ hours from New York City, five hours from Los Angeles, and 10 hours from London or Madrid.

Flights, tours and rail tickets can be booked online at www.lonelyplanet.com/bookings.

AIR

Miami International Airport

Located 6 miles west of Downtown, the busy **Miami International Airport** (MIA; ☎ 305-876-7000; www.miami-airport.com; 2100 NW 42nd Ave) has three terminals and serves over 40 million passengers each year. Around 60 airlines fly into Miami. The airport is open 24 hours and is laid out in a horseshoe design. There are left-luggage facilities on two concourses at MIA, between B and C, and on G; prices vary according to bag size.

From Miami International Airport, taxis charge a flat rate, which varies depending on where you're heading. It's $22 to Downtown, Coconut Grove or Coral Gables; $35 to South Beach; and $44 to Key Biscayne. Count on 40 minutes to South Beach in average traffic, and about 25 minutes to Downtown.

Some hotels offer free shuttles.

Metro buses leave from Miami Airport Station (connected by electric rail to the airport) and run throughout the city; fares are $2.25. The Miami Beach Airport Express (Bus 150) costs $2.65 and makes stops all along Miami Beach, from 41st to the southern tip.

You can also take the **SuperShuttle** (☎ 305-871-8210; www.supershuttle.com) shared-van service, which will cost about $22 to South Beach. Be sure to reserve a seat the day before.

Megabus (p137) offers bus service to Orlando and Tampa. Buses depart from a stop near the airport.

Fort Lauderdale-Hollywood International Airport

Around 26 miles north of Downtown Miami, **Fort Lauderdale-Hollywood International Airport** (FLL; ☎ 866-435-9355; www.broward.org/

airport; 320 Terminal Dr) is a viable gateway airport to the Florida region.

BOAT

Though it's doubtful you'll be catching a steamer to make a trans-Atlantic journey, it is quite possible that you'll arrive in Miami via a cruise ship, as the **Port of Miami** (☎ 305-347-5515; www.miamidade.gov/portmiami), which receives around five million passengers each year, is known as the cruise capital of the world. Arriving in the port will put you on the edge of Downtown Miami; taxis and public buses to other local points are available from nearby Biscayne Blvd.

BUS

For bus trips, **Greyhound** (www.greyhound.com) is the main long-distance operator. **Megabus** (www.us.megabus.com; Miami International Center, 3801 NW 21st St) offers service to Tampa and Orlando.

Greyhound's **main bus terminal** (☎ 305-871-1810; 3801 NW 21st) is near the airport, though additional services also depart from the company's **Cutler Bay terminal** (Cutler Bay; ☎ 305-296-9072; 10801 Caribbean Blvd) and **North Miami terminal** (☎ 305-688-7277; 16000 NW 7th Ave).

If you are traveling very long distances (say, across several states) bargain airfares can sometimes undercut buses. On shorter routes, renting a car can sometimes be cheaper. Nonetheless, discounted (even half-price) long-distance bus trips are often available by purchasing tickets online seven to 14 days in advance.

TRAIN

The main Miami terminal of **Amtrak** (☎ 305-835-1222; www.amtrak.com; 8303 NW 37th Ave, West Little River), about 9 miles northwest of Downtown, connects the city with several other points in Florida (including Orlando and Jacksonville) on the Silver Service line that runs up to New York City. Travel time between New York and Miami is 27 to 31 hours. The Miami Amtrak station is connected by Tri-rail to Downtown Miami and has a left-luggage facility.

ⓘ Getting Around

To/From the Airport
Miami International Airport Taxis charge a flat rate for the 40-minute drive to South Beach ($35). The Miami Beach Airport Express (Bus 150) costs $2.65 and makes stops all along Miami Beach, from 41st to the southern tip. SuperShuttle runs a shared-van service, costing about $22 to South Beach.

Fort Lauderdale-Hollywood International Airport GO Airport Shuttle runs shared vans to Miami, with prices around $25 to South Beach.

A taxi costs around $75 (metered fare) to South Beach and $65 to Downtown.

Bicycle

Citi Bike (☑ 305-532-9494; www.citibike miami.com; 30min/1hr/2hr/4hr/1-day rental $4.50/6.50/10/18/24) is a bike-share program where you can borrow a bike from scores of kiosks spread around Miami and Miami Beach. Miami is flat, but traffic can be horrendous (abundant and fast-moving), and there isn't much biking culture (or respect for bikers) just yet. Free paper maps of the bike network are available at some kiosks, or you can find one online. There's also a handy iPhone app that shows you where the nearest stations are.

For longer rides, clunky Citi Bikes are not ideal (no helmet, no lock and only three gears).

Other rental outfits:

Bike & Roll (p97) Also does bike tours.

Brickell Bikes (☑ 305-373-3633; www. brickellbikes.com; 70 SW 12th St; bike hire 4/8 hours $20/25; ☺10am-7pm Mon-Fri, to 6pm Sat)

Bus

Miami's local bus system is called **Metrobus** (☑ 305-891-3131; www.miamidade.gov/ transit/routes.asp; tickets $2.25) and though it has an extensive route system, service can be pretty spotty. Each bus route has a different schedule and routes generally run from about 5:30am to 11pm, though some are 24 hours. Rides cost $2.25 and must be paid in exact change (coins or a combination of bills and coins) or with an Easy Card (available for purchase from Metrorail stations and some shops and pharmacies). An easy-to-read route map is available online. Note that if you have to transfer buses, you'll have to pay the fare each time if paying in cash. With an Easy Card, transfers are free.

Miami Trolleys

A new free bus service has hit the streets of Miami, Miami Beach, Coconut Grove, Little Havana and Coral Gables, among other locations. The Trolley (www.miamigov.com/trolley) is actually a hybrid-electric bus disguised as an orange and green trolley. There are numerous routes, though they're made for getting around neighborhoods and not *between* them.

The most useful for travelers are the following:

Biscayne Travels along Biscayne Blvd; handy for transport from Brickell to Downtown and up to the edge of Wynwood.

Brickell Connects Brickell area (south of the Miami River in the Downtown area) with the Vizcaya Museum & Gardens.

Coral Way Goes from Downtown (near the Freedom Tower) to downtown Coral Gables.

Wynwood Zigzags through town, from the Adrienne Arsht Center for the Performing Arts up through Wynwood along NW 2nd Ave to 29th St.

Miami Beach Trolleys

Miami Beach has four trolleys (www.miami beachfl.gov/transportation) running along different routes, with arrivals every 10 to 15 minutes from 8am to midnight (from 6am Monday to Saturday on some routes):

Alton-West Loop Runs up (north) Alton Rd and down (south) West Ave between 6th St and Lincoln Rd.

Collins Link Runs along Collins Ave from 37th St to 73rd St. Catch it southbound from Abbott Ave and Indian Creek Dr.

Middle Beach Loop Runs up Collins Ave and down Indian Creek Dr between 20th and 44th Sts (southbound it also zigzags over to Lincoln Rd).

North Beach Loop Runs 65th to 88th St.

Train

The **Metromover** (☑ 305-891-3131; www. miamidade.gov/transit/metromover.asp; ☺5am-midnight Sun-Thu, to 2am Fri & Sat), which is equal parts bus, monorail and train, is helpful for getting around Downtown Miami. It offers visitors a great perspective on the city and a free orientation tour of the area.

Metrorail (www.miamidade.gov/transit/ metrorail.asp; one-way ticket $2.25) is a 21-mile-long heavy-rail system that has one elevated line running from Hialeah through Downtown Miami and south to Kendall/Dadeland. Trains run every five to 15 minutes from 6am to midnight. The one-way fare is $2.25. Pay with either the reloadable Easy Card or single-use Easy Ticket, which are sold from vending machines at Metrorail stations.

The regional **Tri-Rail** (☑ 800-874-7245; www. tri-rail.com) double-decker commuter trains run the 71 miles between Dade, Broward and Palm Beach counties. Fares are calculated on a zone basis; the shortest distance traveled costs $4.40 round-trip; the most you'll ever pay is for the ride between MIA and West Palm Beach ($11.55 round-trip). No tickets are sold on the train, so allow time to make your purchase before boarding. All trains and stations are accessible to riders with disabilities. For a list of stations, log on to the Tri-Rail website.

The Everglades

POP 78,000 / ☎ 305, 736, 239

Best Places to Eat

→ Havana Cafe (p155)

→ Robert is Here (p157)

→ Joanie's Blue Crab Café (p152)

→ Schnebly Redland's Winery (p156)

→ Camellia Street Grill (p155)

→ Oyster House (p155)

Best Places to Sleep

→ Ivey House Bed & Breakfast (p154)

→ Everglades International Hostel (p157)

→ Outdoor Resorts of Chokoloskee (p154)

→ Flamingo Campground (p161)

→ Swamp Cottage (p152)

Why Go?

There is no wilderness in America quite like the Everglades. Called the 'River of Grass' by Native American inhabitants, this is not just a wetland, or a swamp, or a lake, or a river, or a prairie, or a grassland – it is all of the above, twisted together into a series of soft horizons, long vistas, sunsets that stretch across your entire field of vision and the toothy grins of a healthy population of dinosaur-era reptiles.

When you watch anhinga flexing their wings before breaking into a corkscrew dive, or the slow, rhythmic flap of a great blue heron gliding over its domain, or the shimmer of sunlight on miles of untrammeled saw grass as it sets behind hunkering cypress domes, you'll get a glimpse of this park's quiet majesty. In a nation where natural beauty is measured by its capacity for drama, the Everglades subtly, contentedly flows on.

When to Go
Everglades City

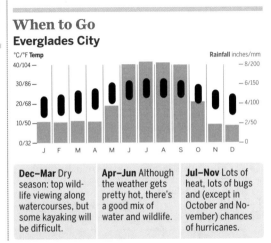

| **Dec–Mar** Dry season: top wildlife viewing along watercourses, but some kayaking will be difficult. | **Apr–Jun** Although the weather gets pretty hot, there's a good mix of water and wildlife. | **Jul–Nov** Lots of heat, lots of bugs and (except in October and November) chances of hurricanes. |

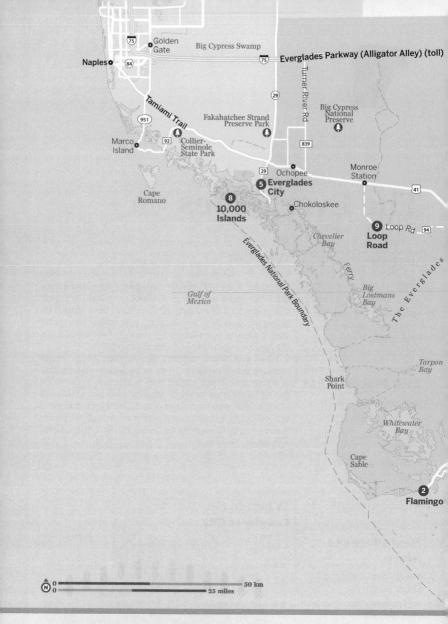

The Everglades Highlights

1 Spotting alligators by day or night, and watching nesting water birds on the **Anhinga Trail** (p159)

2 Hiring a canoe or kayak from **Flamingo** (p160) at the marina and paddling through scenic mangrove-lined waterways.

3 Watching the sun set over the ingress road from the roof of your car at **Pa-hay-okee Overlook** (p160)

4 Walking into the muck at **Slough slog** (p147) amid orchids, birds and towering cypress trees.

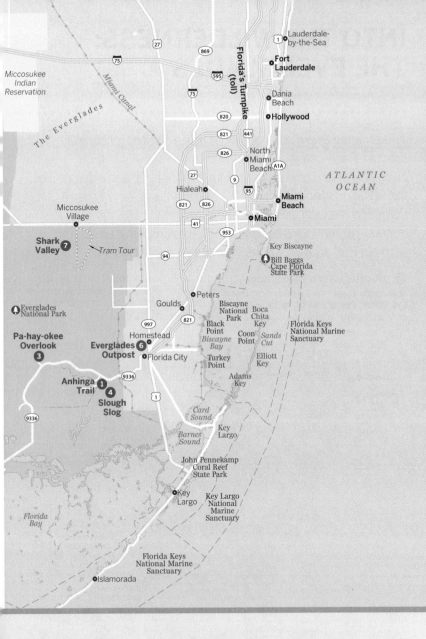

Miccosukee
Indian
Reservation

The Everglades

Miami Canal

Lauderdale-
by-the-Sea

**Fort
Lauderdale**

Florida's Turnpike
(toll)

Dania
Beach

Hollywood

North
Miami
Beach

ATLANTIC
OCEAN

**Miami
Beach**

Miccosukee
Village

Hialeah

Miami

**Shark
Valley** ⑦

Tram Tour

Key Biscayne

Bill Baggs
Cape Florida
State Park

⑨ Everglades
National Park

Peters

Goulds

Biscayne
National
Park

Boca
Chita
Key

**Pa-hay-okee
Overlook**

Homestead

Black
Point

Coon
Point

Sands
Cut

Florida Keys
National Marine
Sanctuary

❸

Biscayne
Bay

**Everglades
Outpost** ⑥

**Anhinga
Trail** ❶

Florida City

Turkey
Point

Elliott
Key

❹

9336

Adams
Key

**Slough
Slog**

9336

①

Card
Sound

Barnes
Sound

Key
Largo

John Pennekamp
Coral Reef
State Park

Florida
Bay

Key
Largo

Key Largo
National
Marine
Sanctuary

Florida Keys
National Marine
Sanctuary

Islamorada

❺ Learning about the
fascinating human settlement
of the Everglades at the
Museum of the Everglades
(p152).

❻ Seeing exotic animal

species – rescued from bad
situations at **Everglades
Outpost** (p156)

⑦ Spying gators and birds
on a bike ride or a tram tour in
Shark Valley (p146)

⑧ Canoeing or kayaking
through the scattered **10,000
Islands** (p154)

⑨ Taking a drive on **Loop
Road** (p150) amid striking
wetland scenery.

INTO THE WILDERNESS: THE EVERGLADES

The enticing Everglades are what make South Florida truly unique. This ecological wonderland is the USA's largest subtropical wilderness, flush with endangered and rare species, including its star attraction, the alligator (and lots of them). It's not just a wetland, swamp, prairie or grassland – it's all of the above, twisted into a series of soft horizons, long vistas and sunsets that stretch across your entire field of vision.

❶ Southeastern Everglades

Begin your Everglades adventure at **Ernest Coe Visitor Center** (p160), with excellent, museum-quality exhibits and tons of information on park activities. Check ahead for a schedule of ranger-led programs, most of which start 4 miles down at **Royal Palm Visitor Center.** (p160) You'll also find the short

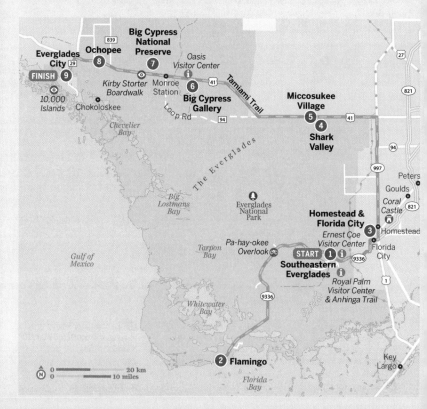

2–3 days; 170 miles/274km

Great for... Outdoors; Families

Best Time to Go December to April for weather and wildlife.

Anhinga Trail (p159) here that offers astounding wildlife-watching opportunities.

Heading further into the park, several trails and scenic viewpoints give you a closer look at the park, including **Pa-hay-okee Overlook** (p160), a raised platform that peeks over one of the prettiest bends in the river of grass, and the challenging Christian Point Trail, which runs through mangrove forest, prairie and hardwood hammock to the edge of Florida Bay.

The Drive > Continue southwest on SR 9336, which takes you past long fields of marsh prairie, white, skeletal forests of bald cypress and dark clumps of mahogany hammock. The Flamingo Visitor Center is 34 miles south of Royal Palm.

❷ Flamingo

You've come this far, and for your efforts you're rewarded with the opportunity to canoe into the bracken heart of the swamp. Hit the **Flamingo Visitor Center** (p159) for a map of local canoe trails, such as Nine Mile Pond, a 5.5-mile loop that leads you into Florida Bay. You can rent canoes and kayaks at **Flamingo Marina** (☑239-695-3101; ⊙store 7am-5:30pm Mon-Fri, from 6am Sat & Sun), and be transported to various trailheads for an additional fee. While you're at the marina, it's worth sticking around to see if any manatees show up. This is also a great spot to see the rare American crocodile.

The Drive > Head back the way you came in; it's the only way out. Six miles past Ernest Coe Visitor Center, go north on Tower Rd. You'll pass Robert Is Here and then Homestead is just a few miles further up.

❸ Homestead & Florida City

Every good road trip needs a kooky tourist attraction, and thus Homestead – in addition to being a good base of operations for the southeastern portion of the Everglades – humbly offers up the **Coral Castle** (p156), which isn't a castle at all but a monument to both unrequited love and all that is weird and wacky about southern Florida.

In the early 20th century, a Latvian man who had been left at the altar channeled his grief into building a sculpture garden out of more than 1000 tons of coral rock. That he did it by himself, in the dead of night (when it was cooler), using no heavy machinery imbues the place with a sense of mystery. At the very least, it's an impressive feat of engineering.

The Drive > Head 20 miles due north on FL 997/177th Ave until you hit the Tamiami Trail, aka US 41. Shark Valley is 18 miles west. Look for alligators (unless you're driving) in the canal that runs alongside the road.

❹ Shark Valley

Alligators, alligators and more alligators! If that's what you've come to find, you won't be disappointed at **Shark Valley** (p146). Kick back and enjoy the view during an excellent two-hour **tram tour** (p146) that follows a 15-mile asphalt trail where you'll see copious amounts of alligators in the winter months.

Not only do you get to experience the park from the shady comfort of a breezy tram, but the tour is narrated by knowledgeable park rangers who give a fascinating overview of the Everglades and its inhabitants. Halfway along the trail the tour stops long enough to let you climb a 50ft-high observation tower, an out-of-place concrete structure that offers a dramatic panorama of the park.

The Drive > Exiting the park, turn left onto Tamiami Trail, then immediately turn back off again. The Miccosukee Village is just past the park entrance.

❺ Miccosukee Village

Not so much a quaint little Native American village as it is a handful of commercial ventures, the Miccosukee Village nonetheless offers insight into Native American life in the Everglades. The centerpiece of the village is the **Miccosukee Indian Museum** (p147), just half a mile down the road from Shark Valley.

Informative and entertaining, this open-air museum showcases the culture of the Miccosukee via guided tours of traditional homes, a crafts gift store, dance and music performances, and live alligator shows in which a tribal member wrestles with a gator, while sharing enlightening facts about these prehistoric creatures. Afterward, visitors are invited to have their picture taken holding a wee gator.

Across the road, catch an airboat ride that includes a stop at a Miccosukee camp that's more than 100 years old.

The Drive > Continuing west on Tamiami Trail, you'll pass trees, trees and more trees. After about 20 minutes you'll see Big Cypress Gallery on your left.

6 Big Cypress Gallery

If you're torn as to the relative beauty of the Everglades, stop by the **Big Cypress Gallery** (p150), featuring the stunning, black-and-white photography of Clyde Butcher. The photographer has been capturing the essence of the Everglades for over 40 years, and there's something about seeing his large-scale prints – some of which are taller than you are – that will make you see the Everglades in a whole new way.

The Drive > The Oasis Visitor Center is on the right, less than a mile west of Big Cypress Gallery.

7 Big Cypress Preserve

North of the Tamiami Trail you'll find this enormous undeveloped preserve that's integral to the Everglades' ecosystem. Encompassing 1139 sq miles, the preserve is indeed big, so where to start? Orient yourself at the **Oasis Visitor Center** (p152). In addition to trail maps you'll find great exhibits for the kids and an outdoor, water-filled ditch popular with alligators.

Further down Tamiami Trail, but still part of the preserve, you'll find the Kirby Storter Boardwalk, a short elevated stroll through a mature cypress dome replete with orchids, bromeliads and the possibility of wildlife that makes you glad it's elevated.

The Drive > Keep going: your next stop is 16 miles west of the Oasis Visitor Center (and 8 miles past Kirby Storter Boardwalk).

8 Ochopee

In tiny Ochopee, you'll find the **Skunk Ape Research Headquarters** (p151), a tongue-in-cheek endeavor dedicated to finding the southeastern USA's version of Bigfoot. The gift shop stocks all your skunk-ape necessities, and there's even a reptile and bird zoo in back run by a true Florida eccentric, the sort of guy who wraps albino pythons around his neck for fun. While there, look into **Everglades Adventure Tours** (p151), offering some of the best private tours of the Everglades, led by some funny guys with great local knowledge.

Ochopee is also home to the Smallest Post Office in the United States, a comically tiny edifice with very limited hours (you try sitting in there for more than a few hours a day). It's a fun photo op, and a great place to mail a postcard.

The Drive > Just over 4 miles west of the post office, turn left onto CR 29 and go 3 miles to reach the not-so-booming town of Everglades City.

9 Everglades City

One of the best ways to experience the serenity of the Everglades is by paddling the network of waterways that skirt the northwest portion of the park. Somehow desolate yet lush, tropical and foreboding, the 10,000 Islands consist of many (but not really 10,000) tiny islands and a mangrove swamp that hugs the southwesternmost border of Florida.

Most islands are fringed by narrow beaches with sugar-white sand, but note that the water is brackish, and very shallow most of the time. It's not Tahiti, but it's fascinating. The Wilderness Waterway, a 99-mile path between Everglades City and Flamingo, is the longest canoe trail in the area. Look for canoe rentals and guided boat trips at the **Gulf Coast Visitor Center** (p153).

Top Alligators, Big Cypress Preserve

Bottom Ochopee Post Office

EVERGLADES NATIONAL PARK

The vast wilderness of Everglades National Park (☎ 305-242-7700; www.nps.gov/ever; 40001 SR-9336, Homestead; vehicle pass $25; ⊘ visitor center 9am-5pm; ♿), encompassing 1.5 million acres, is one of America's great natural treasures. As a major draw for visitors to South Florida, there's much to see and do. You can spy alligators basking in the noonday sun as herons stalk patiently through nearby waters in search of prey, go kayaking amid tangled mangrove canals and on peaceful lakes, or wade through murky knee-high waters amid cypress domes on a rough-and-ready 'slough slog.'

There are sunrise strolls on boardwalks amid the awakening glimmers of birdsong, and moonlit glimpses of gators swimming gracefully along narrow channels in search of dinner. There's backcountry camping, bicycle tours and ranger-led activities that help bring the magic of this place to life.

The big challenge is deciding where to begin. There are three main entrances and three main areas of the park: one along the southeast edge near Homestead and Florida City (Ernest Coe section); a second at the central-north side on the Tamiami Trail (Shark Valley section); and a third at the northwest shore (Gulf Coast section), past Everglades City. The Shark Valley and Gulf Coast sections of the park come one after the other in geographic succession, but the Ernest Coe area is entirely separate. The admission fee ($25 for a vehicle pass, or $8 if you're a cyclist) covers the whole park, and is good for seven consecutive days.

Tamiami Trail

Calle Ocho, in Miami's Little Havana, happens to be the eastern end of the Tamiami Trail/US 41, which cuts through the Everglades to the Gulf of Mexico. So go west, young traveler, along US 41, a few dozen miles and several different worlds away from the city where the heat is on. This trip leads you onto the northern edges of the park, past long landscapes of flooded forest, gambling halls, swamp-buggy tours, roadside food shacks and other Old Florida accoutrements.

As you head west you'll see fields and fields of pine forest and billboards advertising swamp tours. Airboat tours are an old-school way of seeing the Everglades (and there is something to be said for getting a tour from a raging Skynyrd fan with killer tatts and better camo), but there are other ways of exploring the park as well.

◉ Sights

Shark Valley   PARK
(☎ 305-221-8776; www.nps.gov/ever/planyourvisit/svdirections.htm; 36000 SW 8th St, N 25°45.27.60', W 80°46.01.01'; car/cyclist/pedestrian $25/8/8; ⊘ 9am-5pm; ℗♿) ✐ Shark Valley sounds like it should be the headquarters for the villain in a James Bond movie, but it is in fact a slice of National Park Service grounds heavy with informative signs and knowledgeable rangers. Shark Valley is located in the cypress, and hardwood and riverine section of the Everglades, a more traditionally jungly section of the park than the grassy fields and forest domes surrounding the Ernest Coe visitor center.

A 15-mile (24km) paved trail takes you past small creeks, tropical forest and 'borrow pits' (human-made holes that are now basking spots for gators, turtles and birdlife). The pancake-flat trail is perfect for bicycles, which can be rented at the entrance for $9 per hour. Bring water with you.

If you don't feel like exerting yourself, the most popular and painless way to immerse yourself in the Everglades is via the two-hour tram tour (☎ 305-221-8455; www.sharkvalleytramtours.com; adult/child under 12yr/senior $25/19/12.75; ⊘ departures 9:30am, 11am, 2pm, 4pm May-Dec, 9am-4pm Jan-Apr hourly on the hour) that runs along Shark Valley's entire 15-mile trail. If you only have time for one Everglades activity, this should be it, as guides are informative and witty, and you'll likely see gators sunning themselves on the road. Halfway along the trail is the 50ft-high Shark Valley Observation Tower, an ugly concrete tower that offers dramatically beautiful views of the park.

At the park entrance, the easy Bobcat Boardwalk Trail (0.5 miles) makes a loop through a thick copse of tropical hardwoods before emptying you out right back into the Shark Valley parking lot. A little ways past is the Otter Cave Trail (0.25 miles); which heads over a limestone shelf that has been Swiss-cheesed into a porous sponge by rainwater. Animals now live in the eroded holes (although it's not likely you'll spot any) and Native Americans used to live on top of the shelf.

Fakahatchee Strand Preserve   PARK
(☎239-695-4593; www.floridastateparks.org/
fakahatcheestrand; 137 Coastline Dr, Copeland; ve-
hicle/pedestrian/bicycle $3/2/2; ⊙8am-sunset;
P♿) 🖊 The Fakahatchee Strand, besides
having a fantastic name, also houses a 20-
mile by 5-mile estuarine wetland that could
have emerged directly out of the *Jurassic
Park* franchise. A 2000ft boardwalk trav-
erses this wet and wild wonderland, where
panthers still stalk their prey amid the
black waters. While it's unlikely you'll spot
any panthers, there's a great chance you will
see a large variety blooming orchids, bird
life and reptiles ranging in size from tiny
skinks to grinning alligators.

Miccosukee Indian Village   MUSEUM
(☎305-552-8365; www.miccosukee.com; Mile
70, Hwy 41; adult/child/5yr & under $12/6/free;
⊙9am-5pm; P♿) Just west of the turnoff
to Shark Valley, this 'Indian Village' is an
informative open-air museum that showcases the culture of the Miccosukee via guided tours of traditional homes, a crafts gift
store, dance and music performances, and
an airboat ride (additional $20) into a ham-
mock-cum-village of raised *chickee* (wooden
platforms built above the waterline) huts.
There's also an alligator 'wrestling' show.
Thankfully this is more respectful than it
sounds, and is more of a nature demonstra-
tion of this iconic reptile.

Miccosukee Resort & Casino   CASINO
(☎305-222-4600; www.miccosukee.com; 500 SW
177th Ave) Here the long-storied legacy of the
nation's indigenous peoples has culminated
in...slots. Lots of slots, and comatose gam-
blers pouring quarters into them. Still the
Miccosukee and Seminole are cashing in on
this stuff, so more power to them.

ℹ Information

Shark Valley Visitor Center (☎305-221-8776;
www.nps.gov/ever/planyourvisit/svdirections.
htm; national park entry per vehicle/bicycle/
pedestrian $25/8/8; ⊙9am-5pm) A good
place to pick up information about the Everglades, including trails, wildlife watching and
free ranger-led activities.

ℹ Getting There & Away

The Tamiami Trail (US 41) can be accessed in
Miami. You'll need a car to get out this way and
explore. The entrance to Shark Valley is about
40 miles west of Downtown Miami.

Big Cypress & Ochopee

The better part of the Tamiami Trail is
fronted on either side by long cypress trees
overhung with moss. There's endless vistas
of soft prairie, which are flooded in the wet
season into a boggy River of Grass.

BEST FREE PARK ACTIVITIES
....

The $25 entrance fee for the Everglades National Park may seem steep, but it's great
value if you take advantage of the park's many free ranger-led activities. Reserve popular
activities (canoeing, biking) up to one week in advance. Among the highlights:

Slough slog Escape the crowds and immerse yourself in the wilderness on a fascinat-
ing 1–2 mile guided walk/wade through muddy and watery terrain into a cypress dome.
Wear long pants, socks and lace-up shoes that can get wet. Meets at Royal Palm Visitor
Center.

Starlight walk Evening walk along the Anhinga Trail (p159) looking for gators and other
creatures by nightfall. Bring a flashlight (torch).

Bike hike A 2½-hour bike ride exploring the Everglades on two wheels. Bikes and helmets
provided. Departs from Ernest Coe Visitor Center.

Canoe the wilderness A three-hour morning paddle through some of the Everglades'
most sublime scenery. Meets at Flamingo Visitor Center and at Gulf Coast Visitor Center.

Early bird walk Join for a morning hike looking for, and learning about, some of the
Everglades' feathered species. Meets at Flamingo Visitor Center.

Glades glimpse Learn about some of the wonders of the Everglades on a daily talk
given by rangers at the Royal Palm Visitor Center and at the Shark Valley Visitor Center
(typically from 1:30pm to 2pm).

THE EVERGLADES: AN OVERVIEW

It's tempting to think of the Everglades as a swamp, but 'prairie' may be a more apt description. The Glades, at the end of the day, are grasslands that happen to be flooded for most of the year: visit during the dry season (winter) and you'd be forgiven for thinking the Everglades was the Everfields.

So where's the water coming from? Look north on a map of Florida, all the way to Lake Okeechobee and the small lakes and rivers that band together around Kissimmee. Florida dips into the Gulf of Mexico at its below-sea-level tip, which happens to be the lowest part of the state geographically and topographically. Run-off water from central Florida flows down the peninsula via streams and rivers, over and through the Glades, and into Florida Bay. The glacial pace of the flood means this seemingly stillest of landscapes is actually in constant motion. Small wonder the Calusa Indians called the area Pa-hay-okee (grassy water). Beloved conservationist Marjory Stoneman Douglas (1890–1998) called it the River of Grass; in her famous book of the same title, she revealed that Gerard de Brahm, a colonial cartographer, named the region the River Glades, which became Ever Glades on later English maps.

So what happens when nutrient-rich water creeps over a limestone shelf? The ecological equivalent of a sweaty orgy. Beginning at the cellular level, organic material blooms in surprising ways, clumping and forming into algal beds, nutrient blooms and the ubiquitous periphyton, which are basically clusters of algae, bacteria and detritus (ie stuff). Periphyton ain't pretty: in the water they resemble puke streaks and the dried version looks like hippo turds. But you should kiss them when you see them (well, maybe not) because in the great chain of the Everglades, this slop forms the base of a very tall organic totem pole. The smallest tilt in elevation alters the flow of water and hence the content of this nutrient soup, and thus the landscape itself: all those patches of cypress and hardwood hammock (not a bed for backpackers; in this case, hammock is a fancy Floridian way of saying a forest of broadleaf trees, mainly tropical or subtropical) are areas where a few inches of altitude create a world of difference between biosystems.

Fight for the Green Grassy Waters

The Everglades were utter wilderness for thousands of years. Even Native Americans avoided the Glades; the 'native' Seminole and Miccosukee actually settled here as exiles escaping war and displacement from other parts of the country. But following European settlement of Florida, some pioneers saw the potential for economic development of the Grassy Waters.

Cattle ranchers and sugar growers, attracted by mucky waters and Florida's subtropical climate (paradise for sugarcane), successfully pressured the government to make land available to them. In 1905 Florida governor Napoleon Bonaparte Broward personally dug the first shovelful of a diversion that connected the Caloosahatchee River to Lake Okeechobee. Hundreds of canals were cut through the Everglades to the coastline to 'reclaim' the land, and the flow of lake water was restricted by a series of dikes. Farmland began to claim areas previously uninhabited by humans.

Unfortunately the whole 'River of Grass' needs the river to survive. And besides being a pretty place to watch the birds, the Everglades acts as a hurricane barrier and kidney. Kidney? Yup: all those wetlands leached out pollutants from the Florida Aquifer (the state's freshwater supply). But when farmland wasn't diverting the sheet flow, it was adding fertilizer-rich wastewater to it. Result? A very sweaty (and well-attended) biological orgy. Bacteria, and eventually plant life, bloomed at a ridiculous rate (they call it fertilizer for a reason), upsetting the fragile balance of resources vital to the Glades' survival.

Enter Marjory Stoneman Douglas, stage left. Ms Douglas gets the credit for almost single-handedly pushing the now age-old Florida issue of Everglades conservation.

Despite the tireless efforts of Douglas and other environmentalists, today the Florida Aquifer is in serious danger of being contaminated and drying up. The number of wading birds nesting has declined by 90% to 95% since the 1930s. Currently there are over 60 threatened and endangered plant and animal species in the park.

The diversion of water away from the Glades and run-off pollution are the main culprits behind the region's environmental degradation. This delicate ecosystem is the neighbor of one of the fastest-growing urban areas in the USA. The current water-drainage system in South Florida was built to handle the needs of two million people; the local population topped six million in 2010. And while Miami can't grow north or south into Fort Lauderdale or Homestead, it can move west, directly into the Everglades. At this stage, scientists estimate the wetlands have been reduced by 50% to 75% of their original size.

Humans are not the only enemy of the Everglades. Nature has done its share of damage as well. During 2005's Hurricane Wilma, for example, six storm water treatment areas (artificial wetlands that cleanse excess nutrients out of the water cycle) were lashed and heavily damaged by powerful winds. Without these natural filtration systems, the Glades are far more susceptible to nutrient blooms and external pollution. Wildfires also leave ever-increasing swaths of devastation across the state each year. In 2016 nearly 4000 acres went up in flames near Long Pine Key.

Restoration of the Everglades

Efforts to save the Everglades began in the late 1920s, but were sidelined by the Great Depression. In 1926 and 1928, two major hurricanes caused Lake Okeechobee to overflow; the resulting floods killed hundreds. The Army Corps of Engineers did a really good job of damming the lake. A bit too good: the Glades were essentially cut off from their source, the Kissimmee watershed.

In the meantime, conservationists began donating land for protection, starting with 1 sq mile of land donated by a garden club. The Everglades was declared a national park in 1947, the same year Marjory Stoneman Douglas' *The Everglades: River of Grass* was published.

By draining the wetlands through the damming of the lake, the Army Corps made huge swaths of inland Florida inhabitable. But the environmental problems created by shifting water's natural flow, plus the area's ever-increasing population, now threaten to make the whole region uninhabitable. The canal system sends, on average, over 1 billion gallons of water into the ocean every day. At the same time, untreated run-off flows unfiltered into natural water supplies. Clean water is disappearing from the water cycle while South Florida's population gets bigger by the day.

Enter the Comprehensive Everglades Restoration Plan (CERP; www.everglades restoration.gov). CERP is designed to address the root of all Everglades issues: water – where to get it, how to divert it and ways to keep it clean. The plan is to unblock the Kissimmee, restoring remaining Everglades lands to predevelopment conditions, while maintaining flood protection, providing freshwater for South Florida's populace and protecting earmarked regions against urban sprawl. It sounds great, but political battles have significantly slowed the implementation of CERP. The cost of the project has increased over the years, and a mix of political red tape and maneuvering courtesy of federal and state government has delayed CERP's implementation.

Not to throw another acronym at you, but a major portion of the CERP is the Central Everglades Planning Project (CEPP), the rare public works project that is supported by environmentalists and industry alike. The CEPP's aim is to clean polluted water from Florida's agricultural central heartland and redirect it towards the Everglades. The River of Grass would be re-watered, and toxic run-off would no longer flow to the sea. In a bit of good news for the 'Glades, in 2016 the US Congress approved $976 million of funding for CEPP as part of its *Water Infrastructure Improvements for the Nation Act*.

Bringing back the Everglades is one of the biggest, most ambitious environmental restoration projects in US history; one that combines the needs of farmers, fishers, urban residents, local governments and conservationists. The success or failure of the program will be a bellwether for the future of the US environmental movement.

OFF THE BEATEN TRACK

DETOUR: LOOP ROAD

The 24-mile long Loop Rd, off Tamiami Trail (Hwy 41), offers some unique sites. One: the homes of the Miccosukee, some of which have been considerably expanded by gambling revenue. You'll see some traditional chickee-style huts and some trailers with massive add-on wings that are bigger than the original trailer – all seem to have shiny new pickup trucks parked out front. Two: great pull-offs for viewing flooded forests, where egrets that look like pterodactyls perch in the trees, and alligators lurk in the depths below. Three: houses with large Confederate flags and 'Stay off my property' signs; these homes are as much a part of the landscape as the swamp. And four: the short, pleasantly jungly Tree Snail Hammock Nature Trail. Though unpaved, the graded road is in good shape and fine for 2WD vehicles. True to its name, the road loops right back onto the Tamiami; expect a leisurely jaunt on the Loop to add an hour or two to your trip.

◉ Sights & Activities

Big Cypress National Preserve PARK
(☑239-695-4758; www.nps.gov/bicy; 33000 Tamiami Trail E; ⊙24hr; P 🚻) 🎣 FREE The 1139-sq-mile Big Cypress Preserve (named for the size of the park, not its trees) is the result of a compromise between environmentalists, cattle ranchers and oil-and-gas explorers. The area is integral to the Everglades' ecosystem: rains that flood the Preserve's prairies and wetlands slowly filter down through the Glades. About 45% of the cypress swamp (actually mangrove islands, hardwood hammocks, orchid flowers, slash pine, prairies and marshes) is protected.

Great bald cypress trees are nearly gone, thanks to pre-Preserve lumbering, but dwarf pond cypress trees fill the area with their own understated beauty. The helpful Oasis Visitor Center (p152), about 20 miles west of Shark Valley, has great exhibits for the kids and a water-filled ditch that's popular with alligators.

Ah-Tah-Thi-Ki Seminole Indian Museum MUSEUM
(☑877-902-1113; www.ahtahthiki.com; Big Cypress Seminole Indian Reservation, 34725 West Boundary Rd, Clewiston; adult/child/senior $10/7.50/7.50; ⊙9am-5pm) If you want to learn about Florida's Native Americans, come to the Ah-Tah-Thi-Ki Seminole Indian Museum, 17 miles north of I-75. All of the excellent educational exhibits on Seminole life, history and the tribe today were founded on gaming proceeds, which provide most of the tribe's multimillion-dollar operating budget.

The museum is located within a cypress dome cut through with an interpretive boardwalk, so from the start it strikes a balance between environmentalism and education. The permanent exhibit has several dioramas with life-sized figures depicting various scenes out of traditional Seminole life, while temporary exhibits have a bit more academic polish (past ones have included lengthy forays into the economic structure of the Everglades). There's an old-school 'living village' and re-created ceremonial grounds as well. The museum is making an effort to not be a cheesy Native American theme park, and the Seminole tribe has gone to impressive lengths to achieve this.

Kirby Storter Roadside Park NATURE RESERVE
(www.nps.gov/bicy/planyourvisit/kirby-storter-roadside-park.htm; ⊙24hr) FREE Though short in size (1 mile total out and back) this elevated boardwalk leads to a lovely overlook where you can often see a variety of birdlife (ibis and red-shouldered hawks) amid tall cypresses and strangler figs, plus of course alligators.

Big Cypress Gallery GALLERY
(☑239-695-2428; www.clydebutcher.com; 52388 Tamiami Trail; ⊙10am-5pm; P) 🎣 This gallery showcases the work of Clyde Butcher, an American photographer who follows in the great tradition of Ansel Adams. His large-format black-and-white images elevate the swamps to a higher level. Butcher has found a quiet spirituality in the brackish waters. You'll find many gorgeous prints, which make fine mementos from the Everglades experience (though prices aren't cheap).

Private 1½-hour swamp tours through the muck are offered, but the high prices (from $380 for a group of four) keep most would-be swamp-goers away, especially since the national-park service offers free swamp walks out of the Royal Palm Visitor Center.

Skunk Ape Research Headquarters PARK
(☑ 239-695-2275; www.skunkape.info; 40904 Tamiami Trail E; adult/child $12/6; ⊙ 9am-5pm; P) This only-in-Florida roadside attraction is dedicated to tracking down southeastern USA's version of Bigfoot, the eponymous Skunk Ape (a large gorilla-man who supposedly stinks to high heaven). We never saw a Skunk Ape, but you can see a corny gift shop and, in the back, a reptile-and-bird zoo run by a true Florida eccentric, the sort of guy who wraps albino pythons around his neck for fun.

The little zoo is good fun for kids, with tiny alligators and (non-venomous) snakes you can hold, and various large birds, including a blushing blue-and-gold macaw named Patches, and a screechy cockatoo named Sassy. There's also a 22ft Burmese python and a few tortoises.

Ochopee VILLAGE
(38000 Tamiami Trail E, N°25.54.4.64', W°-81.17.50.42'; ⊙ 8-10am & noon-4pm Mon-Fri, 10-11:30am Sat) Drive to the hamlet of Ochopee (population about four)...no...wait...turn around, you missed it! Then pull over and break out the cameras: Ochopee's claim to fame is the country's smallest post office. It's housed in a former toolshed and set against big park skies; a friendly postal worker patiently poses for snapshots.

Florida National Scenic Trail HIKING
(☑ 850-523-8501; www.fs.usda.gov/fnst) There are some 31 miles of the Florida National Scenic Trail within Big Cypress National Preserve. From the southern terminus, which can be accessed via Loop Rd, the trail runs 8.3 miles north to US 41. The way is flat, but it's hard going: you'll almost certainly be wading through water, and you'll have to pick through a series of solution holes (small sinkholes) and thick hardwood hammocks.

There is often no shelter from the sun, and the bugs are...plentiful. There are three primitive campsites with water wells along the trail; pick up a map and a free hiking permit (required) at the Oasis Visitor Center (p152). Most campsites are free, and you needn't register. Monument Lake (p152) has water and toilets.

☞ Tours

Everglades Adventure Tours TOURS
(EAT; ☑ 800-504-6554; www.evergladesadventure tours.com; 40904 Tamiami Trail E; 2hr canoe/pole-boat tour per person $89/109) We already like the EAT guys for being based out of the same headquarters as the Skunk Ape people; we like them even more for offering some of the best private Everglades tours. Swamp hikes, 'safaris,' night tours and being poled around in a canoe or skiff by some genuinely funny guys with deep local knowledge of the Grassy Waters; it's an absolute treat.

THE EVERGLADES TAMIAMI TRAIL

AIRBOATS & SWAMP BUGGIES

Airboats are flat-bottomed skiffs that use powerful fans to propel themselves through the water. Their environmental impact has not been determined, but one thing is clear: airboats can't be doing much good, which is why they're not allowed in the park. Swamp buggies are enormous balloon-tired vehicles that can go through wetlands, creating ruts and damaging wildlife.

Airboat and swamp-buggy rides are offered all along US Hwy 41 (Tamiami Trail). It's recommended to think twice before going on a 'nature' tour. Loud whirring fanboats and marsh jeeps really don't do the quiet serenity of the Glades justice. That said, many tourists in the Everglades are there (obviously) because of their interest in the environment, and they demand environmentally knowledgeable tours. The airboat guys are pretty good at providing these – their livelihood is also caught up in the preservation of the Glades, and they know the backcountry well. We recommend going with the guys at **Coopertown** (☑ 305-226-6048; www.coopertownairboats.com; 22700 SW 8th St; adult/child $23/11; ⊙ 9am-5pm; ♿), one of the first airboat operators you encounter heading west on 41. Just expect a more touristy experience than the national park grounds.

EAT has set up a campsite at Skunk Ape HQ (p151); it costs $25 to camp here ($30 with electricity) and there's wi-fi throughout the camp.

Sleeping & Eating

Swamp Cottage   COTTAGE **$$**
(☎239-695-2428; www.clydebutcher.com/big-cypress/vacation-rentals; 52388 Tamiami Trail; cottage $250-350; 🅿🛜) 🌿 Want to get as close to the swamp as possible without giving up on the amenities? Book a few nights in a bungalow or a two-bedroom cottage, tucked amid lush greenery behind the Big Cypress Gallery (p150). The lodging is comfortably appointed, if not luxurious, and is certainly cozy, though the best feature is having one of America's great wetlands right outside your door.

Monument Lake   CAMPGROUND **$**
(www.recreation.gov; 50215 Tamiami Trail E; tent/RV site per night $24/28; ⊗Aug 15-Apr 15) Reserve months ahead to book one of 10 tent sites (or 26 RV sites) at this appealing campground in the Big Cypress National Preserve. The lake looks quite enticing, but there's no swimming (alligators live here after all).

Joanie's Blue Crab Café   AMERICAN **$$**
(☎239-695-2682; www.joaniesbluecrabcafe.com; 39395 Tamiami Trail E; mains $12-17; ⊗11am-5pm Thu-Tue; closed seasonally, call to confirm; 🌿) This quintessential shack, east of Ochopee, with open rafters, shellacked picnic tables and alligator kitsch, serves filling food of the 'fried everything' variety on paper plates. Crab cakes are the thing to order. There's live music on Saturdays and Sundays from 12:30pm and a rockabilly-loving jukebox at other times.

ℹ Information

Big Cypress Swamp Welcome Center
(☎239-695-4758; www.nps.gov/bicy/planyourvisit/big-cypress-swamp-welcome-center.htm; 33000 Tamiami Trail E; ⊗9am-4:30pm) About 2.5 miles east of the turnoff to Everglades City, this big visitor center is a good one for the kids, with a small nature center where you can listen to recordings of different swamp critters. There's also a viewing platform overlooking a canal where you can sometimes spot manatees. Good spot for information on the reserve.
Oasis Visitor Center (☎239-695-1201; www.nps.gov/bicy; 52105 Tamiami Trail E; ⊗9am-4:30pm; ♿) This visitor center has hands-on exhibits and info on nearby walks in the Big Cypress National Preserve. A platform overlooking a small water-filled ditch is a great spot to see alligators, particularly in the dry season (December to May).

ℹ Getting There & Away

The Oasis Visitor Center is about 20 miles west of the Shark Valley entrance. All of the places mentioned above are spaced along the Tamiami Trail (US 41). There is no public transportation out this way.

Everglades City & Chokoloskee Island

On the edge of Chokoloskee Bay, you'll find an old Florida fishing village of raised houses, turquoise water and scattershot emerald-green mangrove islands. 'City' is an ambitious name for Everglades City, but this is a friendly fishing town where you can easily lose yourself for a day or three. You'll find some intriguing vestiges of the past here, including an excellent regional museum, as well as delicious seafood.

Hwy 29 runs south through town onto the small, peaceful residential island of Chokoloskee, which has some pretty views over the watery wilderness of the 10,000 Islands. You can arrange boating excursions from either Everglades City or Chokoloskee to explore this pristine environment.

◉ Sights

★**Museum of the Everglades**   MUSEUM
(☎239-695-0008; www.evergladesmuseum.org; 105 W Broadway, Everglades City; ⊗9am-4pm Mon-Sat; 🅿) **FREE** For a break from the outdoors, don't miss this small museum run by kindhearted volunteers, who have a wealth of knowledge on the region's history. Located in the town's formerly laundry house, the collection delves into human settlement in the area from the early pioneers of the 1800s to the boom days of the 1920s and its tragic moments (Hurricane Donna devastated the town in 1960), and subsequent transformation into the quiet backwater of today.

Smallwood Store   MUSEUM
(☎239-695-2989; www.smallwoodstore.com; 360 Mamie St, Chokoloskee; adult/child $5/free; ⊗10am-5pm Dec-Apr, 11am-5pm May-Nov) Perched on piers overlooking Chokoloskee Bay, this wooden building dates back to

GLADES GUARDIAN

In a state known for iconoclasts, no one can hold a candle to Marjory Stoneman Douglas – not just for her quirks, but for her drive. A persistent, unbreakable force, she fueled one of the longest conservation battles in US history.

Born in 1890, Douglas moved to Florida after her failed first marriage. She worked for the *Miami Herald* and eventually as a freelance writer, producing short stories that are notable for both the quality of the writing and their progressive themes: *Plumes* (1930) and *Wings* (1931), published in the *Saturday Evening Post,* addressed the issue of Glades bird-poaching when the business was still immensely popular (the feathers were used to decorate ladies' hats).

In the 1940s Douglas was asked to write about the Miami River for the Rivers of America Series and promptly chucked the idea in favor of capturing the Everglades in her classic, *The Everglades: River of Grass*. Like all of Douglas' work, the book is remarkable for both its exhaustive research and lyrical, rich language.

River of Grass immediately sold out of its first print run, and public perception of the Everglades shifted from 'nasty swamp' to 'national treasure.' Douglas went on to be an advocate for environmental causes, women's rights and racial equality, fighting, for example, for basic infrastructure in Miami's Overtown.

Today she is remembered as Florida's favorite environmentalist. Always immaculately turned out in gloves, dress, pearls and floppy straw hat, she would bring down engineers, developers, politicians and her most hated opponents, sugar farmers; by force of her oratory alone. She kept up the fight, speaking and lecturing without fail, until she died in 1998 at the age of 108.

Today it seems every environmental institution in Florida is named for Douglas, but were she around, we doubt she'd care for those honors. She'd be too busy planting herself in the CERP office, making sure everything was moving along on schedule.

1906, when a pioneer by the name of Ted Smallwood opened his rustic trading post, post office and general store. The wooden shelves are lined with antiques and old artifacts, along with descriptions of events and characters from those rough and tumble days of life on a remote island frontier.

👉 Tours

Everglades Adventures　　　　CANOEING
(📞877-567-0679; www.evergladesadventures. com; 107 Camellia St, Everglades City; 3/4hr tour from $89/99, canoe/kayak rental per day from $35/49) 🌿 For a real taste of the Everglades, nothing beats getting out on the water. This highly recommended outfitter offers a range of half-day kayak tours, from sunrise paddles to twilight trips through mangroves that return under a sky full of stars.

Smallwood Store Boat Tour　　　BOATING
(📞239-695-0016; www.smallwoodstoreboattour. com; 360 Mamie St, Chokoloskee; 1hr tour $40; 🚹) Departing from a dock below the Smallwood Store, this small family-run outfit offers excellent private tours taking you out

among the watery wilderness of the 10,000 Islands. You'll see lots and lots of birds, and more than likely a few bottlenose dolphins, who enjoy swimming through the boat's wake.

Gulf Coast Visitor Center　　　BOATING
(📞239-695-2591; www.evergladesnationalpark boattoursgulfcoast.com; 815 Oyster Bar Lane, off Hwy 29; canoe/single kayak/tandem kayak per day $38/45/55; ⏱9am-4:30pm mid-Apr–mid-Nov, from 8am mid-Nov–mid-Apr; 🚹) 🌿 This is the northwestern-most ranger station for Everglades National Park, and provides access to the 10,000 Islands area. Boat tours, lasting just under two hours, depart from the downstairs marina and go either into the mangrove wilderness (adult/child $48/25) or out among the green islands ($38/20), where if you're lucky you may see dolphins springing up beside your craft.

Keep an eye out for manatees in the marina. It's great fun to go kayaking and canoeing around here; boats can be rented from the marina, but be sure to take a map with you (they're available in the visitor center). Boaters will want to reference NOAA Charts 11430 and 11432.

✦ Festivals & Events

Everglades Seafood Festival   FOOD & DRINK
(www.evergladesseafoodfestival.org; ⊘ Feb) In Everglades City, this three-day festival features plenty of feasting, as well as kiddie rides and live music. The star of the show is of course glorious seafood – stone crab, conch fritters, crab cakes, coconut shrimp, mussels and calamari – though there's also fried gator, frog's legs, pulled-pork barbecue and key lime pie on a stick!

🛌 Sleeping

Outdoor Resorts of Chokoloskee   MOTEL $
(☎239-695-2881; www.outdoorresortsofchokolo skee.com; 150 Smallwood Dr, Chokoloskee; r $119; ❄ ⛱) At the northern end of Chokoloskee Island, this good-value place is a big draw for its extensive facilities, including several swimming pools, hot tubs, tennis and shuffleboard courts, a fitness center and boat rentals. The fairly basic motel-style rooms have kitchenettes and a back deck overlooking the marina.

Parkway Motel & Marina   MOTEL $
(☎239-695-3261; www.parkwaymotelandmarina. com; 1180 Chokoloskee Dr, Chokoloskee; r $110-150; P ❄) A friendly couple runs this veritable testament to the old-school Floridian lodge: cute small rooms and one cozy apartment in a one-story motel building. It's in a peaceful spot on the island of Chokoloskee, and owners Bill and Greci have a wealth of knowledge on the region.

Everglades City Motel   MOTEL $$
(☎239-695-4224; www.evergladescitymotel. com; 310 Collier Ave, Everglades City; r $150-250; P ❄ 🛜) With large renovated rooms that have all the mod cons (think flat-screen TVs, fridge, coffeemaker) and friendly staff that can hook you up with boat tours, this motel provides good value for those looking to spend some time near the 10,000 Islands.

Ivey House Bed & Breakfast   B&B $$
(☎877-567-0679; www.iveyhouse.com; 107 Camellia St, Everglades City; inn $100-180, lodge $90-100, cottage $180-230; P ❄ 🛜 ⛱) This friendly, family-run tropical inn offers a variety of well-appointed accommodations: bright spacious inn rooms overlooking a pretty courtyard, cheaper lodge rooms (with shared bathrooms) and a freestanding two-bedroom cottage with a kitchen and screened-in porch. The pool (covered in winter) is a great year-round option for a swim.

This is a top place to book nature trips (p153), from daytime paddles to six-day packages that including lodging, tours and some meals.

🍴 Eating

Sweet Mayberry's   CAFE $
(☎239-695-0092; www.sweetmayberryscafe. com; 207 W Broadway Ave, Everglades City; salads & wraps $10-12; ⊘9am-4pm Tue-Sat; 🛜 ✏) The best cafe in town (not that there's much competition), Sweet Mayberry's is

---

10,000 ISLANDS

One of the best ways to experience the serenity of the Everglades – somehow desolate yet lush, tropical and foreboding – is by paddling the network of waterways that skirt the northwest portion of the park. The 10,000 Islands consist of many (but not really 10,000) tiny islands and a mangrove swamp that hugs the southwestern-most border of Florida.

The Wilderness Waterway, a 99-mile path between Everglades City and Flamingo, is the longest canoe trail in the area, but there are shorter trails near Flamingo. Most islands are fringed by narrow beaches with sugar-white sand, but note that the water is brackish, and very shallow most of the time. It's not Tahiti, but it's fascinating. You can camp on your own island for up to a week.

Getting around the 10,000 Islands is pretty straightforward if you're a competent navigator and you religiously adhere to National Oceanic & Atmospheric Administration (NOAA) tide and nautical charts. Going against the tides is the fastest way to make a miserable trip. The Gulf Coast Visitor Center (p153) sells nautical charts and gives out free tidal charts. You can also purchase charts prior to your visit – call ☎305-247-1216 and ask for charts 11430, 11432 and 11433.

an easygoing charmer, with friendly staff whipping up breakfast bagels, tasty home-made wraps, decadent desserts (try the carrot cake) and proper espressos. Have a seat on the front porch and make yourself at home.

Triad Seafood Cafe   SEAFOOD $
(☑ 239-695-0722; www.triadseafoodmarketcafe.com; 401 School Dr, Everglades City; mains $10-17, stone-crab meals $26-44; ⊙10:30am-6pm Sun-Thu, to 7pm Fri & Sat) Triad is famous for its stone-crab claws, but they serve up all kinds of coastal seafood that you can enjoy on picnic tables perched over the water-front. Should you impress the friendly own-ers with your ability to devour crustaceans (their claws anyway), you get the dubious honor of having your picture hung on the Glutton Board.

★Havana Cafe   LATIN AMERICAN $$
(☑ 239-695-2214; www.havanacafeoftheever Glades.com; 191 Smallwood Dr, Chokoloskee; mains lunch $10-19, dinner $22-30; ⊙7am-3pm Mon-Thu, to 8pm Fri & Sat, closed mid-Apr–mid-Oct) The Havana Cafe is famed far and wide for its deliciously prepared seafood served up with Latin accents. Lunch favorites include stone-crab enchiladas, blackened grouper with rice and beans, and a decadent Cuban sand-wich. The outdoor dining amid palm trees and vibrant bougainvillea – not to mention the incredibly friendly service – adds to the appeal.

Reservations are essential on Friday and Saturday nights, when foodies from out of town arrive for stone-crab feasts. Order in advance the astonishingly good seafood pa-ella or seafood pasta – both $50 but serving at least two people.

★Camellia Street Grill   SEAFOOD $$
(☑ 239-695-2003; 202 Camellia St, Everglades City; mains $13-26; ⊙noon-9pm; ☑) In a barn-like setting with fairy lights strung from the rafters and nautical doodads lining the walls, Camellia is an easygoing spot for a down-home seafood feast. Come before sun-set to enjoy the pretty views from the water-front deck. Don't miss the tender stone-crab claws in season.

Other dishes range from fried baskets of catfish, grouper or shrimp to heartier plates of grilled seafood, barbecue ribs or shrimp and grits. There are also crab-cake sand-wiches, fish tacos and homemade veggie wraps.

Oyster House   SEAFOOD $$
(☑ 239-695-2073; www.oysterhouserestaurant. com; 901 Copeland Ave, Everglades City; mains lunch $12-18, dinner $19-30; ⊙11am-9pm Sun-Thu, to 10pm Fri & Sat; ☑ 🖨) Besides serving the Everglades staples of excellent seafood (oysters, crab, grouper, cobia, lobster), this buzzing, family-run spot serves up alliga-tor dishes (tacos, jambalaya, fried plat-ters) and simpler baskets (burgers, fried seafood), plus not-to-be-missed desserts. The cabin-like interior is decorated with vintage knickknacks and taxidermy, which might make you feel like you're in the deep woods.

🛈 Information

Everglades Area Chamber of Commerce
(☑ 239-695-3941; cnr US Hwy 41 & Hwy 29; ⊙9am-4pm) General information about the region is available here.

🛈 Getting There & Away

There is no public transit out this way. If driving, it's a fairly straight 85-mile drive west from Miami. The trip takes about 1¾ hours in good traffic.

Southern Everglades

Head south of Miami to drive into the heart of the park and the best horizons of the Everglades. Plus there are plenty of side paths and canoe creeks for memorable detours. You'll see some of the most qui-etly exhilarating scenery the park has to offer on this route, and you'll have better access to an interior network of trails for those wanting to push off the beaten track into the buggy, muggy solar plexus of the wetlands.

Homestead & Florida City

Homestead and neighboring Florida City, two miles to the south, aren't of obvious ap-peal upon arrival. Part of the ever-expanding subdivisions of South Miami, this bustling corridor can feel like an endless strip of big-box shopping centers, fast-food joints, car dealerships and gas stations. However, look beneath the veneer and you'll find much more than meets the eye: strange curiosi-ties like a 'castle' built single-handedly by one lovestruck immigrant, an animal rescue center for exotic species, a winery showcas-ing Florida's produce (hint: it's not grapes), an up-and-coming microbrewery, and one of the best farm stands in America. Not to mention that this area makes a great base for forays into the stunning Everglades National Park.

Sights & Activities

★ Coral Castle   CASTLE
(📷 305-248-6345; www.coralcastle.com; 28655 S Dixie Hwy; adult/senior/child $18/15/8; ☺ 8am-6pm Sun-Thu, to 8pm Fri & Sat) 'You will be seeing unusual accomplishment,' reads the inscription on the rough-hewn quarried wall. That's an understatement. There is no greater temple to all that is weird and wacky about South Florida. The legend: a Latvian gets snubbed at the altar. Comes to the USA and settles in Florida. Handcarves, unseen, in the dead of night, a monument to unrequited love.

This rock-walled compound includes a 'throne room,' a sun dial, a stone stockade (an intended 'timeout area' for the child he would never have), a telescope of sorts trained precisely on Polaris, and a revolving boulder gate that can be easily opened with one hand. Even more incredible: all this was built by one small man – the 5ft-tall, 100-pound Edward Leedskalnin – working alone without heavy machinery. He accomplished all this using pulleys, hand tools and other improvised devices, and it took him 28 years to complete his great rock masterpiece.

Schnebly Redland's Winery   WINERY
(📷 305-242-1224; www.schneblywinery.com; 30205 SW 217th Ave; wine tastings/tours $13/8; ☺ 10am-5pm Mon-Thu, to 11pm Fri & Sat, noon-5pm Sun) Tucked along a quiet farm road west of Homestead, Schnebly Redland's Winery has the unusual distinction of being the southernmost winery in America. Given the climate, you won't find malbec, pinot noir or zinfandel here. The name of the game is fruit. Wines here are made of mango, passion fruit, lychee, avocado, coconut and other flavors from the tropics, and are surprisingly good.

Everglades Outpost   WILDLIFE RESERVE
(📷 305-562-8000; www.evergladesoutpost.org; 35601 SW 192nd Ave; adult/child $12/8; ☺ 10am-5:30pm Mon, Tue & Fri-Sun, by appointment Wed & Thu) The Everglades Outpost houses, feeds and cares for wild animals that have been seized from illegal traders, abused, neglected or donated by people who could not care for them. Residents of the outpost include a lemur, wolves, a black bear, a zebra, cobras, alligators and a pair of majestic tigers (one of whom was bought by an exotic dancer who thought she could incorporate it into her act). Your money goes into helping the outpost's mission.

Fruit & Spice Park   PARK
(📷 305-247-5727; www.redlandfruitandspice.com; 24801 SW 187th Ave, Homestead; adult/child/under 6yr $8/2/free; ☺ 9am-5pm; 🅿) Set just on the edge of the Everglades, this 35-acre public park grows all those great tropical fruits you usually have to contract dysentery to enjoy. The park is divided into 'continents' (Africa, Asia etc) and it makes for a peaceful wander past various species bearing in total around 500 different types of fruits, spices and nuts. Unfortunately you can't pick the fruit, but you can eat anything that falls to the ground (go early for the best gathering!).

Downtown Homestead   AREA
(📷 305-323-6564; www.homesteadmainst.org; Krome Ave) You could pass a mildly entertaining afternoon walking around Homestead's almost quaint main street, which essentially comprises a couple of blocks of Krome Ave extending north and south of the Historic Town Hall (📷 305-242-4463; www.townhall museum.org; 41 N Krome Ave; ☺ 1-5pm Tue-Sat). The town hosts one big monthly event from September to April, including concerts, food fests, holiday parades and other events at Losner Park (across the street from the Historic Town Hall). It's a good effort at injecting some character into downtown Homestead.

Garls Coastal
Kayaking Everglades   KAYAKING
(www.garlscoastalkayaking.com; 19200 SW 344th St; single/double kayak per day $40/55, half-/full-day tour $125/150) On the property of the Robert Is Here (p157) fruit stand, this outfitter leads highly recommended excursions into the Everglades. A full-day outing includes hiking (more of wet walk/slog into the lush landscape of cypress domes), followed by kayaking in both the mangroves and in Florida Bay, and, time permitting, a night walk.

For a DIY adventure, you can also hire kayaks as well as other gear – including tents, sleeping bags and fishing gear.

WILDERNESS CAMPING

Three types of **backcountry campsites** (☑ 239-695-2945, 239-695-3311; www.nps.gov/ever/planyourvisit/backcamp.htm; permit Nov-Apr/May-Oct $15/free, plus per person per night $2) are available: beach sites, on coastal shell beaches and in the 10,000 Islands; ground sites, which are basically mounds of dirt built up above the mangroves; and *chickees*; wooden platforms built above the waterline where you can pitch a free-standing (no spikes) tent. *Chickees*, which have toilets, are the most civilized – there's a serenity found in sleeping on what feels like a raft levitating above the water. Ground sites tend to be the most bug-infested.

Warning: if you're paddling around and see an island that looks pleasant for camping but isn't a designated campsite, beware – you may end up submerged when the tides change.

Some backcountry tips:

➡ Store food in a hand-sized, raccoon-proof container (available at gear stores).

➡ Bury your waste at least 10in below ground, but keep in mind some ground sites have hard turf.

➡ Use a backcountry stove to cook. Ground fires are only permitted at beach sites, and you can only burn dead or downed wood.

🛏 Sleeping

★ **Everglades International Hostel** HOSTEL $

(☑ 305-248-1122; www.evergladeshostel.com; 20 SW 2nd Ave, Florida City; camping per person $18, dm $30, d $61-75, ste $125-225; P ❄ 🛜 🛋) Located in a cluttered, comfy 1930s boarding house, this friendly hostel has good-value dorms, private rooms and 'semi-privates' (you have an enclosed room within the dorms and share a bathroom with dorm residents). The creatively configured backyard is the best feature.

There's a tree house; a small rock-cut pool with a waterfall; a Bedouin pavilion that doubles as a dance hall; a gazebo; an open-air tented 'bed room'; and an oven built to resemble a tail-molting tadpole. It all needs to be seen to be believed, and best of all you can crash anywhere in the back for $15. Sleep in a tree house! We should add the crowd is made up of free-spirited international types that made you fall in love with traveling in the first place, and the hostel leads excellent tours into the Everglades.

Hotel Redland HOTEL $

(☑ 305-246-1904; www.hotelredland.com; 5 S Flagler Ave, Homestead; r $110-150; ❄ 🛜) On the edge of Homestead's quaint downtown, the Hotel Redland is set in a 1904 building that has a warm, cozy vibe thanks to its gracious hosts. The 12 rooms are comfortable, but dated in a charming, grandmotherly way (quilted bedspreads, floral curtains, old photos or framed paintings on the walls).

🍴 Eating & Drinking

★ **Robert Is Here** MARKET $

(☑ 305-246-1592; www.robertishere.com; 19200 SW 344th St, Homestead; juices $7-9; ⊗ 8am-7pm) 🍴 More than a farmers' stand, Robert's is an institution. This is Old Florida at its kitschy best, in love with the Glades and the agriculture that surrounds it. You'll find loads of exotic, Florida-grown fruits you won't elsewhere – including black sapote, carambola (star fruit), dragon fruit, sapodilla, guanabana (soursop), tamarind, sugar apples, longans and passion fruit. The juices are fantastic.

There's also a petting zoo and water-play area for the kids (bring your own towels), live music on weekends and plenty of homemade preserves and sauces. Plus Robert is there every day, working the counter and giving insight into these delectable tropical riches.

Gator Grill AMERICAN $

(☑ 786-243-0620; 36650 SW 192nd Ave; mains $9-16; ⊗ 11am-6:30pm) A handy pit stop before or after visiting the Everglades National Park, the Gator Grill is a white shack with picnic tables, where you can munch on all manner of alligator dishes. There are gator tacos,

PYTHONS, GATORS & CROCS, OH MY!

Gators

Alligators are common in the park, although not so much in the 10,000 Islands, as they tend to avoid saltwater. If you do see an alligator, it probably won't bother you unless you do something overtly threatening or angle your boat between it and its young. If you hear an alligator making a loud hissing sound, get the hell out of Dodge. That's a call to other alligators when a young gator is in danger. Finally, never feed an alligator – it's stupid and illegal.

Crocs

Crocodiles are less common in the park, as they prefer coastal and saltwater habitats. They are more aggressive than alligators, however, so the same rules apply. With perhaps only a few hundred remaining in the USA, they are also an endangered species.

Panthers

The Florida panther is critically endangered, and although it is the state's official animal its survival in the wild is by no means assured. There are an estimated 120 to 230 panthers left in the wild, and although that number has increased from around 20 to 30 since the 1980s, it's not cause for big celebration either. As usual, humans have been the culprits behind this predator's demise. Widespread habitat reduction (ie the arrival of big subdivisions) is the major cause of concern. In the past, poor data on panther populations and the approval of developments that have been harmful to the species' survival have occurred; environmental groups contend the shoddy information was linked to financial conflicts of interest. Breeding units, which consist of one male and two to five females, require about 200 sq miles of ground to cover, and that often puts panthers in the way of one of Florida's most dangerous beasts: drivers. Some 31 panthers were killed by cars in 2016.

If you're lucky enough to see one, Florida panthers are rather magnificent brown hunting cats (they are, in fact, cougars). They are extremely elusive and only inhabit 5% of their historic range. Many are relatively concentrated in Big Cypress National Preserve (p150).

Weather

Thunderstorms and lightning are more common in summer than in winter. But in summer the insects are so bad you won't want to be outside anyway. In emergency weather, rangers will search for registered campers, but under ordinary conditions they won't unless they receive information that someone's missing. If camping, have a friend or family member ready to contact rangers if you do not report back by a certain day.

Insects

You can't overestimate the problem of mosquito and no-see-ums (tiny biting flies) in the Everglades; they are, by far, the park's worst feature. While in most national parks there are warning signs showing the forest-fire risk, here the charts show the mosquito level (call ☑ 305-242-7700 for a report). In summer and fall, the sign almost always says 'extremely high.' You'll be set upon the second you open your car door. The only protections are 100% DEET or, even better, a pricey net suit.

Snakes in a Glade!

There are four types of poisonous snake in the Everglades: diamondback rattlesnake (Crotalus adamanteus); pigmy rattlesnake (Sistrurus miliarius); cottonmouth or water moccasin (Agkistrodon piscivorus conanti), which swims along the surface of water; and the coral snake (Micrurus fulvius). Wear long thick socks and lace-up boots – and keep the hell away from them. Oh, and now there are Burmese pythons prowling the water too. Pet owners who couldn't handle the pythons have dumped the animals into the swamp, where they've adapted like...well, a tropical snake to a subtropical forest. The python is an invasive species that is badly mucking up the natural order of things. In 2017 one Palm Beach Post reporter even stumbled upon (and subsequently filmed) one large python devouring an alligator just off the Loop Rd.

gator stir fry, gator kebabs and straight-up fried alligator served in a basket.

Rosita's
MEXICAN $

(☑ 305-246-3114; www.rositasrestaurantfl.com; 199 W Palm Dr, Florida City; mains $8-12; ⊗ 8:30am-9pm) There's a working-class Mexican crowd here, testament to the sheer awesomeness of the tacos and burritos. Everyone is friendly, and the mariachi music adds a festive vibe to the place.

Miami Brewing Company
BREWERY

(☑ 305-242-1224; www.miamibrewing.org; 30205 SW 217th Ave; ⊗ noon-5pm Sun-Thu, to 11pm Fri & Sat) You'll find first-rate craft brews in this enormous warehouse-style tasting room. The brewers here bring more than a hint of Floridian accents in beers like Shark Bait mango wheat ale, Big Rod coconut blond ale and Vice IPA with citrus notes. There's big screens for game days, a pool table, outdoor picnic tables and live music (or DJs) on weekends.

There are also seasonal brews like pumpkin ale, spiced winter ale and a creamy stout with a hint of French vanilla. It's in the same complex (and under the same ownership) as the Schnebly Redland's Winery (p156).

❶ Information

Tropical Everglades Visitor Association (160 N 1st St, Florida City; ⊗ 8am-5pm Mon-Sat, 10am-2pm Sun) Just off the S Dixie Hwy in Florida City, this is the best place in the area for getting info on activities, sites, lodging and dining.

Chamber of Commerce (☑ 305-247-2332; www.southdadechamber.org; 455 N Flagler Ave, Homestead; ⊗ 9am-5pm Mon-Fri) Pick up local info on the area here.

❶ Getting There & Away

Homestead runs a free weekend **trolley bus service** (☑ 305-224-4457; www.cityofhomestead.com; ⊗ Sat & Sun Dec-Apr), which takes visitors from Losner Park (downtown Homestead) out to the **Royal Palm Visitor Center** (p160) in Everglades National Park. It also runs between Losner Park and Biscayne National Park (p161). Call for the latest departure times.

Southern Everglades Highway

As you go past Homestead and Florida City, the farmland loses its uniformity and the flat land becomes more tangled, wild and studded with pine and cypress. In a few miles, you'll reach the entrance post to the southern Everglades. This road is packed with sites, including short nature trails full of great wildlife-watching opportunities, narrow waterways for canoeing, and scenic ponds and lakes. The road ends at Flamingo, where you can arrange boat tours out into Florida Bay, take a coastal walk or simply hang out around the dock looking for manatees and alligators. The 38-mile drive between the park entrance (near Ernest Coe Visitor Center) and Flamingo takes just under an hour, though you could spend many days doing activities (hiking, night walks, canoeing) in this stretch of the national park.

◎ Sights & Activities

★ Anhinga Trail
NATURE RESERVE

(⊗ 24hr) If you do just one walk in the Everglades, make sure it's on the Anhinga Trail. Gators sun on the shoreline, anhinga spear their prey and wading birds stalk haughtily through the reeds. You'll get a close-up view of wildlife on this short (0.8 mile) trail at the Royal Palm Visitor Center. There are various overlooks, where you can sometimes see dozens of alligators piled together in the day.

Come back at night (be sure to bring a flashlight) for a view of the gators swimming along the waterways - sometimes right beside you. The park offers periodic ranger-led walks along the boardwalk at night, though you can always do it yourself. Seeing the glittering eyes of alligators prowling the waterways by flashlight is an unforgettable experience!

Flamingo Visitor Center
VISITOR CENTER

(☑ 239-695-2945; www.nps.gov/ever; State Rd 9336; ⊗ 8am-4:30pm mid-Nov–mid-Apr) At the end of State Rd 9336 is the Flamingo Visitor Center, which overlooks a marina and the watery wilderness beyond. The chief draw here is taking either a boat tour or hiring a kayak or canoe – all arranged through the Flamingo Marina (p160), a short stroll from the visitor center. Do spend some time hanging out near the water's edge. This is a great place for seeing manatees, alligators and even the rare American crocodile.

If you prefer to stay on land, you can hike along the Coastal Prairie Trail (7.5 miles one way) or the shorter, more scenic Bayshore Loop Trail (2 miles) – both reached through the campground. You can

SCENIC HIKES

State Rd 9336 cuts through the soft heart of the park, past long fields of marsh prairie, white, skeletal forests of bald cypress and dark clumps of mahogany hammock. There are plenty of trails to detour down; all of the following are half a mile long. **Mahogany Hammock** leads into an 'island' of hardwood forest floating on the waterlogged prairie, while the **Pinelands** takes you through a copse of rare spindly swamp pine and palmetto forest. Further on, **Pa-hay-okee Overlook** is a raised platform that peeks over one of the prettiest bends in the River of Grass. The **West Lake Trail** runs through the largest protected mangrove forest in the northern hemisphere. Further down you can take a good two-hour, 1.8-mile hike to **Christian Point**. This dramatic walk takes you through several Glades environments: under tropical forest, past columns of white cypress and over a series of mudflats (these are particularly attractive on gray, cloudy days), and ends with a dramatic view of the windswept shores of Florida Bay.

also look for birds (and gators) along the half-mile trail that circles around nearby Eco Pond.

Royal Palm Visitor Center PARK
(☎305-242-7700; www.nps.gov/ever; State Rd 9336; ⊗9am-4:15pm) Four miles past Ernest Coe Visitor Center, Royal Palm offers the easiest access to the Glades in these parts. Two trails, the Anhinga and **Gumbo Limbo** (the latter named for the gumbo-limbo tree, also known as the 'tourist tree' because its bark peels like a sunburned Brit), take all of an hour to walk and put you face to face with a panoply of Everglades wildlife.

Ernest Coe Visitor Center VISITOR CENTER
(☎305-242-7700; www.nps.gov/ever; 40001 State Rd 9336; ⊗9am-5pm mid-Apr–mid-Dec, from 8am mid-Dec–mid-Apr) Near the entrance to the Everglades National Park, this friendly visitor center has some excellent exhibits, including a diorama of 'typical' Floridians (the fisherman looks like he should join ZZ Top).

Flamingo Marina
Rentals & Boat Tours BOATING
(☎239-696-3101; www.evergladesnationalpark boattoursflamingo.com; tours per adult/child $38/18, canoe rental 2/4/8hr $20/28/38, kayak rental half/full day $35/45; ⊗marina 7am-7pm, from 6am Sat & Sun) The most isolated portion of the park is a squat marina where you can go on a backcountry boat tour or rent boats. Due to its isolation, this area is subject to closure during bad weather. You can rent kayaks and canoes here; if you do, you're

largely left to explore the channels and islands of Florida Bay on your own.

Hell's Bay Canoe Trail KAYAKING
Despite the frightening name (and terrible mosquitoes), this can be a magnificent place to kayak. 'Hell to get into and hell to get out of' was how this sheltered launch was described by old Gladesmen, but once inside you'll find a fairly enchanted world: a capillary network of mangrove creeks, saw-grass islands and shifting mudflats, where the brambles form a green tunnel and all you can smell is sea salt and the dark organic breath of the swamp.

Three chickee sites are spaced along the trail. You'll need to pick up a backcountry permit, available at park visitor centers, to camp at one of them. If you're traveling without a boat, you can hire one in Flamingo.

🛏 Sleeping

National Park
Service Campsites CAMPGROUND $
(NPS; www.nps.gov/ever/planyourvisit/camping.htm; campsite $20) There are campgrounds run by the NPS located throughout the park. Sites are fairly basic, though there are showers and toilets. Depending on the time of year, the cold water can be either bracing or a welcome relief. The NPS information offices provide a map of all campsites, as does the park website.

There are also many backcountry campsites ($2 per night). For these you'll also need a permit ($15) and to reserve ahead (at the visitor center) before disembarking. Sites are free during the off season (May to October). Note that these sites are accessible only by canoe or kayak (excepting one site reachable on foot from Flamingo).

Flamingo Campground
CAMPGROUND $

(☑877-444-6777; www.nps.gov/ever/planyourvisit/flamcamp.htm; per campsite without/with electricity $20/30) There are over 200 camping sites at the Flamingo Visitor Center, some of which have electrical hookups. Escape the RVs by booking a walk-in site. Reserve well ahead (via www.reserveamerica.com) for one of the nine waterfront sites.

Long Pine Key Campground
CAMPGROUND $

(☑305-242-7700; www.nps.gov/ever/planyourvisit/longpinecamp.htm; per campsite $20; ⊙closed Jun–mid-Nov) This is a good bet for car campers, just west of Royal Palm Visitor Center. It has 108 sites, available on a first-come basis (no reservations).

BISCAYNE NATIONAL PARK

Just to the east of the Everglades is Biscayne National Park (☑305-230-1144, boat tour 786-335-3644; www.nps.gov/bisc; 9700 SW 328th St; boat tour adult/child $35/25; ⊙7am-5:30pm), or the 5% of it that isn't underwater. In fact, a portion of the world's third-largest reef sits here off the coast of Florida, along with mangrove forests and the northernmost Florida Keys.

A bit shadowed by the Everglades, Biscayne requires a little extra planning, but you get a lot more reward for your effort. The offshore keys, accessible only by boat, offer pristine opportunities for camping. Generally summer and fall are the best times to visit the park; you'll want to snorkel when the water is calm. This is some of the best reef-viewing and snorkeling you'll find in the USA, outside Hawaii and nearby Key Largo.

Fortunately this unique 300-sq-mile park is easy to explore independently with a canoe, or via a boat tour.

Biscayne National Park may not be far from Miami, but it feels like a world removed. Encompassing a vibrant swath of biologically rich coral reef, this park is teeming with life – though you'll have to head on a boat tour, or better yet don snorkel and mask, to see it firsthand. Manatees, dolphins and sea turtles are just a few inhabitants of this diverse ecosystem.

There are also over 500 species of reef fish. Meanwhile, above the surface you'll find neotropical water birds and migratory species.

The best introduction to the area is a boat tour, offered by the park, with a ranger giving an overview of the wildlife and history of the area. Three-hour cruises depart once or twice a day on select Thursdays, Fridays and Saturdays from the Dante Fascell Visitor Center (p162). Call to confirm times and book a spot.

⊙ Sights & Activities

NEC-FLO Paddlesports
KAYAKING

(☑305-390-0393; www.necflo.com; Biscayne National Park, 9700 SW 328th St; ⊙9am-5pm Wed-Sun) This outfit hires out kayaks from its location in Biscayne National Park. Inquire here about boat tours too.

Maritime Heritage Trail
DIVING

The Maritime Heritage Trail takes 'hikers' through one of the only trails of its kind in the USA. If you've ever wanted to explore a sunken ship, this may well be the best opportunity in the country. Six are located within the park grounds; the trail experience involves taking visitors out, by boat, to the site of the wrecks where they can swim and explore among derelict vessels and clouds of fish.

There are even waterproof information site cards placed among the ships. Three of the vessels are suited for scuba divers, but the others – particularly the *Mandalay,* a lovely two-masted schooner that sank in 1966 – can be accessed by snorkelers. Miami outfitters like South Beach Diver & Surf Center (☑305-531-6110; www.southbeachdivers.com; 850 Washington Ave; 2-tank dive trip without/with gear from $90/140, surfboard hire 4hr/all day $30/35; ⊙9am-7pm Mon-Sat, 10am-6pm Sun) lead excursions here.

⊂⇒ Tours

Biscayne National Park Sailing
BOATING

(☑561-281-2689; www.biscaynenationalparksailing.com; 2½/6hr cruise per person $59/149) One of the best ways to experience Biscayne National Park is on this sailing adventure that departs Convoy Point. Full-day sailing trips depart at 10am and cruise along the bay, stopping at Boca Chita or Adams Key, followed by lunch (an extra $25 or you can bring your own), then snorkeling or paddle-boarding in a peaceful spot, and the home-ward journey, arriving around 4pm.

Although somewhat pricey, the tour gets rave reviews from those who've made the trip. Two-person minimum, six-people maximum.

🛏 Sleeping & Eating

Primitive camping (site per night $25, May-Sep free) is available on Elliott and Boca Chita Keys, though you'll need a boat to get there. No-see-ums (tiny flies) are invasive, and their bites are devastating. Make sure your tent is devoid of minuscule entry points.

No food is available in the park, though nearby you'll find an outdoor restaurant at Homestead's Bayfront Park and Marina. You'll find more dining options (and places to pick up supplies) in Florida City, roughly 9 miles west of the park.

ℹ Information

Dante Fascell Visitor Center (🖉 305-230-1144; www.nps.gov/bisc; 9700 SW 328th St; ⊙ 9am-5pm) Located at Convoy Point, this center shows a great introductory film for an overview of the park, and has maps, informa-tion and excellent ranger-led activities. The grounds around the center are a popular picnic spot on weekends and holidays, especially for families from Homestead. Also showcases local artwork. This is the departure point for park-led boat tours.

ℹ Getting There & Away

To get here, you'll have to drive about 9 miles east of Homestead (the way is pretty well sign-posted) on SW 328th St (North Canal Dr) into a long series of green-and-gold flat fields and marsh.

Florida Keys & Key West

POP 77,482 / ☎ 305, 786

Best Places to Eat

➡ Lazy Days (p176)

➡ Square Grouper (p183)

➡ Keys Fisheries (p179)

➡ Key Largo Conch House (p173)

➡ No Name Pub (p182)

Best Places to Sleep

➡ Kona Kai Resort (p172)

➡ Seascape Motel & Marina (p179)

➡ Bay Harbor Lodge (p172)

➡ Deer Run Bed & Breakfast (p182)

➡ Mermaid & the Alligator (p191)

Why Go?

If Florida is a state apart from the USA, the Keys are islands apart from Florida – in other words, it's different down here. This is a place where those who reject everyday life on the mainland escape. What do they find? About 113 mangrove-and-sandbar islands where the white sun melts over tight fists of deep green mangroves; long, gloriously soft mudflats and tidal bars; water as teal as Arizona turquoise; and a bunch of people often like themselves: freaks, geeks and lovable weirdos all.

Key West is still defined by its motto – One Human Family – an ideal that equals a tolerant, accepting ethos where anything goes and life is always a party (or at least a hungover day after). The color scheme: watercolor pastels cooled by breezes on a sunset-kissed Bahamian porch. Welcome to the End of the USA.

When to Go
Key West

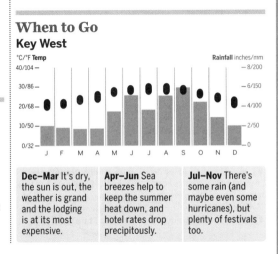

Dec–Mar It's dry, the sun is out, the weather is grand and the lodging is at its most expensive.

Apr–Jun Sea breezes help to keep the summer heat down, and hotel rates drop precipitously.

Jul–Nov There's some rain (and maybe even some hurricanes), but plenty of festivals too.

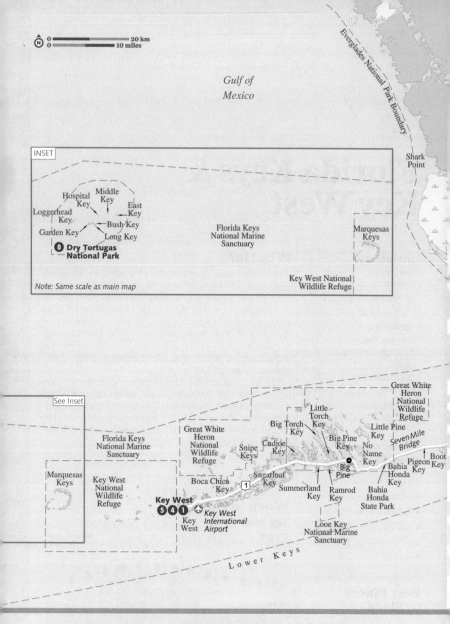

Florida Keys & Key West Highlights

❶ Watching the sun set over the ocean as you sit and take in the raucous show at **Mallory Square** (p184)

❷ Diving around the rainbow reefs at **John Pennekamp Coral Reef State Park** (p170)

❸ Paddling out to the eerie, lonely, beautiful **Indian Key Historic State Park** (p174)

❹ Donning a purple-and-green crocodile costume and partying in the streets of Key West during **Fantasy Fest** (p190)

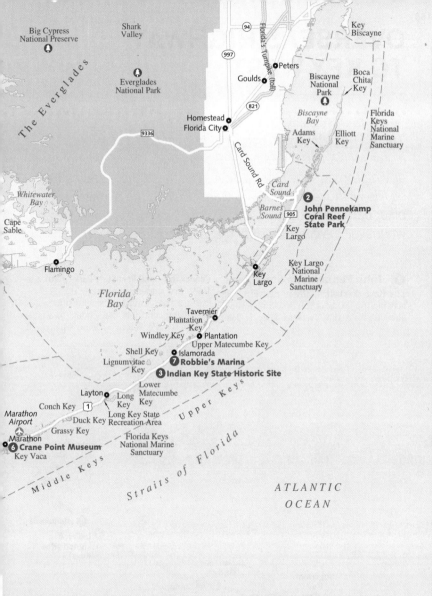

Big Cypress
National Preserve

Shark
Valley

94

Florida's Turnpike (toll)

Key
Biscayne

997

Peters

Goulds

Everglades
National Park

Biscayne
National
Park

Boca
Chita
Key

821

The Everglades

Homestead
Florida City

9336

Adams
Key

Biscayne
Bay

Elliott
Key

Florida
Keys
National
Marine
Sanctuary

Whitewater
Bay

Card Sound Rd

Card
Sound

Cape
Sable

Barnes
Sound

905

**2 John Pennekamp
Coral Reef
State Park**

Key
Largo

Flamingo

Florida
Bay

Key Largo

Key Largo
National
Marine
Sanctuary

Tavernier

Plantation
Key

Windley Key

Plantation

Upper Matecumbe Key

Shell Key

Islamorada

Lignumvitae
Key

7 Robbie's Marina

3 Indian Key State Historic Site

Layton

Long
Key

Lower
Matecumbe
Key

Conch Key

1

Marathon
Airport

Duck Key

Long Key State
Recreation Area

Grassy Key

Upper Keys

Marathon

6 Crane Point Museum

Key Vaca

Florida Keys
National Marine
Sanctuary

Straits of Florida

Middle Keys

ATLANTIC
OCEAN

5 Scratching Papa's six-toed cats behind their ears at **Hemingway House** (p184)

6 Strolling through the palm-hammock and pineland

scrub at **Crane Point Museum** (p177)

7 Feeding the giant tarpon swimming in circles at **Robbie's Marina** (p174)

8 Making an island-hopping day trip and detour to **Dry Tortugas National Park** (p200)

OVERSEAS HIGHWAY TO KEY WEST

There's no better way – short of hopping on a plane – to enjoy such an utter feeling of escape from the mainland as driving through the Florida Keys. The motto here seems to be 'do whatever the hell you want.' Pull off the highway for biker bars, seafood grills and blissful beaches – wherever and whenever the crazy spirit of these islands moves you.

❶ John Pennekamp State Park

The Keys don't dillydally in delivering an oceanic treat. One of the first things you'll encounter on the Overseas Hwy is **John Pennekamp Coral Reef State Park** (p170), the USA's first underwater park.

It's a true jewel box beneath the sea, a vast living coral reef that's home to a panoply of sea life. You never know what you'll

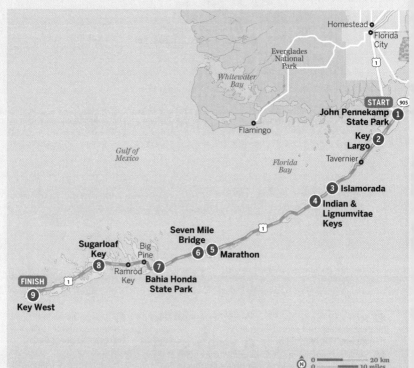

3–5 days; 102 miles/164km

Great for... Outdoors; Food

Best Time to Go December to April for the best weather.

• •

see underwater, except for one predictable favorite: the oft-photographed statue Christ of the Deep, a sunken 4000lb bronze statue.

Your options for exploring the reef include a popular, 2½-hour glass-bottom boat tour on a 65ft catamaran from which you can ooh and aah at filigreed flaps of soft coral, technicolor schools of fish, dangerous-looking barracudas and massive sea turtles.

You can also take a snorkeling or two-tank diving trip, or go DIY and rent a canoe ($20 per hour) or kayak ($12/30 per hour/half day) and journey through a 3-mile network of water trails. Call the park for reservations and departure times.

The Drive > Your instructions for most of this trip will be the same: drive further southwest along the Overseas Hwy. This first leg is a short one; the park and the town of Key Largo are practically spooning.

❷ Key Largo

Key Largo (both the name of the town and the island it's on) is slightly underwhelming at a glance, especially given the romantic notions that may have been placed in your head by hearing it mentioned in pop culture references ranging from Humphrey Bogart to the Beach Boys.

As you drive onto the islands, Key Largo resembles a long line of low-lying hammock and strip development. But that's from the highway. Head down a side road and duck into this warm little bar, or that converted Keys plantation house, and the island idiosyncrasies become more pronounced.

Speaking of pop culture, the actual **African Queen** (p171) – a steamboat used in the 1951 movie starring Humphrey Bogart and Katherine Hepburn – has been restored to her former, er, splendor, and you can relive the movie aboard the tiny vessel on a canal or dinner cruise. If you behave better than Hepburn's character, the captain might even let you take the helm for a bit.

The Drive > Continue south to your next stop, Islamorada, which sounds like an island but is actually a string of several islands. It is here

where the trees open up and you finally start to feel like you're in the islands.

❸ Islamorada

When you reach Islamorada, you'll finally feel like you're in the islands. Here at last are unbroken horizons of sea and sky, one perfect shade of blue mirroring the other. Near mile marker 73.5, sandy **Anne's Beach** (p174) opens upon a sky-bright stretch of calm waters for splashing about beside a tunnel of hardwood hammock. Kids will love getting stuck in the tidal mud flats.

Down the road, **Robbie's Marina** (p174) is a combo tourist shop, fishing marina and cruise-boat operator. From here you can kayak over to the virgin tropical rain forest of Lignumvitae Key, tour Indian Key's historical ruins or go fishing on a party boat. Don't forget to look in on the fearsome tarpon fish before you leave.

㉟ The Drive

You can't drive to your next stop; like many of the Keys, these two can only be reached by boat. You can rent a canoe or kayak or catch a charter from Robbie's Marina.

❹ Indian & Lignumvitae Keys

Take a boat tour or paddle out to either of these remote islands, both of which are on the National Register of Historic Places and offer a serene glimpse into what Florida was like before cars, condos and cheap souvenir T-shirts.

An island ghost town, **Indian Key** (p174) contains the ruins of a 19th-century settlement. In the 1830s it was a thriving town, complete with a warehouse, docks, streets, hotel and about 40 to 50 permanent residents. However, the settlement was wiped out in a Native American attack during the Second Seminole War, and now all that remains are crumbling foundations. It's a serene if sometimes eerie experience, to walk among ruins and paddle around in utter isolation.

On the bay side, the isolated **Lignumvitae Key Botanical State Park** (p174) has virgin tropical forests and the 1919-built Matheson House. Douse yourself in bug spray and consider long sleeves – mosquitoes have overtaken the island – to see some beautifully undeveloped island during weekend tours.

The Drive > From Robbie's Marina, settle in for a half-hour drive to Marathon, the halfway point between Key Largo and Key West.

⑤ Marathon

Marathon sits right on the halfway point between Key Largo and Key West, and is a good place to stop on a road trip across the islands. It's perhaps the most 'developed' key outside Key West, in the sense that it has large shopping centers and a population of a few thousand.

Stop and stretch your legs at **Crane Point Museum** (p177), a nature center with walking trails through a hardwood hammock and wildlife exhibits for kids, including marine touch tanks. And if you're ready to hop in the ocean, **Sombrero Beach** (p178) is a wonderful park with shady picnic areas, nicer-than-you'd-expect bathrooms and a playscape for the kiddos. It's one of the few white-sand, mangrove-free beaches in the Keys.

The Drive > The almost aptly named Seven Mile Bridge starts just past Marathon and continues on for (shhh, don't tell) just under 7 miles.

⑥ Seven Mile Bridge

Take a deep breath because next up on the horizon is the gasp-worthy Seven Mile Bridge. Florida is full of head-spinning causeways, but none longer than this beauty soaring over the Gulf of Mexico. Driving across it provides one of the most memorable stretches of road anywhere.

Parallel to the road is the Old Seven Mile Bridge, a hurricane-battered railway and auto causeway no longer in use. Below the old bridge, about 2 miles from the mainland, **Pigeon Key** (p178) is a National Historic District. Hop on a ferry over to the island to amble around an early-20th-century railroad

workers' village built by real-estate tycoon Henry Flagler, or come just for the snorkeling and sun-splashed beach.

The Drive > Just a couple of miles after the bridge touches down and you're back on land, you'll reach the entrance to Bahia Honda State Park on your left.

⑦ Bahia Honda State Park

This park, with its long, white-sand (and seaweed-strewn) beach is the big attraction in these parts. As Keys beaches go, this one is probably the best natural stretch of sand in the island chain, but we wouldn't vote it best beach in the continental USA (although Condé Nast did...in 1992). As a tourist, the more novel experience is walking a stretch of the old Bahia Honda Rail Bridge, which offers nice views of the surrounding islands. Or check out the nature trails (ooh, butterflies!) and science center, where helpful park employees help you identify stone crabs, fireworms, horseshoe crabs and comb jellies.

The **park concession** (p181) offers daily 1½-hour snorkeling trips at 9:30am and 1:30pm (adult/child $30/25). Reservations are a good idea in high season.

The Drive > Your next stop is another 17 miles along, and you'll need directions to find it. On Sugarloaf Key, turn right at the sign for the Sugarloaf airport, near mile marker 17, then take the right side of the fork in the road.

⑧ Sugarloaf Key

Ready for a little tidbit of randomness? Just off the highway (only about one minute out of your way) you'll find Perky's Bat Tower, a 1920s real-estate-developer's vision gone awry. To eliminate pesky mosquitoes from his planned vacation resort, Richter Perky imported a colony of bats (he'd heard they'd eat mosquitoes) and moved them into a custom-made 35ft tower that resembles an Aztec-inspired fire lookout. The bats promptly flew off, never to return, and the mosquitoes lived happily on. The tower is the only vestige of the development that would have been.

The Drive > Can you feel the excitement? You're only about half an hour away from the end of the road: Key West. Or is that the beginning of the road? US 1 technically begins in Key West, counting up from mile marker zero. Once you hit town, drive all the way to the edge; that's where the heart of Old Town is located.

MATT MUNRO/LONELY PLANET ©

Hemingway House (p184)

❾ Key West

Key West has enjoyed a long and colorful history that includes pirates, sunken treasures, literary legends and lots of ghosts. A visit to **Hemingway Home and Museum** (p184) is practically mandatory, him being the unofficial patron saint of Key West and all. Bearded docents lead tours every half-hour, during which they spin yarns of Papa, his wives and his famous six-toed cats.

Love a good ghost story? Key West is full of them. You might just find out your guesthouse is haunted during the **Key West Ghost & Mysteries Tour** (p190), and you'll hear all about the creepy antics that got Robert the haunted doll confined to **East Martello** (p189).

The Keys are home to the only living coral barrier reef in the United States, which means snorkeling here is excellent. Warm, clear water and white sand make conditions ideal, and the fish are vibrant about a half-hour boat ride from the island.

At sunset, crowds fill **Mallory Square** (p184) for the Sunset Celebration, a nightly festival where you'll see jugglers, fire-eaters and street performers of every stripe. And at the end of the day, bar aficionados flock to the **Green Parrot** (p197), a fine purveyor of old-school Key West ambience. Purported to be the oldest bar on the island, it's also one of the best places in town to hear a live band.

❶ Getting There & Away

Getting here can be half the fun – or, if you're unlucky, a whopping dose of frustration. Imagine a tropical-island hop, from one bar-studded mangrove islet to the next, via one of the most remarkable roads in the world: the Overseas Hwy (US Hwy 1). On a good day, driving along the Overseas with the windows down – the wind in your face and the twin sisters of Florida Bay and the Atlantic stretching on either side – is the US road trip in tropical perfection. On a bad day, you end up sitting in gridlock behind some guy who is riding a midlife-crisis Harley.

Greyhound (www.greyhound.com) buses serve all Keys destinations along US Hwy 1 and depart from Downtown Miami and Key West; you can pick up a bus along the way by standing on the Overseas Hwy and flagging one down. If you fly into Fort Lauderdale or Miami, the **Keys Shuttle** (☑ 888-765-9997; www.keysshuttle.com) provides door-to-door service to most of the Keys ($70/80/90 to the Upper and Middle Keys/Lower Keys/Key West). Reserve at least a day in advance.

❶ Getting Around

Key West Transit (☑ 305-600-1455; www.kwtransit.com; day pass $4-8) operates a commuter bus service runs between Key West and Marathon nine times daily; the fare is just $4. From Marathon you can connect to the 301 **Dade-Monroe Express** ($2.65), operated by Dade County, which travels between Marathon and Florida City 10 times daily; see www.miamidade.gov/transit for a detailed schedule. This route works in the opposite direction as well, which means you can feasibly take public buses from Florida City all the way to Key West, though it's a long day's journey.

UPPER KEYS

No, really, you're in the islands!

It is a bit hard to tell when you first arrive, though. The huge, rooty blanket of mangrove forest that forms the South Florida coastline spreads like a woody morass into Key Largo; little differentiates the island from Florida proper. Keep heading south and the scenery becomes more archipelagically pleasant as the mangroves give way to wider stretches of road and ocean, until all of a sudden you're in Islamorada and the water is everywhere. If you want to avoid traffic on US 1, you can try the less trafficked FL 997 and Card Sound Rd to FL 905 (toll $1), which passes Alabama Jack's (p173).

Key Largo & Tavernier

We're not going to lie: Key Largo (both the name of the town and the island it's on) is slightly underwhelming at a glance. 'Under' is the key word, as its main sights are under the water, rather than above. As you drive onto the islands, Key Largo resembles a long line of low-lying hammock and strip development. But that's just from the highway: head down a side road and duck into this warm little bar, or that converted Keys plantation house, and the island idiosyncrasies become more pronounced.

The 33-mile-long Largo, which starts at Mile Marker 106, is the longest island in the Keys, and those 33 miles have attracted a lot of marine life, all accessible from the biggest concentration of dive sites in the islands. The town of Tavernier (Mile Marker 93) is just south of the town of Key Largo.

◉ Sights

John Pennekamp Coral Reef State Park STATE PARK
(☑ 305-451-6300; www.pennekamppark.com; Mile 102.6 oceanside; admission car with 1/2 people $4.50/9, cyclist or pedestrian $2.50; ☉ 8am-sunset, aquarium to 5pm; 🅿 ♿) ✪ John Pennekamp has the singular distinction of being the first underwater park in the USA. There's 170 acres of dry parkland here and over 48,000 acres (ie 75 sq miles) of wet: the vast majority of the protected area is the ocean. Before you get out in that water, be sure to take in some pleasant beaches and stroll over the nature trails.

The **Mangrove Trail** is a good boardwalk introduction to this oft-maligned, ecologically awesome species (the trees, often submerged in water, breathe via long roots that act as snorkels – neat). Stick around for nightly campfire programs and ranger discussions.

The visitor center is well run and informative and has a small saltwater **aquarium** and nature films that give a glimpse of what's under those waters. To really get beneath the surface, you should take a 2½-hour **glass-bottom boat tour** (adult/child $24/17). You'll be brought out in a safe, modern 38ft catamaran from which you'll get a chance to see filigreed flaps of soft coral, technicolor schools of fish, dangerous-looking barracuda and perhaps massive, yet ballerina-graceful, sea turtles. Besides the swirl of natural coral life, interested divers can catch a glimpse of the *Christ of the Abyss,* an 8.5ft, 4000lb bronze sculpture of Jesus – a copy of a similar sculpture off the coast of Genoa, Italy, in the Mediterranean Sea.

If you want to go even deeper, try straight-up **snorkeling trips** (adult/child $30/25) or **diving excursions** (six-person charter $500, plus equipment rental). DIY-ers may want to take out a canoe ($20 per hour), kayak (from $12/30 per hour/half day) or stand-up paddleboard (from $25/40 per hour/half day) to journey through a 3-mile network of trails. Phone for boat-rental information.

To learn more about the reef in this area, go to www.southeastfloridareefs.net.

Caribbean Club Bar FILM LOCATION
(☎ 305-451-4466; www.caribbeanclubkl.com; Mile 104 bayside; ◷ 7am-4am) Here's one for the movie fans, particularly Bogie buffs: the lively Caribbean Club Bar is, in fact, the only place in Key Largo where *Key Largo*, starring Humphrey Bogart and Lauren Bacall, was filmed (the rest of the island was a Hollywood soundstage). Stop in for drinks, live music (Thursday to Sunday nights) and a dose of old Florida nostalgia – plus great sunsets off the back deck.

If that's not enough, the original *African Queen,* of the same-titled movie, is docked 5 miles south in a channel at the Holiday Inn at Mile Marker 100 – just walk around the back and there she is – assuming the boat's not out for tours.

Laura Quinn Wild Bird Sanctuary WILDLIFE RESERVE
(☎ 305-852-4486; www.keepthemflying.org; 93600 Overseas Hwy, Mile 93.6; donations accepted; ◷ sunrise-sunset; P ♿) ✚ This 7-acre sanctuary serves as a protected refuge for a wide variety of injured birds. A boardwalk leads through various enclosures where you can learn a bit about some of the permanent residents – those unable to be released back in the wild. The species here include masked boobies, great horned owls, green herons, brown pelicans, double-crested cormorants and others. Keep walking along the path to reach a nice vista of Florida Bay and a wading bird pond.

The same organization also runs a bird hospital just south along the main highway. They're the ones to contact if you see injured birds – or have any other bird emergencies – during your travels.

Harry Harris Park PARK
(50 East Beach Rd, Mile 92.6, Tavernier; admission free Mon-Fri, $5 Sat, Sun & holidays; ◷ 7:30am-sunset; ♿ ⛱) This small park is a good place to take the kids – there's a small playground, picnic tables, grills for barbecuing, basketball courts and ball fields. Rarely for the Keys, there's also a good patch of white sand fronting a warm lagoon that's excellent for swimming.

🏃 Activities & Tours

Key Largo Bike and Adventure Tours CYCLING
(☎ 305-395-1551; www.keylargobike.com; 2-day tour from $500) This outfit leads a range of bike outings, including two-day tours from Key Largo to Key West. It also hires out bikes for those who want to go it alone (pick up in in Key Largo or Miami and drop off in Key West).

Key Largo Princess BOATING
(☎ 305-451-4655; Key Largo Holiday Inn, 99701 Overseas Hwy; adult/child from $35/20; ◷ cruises 10am, 1pm & 4pm; ♿) Get a glimpse of the Key's undersea beauty on a glass-bottom boat tour. Popular with families, these 75ft, 129-passenger vessels give you the opportunity to see lots of colorful coral, plus sea fans, sharks, tropical fish and the odd sea turtle winging along.

Snacks and drinks available on the boat.

African Queen BOATING
(☎ 305-451-8080; www.africanqueenflkeys.com; Key Largo Holiday Inn, 99701 Overseas Hwy; canal cruise/dinner cruise $49/89) The steamboat used in the 1951 movie starring Humphrey Bogart and Katherine Hepburn has been restored to its former splendor, and you can relive the movie aboard the tiny vessel on a canal or dinner cruise. If you behave better than Hepburn's character, the captain might even let you take the helm for a bit.

Jacob's Aquatics Center WATER PARK
(☎ 305-453-7946; http://jacobsaquaticcenter. org; 320 Laguna Ave, Mile 99.6; adult/child/ student/family weekday $10/6/8/25, weekend $12/8/10/30; ◷ 10am-7pm May-Sep, to 6pm Oct-Apr; ♿) Jacob's is a complex of all kinds of aquatic fun. There's an eight-lane pool for lap and open swimming, a therapy pool with handicapped access and water aerobic courses. For the kids there's a small water-park with waterslides, a playground and, of course, kiddie-sized pools.

Garl's Coastal Kayaking ECOTOUR
(☎ 305-393-3223; www.garlscoastalkayaking.com; 4hr tours adult/child $75/50, single/double kayak hire per day $40/55) ✚ Garl's is an excellent ecotour operator that gets customers into the Everglades backcountry and mangrove

islets of Florida Bay via kayak and canoe. It also provides reasonable equipment rentals.

🛏 Sleeping

John Pennekamp Coral Reef State Park
CAMPGROUND $

(☎800-326-3521; www.reserveamerica.com; 102601 Overseas Hwy; tent & RV sites $38.50; P) You don't even have to leave Pennekamp at closing time if you opt for tent or RV camping, but you'll need to make a reservation well in advance, as the 47 sites fill up fast. Well-behaved pets are welcome.

Bay Harbor Lodge
MOTEL $$

(☎305-852-5695; www.bayharborkeylargo.com; 97702 Overseas Hwy, bayside; r $150-300; ❄🛜🏊) This lush 2.5-acre property has its own private beach, a temperature-controlled pool and tropical gardens alive with birdsong. The rooms are clean and comfortable, if somewhat dated, but the service is friendly and the homemade scones (served at breakfast) are all the rage. Excellent value.

Hilton Key Largo Resort
HOTEL $$

(☎305-852-5553; www.keylargoresort.com; Mile 102 bayside; r/ste from $200/280; P🛜🏊) This Hilton has a ton of character. Folks just seem to get all laid-back when lounging in clean, designer rooms outfitted in blues and greens with balconies overlooking the water. The grounds are enormous and include an artificial waterfall-fed pool and frontage to a rather large stretch of private white-sand beach. Book online for the best rates.

Kona Kai Resort
HOTEL $$$

(☎305-852-7200; www.konakairesort.com; Mile 97.8 bayside; r $300-440; P🛜🏊) This hideaway is one of the only botanical gardens we can think of that integrates a hotel onto its grounds – or is that the other way around? Either way, this spot, backing onto peaceful waterfront, is lush. The 13 airy rooms and suites (with full kitchens) are all bright and comfortable, with good natural light and an attractive modern design.

Dove Creek Lodge
HOTEL $$$

(☎305-852-6200; www.dovecreeklodge.com; 147 Seaside Ave; r $230-380; P🛜🏊) This mid-sized hotel offers bright rooms decked out in citrus-shaded colors and grounds that front the Atlantic Ocean. It's a family-friendly spot with an old-school resort feel. Can help with booking tours and excursions in the area.

Jules' Undersea Lodge
HOTEL $$$

(☎305-451-2353; www.jul.com; 51 Shoreland Dr, Mile 103.2 oceanside; s/d/tr $675/800/1050) There's lots of talk about underwater hotels getting built in Dubai and Fiji, but as of writing, Jules' Undersea Lodge is still the only place in the world outside of a submarine where you and your significant other can join the 'five-fathom club' (we're not elaborating). Once a research station, this module has been converted into a delightfully cheesy Keys motel, but wetter.

In addition to two private guest rooms, there are common rooms, a kitchen-dining room and a wet room with hot showers and gear storage. Telephones and an intercom

---

FLORIDA KEYS FOR CHILDREN

Check out some of the following options to entertain the kids:

Florida Keys Eco-Discovery Center (p184) Get an understanding of the region's environment.

Glass-bottom boat tours at John Pennekamp Coral Reef State Park (p170) Your own window to the underwater world.

Key West Butterfly & Nature Conservatory (p189) Pretty flying things.

Turtle Hospital (p178) Learn about these fascinating endangered creatures.

Conch Tour Train (p190) Kitschy, corny, enjoyable tour.

Key West Ghost & Mysteries Tour (p190) Only slightly spooky, but younger kids may find this one a bit scary.

Key-deer spotting (p181) Kids go crazy for cute mini-deer.

Key West Cemetery (p185) Get Gothic with these often humorous tombs.

Robbie's Marina (p174) All sorts of activities, including the ever-popular tarpon (giant fish) feeding frenzy.

connect guests with the surface. Guests must be at least 10 years old and you gotta dive to get here – plus, there's no smoking or alcohol. If you just want to visit, you can pop in for a three-hour visit (with pizza!) for $150.

🍴 Eating & Drinking

Harriette's
AMERICAN $
(☎ 305-852-8689; 95710 Overseas Hwy, bayside; mains $7-14; ⊗ 6am-3pm) This sweet, breadbox-sized eatery is famed far and wide for its utterly addictive key lime muffins (so big you'll need a knife and fork to eat them). There's also classic American fare – pancakes, bacon and eggs, and not-to-be-missed fluffy biscuits for breakfast, which is the best time to come. Go early to beat the crowds.

DJ's Diner
AMERICAN $
(☎ 305-451-2999; 99411 Overseas Hwy; mains $8-15; ⊗ 7am-3pm; P 🐕 🖶) You're greeted by a mural of Humphrey Bogart, James Dean *and* Marilyn Monroe – that's a lot of Americana. It's all served with a heapin' helpin' of diner faves amid vinyl-boothed ambience. Breakfast is a big draw with fluffy omelets, eggs Benedict and waffles (including a key lime pie version).

Fish House
SEAFOOD $$
(☎ 305-451-4665; www.fishhouse.com; Mile 102.4 oceanside; mains lunch $12-21, dinner $21-30; ⊗ 11:30am-10pm; P 🖶) The Fish House delivers on the promise of its title – very good fish, bought whole from local fishermen and prepared fried, broiled, jerked, blackened or chargrilled. Because the Fish House only uses fresh fish, the menu changes daily based on what is available.

Shipwreck's Bar & Grill
AMERICAN $$
(45 Garden Cove Dr, oceanside; mains $13-23; ⊗ 11:30am-10pm) Just off the beaten path, Shipwreck's is a local-loving joint littered with nautical gear and dollar bills stapled to the walls, with a breezy open-air deck. Sit at picnic tables over the water, while noshing on fish sandwiches, peel-and-eat shrimp, conch fritters or an excellent blackened mahimahi. It's a dive, but great value for the money.

Key Largo Conch House
FUSION $$
(☎ 305-453-4844; www.keylargoconchhouse.com; Mile 100.2 oceanside; mains lunch $9-16, dinner $16-30; ⊗ 8am-10pm; P 🐕 🖶) This innovative kitchen likes to sex up local classics (mahimahi cooked in a crust of coconut and crushed macadamia nuts or conch with lobster ceviche). Set in a restored old-school

Keys mansion wrapped in a *Gone With the Wind* verandah, it's hard not to love the way the period architecture blends in seamlessly with the local tropical fauna.

Mrs Mac's Kitchen
AMERICAN $$
(☎ 305-451-3722; www.mrsmacskitchen.com; Mile 99.4 bayside; mains breakfast & lunch $9-16, dinner $16-30; ⊗ 7am-9:30pm Mon-Sat; P 🖶) When Applebee's stuffs its wall full of license plates, it's tacky. When Mrs Mac's does it, it's homey. Probably because the service is warm and personable, and the breakfasts are delicious. Plus the food packs in the locals, tourists, their dogs and pretty much everyone else on the island (plus, admittedly, a fair few calories, but that's why it tastes good).

Alabama Jack's
BAR
(58000 Card Sound Rd; ⊗ 11am-7pm) Welcome to your first taste of the Keys: zonked-out fishermen, exiles from the mainland and Harley heads getting drunk on a mangrove bay. This is the line where Miami-esque South Florida gives way to the country-fried American South. Wildlife lovers: you may spot the rare mulleted version of *Jacksonvillia Redneckus*! Everyone raves about the conch fritters; and the fact it has to close because of nightly onslaughts of mosquitoes means this place is as authentically Florida as they come. Country bands take the stage on weekends from 2pm to 5pm. It's just before the tollbooth over the Card Sound Bridge.

ℹ Information
Mariners Hospital (☎ 305-434-3000; www.baptisthealth.net; Mile 91.5 bayside, Tavernier; ⊗ 24hr) The best hospital in the area with a 24-hour emergency room. If you're diving, this is the only place in the Keys that has a hyperbaric chamber.

ℹ Getting There & Away
The Greyhound bus stops at Mile Marker 99.6 oceanside. It stops twice a day traveling between Miami and Key West.

Islamorada
☎ 305 / POPULATION 6600
Islamorada (eye-luh-murr-*ah*-da) is also known as 'The Village of Islands.' Doesn't that sound pretty? Well, it really is. This little string of pearls (well, keys) – Plantation, Upper and Lower Matecumbe, Shell and Lignumvitae (lignum-*vite*-ee) – shimmers as one of the prettiest stretches of the islands. This

is where the scrubby mangrove is replaced by unbroken horizons of ocean and sky, one perfect shade of blue mirroring the other. Islamorada stretches across some 20 miles, from Mile Marker 90 to Mile Marker 74.

◉ Sights

★ Florida Keys History of Diving Museum
MUSEUM

(☑305-664-9737; www.divingmuseum.org; Mile 83; adult/child $12/6; ⊙10am-5pm; P♿) You can't miss the diving museum – it's the building with the enormous mural of whale sharks on the side. The journey into the undersea covers 4000 years, with fascinating pieces like the 1797 Klingert's copper kettle, a whimsical room devoted to Jules Verne's Captain Nemo, massive deep diving suits and an exquisite display of diving helmets from around the world. These imaginative galleries reflect the charming quirks of the Keys.

Windley Key Fossil Reef Geological State Site
STATE PARK

(☑305-664-2540; www.floridastateparks.org/windleykey; Mile 85.5 oceanside; admission/tour $2.50/2; ⊙8am-5pm Thu-Mon) To get his railroad built across the islands, Henry Flagler had to quarry out some sizable chunks of the Keys. The best evidence of those efforts can be found at this former quarry–now–state park. Windley has leftover quarry machinery scattered along an 8ft former quarry wall, with fossilized evidence of brain and staghorn coral imbedded right in the rock. The wall offers a cool (and rare) public peek into the stratum of coral that forms the substrate of the Keys.

There are also various short trails through tropical hardwood hammock that make for a pleasant glimpse into the Keys' wilder side. Borrow a free trail guide from the visitor center. From December to April, ranger-led tours are offered at 10am and 2pm Friday to Sunday for $2.50 per person.

Anne's Beach
BEACH

(Mile 73.5 oceanside; ♿) Anne's is one of the best beaches in these parts. The small ribbon of sand opens upon a sky-bright stretch of tidal flats and a green tunnel of hammock and wetland. Nearby mudflats are a joy to get stuck in, and will be much loved by the kids.

Rain Barrel Sculpture Gallery
ARTS CENTER

(☑305-852-8935; 86700 Overseas Hwy; ⊙9am-5pm) Once you see the giant lobster, you know you've arrived. Welcome to the Rain Barrel, Islamorada's local artists' village, which is packed with souvenir-y tourist tat, island-themed artwork, pottery, glassworks, wood carvings and plenty of other intrigue.

It's a fine place to browse the various studios and galleries, and if nothing else, be sure to snap a few pics of/with the giant crustacean.

Indian Key Historic State Park
ISLAND

(☑305-664-2540; www.floridastateparks.org/indiankey; Mile 78.5 oceanside; $2.50; ⊙8am-sunset) This quiet island was once a thriving city, complete with a warehouse, docks, streets, a hotel and about 40 to 50 permanent residents. There's not much left at the historic site – just the foundation, some cisterns and jungly tangle. Arriving by boat or kayak is the only way to visit. Robbie's Marina hires out kayaks for the paddle out here – around 30 minutes one way in calm conditions.

Lignumvitae Key Botanical State Park
ISLAND

(☑305-664-2540; www.floridastateparks.org/lignumvitaekey; admission/tour $2.50/2; ⊙8am-5pm Thu-Mon, tours 10am & 2pm Fri-Sun Dec-Apr) This key, only accessible by boat, encompasses a 280-acre island of virgin tropical forest and is home to roughly a zillion mosquitoes. The official attraction is the 1919 Matheson House, with its windmill and cistern; the real draw is a nice sense of shipwrecked isolation. From December to April, guided walking tours (1¼ hours) are given at 10am and 2pm Friday to Sunday. You'll have to get here via Robbie's Marina; you can hire kayaks from there (it's about an hour's paddle).

⚐ Activities

★ Robbie's Marina
BOATING

(☑305-664-8070; www.robbies.com; Mile 77.5 bayside; kayak & stand-up paddleboard rentals $45-80; ⊙9am-8pm; ♿) More than a boat launch, Robbie's is a local flea market, tacky tourist shop, sea pen for tarpons (massive fish) and jump-off point for fishing expeditions, all wrapped into one driftwood-laced compound. Boat-rental and tour options are also available. The best reason to visit is to escape the mayhem and hire a kayak for a peaceful paddle through nearby mangroves, hammocks and lagoons.

You can also book a snorkeling trip ($38), which takes you out on a very smooth-riding Happy Cat vessel for a chance to bob amid coral reefs. If you don't want to get on the water, you can feed the freakishly large tarpons from the dock ($3.40 per bucket, $2 to watch). There's also a 'party boat' (half-day/

FLORIDA KEYS OVERSEAS HERITAGE TRAIL
....

One of the best ways to see the Keys is by bicycle. The flat elevation and ocean breezes are perfect for cycling, and the **Florida Keys Overseas Heritage Trail** (☑305-853-3571; www.floridastateparks.org/trail/Florida-Keys) gives gorgeous vantage points along the way. Still under construction, this trail will eventually connect all the islands from Key Largo to Key West. Currently 90 miles of this multi-use trail out of 106 miles are now complete.

If you are keen to ride, it's currently possible to bike through the Keys along portions of this trail, though it's not always easy to follow). In the incomplete parts of the trail, you can ride along the shoulder of the highway if you don't mind traffic whizzing by at 50mph (crossing the Seven-Mile Bridge is particularly harrowing; taxis in Marathon have bike racks, saving you the stress).

For two-day biking trips between Key Largo and Key West, book a tour with Key Largo Bike and Adventure Tours (p171), which leads a range of outings.

night trips $40/45), which is less about revelry and more about catching fish.

🛏 Sleeping

Conch On Inn   MOTEL **$**
(☑305-852-9309; www.conchoninn.com; 103 Caloosa St, Mile 89.5; r $100-180; P🐾) A motel popular with yearly snowbirds, Conch On Inn has simple but cheerfully painted rooms that are clean, comfortable and well equipped. The waterfront deck is a fine spot to unwind – and look for manatees; up to 14 have been spotted off the dock here!

Ragged Edge Resort   RESORT **$$**
(☑305-852-5389; www.ragged-edge.com; 243 Treasure Harbor Rd; apt $100-260; P❄🐾🏊) This low-key and popular apartment complex, far from the maddening traffic jams, has 10 quiet units and friendly hosts. The larger studios have screened-in porches, and the entire vibe is happily comatose. There's no beach, but you can swim off the dock and in the heated pool.

Lime Tree Bay Resort Motel   MOTEL **$$**
(☑305-664-4740; www.limetreebayresort.com; Mile 68.5 bayside; r $180-360; ❄🐾🏊) A plethora of hammocks and lawn chairs provides front-row seats for the spectacular sunsets at this 2.5-acre waterfront hideaway. The rooms are comfortably set, the best with balconies overlooking the water. The extensive facilities include use of tennis courts, bikes, kayaks and stand-up paddleboards.

Casa Morada   HOTEL **$$$**
(☑305-664-0044; www.casamorada.com; 136 Madeira Rd, off Mile 82.2; ste incl breakfast $430-680; P❄🐾🏊) Contemporary chic comes to Islamorada, but it's not gentrifying away the village vibe. Rather, the Casa adds a welcome dab of sophistication to Conch chill: a keystone standing circle, freshwater pool, artificial lagoon, plus a *Wallpaper*-magazine-worthy bar that overlooks Florida Bay – all make this boutique hotel worth a reservation. Go to the bar to catch a drink and a sunset.

Ask about yoga on the pier, private sunset sails on a 30ft Skipjack, and kayak or stand-up paddleboard tours.

🍴 Eating

Bad Boy Burrito   MEXICAN **$**
(☑305-509-7782; www.badboyburrito.com/islamorada; 103 Mastic St, Mile 81.8 bayside; mains $8-15; ⏱10am-6pm Mon-Sat; 🐾) Tucked away in a tiny plaza among a gurgling fountain, orchids and swaying palms, Bad Boy Burrito whips up superb fish tacos and its namesake burritos – with quality ingredients (skirt steak, duck confit, zucchini and squash) and all the fixings (shaved cabbage, chipotle mayo, housemade salsa). Top it off with a hibiscus tea and some chips and guacamole.

Midway Cafe   CAFE **$**
(☑305-664-2622; www.midwaycafecoffeebar.com; 80499 Overseas Hwy; mains $7-10; ⏱7am-3pm Mon-Sat, to 2pm Sun; P🐾) The lovely folks who run this cafe – stuffed with every variety of heart-warming art the coffee-shop trope can muster – roast their own beans, make delectable baked goods and whip up tasty sandwiches, salads, wraps and omelets. You're almost in the Middle Keys: celebrate making it this far with a cup of joe – best enjoyed on the tiny patio beside the cafe.

Bob's Bunz   CAFE **$**
(www.bobsbunz.com; Mile 81.6 bayside; mains $8-15; ⏱6am-2pm; P🐾) The service at this cafe is energetic and friendly in an only-in-America kinda way, and the food is fine, filling and

cheap. Key lime pie is a classic Keys dish and key lime anything at this bakery is highly regarded, so buy that souvenir pie here.

★**Lazy Days**   SEAFOOD **$$**
(☑305-664-5256; www.lazydaysislamorada.com; 79867 Overseas Hwy, oceanside; mains $18-34; ☑🍴) One of Islamorada's culinary icons, Lazy Days has a stellar reputation for its fresh seafood plates. Start off with a conch chowder topped with a little sherry (provided), before moving on to a decadent hogfish Poseidon (fish topped with shrimp, scallops and key lime butter) or a straight-up boiled seafood platter (half lobster, shrimp, catch of the day and other delicacies).

Bayside Gourmet   AMERICAN **$$**
(www.baysidegourmet.com; Mile 82.7 bayside; mains breakfast $8-10, lunch & dinner $10-22; ☑6am-9:30pm Mon-Sat, to 2pm Sun) This stylish, modern, but very friendly deli and restaurant is a family-run affair and feels quite a step up from the average Keys seafood shack. The diverse menu serves up something for all palates, from pancakes and breakfast burritos to grouper sandwiches, lasagna and delicious thin-crust pizzas.

Beach Cafe at Morada Bay   AMERICAN **$$$**
(☑305-664-0604; www.moradabay.com/the-beach-cafe; Mile 81.6 bayside; mains lunch $15-22, dinner $22-39; ☑11:30am-10pm Sun-Thu, to 11pm Fri & Sat; ℗) The Beach Cafe has a lot going for it, namely a lovely, laid-back Caribbean vibe, a powder-white sandy beach, nighttime torches, tapas and fresh seafood. It's also a good place to bring the kids, with room to run around, and the adults can come back for a monthly full-moon party, with live music, special cocktails and a beach barbecue.

🍷 Drinking & Nightlife

Florida Keys Brewing Co   MICROBREWERY
(☑305-916-5206; www.floridakeysbrewingco.com; 200 Morada Way, Mile 81.6; ☑noon-10pm) Of the two microbreweries in Islamorada, this is the one not to miss. It's locally owned and operated, with excellent beer brewed on site. Come in to the friendly tap room, order a flight and have a chat with one of the brewmasters who are usually on hand.

Morada Bay   BAR
(☑305-664-0604; www.moradabay.com; Mile 81.6 bayside; ☑5pm-midnight) As well as top food, Morada Bay holds monthly full-moon parties that attract the entire partying population of the Keys. The whole shebang typically starts

around 9pm and goes until whenever the last person passes out; check website for dates.

🛍 Shopping

Old Road Gallery   ARTS & CRAFTS
(☑305-852-8935; Mile 88.8 oceanside; ☑10am-5pm) Specializing in pottery, painting and sculpture, the Old Road Gallery embodies the Key's most creative side. After browsing the shop, take a stroll through the forested grounds, which are decorated with small, carefully placed works of art. This is one-of-a-kind souvenir shopping.

ℹ Getting There & Away

The Greyhound bus stops at the Burger King at Mile Marker 82.5 oceanside. It goes twice daily to both Key West and Miami.

MIDDLE KEYS

On this stretch of the Keys, the bodies of water get wider, and the bridges get more impressive. This is where you'll find the famous Seven Mile Bridge, one of the world's longest causeways and a natural divider between the Middle and Lower Keys. In this stretch of islands you'll cross specks like Conch Key and Duck Key; green, quiet Grassy Key; as well as Key Vaca, where Marathon, the second-largest town and most Key-sy community in the islands, is located.

Grassy Key

◎ Sights

Curry Hammock State Park   STATE PARK
(☑305-289-2690; www.floridastateparks.org/curryhammock; Mile 56.2 bayside; car/cyclist $5/2; ☑8am-sunset; ℗🍴) 🐾 This park is small but sweet and the rangers are just lovely. Like most parks in the Keys, it's a good spot for preserved tropical hardwood and mangrove habitat – a 1.5-mile hike takes you through both environments. Rent a kayak (single/double for two hours $18/22) or stand-up paddleboard ($22 for two hours). You can also camp at the park for $36 per night – sites have toilets and electric hookups.

🛏 Sleeping & Eating

Rainbow Bend   HOTEL **$$$**
(☑800-929-1505; www.rainbowbend.com; Mile 58 oceanside; r $220-460; ℗🛜🏊) You'll be

experiencing intensely charming Keys-kitsch in these big pink cabanas, where the apartments and suites are bright, the tiki huts are shady and the ocean is right there. Half-day use of the Bend's Boston whalers (motorboats), kayaks and canoes is complimentary. The decor is a bit dated, but the beachfront location is outstanding.

Hawk's Cay Resort RESORT $$$
(☑ 305-743-7000; www.hawkscay.com; 61 Hawk's Cay Blvd, Duck Key, off Mile 61 oceanside; r $390-700; P 🗟 🌊) The Cay is an enormous luxury compound with silky-plush rooms and nicely appointed townhouses, as well as countless island activities. The resort's most concerning feature is the 'Dolphin Connection' program, where guests can interact and swim with captive dolphins. Animal welfare groups claim keeping dolphins inside an enclosed tank is debilitating for the animals, and is made worse by human interaction (p178).

Grassy Key Outpost AMERICAN $$
(☑ 305-743-7373; www.grassykeyoutpost.com; 58152 Overseas Hwy; mains $10-29; ⊙ 8am-9pm, market until 10pm; P ✍) Equal parts market and restaurant, the Outpost is an interesting spot that skews between fine dining and Keys casualness, both in terms of atmosphere and cuisine. There's a Southern flair to the gastronomy; shrimp and grits comes rich and smoky, while the mac 'n' cheese is laced with decadent slathers of rich lobster.

SS Wreck Galley & Grill AMERICAN $$
(☑ 305-517-6484; www.wreckgalleygrill.com; Mile 59 bayside; mains $10-26; ⊙ 11am-9:30pm Tue-Sun; P) The SS Wreck is a Keys classic, where fisherman types knock back brew and feast on wings. It's definitely a local haunt, where island politicos like to prattle about the issues (fishing). The food is excellent: it grills one of the best burgers in the Keys, and fires up excellent daily specials.

Marathon

☑ 305, 786 / POPULATION 8625

Marathon sits right on the halfway point between Key Largo and Key West, and it's a good place to stop on a road trip across the islands. It's perhaps the most 'developed' key outside Key West (that's really pushing the definition of the word 'developed') in the sense that it has large shopping centers and a population of over 8000. Then again it's still a place where exiles from the mainland

fish, booze it up and have a good time, so while Marathon is more family-friendly than Key West, it's hardly G-rated.

◉ Sights

Florida Keys Aquarium Encounters AQUARIUM
(☑ 305-407-3262; www.floridakeysaquarium encounters.com; 11710 Overseas Hwy, Mile 53.1 bayside; adult/child $20/15, animal encounters from $30; ⊙ 9am-5pm; ♿) A visit to this small, interactive aquarium starts with a free 20-minute guided tour of some fascinating marine ecosystems. There are also immersive experiences, where you snorkel in the coral reef aquarium or the tropical fish–filled lagoon. More controversial are the 'animal encounters' and 'touch tanks' where you can handle shallow water marine species and touch stingrays (the barbs have been removed). The stress of human interaction can be detrimental to the well-being of aquatic creatures.

Some of the ecosystems you will encounter include a mangrove-lined basin full of tarpon, a tidal pool tank with queen conch and horseshoe crabs, and a 200,000-gallon coral reef tank with moray eels, grouper and several different shark species.

You can also observe mesmerizing lionfish, a pig-nosed turtle, juvenile alligators and various fish species from the Everglades, plus snowy egrets and little blue herons.

Crane Point Museum MUSEUM
(☑ 305-743-9100; www.cranepoint.net; Mile 50.5 bayside; adult/child $15/10; ⊙ 9am-5pm Mon-Sat, from noon Sun; P ♿ 🐾) 🌿 This is one of the nicest spots on the island to stop and smell the roses. And the pinelands. And the palm hammock – a sort of palm jungle (imagine walking under giant, organic Japanese fans) that only grows between Mile Markers 47

DOLPHINS IN CAPTIVITY

Aquariums and marine life centers are popular destinations in Florida, particularly those with shows featuring dolphins and other marine mammals. Some even offer one-on-one interaction with dolphins. While swimming across a pool being towed by Flipper may sound like a memorable photo op, such practices raise deep ethical concerns.

The harsh reality of life for dolphins in captivity is hidden from visitors. Dolphins are highly intelligent and complex animals, and an artificial environment prevents them from communicating, hunting, playing and mating as they would in the wild. The stress of living in captivity often leads to a greater incidence of illness, disease and behavioral abnormalities. As a result, dolphins in captivity often live much shorter lives than those in the wild. Those dolphins that remain 'voluntarily' in captivity often do so simply to remain close to food.

As more people become aware of the harm caused to marine mammals kept in captivity, some aquariums in the USA are scrapping their dolphin programs. The Baltimore Aquarium, for instance, announced it would remove its dolphins by 2020 and provide a seaside sanctuary for those unable to survive in the wild. For the moment, however, no Florida aquariums have followed suit. You can read more about captive marine life at World Animal Protection (www.worldanimalprotection.us.org), Whale and Dolphin Conservation (www.whales.org/issues/swimming-with-dolphins) and the World Cetacean Alliance (www.worldcetaceanalliance.org).

and 60. There's also the restored Adderly House, a preserved example of a Bahamian immigrant cabin (which must have *baked* in summer) and 63 acres of green goodness (with 1.75 miles of trails) to stomp through.

Pigeon Key National Historic District
ISLAND

(☎305-743-5999; www.pigeonkey.net; Mile 47 oceanside; adult/child $12/9; ☺tours 10am, noon & 2pm) For years tiny Pigeon Key, located 2 miles west of Marathon (basically below the Old Seven Mile Bridge), housed the rail workers and maintenance men who built the infrastructure that connected the Keys. Today you can tour the structures of this National Historic District or relax on the beach and snorkel. Ferries leave from the bright red caboose on Knight's Key (left of the Seven Mile Bridge if you're traveling south to Pigeon).

Call ahead to confirm ferry departure times; the last one returns at 4pm.

Sombrero Beach
BEACH

(Sombrero Beach Rd, off Mile 50 oceanside; ☺7:30am-dusk; P ⓗ ☎) One of the few white-sand, mangrove-free beaches in the Keys. It's a good spot to lounge on the sand or swim, and there's also a small playground.

Turtle Hospital
WILDLIFE RESERVE

(☎305-743-2552; www.theturtlehospital.org; 2396 Overseas Hwy; adult/child $22/11; ☺8:30am-6pm; P ⓗ) ⚲ Be it a victim of disease, boat propeller strike, flipper entanglement with fishing lines or any other danger, an injured sea turtle in the Keys will hopefully end up in this motel-cum-sanctuary. We know we shouldn't anthropomorphize animals, but these turtles just seem so sweet. It's sad to see the injured and sick ones, but heartening to see them so well looked after. Ninety-minute tours are educational, fun and offered on the hour from 9am to 4pm.

Activities

Wheels-2-Go
KAYAKING

(☎305-289-4279; http://wheels-2-go.com; 5994 Overseas Hwy; see-through kayaks/bicycles per day $40/15, single/double kayak per day $30/50; ☺9am-5pm) Friendly kayak- and bicycle-rental services. Staff can advise you of the best spots for kayaking, among mangrove tunnels with some great bird-watching opportunities.

Marathon Kayak
KAYAKING

(☎305-395-0355; www.marathonkayak.com; 3hr tours $70) Does guided mangrove ecotours, sunset tours and boat rentals. The three-hour paddle through a canopy of red mangroves is highly recommended.

Tilden's Scuba Center
DIVING

(☎305-743-7255; www.tildensscubacenter.com; 4650 Overseas Hwy; snorkel/dive trip $60/70, full scuba gear hire $120) This knowledgeable and respected outfit offers snorkeling and diving expeditions through nearby sections of the coral reef. Can also arrange spear-fishing trips.

✈️ Festivals & Events

Marathon Seafood Festival　　FOOD & DRINK
(www.marathonseafoodfestival.com;　⊘mid-Mar)
One of the biggest fests in the Keys is this
food-loving event that takes over Marathon.
You'll find live music, an art and boat show, an
arts and craft market, and ample amusement
for the kids (including rides and games). Also
there's seafood! Loads of stalls selling fresh-
caught delicacies from the ocean.

🛏️ Sleeping

Seascape Motel & Marina　　MOTEL **$$**
(📋305-743-6212;　www.seascapemotelandmarina.
com; 1075 75th St Ocean E, btwn Mile 51 & 52; r
$250-450; 🅿❄🛜🏊) The classy, understated
luxury in this B&B manifests in its 12 rooms,
all of which have a different feel – from
old-fashioned cottage to sleek boutique. It
has a waterfront pool, kayaks and stand-up
paddleboards for guests to use, and its se-
cluded setting will make you feel like you've
gotten away from it all. Seascape also hosts
afternoon wine and snacks (included).

Ranch House Motel　　MOTEL **$$**
(📋305-743-2217; 7251 Overseas Hwy; r $110-200;
❄🛜) For the money, this friendly family-run
place right off the highway is one of the
best-value options in the Keys. The owners
go the extra mile to make guests feel at home.

The rooms are clean and well maintained,
if somewhat frozen in the 1970s: wood-
paneled walls and floral curtains evoke a bit
of Keys nostalgia, while good beds, fridges,
microwaves, coffeepots and wall-mounted
TVs ensure the added features are up to date.

Tropical Cottages　　COTTAGE **$$**
(📋305-743-6048;　www.tropicalcottages.net;　243
61st St; cottages $130-200; 🅿❄🛜🏊) These
pretty pastel cottages are a good option, espe-
cially if you're traveling in a larger group. The
individual cottages aren't particularly plush,
but they're cozy, comfortable and offer a nice
bit of privacy, along with some Old Florida at-
mosphere. There's a small tiki bar where you
can relax with a refreshing cocktail.

Sea Dell Motel　　MOTEL **$$**
(📋305-743-5161; www.seadellmotel.com; 5000
Overseas Hwy; r $130-210; 🅿❄🛜🏊) The Sea
Dell is a Keys classic: bright, low-slung
rooms with a pastel color scheme and floral bedspreads. The rooms are more or less
self-sufficient small apartments, and can
comfortably accommodate small families.
The small pool entices after a day exploring.

Tranquility Bay　　RESORT **$$$**
(📋305-289-0667; www.tranquilitybay.com; Mile
48.5 bayside; r $340-700; 🅿❄🛜🏊) If you're
serious about going upscale, you should
book in here. Tranquility Bay is a massive
condo-hotel resort with plush townhouses,
high-thread-count sheets and all-in-white
chic. The grounds are enormous and activity
filled; they really don't want you to leave.

🍴 Eating

Wooden Spoon　　AMERICAN **$**
(7007 Overseas Hwy; mains $5-12; ⊘5:30am-
1:30pm; 🅿) It's the best breakfast around,
served by sweet Southern women who know
their way around a diner. The biscuits are
fluffy, and they drown so well in that thick,
delicious sausage gravy, and the grits are the
most buttery soft starch you'll ever have the
pleasure of seeing beside your eggs.

★Keys Fisheries　　SEAFOOD **$$**
(📋866-743-4353; www.keysfisheries.com; 3502
Louisa St; mains $12-27; ⊘11am-9pm; 🅿🚻) The
lobster Reuben is the stuff of legend here.
Sweet, chunky, creamy – so good you'll be
daydreaming about it afterward. But you
can't go wrong with any of the excellent seafood here, all served with sass. Expect pleasant levels of seagull harassment as you dine
on a working waterfront.

Sunset Grille　　AMERICAN **$$**
(📋305-396-7235;　www.sunsetgrille7milebridge.
com; 7 Knights Key Blvd, Mile 47 oceanside; mains
lunch $10-16, dinner $19-30; 🚻) Overlooking the
Seven Mile Bridge, this huge, festive spot has
an unbeatable location (it's not called Sun-
set for nothing) and wide-ranging appeal:
namely a huge menu of seafood and grilled
meat dishes, plus a raw bar, sushi and plenty
of kid-friendly options. There's also an ap-
pealing swimming pool (heated in winter)
that's free and open to all.

Burdines Waterfront　　AMERICAN **$$**
(www.burdineswaterfront.com; 1200 Oceanview
Ave, end of 15th St, Mile 48 oceanside; mains
$10-18; ⊘noon-9pm; 🚻) For a taste of old-
school Marathon, head to this barnlike
upper-story shack on the waterfront. It's a
much-loved local haunt where you can take
a seat around the thatch-roof bar or at a
picnic table and take in the breezy views
while feasting on hearty home cooking:
blackened-fish sandwiches, black beans
and rice, handcut fries, shrimp baskets and
stone crab soup.

🍷 Drinking & Nightlife

★ **Hurricane**   BAR

(📞 305-743-2200; Mile 49.5 bayside; ⏱ 11am-midnight) Locals, tourists, mad fishermen and rednecks saddle up here for endless Jägerbombs before dancing the night away to any number of consistently good live acts. With sassy staff and heart-warming (strong) drinks, this is one of the best bars before Key West, and it deserves a visit.

Island Fish Company   BAR

(📞 305-743-4191; Mile 54 bayside; ⏱ 11:30am-10pm) The Island has a friendly staff pouring strong cocktails on a sea-breeze-kissed tiki island overlooking Florida Bay. Chat with your friendly bartender – tip well, and they'll top up your drinks without you realizing it. The laid-back, by-the-water atmosphere is quintessentially Keys. Pretty sunsets and great seafood plates add to the allure.

Brass Monkey   BAR

(📞 305-743-4028; 5561 Overseas Hwy, oceanside; ⏱ 10am-4am) When Colonel Kurtz whispered, 'The horror, the horror,' in *Apocalypse Now* he was probably thinking about the night he got trashed in this scuzziest of dives, the preferred watering hole for off-the-clock bar- and waitstaff in Marathon. Truth be told, there's much fun to be had here, with cheap drinks, a friendly local crowd and live music nightly.

☆ Entertainment

**Marathon Cinema &
Community Theater**   CINEMA

(📞 cinema 305-743-0288, theater 305-743-0994; www.marathontheater.org; 5101 Overseas Hwy) A good, old-school, single-stage theater that shows plays and movies in big reclining seats (with even bigger cup holders).

ℹ️ Information

Fishermen's Hospital (📞 305-743-5533; www.fishermenshospital.org; 3301 Overseas Hwy; ⏱ 24hr) Has a major emergency room, as well as a walk-in clinic for less severe health issues.

ℹ️ Getting There & Away

Fly into the **Marathon Airport** (📞 305-289-6060; Mile 50.5 bayside) or go Greyhound, which stops at the airport. There's also regular bus service to Key West on **Key West Transit** (p170).

LOWER KEYS

The people of the Lower Keys vary between winter escapees and native Conchs. Some local families have been Keys castaways

---

NATURAL WONDERS OF THE KEYS

It's easy to think of the Keys, environmentally speaking, as a little boring. The landscape isn't particularly dramatic (with the exception of those sweet sweeps of ocean visible from the Overseas Hwy); it tends toward low brush and...well, more low brush.

Hey, don't judge a book by its cover. The Keys have one of the most remarkable, sensitive environments in the USA. The difference between ecosystems here is measured in inches, but once you learn to recognize the contrast between a hammock and a wetland, you'll see the islands in a whole new light. Some of the best introductions to the natural Keys can be found at Crane Point Museum (p177) and the Florida Keys Eco-Discovery Center (p184).

But we want to focus on the mangroves – the coolest, if not most visually arresting, habitat in the islands. They rise from the shallow shelf that surrounds the Keys (which also provides that lovely shade of Florida teal), looking like masses of spidery fingers constantly stroking the waters. Each mangrove traps the sediment that has accrued into the land your tiki bar stool is perched on. That's right, no mangroves = no Jimmy Buffett.

The three different types of mangrove trees are all little miracles of adaptation. Red mangroves, which reside on the water's edge, have aerial roots, called propagules, allowing them to 'breathe' even as they grow into the ocean. Black mangroves, which grow further inland, survive via 'snorkel' roots called pneumatophores. Resembling spongy sticks, these roots grow out from the muddy ground and consume fresh air. White mangroves grow furthest inland and actually sweat out the salt they absorb through air and water to keep healthy.

The other tree worth a mention here isn't a mangrove. The lignum vitae, which is limited to the Keys in the USA, is also intriguing. Its sap has long been used to treat syphilis, hence the tree's Latin name, which translates to 'tree of life.'

for generations, and there is somewhat of a more insular feel than other parts of the Overseas Hwy. It's an odd contrast: the islands get at their most isolated, rural and quintessentially 'Keez-y' before opening onto (relatively) cosmopolitan, heterogeneous and free-spirited Key West.

People aside, the big draw in the lower Keys is nature. You'll find the loveliest state park in the Keys here, and one of its rarest species. For paddlers, there is a great mangrove wilderness to explore in a photogenic and pristine environment.

Big Pine Key, Bahia Honda Key & Looe Key

Big Pine is home to endless stretches of quiet roads, Key West employees who found a way around astronomical real-estate rates, and packs of wandering Key deer (p185). Bahia Honda has everyone's favorite sandy beach, while the coral-reef system of Looe offers amazing reef-diving opportunities.

◉ Sights

★ **Bahia Honda State Park**   STATE PARK
(☏ 305-872-3210;   www.bahiahondapark.com; Mile 37; car $4-8, cyclist & pedestrian $2.50; ⊙ 8am-sunset; ♿) ✍ This park, with its long, white-sand (and at times seaweed-strewn) beach, named Sandspur Beach by locals, is the big attraction in these parts. As Keys beaches go, this one is probably the best natural stretch of sand in the island chain. There's also the novel experience of walking on the old Bahia Honda Rail Bridge, which offers nice views of the surrounding islands. Heading out on kayaking adventures (from $12/36 per hour/half day) is another great way to spend a sun-drenched afternoon.

You can also check out the nature trails and science center, where helpful park employees can assist you to identify stone crabs, fireworms, horseshoe crabs and comb jellies. The park concession offers daily 1½-hour snorkeling trips at 9:30am and 1:30pm (adult/child $30/25). Reserve ahead in high season.

No Name Key   ISLAND
Perhaps the best-named island in the Keys, No Name gets few visitors, as it's basically a residential island. It's one of the most reliable spots for Key deer watching. From Overseas Hwy, go on to Watson Blvd, turn right, then left onto Wilder Blvd. Cross Bogie Bridge and you'll be on No Name.

National Key Deer
Refuge Headquarters   WILDLIFE RESERVE
(☏ 305-872-0774; www.fws.gov/refuge/National_ Key_Deer_Refuge; Big Pine Shopping Center, Mile 30.5 bayside; ⊙ 9am-4pm Mon-Fri, 10am-3pm Sat & Sun; ♿) What would make Bambi cuter? Mini Bambi. Introducing the Key deer, an endangered subspecies of white-tailed deer that prance about primarily on Big Pine and No Name Keys. The folks here are an incredibly helpful source of information on the deer and all things Keys. The refuge sprawls over several islands, but the sections open to the public are on Big Pine and No Name.

The headquarters also administers the Great White Heron National Wildlife Refuge – 200,000 acres of open water and mangrove islands north of the main Keys that is only accessible by boat. There's no tourism infrastructure in place to get out here, but you can inquire about nautical charts and the herons themselves at the office.

Blue Hole   LAKE
(off Mile 30.5) This little pond (and former quarry) is now the largest freshwater body in the Keys. That's not saying much, but the hole is a pretty little dollop of blue (well, algal green) surrounded by a small path and information signs. The water is home to turtles, fish and wading birds. A quarter-mile further along the same road is Watson's Nature Trail (less than 1 mile long) and Watson's Hammock, a small Keys forest habitat.

Looe Key National
Marine Sanctuary   PARK
(☏ 305-809-4700;   www.floridakeys.noaa.gov) Looe (pronounced 'loo') Key, located 5 nautical miles off Big Pine, isn't a key at all but a reef, and is part of the Florida Keys National Marine Sanctuary. This is an area of some 2800 sq nautical miles of 'land' managed by the National Oceanic & Atmospheric Administration. The reef here can only be visited through a specially arranged charter-boat trip, best arranged through any Keys diving outfit, the most natural one being Looe Key Dive Center (p182).

Big Pine Flea Market   MARKET
(www.bigpinefleamarket.com; Mile 30.5 oceanside; ⊙ 8am-2pm Sat & Sun, closed Aug & Sep; ℗) **FREE** This market, which attracts folks from across the Keys, rivals local churches for weekly attendance. This is an extravaganza of locally made crafts, vintage clothes, handbags, sunglasses, souvenir T-shirts and beach towels, wood carvings, wind chimes

and hand tools – plus all the secondhand gear you might need for a fishing trip.

🎣 Activities

Serenity Eco Therapy WATER SPORTS
(☎ 305-432-1401; www.serenityecoguides.com; beach yoga from $12, 2hr paddleboard class $85; 🚹) If you're into yoga and/or stand-up paddleboarding – or just curious about trying something completely new – book a class with Serenity. This outfit runs special yoga-SUP classes on the water, as well as beachfront yoga, meditation and sunset paddles. Most classes are held in Bahia Honda State Park.

Old Wooden Bridge Marina BOATING
(☎ 305-872-2241; 1791 Bogie Dr; 2hr single/double kayak ride $25/35, bike hire half/full day $15/20; ⏰ 8am-5pm Sun-Thu, to 6pm Fri & Sat) At the foot of the bridge that takes you over to No Name Key, there's a little wooden shack on the marina where you can hire kayaks and bicycles for the day (plus get staples like beer inside the shop). This is a lovely area to explore either on the water or on two wheels.

Looe Key Dive Center DIVING
(☎ 305-872-2215; www.diveflakeys.com; snorkel/dive from $40/70) Located in a resort of the same name, the Looe Key Dive Center on Ramrod Key runs recommended day trips out to Looe Key departing in morning (at 8am) and afternoon (12:45pm). This two-tank/two-location dive is $70 plus gear for scuba divers, $40 plus gear for snorkelers, and $25 for 'bubblewatchers' who want to come along for the ride.

🛏 Sleeping

⭐ **Bahia Honda State Park Campground** CAMPGROUND $
(☎ 800-326-3521; www.reserveamerica.com; Mile 37, Bahia Honda Key; campsites/cabins $40/160; 🅿️🛜) 🌿 Bahia Honda has the best camping in the Keys. There's nothing quite like waking up to the sky as your ceiling and the ocean as your shower (and: Ow! Sand flies. OK, it's not paradise...). The park has six cabins, each sleeping six people, and 80 campsites a short distance from the beach. Reserve months in advance.

Barnacle Bed & Breakfast B&B $$
(☎ 305-872-3298; www.thebarnacle.net; 1557 Long Beach Dr, Big Pine Key; r $220-290; 🅿️❄️🛜) The Barnacle welcomes you into its atrium with the promise of fresh ocean breezes. Wander around the pond and Jacuzzi, past the swinging hammocks, and into highly individualized rooms that all share a lovingly

mad design sense. Tropical knickknacks and big windows that let in lots of Keys sunlight are standard. Meals should be enjoyed on the deck, which overlooks the sea.

⭐ **Deer Run Bed & Breakfast** B&B $$$
(☎ 305-872-2015; www.deerrunfloridabb.com; 1997 Long Beach Dr, Big Pine Key, off Mile 33 oceanside; r $300-480; 🅿️❄️🛜🏊) 🌿 This state-certified green lodge and vegetarian B&B is isolated on a lovely stretch of Long Beach Dr. It's a garden of quirky delights, complemented by love-the-earth paraphernalia, street signs and four simple but cozy rooms. The helpful owners will get you out on a boat or into the heated pool for relaxation while they whip up delicious vegetarian meals.

🍴 Eating & Drinking

No Name Pub PIZZA $
(☎ 305-872-9115; www.nonamepub.com; N Watson Blvd, Big Pine Key, off Mile 30.5 bayside; mains $10-21; ⏰ 11am-10pm; 🅿️) The No Name's one of those off-the-track places that everyone seems to know about. Despite the isolated location, folks come from all over to this divey spot to add their dollar bills to the walls, drink locally brewed beer, enjoy a little classic rock playing overhead, and feast on excellent pizzas, burgers and pub grub.

Good Food Conspiracy VEGETARIAN $
(☎ 305-872-3945; Big Pine Key, Mile 30 oceanside; sandwiches $8-14; ⏰ 9:30am-7pm Mon-Sat, 11am-5pm Sun; 🅿️🌿) 🌿 Rejoice health-food lovers: all the greens, sprouts, herbs and tofu you've been dreaming about during that long, fried-food-studded drive down the Overseas Hwy are available at this friendly little macrobiotic organic shop. There is a good sandwich and fresh-juice bar on site, where you can get avocado melts, fresh salads, veggie burgers, homemade soup and fruit smoothies.

Kiki's Sandbar BAR
(☎ 305-872-4500; www.kikissandbar.com; 183 Barry Ave, Mile 28.3 bayside; ⏰ 8am-midnight) For drinks with a view, Kiki's is hard to beat. You can have a chat around the bar or retreat for a bit of sunset watching or stargazing from one of the picnic tables on the waterfront lawn – or better yet stroll to the pier, which can be a magical setting when the moon is on the rise.

ℹ Getting There & Away

Greyhound (www.greyhound.com) has two buses daily that stop in Big Pine Key on the run between Miami and Key West (oneway from $9).

Key West Transit (p170) runs nine buses daily between Key West and Marathon, stopping in Big Pine Key. The one-way fare is $4.

Sugarloaf Key & Boca Chica Key

This is the final stretch before the holy grail of Key West. There's not much going on – just bridges over lovely swaths of teal and turquoise, a few good eats and a thoroughly batty roadside attraction.

This lowest section of the Keys goes from about Mile Marker 20 to the start of Key West.

⊙ Sights

Sheriff's Animal Farm ZOO

(Monroe County Sheriff's Office Animal Farm; ☑ 305-293-7300; 5501 College Rd, Stock Island; ⊙ 1-3pm 2nd & 4th Sun of the month or by appointment; P 🚻) ✔ FREE Just before you hit Key West, you may be tempted to stop at this farm, located near the Monroe County Sheriff's Office and Detention Center (seriously). This shelter for Monroe County animals that have been abandoned or given up is a lovely place to take the kids (call ahead to visit and farmer Jeanne Selander will be happy to show you around).

Sugarloaf Key Bat Tower LANDMARK

(Sugarloaf Key, Mile17) It resembles an Aztec-inspired fire lookout, but this wooden tower is actually one real-estate developer's vision gone utterly awry. In the 1920s Richter C Perky had the bright idea to transform this area into a vacation resort. There was just one problem: mosquitoes. His solution? Build a 35ft tower and move in a colony of bats (he'd heard they eat mosquitoes). He imported the flying mammals, but they promptly took off, leaving the tower empty.

The tower is in bad shape, and there's no access to the top.

🛏 Sleeping

Sugarloaf Lodge MOTEL $$

(☑ 305-745-3211; www.sugarloaflodge.net; Sugarloaf Key, Mile 17; r $150-240; P ❄ 🛜 🏊) The 55 motel-like rooms are nothing special, though every single one has an excellent bay view from the balcony or patio (1st floor). There is also an on-site restaurant, a tiki bar, a marina and an airstrip, from which you can charter a seaplane tour or go skydiving. Friendly service.

✖ Eating & Drinking

Baby's Coffee CAFE $

(☑ 305-744-9866; Mile 15 oceanside; ⊙ 6:30am-8pm Mon-Sat, 7am-5pm Sun) This very cool coffee counter has an on-site bean-roasting plant and sells bags of the aromatic stuff along with excellent hot and cold java brews – many locals consider this to be some of the best coffee in the islands. Other essentials are sold, from yummy baked goods to fruit smoothies.

Mangrove Mama's CARIBBEAN $$

(☑ 305-745-3030; www.mangrovemamas20. com; Mile 20 bayside; lunch $10-15, dinner $15-29; ⊙ 8am-10pm; P 🚻) This groovy roadside eatery serves Caribbean-inspired seafood – coconut shrimp, plantain-crusted hogfish, cracked conch sandwiches – best enjoyed on the backyard patio and accompanied by a little live music (daily from 5:30pm).

Square Grouper MODERN AMERICAN $$$

(☑ 305-745-8880; www.squaregrouperbarandgrill. com/menu; Mile 22.5 oceanside, Cudjoe Key; mains $22-39; ⊙ 11am-2:30pm & 5-10pm Tue-Sat; 🚻) ✔ One of the most talked-about restaurants in the Keys, Square Grouper hits all the right notes with fresh, locally sourced ingredients, innovative recipes and great service, all dished up in one elegant but unpretentious dining room. Local fish-of-the-day tacos, seared sesame-encrusted tuna loin and a rich seafood stew are among the highlights, though it's worth investigating daily specials.

Reserve ahead. And don't forget to have a pre- or post-dinner drink in the upstairs lounge My New Joint.

★ My New Joint COCKTAIL BAR

(☑ 305-745-8880; www.mynewjoint420lounge.com; Mile 22.5, Cudjoe Key; ⊙ 4:20pm-midnight Mon-Sat) My New Joint brings a serious dash of style to the Lower Keys. This spacious, warmly lit lounge has artfully made cocktails, excellent brews on tap (including local varieties), great tapas plates and platters of oysters, and live music most nights (from 7pm or 8pm). Nibble on house-smoked fish, charred Brussels sprouts, soft-shell crab steamed buns and other gourmet sharing plates.

❶ Getting There & Away

Key West Transit (p170) runs nine buses a day between Key Wet and Marathon, stopping in both Boca Chica and Sugarloaf Key. The one-way fare is $4.

KEY WEST

📖 305, 786 / POPULATION 26,000

Key West is the far frontier, edgier and more eccentric than the other keys, and also far more captivating. At its heart, this 7-sq-mile island feels like a beautiful tropical oasis, where the moonflowers bloom at night and the classical Caribbean homes are so sad and romantic it's hard not to sigh at them.

While Key West has obvious allure, it's not without its contradictions. On one side of the road, there are literary festivals, Caribbean villas, tropical dining rooms and expensive art galleries. On the other, an S&M fetishist parade, frat boys passing out on the sidewalk and grizzly bars filled with bearded burnouts. With all that in mind, it's easy to find your groove in this setting, no matter where your interests lie.

As in other parts of the Keys, nature plays a starring role here, with some breathtaking sunsets – cause for nightly celebration down on Mallory Sq.

⊙ Sights

★ Mallory Square   SQUARE

(www.mallorysquare.com; 🚻) Take all those energies, subcultures and oddities of Keys life and focus them into one torchlit, family-friendly (but playfully edgy), sunset-enriched street party. The child of all these raucous forces is Mallory Sq, one of the greatest shows on Earth. It begins in the hours leading up to dusk, the sinking sun a signal to bring on the madness. Watch a dog walk a tightrope, a man swallow fire, and British acrobats tumble and sass each other.

★ Museum of Art & History
at the Custom House   MUSEUM

(📞 305-295-6616; www.kwahs.com; 281 Front St; adult/child $10/5; ⊙9:30am-4:30pm) Those wanting to learn a bit about Key West history shouldn't miss this excellent museum at the end of the road. Among the highlights: photographs and archival footage from the building of the ambitious Overseas Hwy (and the hurricane that killed 400 people), a model of the ill-fated USS *Maine* (sunk during the Spanish-American War) and the Navy's role in Key West (once the largest employer), and exhibits on the 'wreckers' of Key West, who made their fortune scavenging sunken treasure ships.

★ Nancy Forrester's
Secret Garden   GARDENS

(www.nancyforrester.com; 518 Elizabeth St; adult/child $10/5; ⊙10am-3pm; 🚻) Nancy, an environmental artist and fixture of the Keys community, invites you into her backyard oasis where chatty rescued parrots and macaws await visitors. Come at 10am when Nancy gives an overview of these marvelously intelligent and rare birds ('Parrot 101' as she calls it). At other times, Nancy is on hand to answer questions and share insight on parrot life. It's a great place for kids, who often leave inspired by the hands-on interactions.

Musicians are welcome to bring their instruments to play in the yard. The birds love it – particularly flutes!

Duval Street   AREA

Key West locals have a love-hate relationship with the most famous road in Key West (if not the Keys). Duval, Old Town Key West's main strip, is a miracle mile of booze, tacky everything and awful behavior. But it's fun. The 'Duval Crawl' is one of the wildest pub crawls in the country. The mix of neon drink, drag shows, T-shirt kitsch, local theaters, art studios and boutiques is more charming than jarring.

Hemingway House   HOUSE

(📞 305-294-1136; www.hemingwayhome.com; 907 Whitehead St; adult/child $14/6; ⊙9am-5pm) Key West's biggest darling, Ernest Hemingway, lived in this gorgeous Spanish colonial house from 1931 to 1940. Papa moved here in his early 1930s with wife No 2, a *Vogue* fashion editor and (former) friend of wife No 1 (he left the house when he ran off with wife No 3). *The Short Happy Life of Francis Macomber* and *The Green Hills of Africa* were produced here, as well as many six-toed cats, whose descendants basically run the grounds.

Florida Keys Eco-Discovery Center   MUSEUM

(📞 305-809-4750; http://eco-discovery.com/ecokw.html; 35 East Quay Rd; ⊙9am-4pm Tue-Sat; 🅿 🚻) 🎟 FREE This 6000-sq-ft center is one of the best places in the Keys to learn about the extraordinary marine environments of South Florida. Start off with the 20-minute film which has some beautiful footage of life among the reefs, hardwood hammocks, seagrass beds and mangroves. Continue to the exhibits of life above the waterline, then look at sea creatures in the small aquarium tanks that make up the 'Living Reef' section.

KEY DEER

••

While we can't guarantee you'll see one, if you head down the side roads of Big Pine Key, there's a pretty good chance you'll spot the Key deer, a local species roughly the size of a large dog. Once mainland dwellers, the Key deer were stranded on the Keys during the formation of the islands. Successive generations grew smaller and had single births, as opposed to large litters, to deal with the reduced food resources in the archipelago. While you won't see thundering herds of dwarfish deer, they are pretty easy to spot if you're persistent and patient. In fact, they're so common you need to pay careful attention to the reduced speed limits. Note: speed limits drop further at night, because cars are still the biggest killer of Key deer. Sadly, Key deer are endangered, with fewer than 1000 left in the wild.

To visit the official Key deer refuge (although the deer can be spotted almost anywhere on Big Pine) take Key Deer Blvd (it's a right at the lights off the Overseas Hwy at the southern end of Big Pine) north for 3.5 miles from Mile Marker 30.5.

Studios of Key West GALLERY
(TSKW; ☑ 305-296-0458; www.tskw.org; 533 Eaton St; ⊙ 10am-4pm Tue-Sat) FREE This nonprofit showcases about a dozen artists' studios in a three-story space, and hosts some of the best art openings in Key West on the first Thursday of the month. Besides its public visual-arts displays, TSKW hosts readings, literary and visual workshops, concerts, lectures and community discussion groups.

Key West Cemetery CEMETERY
(www.friendsofthekeywestcemetery.com; cnr Margaret & Angela Sts; ⊙ 7am-6pm; ⊕) A darkly alluring Gothic labyrinth beckons at the center of this pastel town. Built in 1847, the cemetery crowns Solares Hill, the highest point on the island (with a vertigo-inducting elevation of 16ft). Some of the oldest families in the Keys rest in peace – and close proximity – here. With body space at a premium, mausoleums stand practically shoulder to shoulder. Island quirkiness penetrates the gloom: seashells and macramé adorn headstones with inscriptions like, 'I told you I was sick.'

Get chaperoned by a guide from the Historic Florida Keys Foundation (☑ 305-292-6718), with guided tours ($15 per person) that usually go at 9:30am on Tuesdays and Thursdays. Call to reserve a spot.

Fort Zachary Taylor State Park STATE PARK
(☑ 305-292-6713; www.floridastateparks.org/fort-taylor; 601 Howard England Way; vehicle/pedestrian/bicycle $7/2.50/2.50; ⊙ park 8am-sunset, fort 8am-5pm) 'America's Southernmost State Park' is home to an impressive fort, built in the mid-1800s that played roles in the American Civil War and in the Spanish-American War. The beach here is the best one Key West has to offer – it has white sand to lounge on (but is rocky in parts), water deep enough to swim in and tropical fish under the waves. Learn more about the fort on free guided tours offered at 11am.

The beach is also a great spot to watch the sunset – a fine alternative to the mayhem of Mallory Sq. But you won't be able to stick around and watch the colors light up the sky: all visitors are ushered out right after the sun sinks below the sea. If coming by foot, it's about a half-mile walk (12 minutes) from the entrance to the beach.

Mel Fisher Maritime Museum MUSEUM
(www.melfisher.org; 200 Greene St; adult/child $15/12; ⊙ 8:30am-5pm Mon-Fri, from 9:30am Sat & Sun) For a fascinating glimpse into Key West's complicated history, pay a visit to this popular museum near the waterfront. It's best known for its collection of gold coins, rare jewels and other treasures scavenged from Spanish galleons by Mel Fisher and crew. More thought-provoking is the exhibition devoted to the slave trade, with artifacts from the wreck of the *Henrietta Marie,* a merchant slave ship that sank in 1700.

Key West First Legal Rum DISTILLERY
(☑ 305-294-1441; www.keywestlegalrum.com; 105 Simonton St; ⊙ 10am-8pm Mon-Sat, to 6pm Sun, tours 1pm, 3pm & 5pm Mon-Fri, 1pm & 3pm Sat) Opened in 2013 by a kitesurfing pioneer, this distillery makes some mighty fine rums, which are made with Florida sugarcane and infused with coconut, vanilla and key lime. Try up to eight rums in the shop for $11, which includes a shot glass. You can also take a self-guided audio tour of the small one-room operation, or come for a livelier chef-guided tour held throughout the week.

Key West

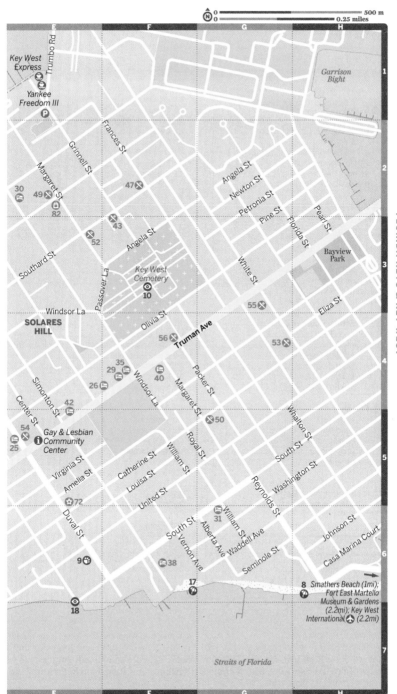

Key West

Key West Distilling   DISTILLERY
(☎305-295-3400; www.kwdistilling.com; 524 Southard St; ☺10am-5pm Mon-Sat) This tiny craft distiller, basically a one-man operation, creates some excellent rums, two types of vodka (including one with horseradish), one gin and one whiskey. The focus is on quality (rather than quantity), and you won't find a better spiced rum in South Florida than its Rambunctious Rum. Stop in for a free tasting and a tour.

Fort East Martello Museum & Gardens
MUSEUM

(☑305-296-3913; www.kwahs.org/museums/fort-east-martello/history; 3501 S Roosevelt Blvd; adult/child $10/5; ☺9:30am-4:30pm) This old fortress was built to resemble an old Italian Martello-style coastal watchtower (hence the name), a design that quickly became obsolete with the advent of the explosive shell. Now the fort serves a new purpose: preserving the old. There's historical memorabilia, artifacts, the folk art of Mario Sanchez and 'junk' sculptor Stanley Papio, who worked with scrap metal; plus a genuinely creepy haunted doll.

Perhaps the most haunted thing in Key West, 'Robert the doll' is a terrifying child's toy from the 19th century who reportedly causes much misfortune to those who question his powers. Honest, he looks like something out of a Stephen King novel; see www.robertthedoll.org for more information.

Little White House
HISTORIC BUILDING

(☑305-294-9911; www.trumanlittlewhitehouse.com; 111 Front St; adult/child 5-12yr/senior $16/5/14; ☺9am-4:30pm) This is where President Harry S Truman used to vacation when he wasn't molding post-WWII geopolitics. It's beautifully preserved and open only for guided tours, although you are welcome to visit one small gallery with photographs and historical displays (and a short video) on the ground floor.

Key West Lighthouse
LIGHTHOUSE

(☑305-294-0012; www.kwahs.org/museums/lighthouse-keepers-quarters/history; 938 Whitehead St; adult/child/senior $10/5/9; ☺9:30am-4:30pm) You can climb up 88 spiraling steps to the top of this snowy white lighthouse, built in 1846, for a decent view (perhaps not as enjoyable as it was in the days when a men's clothing-optional resort was next door, but we digress...). Aside from the views, you can also visit the lighthouse keeper's cottage, which has photographs and artifacts with historical tidbits on life for the keepers of the light.

Key West Butterfly & Nature Conservatory
WILDLIFE RESERVE

(☑305-296-2988; www.keywestbutterfly.com; 1316 Duval St; adult/4-12yr $12/8.50; ☺9am-5pm; ⊞) This vast domed conservatory lets you stroll through a lush, enchanting garden of flowering plants, tiny waterfalls, colorful birds and up to 1800 fluttering butterflies made up of over 50 different species – all live imports from around the globe.

Southernmost Point
LANDMARK

(cnr South & Whitehead Sts) This red-and-black buoy is the most-photographed spot on the island, but it isn't even the southernmost point in the USA (that's in the off-limits naval base around the corner). This is the most-overrated attraction in Key West.

🏃 Activities

Nomadic Standup Paddleboard
WATER SPORTS

(☑305-395-9494; www.nomadicsup.com; 3hr paddleboard tour $65) You can't leave the Keys without getting out on the water. This outfit provides one of the best ways to experience the sublime beauty: on a guided paddleboard outing. Cody will pick you up at your hotel and take you and other guests out to some lovely spots where you will paddle peaceful waterways amid the pristine mangroves northeast of Key West.

Yoga on the Beach
YOGA

(☑305-296-7352; www.yogaonbeach.com; Fort Zachary Taylor State Park; class $18; ☺8:15am-9:45am) If you're a yoga fan, you won't want to miss a session on the beach at Fort Zachary Taylor State Park (p185). The daily 90-minute class, held on the sands overlooking gently lapping waves, is simply exhilarating. Class fee includes park admission for the day, and mats are available.

Reelax Charters
KAYAKING

(☑305-304-1392; www.keyskayaking.com; Sugarloaf Key Marina, Mile 17; all-inclusive kayak trips from $240) Get your paddle on and slip silently into the surrounding mangroves and mudflats of the Lower Keys with Andrea Paulson. Based on Sugarloaf Key, about 17 miles northeast of Key West

Keys Association of Dive Operators
DIVING

(www.divekeys.com) The Key West Association of Dive Operators website is a clearing house for information on diving opportunities in the islands; they also work on enhancing local sustainable underwater activities by creating artificial reefs and encouraging safe boating and diving practices.

Jolly Rover
CRUISE

(☑305-304-2235; www.schoonerjollyrover.com; Schooner Wharf, cnr Greene & Elizabeth Sts; day cruise adult/child $45/25, sunset cruise $59/29) This outfit has a gorgeous, tanbark (reddish-brown) 80ft schooner that embarks on daily two-hour cruises under sail. It looks like a pirate ship and has the cannons to back the

BEACHES IN KEY WEST

Key West is *not* about beachgoing. In fact, for true sun 'n' surf, locals go to Bahia Honda whenever possible. Still, the three city beaches on the southern side of the island are lovely and narrow, with calm and clear water. Tiny South Beach is at the end of Simonton St. Higgs Beach (Reynolds St), at the end of Reynolds St and Casa Marina Ct, has barbecue grills, picnic tables and a large pier for watching the sunset. Smathers Beach (S Roosevelt Blvd; P), further east, is a longer stretch of sand, though not easily accessible if you're coming on foot. The best local beach, though, is at Fort Zachary Taylor (p185); it's worth the admission to enjoy the white sand and relative calm.

image up. You can bring your own food and drink (including alcohol) – small coolers only.

Tours

Conch Tour Train   TOURS
(☎888-916-8687; www.conchtourtrain.com; cnr Front & Duval Sts; adult/senior/child under 13yr $32/29/free; ⊙tours 9am-4:30pm; ☕) This tour outfit seats you in breezy linked train cars on a 90-minute narrated tour; there are three stops (including one near the Hemingway House), where you can hop off and take a later train. Offers discounted admission to the Hemingway House as well as Ghosts and Graveyards night tours. The best place to board is at the Front St depot.

Old Town Trolley Tours   TOURS
(☎855-623-8289; www.trolleytours.com/key-west; adult/child/senior $32/11/29; ⊙tours 9am-4:30pm; ☕) These tours are a great introduction to the city. The 90-minute, hop-on, hop-off narrated tram tour starts at Mallory Sq and makes a loop around the whole city, with 12 stops along the way. Trolleys depart every 15 to 30 minutes from 9am to 4:30pm daily. The narration is hokey, but you'll get a good overview of Key West history.

Key West Ghost & Mysteries Tour   TOURS
(☎786-530-3122; www.keywestghostandmysteries tour.com; tours depart from Duval & Caroline Sts; adult/child $18/10; ⊙tours 9pm) A playfully creepy ghost tour that's as family-friendly as this sort of thing gets – in other words, no big chills or pop-out screaming.

Festivals & Events

★ Fantasy Fest   CULTURAL
(www.fantasyfest.net; ⊙late Oct) Akin to New Orleans' riotous Mardi Gras revelry, Fantasy Fest is 10 days of burlesque parties, parades, street fairs, concerts and loads of costumed events. Bars and inns get competitive about decorating their properties, and everyone gets decked out in the most outrageous costumes they can cobble together (or get mostly naked with daring body paint).

Womenfest   LGBT
(www.womenfest.com; ⊙Sep) One of North America's biggest lesbian celebrations, Womenfest is four days of merrymaking, with pool parties, art shows, roller derby, drag brunches, sunset sails, flag football, and a tattoo and moustache bicycle ride. It's great fun, with thousands descending on Key West from all corners of the USA and beyond.

Key West Literary Seminar   LITERATURE
(www.kwls.org; ⊙Jan) A feast for the literary minded, this four-day yearly event draws top novelists, poets and historians from around the country (although it costs hundreds of dollars to attend). Most book signings and presentations take place in the San Carlos Institute (☎305-294-3887; www.institutosan-carlos.org; 516 Duval St; ⊙noon-5pm Fri-Sun).

Goombay Festival   CULTURAL
(www.goombay-keywest.org; ⊙late Oct; ☕) Held during the same out-of-control week as Fantasy Fest, this is a Bahamian celebration of food, crafts and culture. The family-friendly event runs over two days (typically a Friday and Saturday).

Hemingway Days Festival   CULTURAL
(www.fla-keys.com/hemingwaymedia/; ⊙late Jul) This long-running fest brings parties, a 5km run, a fishing tournament, arm-wrestling contests, a 'Papa' look-alike contest and the running of the bulls (with mock animals pulled on wheels).

Conch Republic
Independence Celebration   CULTURAL
(www.conchrepublic.com; ⊙Apr) A 10-day tribute to Conch Independence; vie for (made-up) public offices and watch a drag queens' foot-race.

Sleeping

There's a glut of boutique hotels, cozy B&Bs and four-star resorts here at the end of the USA. Unfortunately, the one thing lacking is inexpensive lodging. Aside from sleeping in the town's only hostel, it's not easy finding a place for under $300 a night during the high season. Although some options are more central than others, any hotel in Old Town is within walking distance of all the action.

Casablanca Key West
GUESTHOUSE **$$**
(☎305-296-0815; www.keywestcasablanca.com; 900 Duval St; r $180-400; ❇☎☀) On the quieter end of Duval St, the Casablanca is a friendly eight-room guesthouse with a delightful tropical elegance. The inn, once a private house, was built in 1898 and hosted a few luminaries over the years, including Humphrey Bogart who stayed here in 1937. The rooms are bright with polished wood floors and comfy beds; and some have little balconies.

Old Town Manor
BOUTIQUE HOTEL **$$**
(☎305-292-2170; www.oldtownmanor.com; 511 Eaton St; $200-310; ❇☎☀) While it bills itself as a B&B (and breakfast is included), the Old Town feels more like a boutique operation that offers a wide variety of rooms – 14, to be exact, spread amid lush gardens. The digs come in the usual tropically inspired palette (the lime-green walls in some rooms may be too much for some), with quality furnishings.

L'Habitation
GUESTHOUSE **$$**
(☎305-293-9203; www.lhabitation.com; 408 Eaton St; r $200-250; ❇☎) A beautiful, classical Keys cottage, L'Habitation has fine rooms kitted out in light tropical shades, with lamps that look like contemporary art pieces and cozy quilts. The friendly bilingual owner welcomes guests in English or French. The front porch, shaded by palms, is a perfect place to stop and engage in Keys people-watching.

Key West Bed & Breakfast
B&B **$$**
(☎305-296-7274; www.keywestbandb.com; 415 William St; r $90-280; ❇☎) Sunny, airy and full of artistic touches: hand-painted pottery here, a working loom there – is that a ship's masthead in the corner? There is also a range of rooms to fit every budget.

Key Lime Inn
HOTEL **$$**
(☎800-549-4430; www.historickeywestinns.com; 725 Truman Ave; r from $200; P❇☀) These cozy rooms are all scattered around a tropical hardwood backdrop. Inside, the blissfully cool rooms are greener than a jade mine, with tiny flat-screen TVs and artwork on the walls – plus French doors opening onto balconies in some. Start the morning with coffee and breakfast by the pool.

Chelsea House
HOTEL **$$**
(☎305-294-5229; www.historickeywestinns.com/the-inns/chelsea-house; 707 Truman Ave; r low season/high season from $200/$250; P❇@☎☀) This perfect pair of Victorian mansions beckons with big, comfy beds and classy decor. The old-school villa ambience clashes – in a nice way – with the happy vibe of the guests and the folks at reception. Some rooms are quite small and lack windows; make sure you inquire before booking. The tropical gardens make a peaceful setting after a day of exploring.

Caribbean House
GUESTHOUSE **$$**
(☎305-296-0999; www.caribbeanhousekw.com; 226 Petronia St; r from $159; P❇☎) This is a cute, dollhouse-like Caribbean cottage in the heart of Bahama Village. The 10 small, brightly colored guest rooms aren't too fancy, but it's a happy, cozy bargain for Key West. The best rooms have small balconies.

Key West Youth Hostel & Seashell Motel
HOSTEL **$$**
(☎305-296-5719; www.keywesthostel.com; 718 South St; dm $55, d $120-240; P❇☎) This place isn't winning any design awards, but the staff are kind, and it's one of the only lower-priced choices on the island. The dorms and motel rooms have plain white tile floors, though the cheery paint job in some rooms (yellow or blue and white) somewhat breaks the monotony. The patio in the back is a fine place to meet other travelers.

★Mermaid & the Alligator
GUESTHOUSE **$$$**
(☎305-294-1894; www.kwmermaid.com; 729 Truman Ave; r winter $330-380, summer $230-290; P❇☎☀) It takes a real gem to stand out amid the jewels of Keys hotels, but this place, in a 1904 mansion, more than pulls off the job. Each of the nine rooms is individually designed with a great mix of modern comfort, Keys Colonial ambience and playful laughs.

Tropical Inn
BOUTIQUE HOTEL **$$$**
(☎888-611-6510; www.tropicalinn.com; 812 Duval St; r $275-500; ❇☎☀) The Tropical Inn has excellent service and a host of individualized rooms spread out over a historic home property. Each room comes decked out in bright pastels and shades of mango, lime and seafoam. A delicious breakfast is included and can be enjoyed in the jungly courtyard next to a lovely sunken pool.

Gardens Hotel HOTEL **$$$**
(☑305-294-2661; www.gardenshotel.com; 526 Angela St; r $400-700; [P][✳][🛜][≋]) Would we be stating the obvious if we mentioned this place has really nice gardens? In fact, the rooms are located in the Peggy Mills Botanical Gardens, which is a longish way of saying 'tropical paradise.' Inside, Caribbean accents mesh with antique furniture, polished wood floors, designer linens and marble bathrooms to make for some of Key West's most enticing rooms.

Saint Hotel BOUTIQUE HOTEL **$$$**
(☑305-294-3200; www.thesainthotelkeywest.com; 417 Eaton St; r $360-700; [✳][🛜][≋]) Despite its proximity to Duval St, the Saint feels like a world removed with its plush rooms, chic minimalist lobby, photogenic pool with small cascading waterfall, and artfully designed bar. The best rooms have balconies overlooking the pool.

Seascape Tropical Inn B&B **$$$**
(☑305-296-7776; www.seascapetropicalinn.com; 420 Olivia St; r $250-425; [✳][🛜][≋]) Had this B&B existed back in the day, Hemingway could have stumbled into it after one of his epic drinking binges – it's within hollering distance of his old house. Now you can crash in one of seven rooms, each uniquely designed with floral comforters and artwork on the walls. The best rooms have French doors opening onto private terraces.

Silver Palms Inn BOUTIQUE HOTEL **$$$**
(☑305-294-8700; www.silverpalmsinn.com; 830 Truman Ave; r $280-400; [P][✳][🛜][≋]) 🐾 Royal blues, sweet teals, bright limes and lemon-on-yellow color schemes douse the interior of this boutique property, which also boasts bicycle rentals, a saltwater swimming pool and a green certification from the Florida Department of Environmental Protection. Overall the Silver Palms offers more of a modern, large-hotel vibe with a candy-colored dose of Keys tropics attitude.

Lighthouse Court Inn BOUTIQUE HOTEL **$$$**
(☑305-294-5229; www.historickeywestinns.com/the-inns/lighthouse-court; 902 Whitehead St; r from $260; [✳][🛜][≋]) The rooms at the Lighthouse Court are among the most handsomely appointed in town. They're elegant in their simplicity, with the warm earth tones of hardwood floors set off by just the right amount of tropical breeziness and cool colors. Affiliated with Historic Key West Inns.

Mango Tree Inn B&B **$$$**
(☑305-293-1177; www.mangotree-inn.com; 603 Southard St; r $235-400; [✳][🛜][≋]) This down-to-earth B&B offers a courtyard pool and attractive accommodation in a number of airy rooms, each decorated with swaths of tropical-chic accoutrements, from rattan furniture to flowering hibiscus. Rates dip as low as $150 in the low season.

Santa Maria Suites Resort BOUTIQUE HOTEL **$$$**
(☑305-296-5678; www.santamariasuites.com; 1401 Simonton St; r from $450; [P][✳][🛜][≋]) With its marvelous deco facade, the Santa Maria looks like it took a wrong turn on South Beach, Miami, and ended up in Key West. The suites themselves – all two-bedroom – also show elements of Miami decadence, with spacious sun-drenched interiors, designer kitchens and stylish living rooms that open onto terraces.

Curry Mansion Inn HOTEL **$$$**
(☑305-294-5349; www.currymansion.com; 511 Caroline St; r $250-390; [P][✳][🛜][≋]) In a city full of stately 19th-century homes, the Curry Mansion is especially handsome. All the elements of an aristocratic American home come together here, from plantation-era Southern colonnades to a New England–style widow's walk and, of course, bright Floridian rooms with canopied beds. Enjoy bougainvillea and breezes on the verandah.

Truman Hotel HOTEL **$$$**
(☑305-296-6700; www.trumanhotel.com; 611 Truman Ave; r $320-400; [P][✳][🛜][≋]) Close to the main downtown drag, these playful rooms have huge flat-screen TVs, kitchenettes, zebra-print throw rugs and mid-century modern furniture. Try to score an upstairs room overlooking the pool (and away from Truman Ave) for the best light and least noise. The pool, fringed with palm trees, is particularly inviting.

✕ Eating

BO's Fish Wagon SEAFOOD **$**
(www.bosfishwagon.com; 801 Caroline St; mains $12-19, lunch specials $11-17; ⊙11am-9:30pm) Looking like a battered old fishing boat that smashed onto the shore, BO's is awash with faded buoys, lifesavers and rusting license plates strung from its wooden rafters, and in some spots you needn't step outside to peer up at the moon. Regardless, the seafood is fantastic – with rich conch fritters, softshell crab sandwiches and tender fish tacos.

THE CONCH REPUBLIC: ONE HUMAN FAMILY

Conchs (pronounced 'conk' as in 'bonk,' not 'contsh' as in 'bunch') are people who were born and raised in the Keys. It's a rare title to achieve. Even transplants can only rise to the rank of 'freshwater Conch.' You will hear reference to, and see the flag of, the Conch Republic everywhere in the islands, which brings us to an interesting tale.

In 1982 US border patrol and customs agents erected a roadblock at Key Largo to catch drug smugglers and illegal aliens. As traffic jams and anger mounted, many tourists disappeared. They decided they'd rather take the Shark Valley Tram in the Everglades, thank you very much. To voice their outrage, a bunch of fiery Conchs decided to secede from the USA. After forming the Conch Republic, they made three declarations (in this order): secede from the USA; declare war on the USA and surrender; and request $1 million in foreign aid. The roadblock was eventually lifted, and every February, Conchs celebrate the anniversary of those heady days with nonstop parties, and the slogan 'We Seceded Where Others Failed.'

Today the whole Conch Republic thing is largely a marketing gimmick, but that doesn't detract from its official motto: 'One Human Family.' This emphasis on tolerance and mutual respect has kept the Keys' head and heart in the right place, accepting gays, straights and peoples of all colors and religions.

FLORIDA KEYS & KEY WEST KEY WEST

Date & Thyme
HEALTH FOOD $

(☑ 305-296-7766; www.helpyourselffoods.com; 829 Fleming St; ⊗ cafe 8am-4pm, market to 6pm; ⚐) ⚑ Equal parts market and cafe, Date & Thyme whips up deliciously guilt-free breakfast and lunch plates, plus energizing smoothies and juices. Try the açai bowl with blueberry, granola and coconut milk for breakfast, or lunch favorites like Thai coconut curry with mixed vegetables and quinoa. There's a shaded patio in front, where roaming chickens nibble underfoot (don't feed them).

5 Brothers Grocery & Sandwich Shop
DELI $

(930 Southard St; sandwiches $4-8; ⊗ 6:30am-3pm Mon-Sat) A Key West icon, this tiny grocery store and deli fires up some of the best Cuban-style espresso this side of Miami. Join locals over early-morning *cafe con leche*, guava pastries and bacon and egg rolls, or stop in later for delectable roast pork sandwiches.

Garbo's Grill
FUSION $

(www.garbosgrillkw.com; 409 Caroline St; mains $10-14; ⊗ 11am-10pm Mon-Sat) Just off the beaten path, Garbo's whips up delicious tacos with creative toppings like mango ginger habanero-glazed shrimp, Korean barbecue, and fresh mahimahi with all the fixings, as well as gourmet burgers and hot dogs. It's served out of a sleek Airstream trailer, which faces onto a shaded brick patio dotted with outdoor tables.

Pierogi Polish Market
EASTERN EUROPEAN $

(☑ 305-292-0464; 1008 White St; mains $5-11; ⊗ pierogi counter 11am-7pm Mon-Sat, shop 10am-8pm Mon-Sat, noon-6pm Sun; ℗⚐) The Keys have an enormous seasonal population of temporary workers largely drawn from Central and Eastern Europe. This is where those workers can revisit the motherland, via pierogies, dumplings, blinis and a great sandwich selection. Although it's called a Polish market, there's food here that caters to Hungarians, Czechs and Russians (among others).

Glazed Donuts
BAKERY $

(☑ 305-294-9142; 420 Eaton St; doughnuts $2-4; ⊗ 7am-3pm Tue-Sun; ⚐🍴) Doughnuts make the world go round, and you'll find some excellent varieties at this cute bakery. The flavors are as eccentric as Key West itself, and reflect the seasons: strawberry shortcake, blood orange marmalade, mango hibiscus and (of course) key lime. Good coffees complete the perfect combo.

★ Thirsty Mermaid
SEAFOOD $$

(☑ 305-204-4828; www.thirstymermaidkeywest.com; 521 Fleming St; mains $12-28; ⊗ 11am-11:30pm; ⚐) Aside from having a great name, the pint-sized Thirsty Mermaid deserves high marks for its outstanding seafood and stylish but easygoing atmosphere. The menu is a celebration of culinary treasures from the sea, with a raw bar of oysters, ceviche, middleneck clams and even caviar. Among the main courses, seared diver scallops or togarashi-spiced tuna with jasmine rice are outstanding.

The Café
VEGETARIAN $$

(☑ 305-296-5515; www.thecafekw.com; 509 Southard St; mains $12-22; ⊗ 9am-10pm; ⚐) The oldest vegetarian spot in Key West is a sunny

LAZY DAYS

. . . .

With its walkable town center, easygoing bars and friendly locals happy to share a story or two, Key West seems like it was made for lazy days. After you've seen the sights, take a day for seaside relaxing and enjoying the Keys' lesser-known charms.

BEACH LOUNGING

Although not known as a beach destination, Key West has some pretty spots for a day by the ocean. **Fort Zachary Taylor State Park** (p185) has a stretch of white sands and clear water, plus snorkel gear for hire and a peaceful cafe.

NO NAME KEY

An easy 45-minute drive from Key West is **No Name Key** (p181), where endangered Key Deer feed in the forests near the road. Take short walks in the **National Key Deer Refuge** (p181) and stop for a meal at the famous **No Name Pub** (p182).

BRUNCH & COCKTAILS

The classic way to start the day in Key West is over a long leisurely brunch. You can join the roosters for a bit of backyard nibbling at **Blue Heaven** (p196), or make your own Bloody Marys at **Blue Macaw** (p196). Speaking of Bloodies, you can drink (and eat) your way through the town's best at **Pilar Bar** (p197).

BACKYARD OASIS

At **Nancy Forrester's Secret Garden** (p184), Nancy happily introduces visitors to her remarkable parrots and macaws, all with unique personalities. If you play an instrument, these birds always enjoy a concert!

1. Fort Zachary State Park Beach
2. Deer, National Key Deer Refuge
3. Blue Heaven restaurant

CHUCK WAGNER/SHUTTERSTOCK ©

luncheonette by day that morphs into a buzzing, low-lit eating and drinking spot by night. The cooking is outstanding, with an eclectic range of dishes: Thai curry stir fries, Italian veggie meatball subs, pizza with shaved Brussels sprouts, and a famous veggie burger.

Mangia Mangia
ITALIAN $$

(📋 305-294-2469; www.mangia-mangia.com; 900 Southard St; mains $18-29; ⊘ 5:30-10pm) On a peaceful stretch of Southard St, Mangia Mangia cooks up fresh pastas, made in-house from scratch, paired with delicacies such as mixed seafood, lobster and sea scallops (there's also grilled fish and meat dishes). The comfy setting has an old-school vibe, with wood-paneled walls and tropical paintings, though you can also dine in the pleasant side garden.

Six Toed Cat
AMERICAN $$

(📋 305-294-3318; 823 Whitehead St; mains $12-21; ⊘ 8:30am-5pm) Simple, fresh and filling breakfast and lunch fare is served just a stone's throw from the Hemingway House (p184; and is indeed named for the author's six-toed felines). A lobster Benedict with avocado should satisfy the day's protein needs, but if you're here for lunch, don't miss the lovely fried shrimp sandwich.

Point5
FUSION $$

(📋 305-296-0669; 915 Duval St; small plates $5-17; ⊘ 6pm-midnight; 📋) Point5 is a good deal more sophisticated than the typical Duval St drinkery. It trades in fusion-style tapas with global influence, ranging from marinated octopus salad to Sichuan eggplant and chipotle pork tacos. All go nicely with the wines by the glass and creative cocktail selections.

Blue Macaw
AMERICAN $$

(📋 305-440-3196; www.bluemacawkeywest.com; 804 Whitehead St; mains lunch $12-16, dinner $19-34; ⊘ 9am-10pm; 📋) Blue Macaw serves nicely executed fish and chips, portabello quesadillas, rack of ribs and sesame-seared tuna, though it's the atmosphere that brings in most people. Its open-air tables are set on a patio trimmed with tropical plants, and there's live music from 11am onward. The other draw: the make-your-own Bloody Marys, a great way to start the day.

Croissants de France
FRENCH $$

(📋 305-294-2624; www.croissantsdefrance.com; 816 Duval St; mains $12-19; ⊘ 7:30am-9pm; 📋) France comes to the Caribbean at this lovely bistro, with tasty results. Stop by for eggs Benedict, cinnamon brioche French toast or lovely pastries at breakfast, then pop back at lunch for baguette sandwiches, quiche and berry-filled sweet crepes. The setting perfectly seizes Key West's cozy-Caribbean-chic aesthetic.

Mo's Restaurant
CARIBBEAN $$

(📋 305-296-8955; 1116 White St; mains $10-21; ⊘ 11am-10pm Mon-Sat) The words 'Caribbean,' 'home' and 'cooking,' when used in conjunction, are generally always enough to impress. But it's not just the genre of cuisine that wins us over at Mo's – it's the execution.

The dishes are mainly Haitian, and they're delicious – the spicy pickles will inflame your mouth, which can get cooled down with a rich vegetable 'mush' over rice, or try the incredible signature snapper.

El Siboney
CUBAN $$

(📋 305-296-4184; www.elsiboneyrestaurant.com; 900 Catherine St; mains $8-19; ⊘ 11am-9:30pm) This is a rough-and-ready Cuban joint where the portions are big and there's no messing around with high-end embellishment or bells and whistles. It's classic ingredients: rice, beans, grilled grouper, roasted pork, barbecue chicken, sweet plantains – all cooked with pride to belly-filling satisfaction.

Seven Fish
SEAFOOD $$

(📋 305-296-2777; www.7fish.com; 921 Truman Ave; mains $20-34; ⊘ 6-10pm Wed-Mon) This simply designed spot on busy Truman Ave specializes in the culinary hits from the sea – delectably prepared freshly caught fish and seafood dished up with care. Try the crab and shiitake mushroom pasta, the sea scallops or the straight-up fresh fish of the day. You can't go wrong here.

★ Blue Heaven
AMERICAN $$$

(📋 305-296-8666; www.blueheavenkw.com; 729 Thomas St; mains breakfast & lunch $10-17, dinner $22-35; ⊘ 8am-10:30pm; 📋) Proof that location is *nearly* everything, this is one of the quirkiest venues on an island of oddities. Customers (and free-roaming fowl) flock to dine in the ramshackle, tropical plant-filled garden where Hemingway once officiated boxing matches. This place gets packed with customers who wolf down delectable breakfasts (blueberry pancakes) and Keys cuisine with French touches (like yellowtail snapper with citrus beurre blanc).

Nine One Five
FUSION $$$

(📋 305-296-0669; www.915duval.com; 915 Duval St; mains lunch $14-22, dinner $26-45; ⊘ 5-11pm Mon & Tue, 11:30am-11pm Wed-Sun; 📋) Classy

Nine One Five certainly stands out from the nearby Duval detritus of alcoholic aggression and tribal-band tattoos. Ignore all that and enter this modern and elegant space, which serves a creative, New American-dips-into-Asia menu. It's all quite rich – imagine a wild salmon with pearl barley, leeks and beurre blanc, or tortelloni with pecorino cream sauce and shaved black truffle.

Café Solé FRENCH $$$
(☑ 305-294-0230; www.cafesole.com; 1029 Southard St; mains $25-38; ☺ 5-10pm) Conch carpaccio with capers? Lobster bouillabaise? Yes indeed. This locally and critically acclaimed venue is known for its cozy back-porch ambience and innovative menus, cobbled together by a chef trained in southern French techniques who works with island ingredients.

🍸 Drinking & Nightlife

Basically Key West is a floating bar. 'No it's a nuanced, multilayered island with a proud nautical and multicultural histo–' *Bzzzt!* Floating bar. Bars close around 4am. Duval is the famed nightlife strip, which is lined with all manner of drinking dens – from frat boy party hubs to raucous drag-loving cabarets. Live music is a big part of the equation.

★ Green Parrot BAR
(☑ 305-294-6133; www.greenparrot.com; 601 Whitehead St; ☺ 10am-4am) The oldest bar on an island of bars, this rogues' cantina opened in the late 19th century and hasn't closed yet. Its ramshackle interior – complete with local artwork littering the walls and a parachute stretched across the ceiling – only adds to the atmosphere, as does the colorful crowd, obviously out for a good time.

The Green Parrot books some of the best bands – playing funk-laden rock, brassy jazz, juke-joint blues and Latin grooves – that hail from Miami, New Orleans, Atlanta and other places. There's never a cover.

Pilar Bar BAR
(☑ 305-294-3200; www.thesainthotelkeywest.com/pilar-bar; 417 Eaton St; ☺ 1-11pm) Inside the Saint Hotel, this small, convivial bar deserves special mention for its outstanding Bloody Marys – among the best you'll find in this country. It's also a great setting for a cocktail and high-end pub grub – and feels secreted away from the chaos of nearby Duval St.

About that Bloody Mary… Bartender Paul Murphy, an expat from London, created 'the Almighty,' featuring specially infused Austral-ian vodka and topped with a veritable meal, including Yorkshire pudding, prime rib parcel with horseradish cream, peppered bacon, a blue cheese-stuffed meatball and other ingredients, plus topped with a Key West shrimp.

Porch BAR
(☑ 305-517-6358; www.facebook.com/theporchkw; 429 Caroline St; ☺ 11am-4am) For a break from the frat-boy bars on the Duval St strip, head to the Porch. Inside a lovely Caribbean-style mansion, this two-part bar serves up craft beer and wine on one side (left entrance) and creative cocktails (right entrance) in a handsomely designed but laid-back setting.

Vinos on Duval WINE BAR
(☑ 305-294-7568; www.vinosonduval.com; 810 Duval St; ☺ 1pm-1am) On the less rowdy end of Duval St, Vinos pours a good selection of wines from around the globe – Spanish tempranillos, Argentine malbecs, Californian cabs – in a cozy setting with a touch of Key West eccentricity. Grab a seat at the bar and have a chat with the knowledgeable staff, or retreat to one of the tables on the porch.

Captain Tony's Saloon BAR
(☑ 305-294-1838; www.capttonyssaloon.com; 428 Greene St; ☺ 10am-2am) Propagandists would have you believe the nearby megabar complex of Sloppy Joe's was Hemingway's original bar, but the physical place where the old man drank was right here, the original Sloppy Joe's location (before it was moved onto Duval St and into frat-boy hell). Hemingway's third wife (a journalist sent to profile Papa) seduced him in this very bar.

Conch Republic BAR
(☑ 305-294-4403; www.conchrepublicseafood.com; 631 Greene St; ☺ noon-midnight) Overlooking the waterfront, this sprawling open-sided eatery and drinking space is a fun place to get you in the Key West spirit. The allure: a festive happy hour, the chatty laid-back crowd, island breezes and live music (nightly from 6pm to 10pm, plus afternoons on Friday and Saturday). The seafood is also quite good (mains $15 to $30).

Vivez Joyeux WINE BAR
(☑ 305-517-6799; www.vivez-joyeux.com; 300 Petronia St; ☺ 3-10pm) This French-run wine bar is tiny but utterly charming, with velvety red wines by the glass or bottle from an impressive rotation of French and American wine growers. You can pair those wines with first-rate cheese, charcuterie and other snacks.

GAY & LESBIAN KEY WEST

Key West's position at the edge of the USA has always attracted artists and eccentrics, and with them a refreshing dose of tolerance. The island had one of the earliest 'out' communities in the USA, and though less true than in the past, visiting Key West is still a rite of passage for many LGBTQI Americans. In turn, this community has had a major impact on the local culture. A good first stop for visitors is at the Key West Business Guild, which represents many gay-owned businesses; the guild is housed at the Gay & Lesbian Community Center (p199), where you can pick up loads of information about local gay life. For details on gay parties and events, log onto www.gaykeywestfl.com.

Gay nightlife, in many cases, blends into mainstream nightlife, with everybody kind of going everywhere these days. But the backbone of the gay bar scene can be found in a pair of cruisey watering holes that sit across the street from one another, Bourbon St Pub and 801 Bourbon Bar (☑305-294-4737; www.801bourbon.com; 801 Duval St; ⊙9am-4am), and can be summed up in five words: drag-queen-led karaoke night. For a peppier scene that includes dancing and occasional drag shows, men and women should head to Aqua. There's also the fun scene at La Te Da, which is best known for its Sunday-afternoon dance parties.

Most hotels in Key West are gay friendly.

Bourbon St Pub   GAY & LESBIAN
(☑305-294-9354; www.bourbonstpub.com; 724 Duval St; ⊙10am-4am) A celebratory crowd, great DJs and striking male dancers (who shimmy on top of the bar from 10pm onward) keep the party going at this iconic spot on Duval St. The garden bar in back, with pool and Jacuzzi, is open to men only, and occasionally hosts clothing-optional afternoon parties.

Garden of Eden   BAR
(224 Duval St; ⊙noon-4am) Go to the top of this building and discover Key West's own clothing-optional drinking patio. Lest you get too excited, cameras aren't allowed and most people come clothed. Regardless, the views are great, the mixed crowd is up for a fun time, and it's an obligatory stop when bar-hopping along Duval.

If you go, don't be a voyeuristic wallflower. Get out there and dance!

Aqua   GAY & LESBIAN
(☑305-294-0555; www.aquakeywest.com; 711 Duval St; ⊙3pm-2am) Aqua hosts some of the best drag shows on the island that attracts all types – gay, lesbian, straight, young, old, couples, groups – all wanting to see what the excitement is about. There's also karaoke several nights a week (currently Monday through Wednesday), so if you can sing, get in on the action!

Hog's Breath   BAR
(☑305-296-4222; www.hogsbreath.com; 400 Front St; ⊙10am-2am) A good place to start the infamous Duval Pub Crawl, the Hog's Breath is a rockin' outdoor bar with good live bands and better cold Coronas.

☆ Entertainment

La Te Da   CABARET
(☑305-296-6706; www.lateda.com; 1125 Duval St; ⊙shows 8:30pm) While the outside bar is where locals gather for mellow chats over beer, you can catch high-quality drag acts – big names come here from around the country – upstairs at the fabulous Crystal Room on weekends (admission $26). More low-key cabaret acts grace the downstairs lounge.

The Sunday tea dance – an afternoon dance party (from 4pm to 7pm) by the pool – is a great way to end the weekend.

Virgilio's   LIVE MUSIC
(☑305-296-1075; 524 Duval St; ⊙7pm-3am, to 4am Thu-Sat) This bar-stage is as un-Keys as they come, and frankly, thank God for a little variety. This town needs a dark, candlelit martini lounge where you can chill to blues or jazz and get down with some salsa, which Virgilio's handsomely provides. Enter on Applerouth Lane.

Tropic Cinema   CINEMA
(☑877-761-3456; www.tropiccinema.com; 416 Eaton St) Great art-house movie theater with deco frontage.

Waterfront Playhouse   THEATER
(☑305-294-5015; www.waterfrontplayhouse.org; 310 Wall St, Mallory Sq) Catch high-quality musicals and dramas from the oldest-running

theater troupe in Florida. The season runs November through April.

Red Barn Theatre   THEATER
(☑ 305-296-9911; www.redbarntheatre.com; 319 Duval St; ⊙ box office 1-8pm Tue-Fri, 4-8pm Sat & Sun) An occasionally edgy and always fun, cozy little local playhouse.

🛍 Shopping

Salt Island Provisions   GIFTS & SOUVENIRS
(☑ 305-896-2980; 830 Fleming St; ⊙ 10am-6pm) This crafty little shop is a fun place to browse for gift ideas. You'll find delicate jewelry made by local artisans, beeswax candles, organic coffee, Florida-related photography books and, of course, salt in its many incarnations: namely salt scrubs and gourmet cooking salts in infusions of merlot, sriracha, curry and white truffle.

Petronia Island Store   ARTS & CRAFTS
(801 Whitehead St; ⊙ 10am-4pm Thu-Sun) On a shop- and gallery-lined stretch of Whitehead St, this small sunlit store carries a well-curated selection of handmade soaps, jewelry, candles, pretty stationery and organic cotton clothes (with mermaids, mariners and octopi) for the young ones. Run by artists, the hip little outpost carries unique pieces that seem imbued with the creative, crafty ethos of Key West.

Books & Books   BOOKS
(☑ 305-320-0208; www.booksandbookskw.com; 533 Eaton St; ⊙ 10am-6pm) Miami's best indie bookshop has a branch in Key West, and it's a magnet for the literary minded. You'll find plenty of titles of local interest (particularly strong on Key West and Cuba), great staff picks and thought-provoking new releases. Regular book signings and author readings take place throughout the year.

Kermit's   FOOD
(www.keylimeshop.com; 200 Elizabeth St; ⊙ 9am-9:30pm) Satisfy your cravings for all things key lime–related at this long-running institution near the waterfront. You'll find salsa, barbecue sauce, candies, ice cream, dog biscuits and even wine all bearing that distinctive key lime flavor. Purists may prefer to settle for a pie (mini pies available) or perhaps a chocolate-dipped key lime popsicle.

Key West Dream Collection   CLOTHING
(☑ 305-741-7560; 613 Simonton St; ⊙ 10am-3pm) This wonderfully eclectic store is a showcase for Key West's creative side with eye-catching

vintage apparel, African textiles and glass beads, books and artwork by local writers and artists, and even CDs by homegrown Key West bands.

Leather Master   FASHION & ACCESSORIES
(418 Applerouth Lane; ⊙ 11am-10pm Mon-Sat, noon-5pm Sun) Besides the gladiator outfits, studded jockstraps and S&M masks, they do very nice bags and shoes here. Which is what you came for, right?

ℹ Information

Key West Chamber of Commerce (☑ 305-294-2587; www.keywestchamber.org; 510 Greene St; ⊙ 9am-6pm) An excellent source of info.

Lower Keys Medical Center (☑ 305-294-5531; www.lkmc.com; 5900 College Rd, Mile 5, Stock Island) Has a 24-hour emergency room.

Gay & Lesbian Community Center (☑ 305-292-3223; 513 Truman Ave; ⊙ 9am-5pm) Serves as a welcome center for LGBT travelers. Loads of great tips on restaurants, bars, lodging and outdoor activities in Key West.

ℹ Getting There & Away

Key West International Airport (EYW; ☑ 305-809-5200; www.eyw.com; 3491 S Roosevelt Blvd) is off S Roosevelt Blvd on the east side of the island. You can fly into Key West from some major US cities, such as Miami or New York. Flights from Los Angeles and San Francisco usually have to stop in Tampa, Orlando or Miami first. American Airlines (www.aa.com) has several flights a day. From Key West airport, a quick and easy taxi ride into Old Town will cost about $22.

Greyhound (☑ 305-296-9072; www.greyhound.com; 3535 S Roosevelt Blvd) has two buses daily between Key West and Downtown Miami. Buses leave Miami for the 4¼-hour journey at 12:35pm and 6:50pm and Key West at 8:55am and 5:45pm going the other way (from $10 to $40 each way).

You can boat from Miami to the Keys on the **Key West Express** (☑ 239-463-5733; www.seakeywestexpress.com; 100 Grinnell St, Key West; adult/senior/junior/child round-trip $155/145/92/62, one way $95/95/68/31), which departs from Fort Myers beach daily at 8:30am and does a 3½-hour cruise to Key West. Returning boats depart the seaport at 6pm. You'll want to show up 1½ hours before your boat departs. During winter the *Express* also leaves several times a week from Marco Island (the prices and sailing time are identical to Fort Myers departures).

ℹ Getting Around

Once you're in Key West, the best way to get around is by bicycle (rentals from the Duval St area, hotels and hostels cost from $10 a day). For transport within the Duval St area, the free Duval Loop shuttle (www.carfreekeywest.com/duval-loop) runs from 6pm to midnight.

Other options include the **Key West Transit** (p170), with color-coded buses running about every 15 minutes; mopeds, which generally cost from $35 per day ($60 for a two-seater); or the open-sided electric tourist cars, aka 'Conch cruisers,' which travel at 35mph and cost about $140/200 for a four-seater/six-seater per day.

A&M Scooter Rentals (☑ 305-896-1921; www.amscooterskeywest.com; 523 Truman Ave; bicycle/scooter/electric car per day from $10/35/140; ☺ 9am-7pm) rents out scooters and bikes, as well as open-sided electric cars that can seat from two to six, and offers free delivery.

Parking can be tricky in town. There's a free **parking lot** on Fort St off Truman Ave.

DRY TORTUGAS NATIONAL PARK

After all those keys, connected by that convenient road, the nicest islands in the archipelago require a little extra effort.

Dry Tortugas National Park (☑ 305-242-7700; www.nps.gov/drto) is open for day trips and overnight camping, which provides a rare phenomenon: a quiet Florida beach. Reserve months in advance through the Yankee Freedom III, which provides ferry service to the island. The sparkling waters offer excellent snorkeling and diving opportunities. A visitor center is located within fascinating Fort Jefferson.

Dry Tortugas National Park is America's most inaccessible national park. Reachable only by boat or seaplane, it rewards you for your effort in getting there with amazing snorkeling amid coral reefs full of marine life. You'll also get to tour a beautifully preserved 19th-century brick fort, one of the largest such fortifications in the USA despite its location 70 miles off the coast of Key West.

On paper, the Dry Tortugas covers an extensive area – over 70 sq miles. In reality only 1% of the park (about 143 acres) consists of dry land, so much of the park's allure lies under the water. The marine life is quite rich here, with the opportunity to see tarpon, sizable groupers and lots of colorful coral and smaller tropical fish, plus the odd sea turtle gliding through the sea.

Explorer Ponce de León named this seven-island chain Las Tortugas (The Turtles) for the sea turtles spotted in its waters. Thirsty

mariners who passed through and found no water later affixed 'dry' to the name. In subsequent years, the US Navy set an outpost here as a strategic position into the Gulf of Mexico. But by the Civil War, Fort Jefferson, the main structure on the islands, had become a prison for Union deserters and at least four other people, among them Dr Samuel Mudd, who had been arrested for complicity in the assassination of Abraham Lincoln. Hence a new nickname: Devil's Island. The name was prophetic: in 1867 a yellow-fever outbreak killed 38 people, and after an 1873 hurricane the fort was abandoned. It reopened in 1886 as a quarantine station for smallpox and cholera victims, was declared a national monument in 1935 by President Franklin D Roosevelt, and was upped to national park status in 1992 by George Bush Sr.

You can come for the day or overnight if you want to camp. Garden Key has 10 campsites ($15 per person, per night), which are given out on a first-come, first-served basis. You'll need to reserve months ahead through the ferry Yankee Freedom III, which takes passengers to and from the island. There are toilets, but no freshwater showers or drinking water; bring everything you'll need. You can stay up to four nights. The sparkling waters offer excellent snorkeling and diving opportunities.

In March and April, there is stupendous bird-watching, including aerial fighting. Stargazing is mind-blowing any time of the year.

❶ Getting There & Away

If you have your own boat, the Dry Tortugas are covered under National Ocean Survey chart No 11438. **Key West Seaplanes** (☑ 305-293-9300; www.keywestseaplanecharters.com; half-day trip adult/child $330/265, full-day trip $578/462) can take up to 10 passengers (flight time 40 minutes each way). The half-day tour is four hours, allowing 2½ hours on the island. The eight-hour full-day excursion gives you six hours on the island. Again, reserve at least a week in advance. Passengers over age 16 arriving by plane also need to pay an added $10 park admission fee (cash only). Flights depart from West International Airport.

Yankee Freedom III (☑ 800-634-0939; www.drytortugas.com; Key West Ferry Terminal, 100 Grinell St; adult/child/senior $175/125/165) Operates a fast ferry departing from the Historic Seaport (at the northern end of Margaret St). Round-trip fares cost $170/125 per adult/child. Reservations are recommended. Continental breakfast, a picnic lunch, snorkeling gear and a 45-minute tour of Fort Jefferson are all included.

Understand Miami & the Keys

Miami & the Keys Today

South Florida is thriving: a diverse and open-minded population, low unemployment and a strong economy – which, after a string of high-performing years, will reach $1 trillion by 2018. Yet climate change poses significant threats to Miami Beach and the Keys, and the ever-expanding population places increasing stress on critically threatened ecosystems like the Everglades. Rather than bury their heads in the sand, Floridians are facing these issues head-on and working to find solutions to the biggest challenges of today.

Best on Film

Moonlight (2016) Poignant, Oscar-winning coming-of-age tale set in a housing project in Miami.
Wind Across the Everglades (1958) Offbeat story of warden versus poacher, against a Glades backdrop.
Key Largo (1948) Bogart, Bacall and neon-soaked noir.
Adaptation (2002) Surreal adaption of *The Orchid Thief*.
The Birdcage (1996) Robin Williams and Nathan Lane as gay lovers.
Scarface (1983) Al Pacino turns the American Dream into a nightmare.

Best in Print

Birds of Paradise (Diana Abu-Jaber; 2011) Beautifully captures Miami's complexity in a story about a broken couple and the estranged children.
Swamplandia! (Karen Russell; 2011) Tragicomic saga of a family of Everglades alligator wrestlers.
Miami (Joan Didion; 1987) Portrait of life among Cuban exiles in the 1980s.
The Everglades: River of Grass (Marjory Stoneman Douglas; 1947) Rich tribute to the Glades.
Shadow Country (Peter Matthiessen; 2008) The American Western reframed in the Florida swamps.

Confronting Climate Change

While the US government does its best to deny climate change, South Florida is already feeling the effects of a hotter planet. What scientists warned about years ago is becoming increasingly evident in the bottom half of Florida: namely that with higher temperatures, the sea levels would rise, and powerful storms would become more frequent. Coastlines would be particularly imperiled.

While bureaucrats continue to obfuscate the facts in Washington, down in South Florida, the citizens have already seen enough evidence – commonplace floods on streets that were always dry in the past, and cars and lawns ruined by seawater as sea-level rise has tripled in the last decade. Under mounting pressure from residents, Miami Beach has sprung into action, unveiling a $400 million plan that includes funding to elevate streets, build higher seawalls and add dozens of new pumps to deal with the inundations. The plan is especially ambitious considering Florida's governor Rick Scott refuses to even acknowledge climate change.

Luckily Miami Beach Mayor Philip Levine sees things differently, committing his city to a robust plan of fortifying itself against rising seas over the long term. Advocates of the plan tout not only the importance of investing in a more resilient city of the future, but its potential as a job-creating engine – putting people to work in an overhaul of aging infrastructure. The big question, though, is whether or not South Florida will be able to keep up with the threats that lie ahead.

Regrowing the Reef

As the oceans warm, the world's coral reefs remain gravely threatened. Even small fluctuations in temperatures can lead to huge swaths of coral bleaching and die-offs. In back-to-back years (2015 and 2016) the Florida Keys experienced unprecedented die-offs, wiping out some corals that had survived for over 300 years. Though small in size, reefs play an outsized role, protecting coastlines from storms and damaging waves. They also harbor over 25% of the world's marine species, and provide jobs in fishing, recreation and tourism. According to the National Oceanic and Atmospheric Administration (NOAA), the Florida Keys have an estimated asset value of over $7 billion.

With all that in mind, it becomes increasingly obvious that something must be done to save the world's coral reefs. In 2016, the Florida-based Mote Marine Laboratory, in partnership with the Nature Conservancy, announced a plan to do just that. It would embark on a 15-year initiative to restore more than one million corals across the region. Mote, a nonprofit marine science institute, has been one of the pioneers in coral research. After developing a groundbreaking method of growing coral, it planted some 200,000 corals onto depleted reefs around the Florida Keys. The research facility on Summerland Key will play a pivotal role in the future, using its campus – which saw a 19,000-sq-ft expansion in 2017 – as a base of operations to restore coral colonies up and down the Keys.

Restoring the Glades

Restoration of the Everglades is another big topic in South Florida. One of Florida's most biologically rich ecosystems remains gravely threatened. The flow of water into the Glades (syphoned away to create subdivisions and farms) has fallen by 60% compared to a century ago. This, coupled with nutrient pollution, has led to a decline in marine habitats and native species. Today the Glades, which once covered 4000 sq miles, are only half of their original size. Some 90% of its wading birds are gone, and over 70 plant and animal species are listed as threatened or endangered.

The long-term Comprehensive Everglades Restoration Plan (CERP), first unveiled in 2000, aims to help restore this threatened wetland, through a series of big engineering projects that would deliver the right amount of water through the Glades at the right time of year. While funding has been hit-or-miss in subsequent state administrations over the years, things were looking somewhat more promising in early 2017, with the Florida legislature debating plans to buy up some 60,000 acres of farmland and build a $120-billion-gallon reservoir. Big challenges remain: namely whether funding will get federal approval. Increasingly, more and more people are seeing the importance of the Glades – including bureaucrats who once voted against the restoration.

POPULATION: **860,000**

AREA: **10,600 SQ MILES**

PERCENTAGE OF FOREIGN-BORN CITIZENS: **37%**

MEDIAN HOUSEHOLD INCOME : **$41,900**

PERCENTAGE OF HOUSEHOLDS LIVING IN POVERTY: **21.3%**

if Miami were 100 people

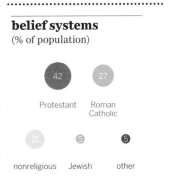

65 would be Hispanic
15 would be Caucasian (non-Hispanic)
19 would be black
1 would be Asian

belief systems
(% of population)

42 Protestant
27 Roman Catholic
21 nonreligious
5 Jewish
5 other

population per sq mile

MIAMI　USA　FLORIDA

† ≈ 90 people

History

South Florida was built on a cycle of boom and bust, by dreamers who took advantage of nice weather and opportunists who took advantage of natural disasters – nothing clears out old real estate like a hurricane, after all. Every chapter of the region's saga has been closed by a hurricane, building boom or riot. South Florida has historically treated slow growth with contempt, and this attitude has paid with huge financial dividends on the one hand, and economic and environmental catastrophes on the other.

Spain, Britain & Spain Again

The Spanish settled Florida in 1565, several decades before Pilgrims landed on Plymouth Rock and English aristocrats starved in Jamestown, Virginia. The territory changed hands from Spain (until 1763) to Britain (1763–83) and back to Spain again (1783–1821). And then came American Independence. The Spanish had to deal with a big, land-hungry new nation lying just to the north.

Relations chilled when escaped American slaves made for Spanish Florida, where slavery was illegal and freed slaves were employed as standing militia members. White American Southerners saw armed black militia and started sweating the notion of slave revolts in their back plantation yard. By 1821 the USA had purchased Florida from Spain; concurrently, businessman John W Simonton bought the island of Key West from Spanish artillery officer Juan Pablo Salas.

The island was deemed the 'Gibraltar of the West' for its command of the Straits of Florida, which sit between the Atlantic Ocean and the Gulf of Mexico. In 1823 Commodore David Porter of the US Navy took over the island, administering it as a base from which to track down illegal slave ships.

The Unconquered People

In the late 18th century, elements of the Creek nation in Georgia and other tribes from the north migrated to Florida. These tribes intermingled and intermarried, and in the late 1700s were joined by runaway black slaves. Black newcomers were generally welcomed into Native American

TIMELINE	10,000 BC	2000 BC	500 BC
	After crossing the Bering Strait from Siberia some 50,000 years earlier, humans arrive in Florida, hunting mastodon and saber-toothed tigers, at the end of the last Ice Age.	The earliest period in which archaeologists can find evidence of the creation of fired pottery in the state of Florida.	Pottery from this period is attributed to the Glades Culture, which stretches from the Keys to present-day Martin county, north of Miami. The Glades Culture does not survive European contact.

society and were occasionally kept as slaves, although this slavery was more akin to indentured servitude (slaves, for example, had their own homes that they inhabited with their families).

At some point, these fugitive, mixed peoples occupying Florida's interior were dubbed 'Seminoles,' a corruption of the Spanish word *cimarrones,* meaning 'free people' or 'wild ones.' Defying European rule and ethnic category, they were soon considered too free for the newly independent United States, which coincidentally was growing hungrier for land.

When the majority of the Creek were forced west across the Mississippi River in 1817, Americans figured everything east of that body of water was now theirs for the settling. But the Seminoles had no intention of leaving their homes.

Bad blood and sporadic violence between Americans and Seminoles eventually gave the USA the excuse it needed to make a bid for Florida, which was finally bought from Spain in 1821. Before and after that the US military embarked on several campaigns against the Seminoles and their allies, who took to the swamps, fought three guerrilla wars, and scored a respectable amount of victories against an enemy several times their size. In fact, the Second Seminole War (1835–42) was the longest in American history between the American Revolution and the Vietnam War.

Indeed, operationally the Seminole wars were a 19th-century version of Vietnam, a never-ending parade of long, pointless patrols into impenetrable swamps, always searching for an ever-invisible enemy. By 1830 Congress came up with the shocking *Removal Act*, a law that told Native Americans to pack up their things and move across the country to Oklahoma. Seminole Chief Osceola and his band (never exceeding more than 100 warriors) refused to sign the treaty and fled into the Everglades. After keeping thousands of soldiers jumping at the barest hint of his presence for years, Osceola was captured under a false flag of truce in

HISTORY THE UNCONQUERED PEOPLE

Native American Resources

Ah-Tah-Thi-Ki Museum (www. ahtahthiki.com)

Tequesta Indians (www.floridianna-ture.com/tequesta. htm)

Heritage of the Ancient Ones (www. ancientnative.org)

Miccosukee Tribe (www.miccosukee. com/tribe)

TEQUESTA INDIANS

In 1998, 24 holes, inscribed in bedrock and arranged in the shape of a perfect circle, were found in Downtown Miami. The 'Miami Circle,' as it was dubbed, is thought to be the foundations of a permanent structure and, at some 2000 years old, it's the oldest contender for that title on the US East Coast.

Archaeologists think the Circle was built by Miami's earliest known inhabitants, the Tequesta (Tekesta) Indians, who are otherwise a mystery. The tribe was mostly wiped out by Spanish first contact, which brought violence and disease, and survivors likely melted into the Miccosukee and Seminole nations.

AD 500	1513	1702	1763
The Caloosahatchee Culture develops and thrives in the area that now includes the western Everglades and 10,000 Islands. This complex society lasts till 1750.	Ponce de León 'discovers' Florida, landing south of Cape Canaveral, believing it to be an island. Since it's around Easter, he names it La Florida, 'The Flowery Land' or 'Feast of Flowers.'	In their ongoing struggle with Spain and France over New World colonies, the British burn St Augustine to the ground; two years later they destroy 13 Spanish missions in Florida.	The mixed Spanish–Native American community in Key West is resettled in Havana after the island is seized by the British. For years, the island has little real authority.

1837. Yet resistance continued, and while the Seminoles gave up fighting, the government gave up on moving them west.

By 1842 the warring had ended, but no peace treaty was ever signed, which is why the Seminoles to this day call themselves 'the unconquered people.' Those Seminoles who remained in Florida are now organized under a tribal government and run the Ah-Tah-Thi-Ki Museum and the Hard Rock Cafe. Not one Hard Rock Cafe: the entire chain, bought for $965 million in 2007 with money made from gambling revenue. The Seminoles were the first Native American tribe to cash in on gambling, starting with a bingo hall in 1979 that has since expanded to a multi-billion-dollar empire. Not bad for a Seminole population of a little over 3000.

A Freeze Brings Flagler & the Railway

For decades, Florida was farming country: sugar, citrus and drained swamps. In 1875 Julia Tuttle and her tubercular husband arrived in this agricultural empire from Cleveland, Ohio. After his death she moved to South Florida to take over the land she had inherited as a widow. Proving her worth as a true Floridian, over the next 20 years she proceeded to buy more and more property.

In the meantime, Henry Morrison Flagler, a business partner of John D Rockefeller, realized Florida's tourism potential. Flagler had been busy developing the northern Florida coast in St Augustine and Palm Beach, and he also built the Florida East Coast Railroad, which extended down as far as Palm Beach. Tuttle saw a business opportunity and contacted Flagler with a proposition: if he would extend his railroad to Miami,

FIVE WHO SHAPED SOUTH FLORIDA

Henry Morrison Flagler The developer whose Florida East Coast Railroad brought scores of visitors to sunny paradise.

Julia Tuttle The woman behind Flagler, who (supposedly) lured the skeptical developer to Miami with a handful of orange blossoms.

Fidel Castro He may have been reviled by local Cubans, but then again, said Cubans wouldn't be here if it wasn't for the bushy-bearded Caribbean communist leader.

Morris Lapidus The Fontainebleau, Eden Roc, Lincoln Rd Mall...is there anything this MiMo (Miami Modern) god didn't design?

Pardon C Greene One of the founding fathers of Key West; also a member of the city council and (briefly) mayor of the town.

1776	Late 1700s	1818	1822
The American Revolution begins, but Florida's two colonies don't rebel. They remain loyal to the British crown, and soon English Tories flood south into Florida to escape the fighting.	Elements of the Creek Nation, supplemented by black runaway slaves and their descendants, begin settling in South Florida, displacing local Calusa and Mayaimi Indians.	Andrew Jackson invades Western Florida after violence between settlers and a coalition of Native Americans and blacks. The First Seminole War essentially ends when the USA buys Florida from Spain.	Commodore Matthew C Perry lands on Key West and plants the American flag, claiming the entire Keys island chain for the USA.

Tuttle would split her property with him. Miami? Way down at the end of nowhere? Flagler wasn't interested.

Then, in 1895, a record freeze enveloped most of Florida (but not Miami), wiping out citrus crops and sending vacationers scurrying. Legend has it that Tuttle – who is said to have been rather quick both on the uptake and with an 'I told you so' – went into her garden at Fort Dallas on the Miami River, snipped off some orange blossoms and sent them to Flagler, who hightailed it down to Miami to see for himself.

Flagler was hooked. He and Tuttle came to terms, and all those Floridians whose livelihoods had been wiped out by the freeze followed Flagler south. Passenger-train services to Miami began on April 22, 1896, the year the city of Miami became incorporated. Incidentally, this was the same year John S Collins began selling lots out of a 5-mile strip between the Atlantic and Biscayne Bay, or what is now 14th to 67th Sts on Miami Beach (ie most of the city).

Of Miami's 502 original inhabitants, 100 of them were black, conscripted for hard labor and regulated to the northwest neighborhood of Colored Town.

During this period, a frenzy of activity was underway to prepare South Florida for extensive settlement. In 1900 Governor Napoleon Bonaparte Broward, envisioning an 'Empire of the Everglades,' set in motion a frenzy of canal building. Over the next 70 years some 1800 miles of canals and levees were etched across Florida's porous limestone. These earthworks drained about half the Everglades (about 1.5 million acres) below Lake Okeechobee, replacing it with farms, cattle ranches, orange groves, sugarcane and suburbs.

Caribbeans & Confederates

For most of the second half of the 19th century, Key West was the largest, wealthiest city in Florida. How did the little island do so well? Wrecking and sponges. Wrecking is the art of salvaging shipwrecks; local boosters liked to make out this was an altruistic act, and many sailors were pulled from the sea, but the cargo on their boats was sold by Keys merchants. Sponges are just that – undersea sponges that became the backbone of the actual American sponge industry for decades.

The population of the island consisted largely of Caribbean emigres, but mainland Floridians attracted by business opportunities also made their way here. While the presence of a US Naval Base kept Key West in the Union during the American Civil War, many island residents overtly sympathized with the Confederacy.

HISTORY CARIBBEANS & CONFEDERATES

The main (Downtown) branch of the Miami-Dade Public Library has an extensive Florida collection that constitutes one of the best repositories of state history anywhere. The collection includes some 17,000 photos by Gleason Romer, who snapped South Florida as a photojournalist and amateur shooter from 1925 to the 1950s.

1835	1845	1861	1868
In attacks coordinated by Seminole leader Osceola, Seminoles destroy five sugar plantations on Christmas Day and soon after kill 100 US soldiers marching near Tampa, launching the Second Seminole War.	Florida is admitted to the Union as the 27th state. Since it is a slave state, its admission is balanced by that of Iowa, a free state.	Voting 62 to 7, Florida secedes from the USA, raising its fifth flag, the stars-and-bars of the Confederacy. Florida's farms and cattle provide vital Confederate supplies during the ensuing Civil War.	Florida is re-admitted to the United States, but racial tensions between Southern whites and freed blacks run high, resulting in discriminatory 'Jim Crow' legislation.

The First Big Booms

The promise of money and the expansion of Flagler's railway fueled waves of settlement. Population growth peaked during WWI, when the US military established an aviation training facility in Miami. Many of the thousands who came to work and train figured, 'Hey, the weather's nice,' and Miami's population shot from 1681 people in 1900 to almost 30,000 by 1920. The new Floridians wrote home and got relatives in on the act, and after the war came the first full-fledged Miami boom (1923–25), when Coconut Grove and Allapattah were annexed into what was dubbed, for the first time, Greater Miami.

Even then, Miami was built for good times. People wanted to drink and gamble, because although it was illegal, liquor flowed freely here throughout the entire Prohibition period.

Historic Homes
....
Merrick House
(Coral Gables)
....
Vizcaya Museum &
Gardens (Coconut
Grove)
....
Biltmore Hotel
(Coral Gables)
....
Hemingway House
(Key West)

Depression, Deco & Another World War

Miami's growth was astronomical, and so was its eventual fall: the Great Miami Hurricane of 1926, which left about 220 people dead and up to 50,000 homeless; and the Great Depression. But it's in Miami's nature to weather every disaster with an even better resurgence, and in the interwar period Miami's phoenix rose in two stages. First, Franklin Roosevelt's New Deal brought the Civilian Conservation Corps, jobs and a spurt of rise-from-the-ashes building projects.

Then, in the early 1930s, a group of mostly Jewish developers began erecting small, stylish hotels along Collins Ave and Ocean Dr, jump-starting a miniboom that resulted in the creation and development of Miami Beach's famous art-deco district. This led to a brief rise in anti-Semitism, as the Beach became segregated and 'Gentiles Only' signs began to appear. The election of a Jewish governor of Florida in 1933 led to improvement, as did airplane travel, which brought plenty of Jewish visitors and settlers from the north.

During WWII, Miami was a major military training ground, and afterward many of those GIs returned with their families to enjoy Florida's sandy beaches at their leisure. This marked the real beginning of tourism in Florida, and large-scale settlement of South Florida in particular.

Cuba Comes Over

During the 1950s progress seemed inexorable; in 1954 Leroy Collins became the first Southern governor to publicly declare racial segregation 'morally wrong,' while an entire 'Space Coast' was created around Cape Canaveral (between Daytona and Miami on the east coast) to support the development of the National Aeronautics & Space Administration (NASA).

1894–5	1905	1912	1925
The Great Freeze wipes out crops in Central Florida. Farmers and developers look to South Florida for year-long growing conditions.	The first of many attempts to drain the Everglades begins. In coming decades, thousands of acres are destroyed as water is diverted from its natural flow from Lake Okeechobee.	'Flagler's Folly,' Henry Flagler's 128-mile overseas railroad connecting the Florida Keys, reaches Key West. It's hailed as the 'Eighth Wonder of the World,' but is destroyed by a 1935 hurricane.	Coral Gables, one of the first planned communities in the USA, is officially founded. The 'City Beautiful' was designed by real-estate developer George Edgar Merrick.

Then, in 1959, Fidel Castro marched onto the 20th-century stage and forever changed the destiny of Cuba and Miami.

As communists swept into Havana, huge portions of the upper and middle classes of Cuba fled north and established a fiercely anti-Castro Cuban community, now as angry as ever about the regime to the south. At the time, counter-revolutionary politics were discussed, and a group of exiles formed the 2506th Brigade, sanctioned by the US government, which provided weapons and Central Intelligence Agency (CIA) training for the purpose of launching a US attack on Cuba.

The resulting badly executed attack is remembered today as the Bay of Pigs fiasco. The first wave of counter-revolutionaries, left on the beach without reinforcements or supplies, were all captured or killed. All prisoners were released by Cuba about three months later.

In the meantime, Castro attracted Soviet missiles to his country, but couldn't keep his people. In 1965 alone some 100,000 Cubans hopped the 'freedom flight' from Havana to Miami.

Racial Tensions

Riots and skirmishes broke out between Cubans and blacks, and blacks and whites, in Miami. In 1968 a riot broke out after it was discovered that two white police officers had arrested a 17-year-old black male, stripped him naked and hung him by his ankles from a bridge.

In 1970 the 'rotten meat' riot began when black locals picketed a white-owned shop they had accused of selling spoiled meat. After three days of picketing, white officers attempted to disperse the crowds and fired on them with tear gas. During the 1970s there were 13 other race-related violent confrontations.

Racial tensions exploded on May 17, 1980, when four white police officers, being tried on charges that they beat a black suspect to death while he was in custody, were acquitted by an all-white jury. When the verdict was announced, race riots broke out all over Miami and lasted for three days.

The Mariel Boatlift

In the late 1970s, Fidel suddenly declared that anyone who wanted to leave Cuba had open access to the docks at Mariel Harbor. Before the ink was dry on the proclamation, the largest flotilla ever launched for non-military purposes set sail (or paddled) from Cuba in practically anything that would float the 90 miles between Cuba and the USA.

The Mariel Boatlift, as the largest of these would be called, brought 125,000 Cubans to Florida, including an estimated 25,000 prisoners and mental patients. Mariel shattered the stereotype of the wealthy Batista-exiled Cuban. The resulting strain on the economy, logistics

After WWII, the advent of effective bug spray and affordable air-conditioning did more for Florida tourism than anything else. With these two technological advancements, Florida's subtropical climate was finally safe for delicate Yankee skin.

1926	1928	1920s–30s	1933–40
The Great Miami Hurricane devastates South Florida, killing 220 people, leaving up to 50,000 homeless and causing some $100 million in damages. The Great Depression slows recovery.	Ernest Hemingway pens *A Farewell to Arms* in Key West, supposedly while awaiting the delivery of a car. His wife's uncle gives the Hemingways a local house in 1931.	A small spit of land located across Biscayne Bay, known as Miami Beach, becomes dotted with hotels and resorts, presaging its emergence as a tourism hot spot.	New Deal public-works projects employ 40,000 Floridians and help save Florida from the Depression. The most notable construction project is the Overseas Hwy through the Keys.

and infrastructure of South Florida added to still-simmering racial tensions; by 1990 it was estimated that 90% of Miami's Caucasian populace was Hispanic.

The tension carried over from Hispanic-Anglo divisions to rifts between older Cubans and the new *Marielitos*. The middle- to upper-class white Cubans of the 1960s were reintroduced to that nation in the form of thousands of Afro-Cubans and *santeros,* or worshippers of Santeria, Cuba's version of *vodou* (voodoo).

Miami Not So Nice

In the 1980s Miami became the major East Coast entry port for drug dealers and their product and earned the nickname 'Mi-Yay-Mi' – 'yay' being slang for cocaine. As if to keep up with the corruption, many savings and loans (S&Ls) opened in newly built Miami headquarters. While *Newsweek* magazine called Miami 'America's Casablanca,' locals dubbed it the 'City with the S&L Skyline.'

A plethora of businesses – legitimate concerns as well as drug-financed fronts – and buildings sprang up all over Miami. Downtown was completely remodeled. But it was reborn in the grip of drug smugglers: shootouts were common, as were gangland slayings by cocaine cowboys. At one stage, up to three people per week were being killed in cocaine-related clashes.

The police, Coast Guard, Drug Enforcement Agency (DEA), Border Patrol and the Federal Bureau of Investigation (FBI) were trying to keep track of it all. Roadblocks were set up along the Overseas Hwy to Key West (prompting the quirky and headstrong residents down there to call for a secession, which eventually sent the police on their way).

Miami Vice was single-handedly responsible for Miami Beach rising to international fabulousness in the mid-1980s, its slick soundtrack and music-video-style montages glamorizing the rich South Florida lifestyle. Before long, people were coming down to check it out for themselves – especially photographer Bruce Weber, who began using South Beach as a gritty and fashionable backdrop for modeling shoots in the early 1980s.

Celebrities were wintering in Miami, international photographers were shooting here, and the Art Deco Historic District, having been granted federal protection, was going through renovation and renaissance. Gay men, always on the cutting edge of trends, discovered South Beach's gritty glamour. The city was becoming a showpiece of fashion and trendiness.

The 1990s & 2000s

A combination of Hurricane Andrew and a crime wave against tourists, particularly carjackings, equaled a drop in visitors, until tourist-oriented

Miami Histories

Miami (1987; Joan Didion)

The Corpse Had a Familiar Face (1987; Edna Buchanan)

Black Miami in the Twentieth Century (1997; Marvin Dunn)

This Land Is Our Land: Immigrants and Power in Miami (2003; Alex Stepick)

Miami, USA (2000; Helen Muir)

1941–45	1942	1947	1961
USA enters WWII. Two million men and women receive basic training in South Florida. At one point, the army commandeers 85% of Miami Beach hotels to house personnel.	From January to August, German U-boats sink more than two dozen tankers and ships off Florida's coast. By war's end, Florida holds nearly 3000 German POWs in 15 labor camps.	Everglades National Park is established, successfully culminating a 19-year effort, led by Ernest Coe and Marjory Stoneman Douglas, to protect the Everglades from the harm done by dredging and draining.	Brigade 2506, a 1300-strong volunteer army, invades Cuba's Bay of Pigs on April 16. President Kennedy withholds air support, leading to Brigade 2506's immediate defeat and capture by Fidel Castro.

community policing and other visible programs reversed the curse. Miami went from being the US city with the most violent crime to one with average crime statistics for a city its size. From 1992 to 1998, tourist-related crimes decreased by a whopping 80%.

The Cuban-American population dominated headlines again during the Elián Gonzalez nightmare, an international custody fight that ended with heavily armed federal agents storming the Little Havana house where the seven-year-old was staying to have him shipped back to Cuba while anti-Castro Cubans protested in Miami streets.

On the bright side, corruption was slightly cleaned out after the removal of Mayor Xavier Suarez in 1998, whose election was overturned following the discovery of many illegal votes. Manuel 'Manny' Diaz, who had been a lawyer for the Miami-based Gonzalez family, followed Suarez as mayor and pushed for cementing ties between Miami and the Latin American world – he was fond of saying, 'When Venezuela or Argentina sneezes, Miami catches a cold.'

During the 2000s Miami proper underwent more 'Manhattan-ization,' with more and more skyscrapers altering the city skyline. There are currently 307 high-rise buildings in Miami, 59 of which stand taller than 400ft. At the same time, Diaz began working to use arts districts and buildings – the former represented by Wynwood and Midtown, the latter by the Adrienne Arsht Center for the Performing Arts – to revitalize blighted areas of town.

Water and a lack of it have always been nagging fears in South Florida, one of the fastest-growing population areas of the country, but the issue took on new urgency in the 2000s. By the late 1990s, the South Florida aquifer seemed in danger of depletion. The solution seemed to rest in the Comprehensive Everglades Restoration Plan (CERP), which was passed in 2000. Said project is aimed at restoring the flow of water to the Everglades from Lake Okeechobee, which would subsequently help replenish the South Florida aquifer and the state's most iconic wilderness space. At the time of research, the US National Research Council had determined that progress toward restoring the core of the Glades was proceeding very slowly, and quicker action was needed.

In the normally placid Keys, protests, heated town-hall meetings and various civic master plans tried to address the impact of skyrocketing costs of living on an island chain where there isn't much room to build new houses. During this period, commuter buses running from Homestead were packed full of the service industry workers, teachers and other backbone members of the community who could no longer afford a trailer or apartment in the Keys. Today there is high pressure on new housing projects in the islands to provide affordable units.

HISTORY THE 1990S & 2000S

Richard Heyman, who served two terms as mayor of Key West (1983–85 and 1987–89), was perhaps the first openly gay mayor of a sizable US town (and perhaps any US town). In 2010 a documentary on his life, *The Newcomer*, was released. Heyman died of AIDS-related pneumonia in 1994.

May 1980	1980	1992	1999
In the McDuffie trial, white police are acquitted of wrongdoing in the death of a black man, igniting racial tensions and Miami's Liberty City riots; 18 people are killed.	Cuba's Castro 'opens the floodgates.' The USA's ensuing Mariel Boatlift rescues 125,000 *Marielitos*, who face intense discrimination in Miami.	On August 24, Hurricane Andrew devastates Dade County, leaving 41 people dead, more than 200,000 homeless and causing about $15.5 billion in damage.	On Thanksgiving, five-year-old Elián González is rescued at sea, his Cuban mother having died en route. Despite wild protests by Miami's Cuban exiles, the USA returns the then seven-year-old Elián to his father in Cuba.

The Recent Past

The Cuban American and former journalist Tomás Regalado was elected mayor of Miami in 2009 in the wake of a financial crisis and recession (he was re-elected in 2013). Florida led the Eastern USA in foreclosures, and the evidence was visible across South Florida in the form of double-digit home vacancy rates. But for every burst bubble, there is re-inflation, and at the time of writing the real estate market was in comeback mode; from Miami to Key West, condos were getting occupied, and condo rents were rising as fast as condo towers.

Miami is still, by far, the largest Cuban city outside Cuba, and most Cubans here were adamantly anti-Castro. When Fidel died in 2016, there was much rejoicing – especially for those who'd lost property or seen relatives imprisoned during the most authoritarian days of the Castro regime. Although a Castro (Fidel's brother Raúl) is still at the helm, there is more hope than ever before for exiles to reconnect with their ancestral homeland – particularly now that Cuban-US diplomatic ties have been reestablished.

2000	2009	2010	2014
The Comprehensive Everglades Restoration Plan (CERP) is put into action. The 30-year plan aims to restore natural water flow to the Everglades and replenish South Florida's water reservoirs.	Tomas Regalado, a former journalist and centrist Republican, is elected the 33rd mayor of Miami by a 72% margin.	The *Deepwater Horizon/* BP oil disaster results in 11 deaths and 4.9 million barrels of oil being spilled into the Gulf of Mexico.	Flooding on Alton Rd causes the city of Miami Beach to fund both flood-relief programs and climate-change impact assessments.

Multiculturalism & the Arts

South Florida is an intersection of Middle America, Latin America and the Caribbean, a clash of idiosyncratic types who decided miles of marshland, beach, mangroves and islets were a place where the American dream could be realized to subtropical perfection. It's also a place often misunderstood by outsiders, though the region's burgeoning arts scene – music, film, literature and the plastic arts – helps shed a light on its multilayered complexity.

Greater Multicultural Miami

Contemporary South Florida is certainly more than Miami, but if the local distinct regional identity has an anchor city, Miami is that town. With that said, while Miami's energy impacts the Keys and the Glades (particularly the former), these other areas are more demographically homogenous, and in the case of Key West, have their own unique histories of settlement and demographic shift.

Miami

It would still be silly not to recognize Miami as the center of South Florida's cultural gravity. Which begs the question: what makes Miami, well, Miami? Basically it's the mix: that conspicuous jumble of Cubans, Haitians, Anglos, Jews, Asians, and South and Central Americans of all stripes. Miami possesses the best and worst of its parent cultures: immigrant and migrant narratives that are embraced and rejected and spliced and diced into entirely new paradigms. How else does a Cuban American proudly show off an inherited Matanzas accent on the one hand while shrugging off the pork and rum of their island ancestors in favor of vegetarianism and yoga? As they say here, only in Miami. Or if you prefer, *solamente en Miami.*

Florida's Division of Cultural Affairs (www.florida-arts.org) is a great resource for statewide arts organizations and agencies. Its Florida Artists Hall of Fame memorializes the Sunshine State's creative legacy.

It can be difficult to meet someone from Miami who has more than two generations of connection to the city. At the negative end, this lack of connection can manifest as a detached sense of place and resentment toward other newcomers. Miami is not without tensions between its myriad communities. On the positive side are those Miamians concerned with building an identity for their town; the ones who patronize local sport and arts, and extend a helping hand toward newcomers from across America or the Gulf of Mexico.

It almost goes without saying, but Miami's cultural capital, even among Asian and Anglo citizens, is largely derived from the Caribbean and Latin America. There's an energy here that is cheerful, loud and colorful. It infects the place, and it will get under your skin the longer you stay.

The Everglades

Rural Florida can still evoke America's western frontier, and the Everglades, the wildest part of the state, remains very much a hinterland populated by either frontier types or people who self-conceptualize as frontier types. The Old West trope is exacerbated by the fact there is still a settlement pattern here of colonizers and Native Americans; the Seminole and Miccosukee tribes constitute a major part of the 'Glades' population. Their neighbors in Homestead and Everglades City are largely descended from those who came here in the 19th century, after the West was won, when Florida became one of the last places where pioneers could simply plant stakes and make a life on ostensibly unclaimed land (well, unclaimed if you weren't Native American).

These pioneers became Florida's 'Crackers,' the poor rural farmers, fisherfolk, cowhands and outlaws who traded the comforts of civilization for independence on their terms. Many Crackers came from the old Southern states, and created a culture not too far removed, geographic or otherwise, from the Confederacy. In parts of southern America, the term cracker is pejorative, but it has a specific connotation in Florida that is a badge of honor, as evidenced by the annual Cracker Storytelling Festival and *Crackers in the Glade*, a classic illustrated account of growing up in the Everglades region, among other cultural ephemera.

A bit of Southern-fried hospitality and Western independence is a feisty combination, but therein lie the roots of many Glades citizens. Even the local Native Americans share these qualities; it may surprise you to see large Confederate flags and Ford F-250 pickup trucks jamming many a Seminole nation parking lot, although many Seminole and Miccosukee also retain elements of indigenous culture. Most Everglades citizens, like rural people in much of the USA, place a high value on self-reliance and perceived freedom from government.

Finally we'd be remiss not to mention the large number of Mexicans who now call Homestead home, the majority attracted by jobs working on nearby farms. As you drive south from Miami, the shift from Cuban Spanish to Mexican Spanish is quite distinct, even to an untrained ear.

The Keys

The Keys constitute a fascinating combination of white Floridians, Caribbean islanders and just about anyone attracted to living an island lifestyle that's still technically in the borders of the USA. As the Keys have been settled by non–Native Americans longer than Miami, there is a distinct local culture that's a little bit country in the Outer Keys, and elegantly eccentric in Key West. Regardless of where you're from, if you're born in the Keys, you're considered a Conch – one of the members of a tribe whose bond is life amid the islands.

There's a great deal of pride in the Keys themselves and their independence from the mainland. And while many people, especially in the Outer Keys, have conservative attitudes on gun control and the environment (ie less regulation related to both), there's also a great deal of tolerance for alternative lifestyles. Maybe because just choosing to live out here is an alternative lifestyle decision.

The search for an alternative lifestyle, plus geographic isolation, led many gay people to Key West. Richard Heynman, who was mayor of the city from 1983–85 and 1987–89, was one of the first openly gay mayors of an American city. The *Key West Citizen* has even argued that, in regards to LGBT politics, Key West is essentially post-sexual identity. Anything has gone for so long that nothing (between consenting adults) is off-limits.

The Arts in South Florida

Art, music and literature permeate South Florida's daily life. Because this region has a pretty face, many people think it has a correspondingly shallow mind. The stereotype isn't fair. Because what makes South Florida beautiful, from the bodies on the beach to the structure of the skyline, is diversity. The energies of the western hemisphere have been channeled

BRIGHT BRITTO

If the top public artist of a given city determines how said city sees itself, we must conclude Miami is a cartoon-like, cubist, chaotic place of bright, happy, shiny joy.

That's the aesthetic legacy Romero Britto is leaving this town. The seemingly perpetually grinning Brazilian émigré, clad in jackets leftover from a 1980s MTV video, was the hot face of public art in the 2000s, having designed the mural of the **Miami Children's Museum** (p75), the 'Welcome' structure at Dadeland North Station, the central sculpture at the shops at Midtown and many others. You might need sunglasses to appreciate his work, which appeals to the islander in all of us: Saturday-morning cartoon brights, sharp geometric lines and loopy curls, inner-child character studies and, underlying everything, a scent of teal oceans on a sunny day.

Gloria Estefan loves the guy, and former governor Jeb Bush gave Tony Blair an original Britto when the ex-PM visited Miami in 2006. However, not everyone feels the Romero love; plenty of critics have dubbed Britto more commercial designer than pop artist (but, like, what is art man?). Rather than get mired in the debate, we suggest you check out a Britto installation for yourself, or the **Britto Central** gallery at 818 Lincoln Rd. The man's work is as ubiquitous as palm trees and, hey, if you've got a spare $20,000, you can buy an original (a small one) before you go home.

into this Gateway to the Americas, and a lot of that drive is rooted in creativity and a search for self-expression.

This artistic impulse tends to derive from the immigrant experience – which this region has in spades. The pain of exile, the flush of financial success and the frustration of being shut out of the often callous American dream provide ample inspiration for the arts. Living in a country where you can't be arrested for public expression helps too. Miami's greatest quality, its inborn tolerance for eccentricity, is at the root of such public innovations as the Arab fantasy-land architecture of Opa Locka, the modernistic design of the Art Deco Historic District and the condominium-lined skyscraper corridors of Brickell.

In addition, there is always a sense of the possible coupled with the fantasy of excess. Plenty of people dismiss Coral Gables and the Vizcaya as gauche and tacky, and through modern eyes they may appear as such. But they were revolutionary for their time. During the early 20th century, concepts such as a Mediterranean-Revival village that served as a bulwark against sprawl, or an Italianate villa carved out of the seashore, would not have flown in the aesthetically conservative Northeast, but they found legs here.

Putting Miami on the Arts Map

Miami's citizens and their memories, realities and visions have created a burgeoning art scene that truly began to be noticed with the 2002 introduction of Art Basel Miami Beach (p100), the US outpost of an annual erudite gathering that's based in Switzerland. By its second year, the event had created a buzz throughout the national art world – and had succeeded in wooing 175 exhibitors, more than 30,000 visitors and plenty of celebs to take over the galleries, clubs and hotels of South Beach and the Design District. It has grown, in both size and strength, each year since, and its impact on the local art scene cannot be overstated; today Art Basel Miami Beach is the biggest contemporary arts festival in the western hemisphere.

Public Art

This city has always been way ahead of the curve when it comes to public art. Miami and Miami Beach established the Art in Public Places program back in 1973, when it voted to allocate 1.5% of city construction funds to the fostering of public art; since then more than 700 works – sculptures, mosaics, murals, light-based installations and more – have been created in public spots.

Barbara Neijne's *Foreverglades,* in Concourse J of Miami International Airport, uses mosaic, art-installed text from *River of Grass* (by Marjory Stoneman Douglas) and waves representing the movement of water over grass to give new arrivals a sense of the flow of Florida's unique ecosystem. A series of handprints representing Miami's many immigrant communities link into a single community in *Reaching for Miami Skies,* by Connie Lloveras, which greets Metromover commuters at Brickell Station. In Miami-Dade Library, the floating text of *Words Without Thought Never to Heaven Go* by Edward Ruscha challenges readers to engage in thought processes that are inspired by, but go beyond, the books that surround them. The team of Roberto Behar and Rosario Marquardt, hailing from Argentina, have been among the most prolific public artists in town, to the degree that their work is deliberately meant to warp conceptions of what is or isn't public space; they created the giant red *M* at the Metromover Riverwalk Station for the city's centennial back in 1996.

> You can count among Florida's snowbirds some of the USA's best writers, such as Robert Frost, Isaac Bashevis Singer and Annie Dillard, and every January, the literati of the USA holds court at the Annual Key West Literary Seminar.

Literature

Writers need to be around good stories to keep their narrative wits sharp, and no place provides stories quite like South Florida, where farmers clash with environmentalists who fight financiers, while immigrants arrive from a hundred different countries and, every summer, a hurricane hits. This proximity to real-life drama means, unsurprisingly, many of Miami's best authors cut their teeth in journalism. As a result, there's a breed of Miami prose that has the terse punch of the best newspaper writing. Beginning with former *Miami Herald* crime-beat reporters Edna Buchanan and Carl Hiaasen, and leading to new names like Jeff Lindsay, the Miami crime-writing scene is alive and well.

On the other hand, local immigrant communities have lent this town's literature the poetry of exiled tongues, narratives that find a thread

CARL HIAASEN: LOVING THE LUNACY

In Carl Hiaasen's Florida the politicians are corrupt, the rednecks are violent, the tourists are clueless, the women are fast and the ambience is smoky noir, brightened by a few buckets of loony pastel. Some would say the man knows his home state.

Hiaasen, who worked at the *Miami Herald* for decades and is now a Keys resident (he met his wife while reading in the Keys bar she managed), is both a writer gifted with crisp prose and a journalist blessed by a reporter's instinct for the offbeat. His success has rested in his ability to basically take the hyperbolic reality that is Florida and tell it to the world. Although his fiction is just that, in many ways it simply draws off the day-to-day eccentricities of the Sunshine State and novelizes them. In *Tourist Season* Hiaasen turns his pen on ecozealots with a story about a terrorist group that tries to dissuade tourists from coming to Florida and further wrecking the state – namely, by feeding them to a crocodile named Pavlov. In complete thematic contrast comes *Hoot,* a heart-warming tale (odd for Hiaasen) catering to young adults about a 12-year-old boy's fight against a corporation that threatens to pave over a Coconut Grove colony of burrowing owls. *Stormy Weather* takes on the corruption, bureaucracy and disaster tourism that fills the vacuum of the devastation trail left by a hurricane.

Hiaasen's work tends to career between satire and thriller, and betrays both an unceasingly critical eye and deep affection for all of Florida's quirks. Which ironically makes Hiaasen – enemy of almost every special-interest group in the Sunshine State – the state's biggest promoter. He is a man who loves Florida despite its warts and that, folks, is true romance.

through the diaspora alleyways that underline Florida's identity. Look out for Carolina Garcia-Aguilera, Edwidge Danticat and Diana Abu-Jaber. And finally, the subtle beauty of South Florida has produced a certain breed of nature writer that is able to capture the nuances of the region's subdued scenery while explaining the complicated science that runs through it all – Marjory Stoneman Douglas and Ted Levin spring to mind. Pulitzer Prize-finalist Karen Russell often combines sensuous nature imagery with a sprinkling of sometimes-funny, sometimes-ominous magical realism.

Music

As in all things, it's the mad diversity of Miami that makes its music so appealing. The southbound path of American country and Southern rock, the northbound rhythms of the Caribbean and Latin America, and the homegrown beats of Miami's African American community get mixed into a musical crossroads of the Americas. Think about the sounds the above influences produce, and you'll hear a certain thread: bouncy and percussive with a tune you can always dance to.

The above sounds, rooted in the New World, are fighting against interlopers from a far shore: Europeans and their waves of techno, house and EDM. In the narrative of Miami immigrants, we can't leave out the gay community and the Euro-expats. The latter have brought a strong club-music scene, best evidenced by the annual Winter Music Conference in March, which brings thousands of DJs and producers to town. The gay community has traditionally been a receptive audience for club music, and many club nights have crossover with gay parties.

Miami's heart and soul is Latin, and that goes for its music as well. Producers and artists from across Latin America come here for high-quality studio facilities, the lure of global distribution and the Billboard Latin Music Conference & Awards, held here each April. The Magic City has been the cradle of stars such as Gloria Estefan, Ricky Martin and Albita, and a scan over the local airwaves always yields far more Spanish-language stations than English, playing a mix of salsa, *son* (an Afro-Cuban-Spanish mélange of musical styles), conga and reggaeton. A night out in La Covacha is a good intro to the scene.

Here's a quick crib sheet for your Miami nightclub explorations.

Salsa is the most commonly heard word used to reference Latin music and dance. This makes sense as it's a generic term developed in the mid-1960s and early '70s to pull all Latin sounds under one umbrella name for gringos who couldn't recognize the subtle differences between beats. From the Spanish word for 'sauce,' salsa has its roots in Cuban culture and has a sound that's enhanced by textures of jazz. Music that lends itself to salsa dancing has four beats per bar of music.

One specific type of Cuban salsa is *son* – a sound popularized by the release of 1999's *Buena Vista Social Club*. It has roots in African and Spanish cultures and is quite melodic, usually incorporating instruments including the *tres* (a type of guitar with three sets of closely spaced strings), standard guitars and various hand drums.

Merengue originates from the Dominican Republic and can be characterized by a very fast beat, with just two beats to each bar. It's typically played on the tamboura, guiro (a ridged cylindrical percussion instrument made of metal or dried gourd) and accordion.

Hailing from the Andalusian region of Spain is the folk art of flamenco, which consists of hand clapping, finger snapping, vocals, guitar and the flamboyant dance. Miami's Argentines love to tango, a Buenos Aires invention that draws off European classical dance and the immigrant experience of South America's French, Italian, African and indigenous ethnic enclaves.

MULTICULTURALISM & THE ARTS THE ARTS IN SOUTH FLORIDA

Naked Came the Manatee (1998) is a collaborative mystery novel by a constellation of famous Florida writers: Carl Hiaasen, Dave Barry, Elmore Leonard, James Hall, Edna Buchanan and more. It's like nibbling a delectable box of cyanide-laced chocolates.

EXPERIENCING MULTICULTURAL MIAMI

The following guide may help you understand some of Miami's most prominent ethnic groups.

Cuban Miami

Cuban Miami is stereotypically associated with Little Havana, but to be fair, so much of Miami is Cuban it's more accurate to refer to Cubans as the norm, the default ethnicity. With that said, the most important cultural symbols of Cuban Miami are concentrated in Little Havana, particularly near 8th St/Calle Ocho. Other parts of town where you can get a strong sense of Cuban identity include Hialeah, where over 90% of the population speaks Spanish as a first language.

Little Havana (p79) The old heart of Cuban Miami.

Viernes Culturales (p101) A regular Latin street celebration.

Versailles (p120) The most storied standby of culinary Cuban Florida.

Cubaocho (p132) Meeting point of the Cuban disaspora, who come for (great) intimate concerts and art exhibitions.

Máximo Gómez Park (p79) Watch old Cubans trade dominoes and jibes.

Haitian Miami

Haitian Miamians speak Creole (also spelled 'Kreyol'), which is related to French. If you speak French, you may be able to converse with local Haitians, but as Kreyol is its own language, with its own grammar and syntax, French alone may not get you far. Little Haiti is by far one of the most colorful neighborhoods in the city, but it can be rough after dark, so try and visit during the day, unless the **Sounds of Little Haiti** (p98) monthly street party is happening.

Tap Tap (p115) Haitian cuisine, South Beach setting.

Libreri Mapou (p135) A Haitian-related library.

Little Haiti Cultural Center (p77) Community center for Haitian Miami.

Chef Creole (p120) Traditional Haitian food in Little Haiti.

Jewish Miami

Jews were some of the first developers and residents of Miami Beach. They've maintained a strong presence here for decades, which helps explain why the Miami metro area has the nation's second-largest concentration of Jews. While many of these Jews are descended from northeast families, many are also the children of Latin American exiles. There is a significant Cuban, Puerto Rican, Brazilian and Colombian Jewish presence in Miami. The area around 41st St in North Miami Beach, and 95th and Harding in Surfside are both streets where you'll see lots of Jewish businesses and community organizations.

Jewish Museum of Florida-FIU (p59) Center for research on Jewish Florida.

Temple Emanu-El (p63) One of the area's largest synagogues.

Lots of Lox (p125) Old-school Jewish deli.

Roasters 'n Toasters (p115) A favorite Jewish deli.

Argentine Miami

Argentines are mainly concentrated in Northern Miami Beach, although they are not restricted to any one part of the city. In South America, Argentines are often stereotyped as snooty compared to other South American nationalities. Many Spanish-speaking Miamians, especially ones from South America, like to riff on this cliché with their Argentine friends, but the comments are almost always good-natured teasing and taken as such. North Miami Beach is also home to a good number of Uruguayans, who have cultural and geographic ties to their Argentine neighbors.

Spanish Miami

When we say Miami is a capital of the Spanish-speaking world, that applies to the home of the mother tongue as well. Spaniards have been settling in Miami in large numbers for the past few decades. There is no one part of Spain that produces these new arrivals; in one part of Miami you'll find people from the Basque country who resent being called 'Spanish,' while in another you may break bread with Catalans in one restaurant and Castillians in another. Many of the best high-end grocery stores, bakeries, cheese shops and meat shops in Miami are run by Spaniards.

El Carajo (p121) A semi-hidden tapas joint beloved by Spanish expats.

Japanese Miami

Miami does not have a particularly large Japanese community, but there are some Japanese here. Many are businesspeople participating in the global economy and international commerce, but there is also a large amount of contemporary artists and designers who are attracted by Miami's growing cultural credibility. No one neighborhood in Miami can be said to be Japanese.

Matsuri (p123) A popular sushi spot for expat Japanese.

Brazilian Miami

Miami's Brazilians are mainly found in Northern Miami Beach: working, partying, eating and blending into the Miami milieu. Well, those Brazilians who live in Greater Miami, that is. There is also a noticeably large population of temporary Brazilians in the city, including shoppers who come here to buy electronics and clothes that lack Brazil's import duties, and a glut of designers, DJs, musicians, fashionistas, models and their respective entourages; these Brazilians tend to base themselves in South Beach with the other jet-setters.

Boteco (p129) Popular Brazilian watering hole.

Colombian Miami

You'll find many Colombians with their South American brethren in Northern Miami Beach, but there are also plenty of Colombians in Coral Gables (where the Colombian consulate is located). A poorer component of the Colombian population lives in parts of Downtown and in the city's vast suburbs. Colombian politics are difficult to pigeonhole, as Colombian migrants have come to the USA fleeing from both left- and right-wing overthrows.

La Moon (p116) Late-night Colombian eats attract the Colombian community.

San Pocho (p121) Classic Colombian eatery in Little Havana.

Nicaraguan Miami

Central Americans make up a large percentage of the population of 'Cuban' areas such as Little Havana, with Nicaragua leading the way – currently, Nicaraguans represent nearly half of the Central American population in Miami.

Yambo (p121) An enormously good-value *fritanga* (Nicaraguan diner).

MIAMI TRACKS (& WHERE TO PLAY THEM)

....

'Conga' Gloria Estefan & the Miami Sound Machine – Ocean Dr

'Rakata' Wisin y Yandel – Little Havana

'Moon Over Miami' Joe Burke and Edgar Leslie – Julia Tuttle Causeway

'Miami' Will Smith – I-95 past Downtown

'Miami' U2 – Wynwood or North Miami Beach

'Save Hialeah Park' Los Primeros – Hialeah

'Swamp Music' Lynyrd Skynyrd – Tamiami Trail to Everglades City

'Jaspora' Wyclef Jean – Little Haiti

'Your Love' the Outfield – A1A

The popular reggae sound, originating in Jamaica and having strong Rastafarian roots, is a total movement most popularly associated with Bob Marley. It's characterized by rhythm chops on a backbeat and, at least in its beginnings, a political-activist message. There are various styles within reggae, including roots (Marley's sound), dancehall (ie Yosexygirlwannagetboomshackalacka), raga and dub.

But it's rare to just hear one of the above. Miami is a polyglot kind of town, and it loves to blend techno with *son,* give an electronic backbeat to salsa, and overlay everything with dub, hip-hop and *bomba* (African-influenced Puerto Rican dance music). This mixed marriage produces a lot of musical children, and the most recognizable modern sound derived from the above is reggaeton, a driving mash-up that plays like Spanish rap shoved through a sexy backbeat and thumpin' dancehall speakers. Pioneers of the genre include Daddy Yankee, Don Chezina, Tito El Bambino, Wisin Y Yandel, Calle 13 and producers such as Luny Tunes and Noriega. Although it largely originated in Puerto Rico, reggaeton is one of the few musical styles that can get Latinos from across the Americas – from Nicaraguans to Mexicans to Colombians – shaking it.

Miami's hip-hop has had a bit of a circular evolution, from early '90s Miami bass (dirty-dance music, exemplified by 2 Live Crew) to more aggressive, street-style rap, which has blended and morphed into today's club-oriented tracks. These modern sounds draw off the crunk beats, Southern drawls and Atlanta overproduction of the Dirty South sound. The hit 2008 single 'Low' by Flo Rida encapsulates the genre, which sounds, in a lot of ways, like the club child of Miami bass and everything that has come since. Local hip-hop heroes work hard to keep Miami on the map and strongly rep neighborhoods such as Opa Locka, Liberty City and Overtown; artists to listen for include DJ Smallz, Rick Ross, Flo Rida and Uncle Luke. We'd be remiss not to mention Pitbull, who has successfully branded his sound as a bridge between reggaeton, hip-hop and pop.

There has been a small but strong indie-rock boom over the past decade, mainly centered on Sweat Records and Churchill's in Little Haiti. The crop of homegrown bands is growing; events such as Sweatstock are a good means of accessing the scene. Besides Churchill's, other good spots to see the cutting edge of Miami rock are Bardot, Ball & Chain, Gramps and Lagniappe.

Film & TV

Crime sells this city – at least cinematically. Sam Katzman chose Miami for B-movies about gang wars, and several (lowbrow) classics – as well as the *Jackie Gleason Show* – in the 1960s. *Scarface,* Brian DePalma's over-the-top story of the excesses of capitalism, entered Miami into hip-hop's common lexicon; and *Miami Vice,* the 1980s TV series about a couple of pastel-clad vice-squad cops, put Miami on the international map. The images – of murders, rapes and drug-turf wars – were far from positive, and the powers-that-be in the city were not initially happy. But *Vice* was more about Ferraris, speedboats and booty than gang-banging, and as branding goes, it depicted Miami as more than a high-crime slum where everyone's grandparents retired. As William Cullom, a president of the Greater Miami Chamber of Commerce put it, '*[Miami Vice]* has built an awareness of Miami in young people who had never thought of visiting Miami.' A pretty mediocre Hollywood film version starring Colin Farrell and Jamie Foxx, released in 2006, capitalized on the '80s nostalgia market. There have been loads of comedies filmed here as well, but for our money, *The Birdcage* best captures the fabulousness and, yes, even community vibe, of South Beach.

One of the best American films of recent years shines a spotlight on a community often overlooked in Miami. *Moonlight,* ostensibly a coming-of-age tale, shows what it's like to grow up poor, black and gay in a Miami housing project. It's a beautifully shot film, intensely personal and full of beauty and complexity (drug dealers as father figures, close friends as betrayers). It garnered much critical praise after its 2016 release, winning three Oscars including the 2017 Oscar for Best Picture.

Fashion

With Miami a trendsetter in the realm of cuisine, nightlife and the arts, it makes sense that the city would gain acclaim in the world of fashion. And it has, with the annual Miami Fashion Week drawing attention from across the globe. These days the focus is on resort wear, which fits well with the city's aesthetic – since Miami is a beach-loving kind of city. The week long event leans heavily toward Latin American designers, representing both well-known brands and up-and-coming labels.

Miami has also gained cred among European designers (ironically ever since one of them, Gianni Versace, was killed here) and draws mavens from all over the Old World who find something inspiring in the combination of a Latin emphasis on appearance versus the American love of comfort and the dare-to-bare styles inspired by the sunny weather. Today Miami is the base city for Perry Ellis International.

So what defines the 'Miami look'? On the one hand, you'll see a desperate desire for brand-name cred, of Louis Vuitton–endowed affirmation. But on the flip side is the understated sense of cool that comes from all that heat, exemplified by a casual dressiness the best-looking Miamians accomplish without any apparent effort. Note, for example, the older Cuban man lounging in his *guayabera,* an elegant but simple brocaded men's shirt; he's classy because he's looking good without seeming to try.

There is a distinctive South Beach style and there's no better place to buy it than at the source, but be warned: you must be bold, unabashed and bikini-waxed to pull off some of the more risqué outfits on display.

Two of the best film festivals in Florida are the Miami International Film Festival (www. miamifilmfestival. com), which is a showcase for Latin cinema (March), and the up-and-coming Florida Film Festival (www. floridafilmfestival. com) in Orlando (April).

Environment

Naturalist Marjory Stoneman Douglas called Florida 'a long pointed spoon' that is as 'familiar as the map of North America itself.' On that map, the shapely Floridian peninsula represents one of the most ecologically diverse regions in the world. A confluence of porous rock and subtropical climate gave rise to a watery world of uncommon abundance and lush beauty, but this unique ecosystem could be undone by human hands in the geological blink of an eye.

The Land

Above Everglades National Park (p146)

Florida is many things, but elevated it is not. This state is as flat as a pancake, or as Douglas says, like a spoon of freshwater resting delicately in a bowl of saltwater – a spongy brick of limestone hugged by the Atlantic Ocean and the Gulf of Mexico. The highest point, the Panhandle's Britton Hill, has to stretch to reach 350ft, which isn't half as tall as the buildings of Downtown Miami. This makes Florida officially the nation's flattest state, despite being 22nd in total area with 58,560 sq miles.

However, more than 4000 of those square miles are water; lakes and springs pepper the map like bullet holes in a road sign. To the south is Lake Okeechobee, the 9th largest freshwater lake in North America. This sounds impressive, but the bottom of the lake is only a few feet above sea level, and it's so shallow you can practically wade across.

Every year Lake Okeechobee ever so gently floods the southern tip of the peninsula. Or it wants to; canals divert much of the flow to either irrigation fields or Florida's bracketing major bodies of water – the Gulf of Mexico and the Atlantic Ocean. But were the water to follow the natural lay of the land, it would flow down: from its center, the state of Florida inclines about 6in every 6 miles until the peninsula can't keep its head above water anymore. What was an unelevated plane peters out into the 10,000 Islands and the Florida Keys, which end with a flourish in the Gulf of Mexico. Key West, the last in the chain, is the southernmost point in the continental USA.

Incidentally, when the waters of Okeechobee do flood the South Florida plane, they interact with the local grasslands and limestone to create a wilderness unlike any other: the Everglades. They also fill up the freshwater aquifers that are required to maintain human existence in the ever-urbanizing Miami area. Today numerous plans, which seem to fall prey to numerous private interest and public bureaucratic roadblocks, are discussed for restoring the original flow of water from Central to South Florida, an act that would revitalize the Glades and, to some degree, address the water supply needs of Greater Miami.

What really sets Florida apart, though, is that it occupies a subtropical transition zone between northern temperate and southern tropical climates. This is key to the coast's florid coral-reef system, the largest in North America, and the key to Florida's attention-getting collection of surreal swamps, botanical oddities and monstrous

The Everglades once stretched over some 11,000 square miles, but today the wetlands are less than half the size they were a century ago.

ENVIRONMENT THE LAND

KEEPERS OF THE EVERGLADES

Anyone who has dipped a paddle among the saw grass and hardwood hammocks of Everglades National Park wouldn't quibble with the American alligator's Florida sobriquet, 'Keepers of the Everglades.' With snout, eyeballs and pebbled back so still they hardly ripple the water's surface, alligators have watched over the Glades for more than 200 million years.

It's impossible to count Florida's wild alligators, but estimates are that 1.5 million lumber among the state's lakes, rivers and golf courses. No longer officially endangered, they remain protected because they resemble the still-endangered American crocodile. Alligator served in restaurants typically comes from licensed alligator farms, though since 1988 Florida has conducted an annual alligator harvest, open to nonresidents, that allows two alligators per person.

Alligators are alpha predators that keep the rest of the food chain in check, and their 'gator holes' become vital water cups in the dry season and during droughts, aiding the entire wetlands ecosystem. Alligators, which live for about 30 years, can grow up to 14ft long and weigh 1000lb.

A vocal courtship begins in April, and mating takes place in May and June. By late June, females begin laying nests of 30 to 45 eggs, which incubate for two months before hatching. On average, only four alligators per nest survive to adulthood.

Alligators hunt in water, often close to shore; typically, they run on land to flee, not to chase. In Florida an estimated 15 to 20 nonfatal attacks on humans occur each year, and there have been 22 fatal attacks since 1948.

Some estimate an alligator's top short-distance land speed at 30mph, but it's a myth that you must zigzag to avoid them. The best advice is to run in a straight line as fast as your little legs can go.

critters. The Everglades gets the most press, and as an International Biosphere, World Heritage Site and national park, this 'river of grass' deserves it.

But the Keys are a crucially important, vital and unique treasure as well. To explore these islands is to enter genuine jungle while still technically within the Lower 48 (admittedly, as low as you can get in that Lower 48). The teal and blue waterways that separate the Keys are as fascinating as the islands themselves; here the water gets so shallow that you can sometimes wade from key to key. Couple this shallow shelf with the rich sunlight of South Florida and you get one of the world's most productive aquatic biomes.

Wildlife

Get outside Miami's concrete jungle and you'd be forgiven for thinking you'd entered a real one. Alligators prowl the swamps, the USA's only crocodiles nest in the Keys, birds that resemble pteranodons flap over it all, and underneath rolls that gentle giant, the manatee.

Birds

Audubon of Florida (www.fl.audubon.org) is perhaps Florida's leading conservation organization. It has tons of birding and ecological information, and it publishes *Florida Naturalist* magazine.

Nearly 500 avian species have been documented in Florida, including some of the world's most magnificent migratory water birds: ibis, egrets, great blue herons, white pelicans and whooping cranes. .

Nearly 350 species spend time in the Everglades, the prime birding spot in Florida. In fact, much of the initial attention to conservation that first popped up here was related to the illegal poaching of Everglades' wading birds; the beautiful beasts were being killed so their plumage could decorate fashionable women's hats in the early 20th century.

Songbirds and raptors fill Florida skies, too. The state has over 1000 mated pairs of bald eagles, the most in the southern USA, and peregrine falcons, who can dive up to 150mph, migrate through in spring and fall.

The Everglades aren't the only place to bird-watch around here. Completed in 2006, the Great Florida Birding Trail (http://floridabirdingtrail.com) runs 2000 miles across the entire state and includes nearly 500 bird-watching sites, including many South Florida stops outside the Glades. Other good spots for birding in the region:

➡ Oleta River State Park (p68)

➡ Arch Creek Park (p92)

➡ Haulover Beach Park (p69)

➡ Bill Baggs Cape Florida State Park (p89)

➡ Crandon Park (p91)

➡ Indian Key Historic State Park (p174)

➡ Lignumvitae Key State Botanical Site (p174)

➡ Curry Hammock State Park (p176)

➡ Crane Point Museum (p177)

➡ Bahia Honda State Park (p181)

We'd be remiss not mention the Laura Quinn Wild Bird Sanctuary (p171) in the Upper Keys, where injured birds are nursed back to health by a lovely team of volunteers. Guests are welcome to walk the paths that meander past the hurt bird life.

Land Mammals

Florida's most endangered mammal is the Florida panther. Before European contact, perhaps 1500 roamed the state. The first panther bounty ($5 a scalp) was passed in 1832, and over the next 130 years

STEVE BOWER/SHUTTERSTOCK ©

Great Blue Heron

they were hunted relentlessly. Though hunting was stopped in 1958, it was too late for panthers to survive on their own. Without a captive breeding program, begun in 1991, the Florida panther would now be extinct and with only some 120 known to exist, they're not out of the swamp yet.

The biggest killers of the panthers are motor vehicles. Every year a handful – sometimes more – of panthers are killed on the road; pay particular attention to speed limits posted in areas like the Tamiami Trail, which cuts through Everglades National Park and the Big Cypress Preserve.

Easy to find, white-tailed deer are a common species that troubles landscaping. Endemic to the Keys are Key deer, a Honey-I-Shrunk-the-Ungulate subspecies: less than 3ft tall and lighter than a 10-year-old boy, they live mostly on Big Pine Key.

Although they are ostensibly native to the American West, the adaptable coyote has been spotted across Florida, appearing as far south as the Florida Keys.

Shy, timid and not to be messed with if encountered, there are several hundred specimens of the Florida black bear in Everglades National Park and the Big Cypress Preserve.

Reptiles & Amphibians

Boasting an estimated 184 species, Florida has the nation's largest collection of reptiles and amphibians, and unfortunately, it's growing. No, we're not antireptile, but invasive scaly species are wreaking havoc with Florida's delicate, native ecosystem. Uninvited guests add to the total regularly, many establishing themselves after being released by pet owners. Some of the more dangerous, problematic and invasive

Green Reads

The Swamp, Michael Grunwald

Losing It All to Sprawl, Bill Belleville

Zoo Story, Thomas French

Green Empire, Kathryn Ziewitz and June Wiaz

Manatee Insanity, Craig Pittman

species include Burmese pythons, black and green iguanas, and Nile monitor lizards.

The American alligator is Florida's poster species, and they are ubiquitous in Central and South Florida. They don't pose much of a threat to humans unless you do something irredeemably stupid, like feed or provoke them. With that said, you may want to keep small children and pets away from unfamiliar inland bodies of water.

South Florida is also home to the only North American population of American crocodile. Florida's crocs number around 1500; they prefer saltwater, and to distinguish them from gators, check their smile – a croc's snout is more tapered and its teeth stick out.

Turtles, frogs and snakes love Florida, and nothing is cuter than watching bright skinks, lizards and anoles skittering over porches and sidewalks. Cute doesn't always describe the state's 44 species of snakes – though Floridian promoters emphasize that only six species are poisonous, and only four of those are common. Feel better? Of the baddies, three are rattlesnakes (diamondback, pygmy, canebrake), plus copperheads, cottonmouths and coral snakes. The diamondback is the biggest (up to 7ft), most aggressive and most dangerous. But rest assured, while cottonmouths live in and around water, most Florida water snakes are not cottonmouths. Whew!

If you're not daunted by the prospect of playing with some of South Florida's scaliest citizens, head to the delightful Skunk Ape Research Headquarters (p151) in the Everglades. The zoo out back has to be one of the finest amateur reptile collections anywhere, and you may just spot the eponymous Skunk Ape, the American South's version of Bigfoot/Yeti.

Sea Turtles

Most sea-turtle nesting in the continental USA occurs in Florida. Predominantly three species create over 80,000 nests annually, mostly on southern Atlantic Coast beaches but extending to all Gulf Coast beaches. Most are loggerhead, followed by far fewer green and leatherback, and historically hawksbill and Kemp's ridley as well; all five species are endangered or threatened. The leatherback is the largest, attaining 10ft and 2000lb.

During the May-to-October nesting season, sea turtles deposit 80 to 120 eggs in each nest. The eggs incubate for about two months, and then the hatchlings emerge all at once and make for the ocean. Contrary to myth, hatchlings don't need the moon to find their way to the sea. However, they can become hopelessly confused by artificial lights and noisy human audiences. For the best, least-disruptive experience, join a sanctioned turtle watch; for a list, visit www.myfwc.com/seaturtle, then click on 'Educational Information' and 'Where to View Sea Turtles.'

The Keys contain its very own Turtle Hospital (p178), a sanctuary for sick and injured gentle shelled giants. They're keen on visitors, so if you're rolling through Marathon, drop by.

Naturalist Doug Alderson helped create the Big Bend Paddling Trail, and in *Waters Less Traveled* (2005) he describes his adventures: dodging pygmy rattlesnakes, meeting Shitty Bill, discussing Kemp's ridley turtles and pondering manatee farts.

Marine Mammals

Florida's coastal waters are home to 21 species of dolphins and whales. By far the most common is the bottlenose dolphin, which is highly social, extremely intelligent and frequently encountered around the entire peninsula. Bottlenose dolphins are the species most often seen in captivity.

Winter is also the season for manatees, who seek out Florida's warm-water springs and power-plant discharge canals beginning in November. These lovable, lumbering creatures are another iconic Florida species whose conservation both galvanizes and divides state residents.

FLORIDA'S MANATEES

It's hard to believe Florida's West Indian manatees were ever mistaken for mermaids, but it's easy to see their attraction: these gentle, curious, colossal mammals are as sweetly lovable as 10ft, 1000lb teddy bears. Solitary and playful, they have been known to 'surf' waves, and every winter, from November to March, they migrate into the warmer waters of Florida's freshwater estuaries, rivers and springs. Like humans, manatees will die if trapped in 62°F water for 24 hours, and in winter Florida's eternally 72°F springs are balmy spas.

Florida residents for over 45 million years, these shy herbivores have absolutely no defenses except their size (they can reach 13ft and 3000lb), and they don't do much, spending most of each day resting and eating the equivalent of 10% of their body weight. Rarely moving faster than a languid saunter, manatees even reproduce slowly; females birth one calf every two to five years. The exception to their docility? Mating. Males are notorious for their aggressive sex drive.

Florida's manatees have been under some form of protection since 1893, and they were included in the first federal endangered species list in 1967. Manatees were once hunted for their meat, but today collisions with boats are a leading cause of manatee death, accounting for over 20% annually. Propeller scars are so ubiquitous among the living that they are the chief identifying tool of scientists.

Manatees also face other environmental dangers. In 2013 a bloom of red tide algae in southwest Florida, as well as illnesses, caused the death of more than 800 manatees. All the same, there has been good news in terms for the manatee population, with consistent growth in recent years. Over 6600 were counted in aerial suveys in 2017, compared to 6250 in 2016 and 6063 the year before. Owing to these encouraging figures, in 2017 the US Fish and Wildlife Service removed the manatee from the endangered list, downgrading it to 'threatened' status.

Plants

The diversity of the peninsula's flora, including more than 4000 species of plants, is unmatched in the continental USA. Florida, especially South Florida, contains the southern extent of temperate ecosystems and the northern extent of tropical ones, which blend and merge in a bewildering, fluid taxonomy of environments. Interestingly, most of the world at this latitude is a desert, which Florida most definitely is not.

Wetlands & Swamps

It takes special kinds of plants to thrive in the humid, waterlogged and sometimes salty marshes, sloughs, swales, seeps, basins, marl prairies and swamps of Florida. Much of the Everglades is dominated by vast expanses of saw grass, which is actually a sedge with fine toothlike edges that can reach 10ft high. South Florida is a symphony of sedges, grasses and rushes. These hardy, water-tolerant species provide abundant seeds to feed birds and animals; they also protect fish in shallow water; and pad out wetlands for birds and alligators.

The strangest plants are the submerged and immersed species that grow in, under and out of the water. Free-floating species include bladderwort and coontail, a species that lives, flowers and is pollinated entirely underwater. Florida's swamps are abundant with rooted plants with floating leaves, such as the pretty American lotus, water lilies and spatterdock (if you love names, you'll love Florida botany). Another common immersed plant, bur marigold, can paint whole prairies yellow.

A dramatic, beautiful tree in Florida's swamps is the bald cypress, which is the most flood-tolerant tree. It can grow 150ft tall, with buttressed trunks and roots with 'knees' that poke above the drenched soil.

GHOST HUNTERS

Florida has more species of orchids than any other state in the USA, and orchids are themselves the largest family of flowering plants in the world, with perhaps 25,000 species. When it comes to botanical fascination, orchids rate highly, and the Florida species that inspires the most intense devotion is the extremely rare ghost orchid.

This bizarre epiphytic flower has no leaves and usually only one bloom, which is of course deathly white with two long thin drooping petals that curl like a handlebar moustache. The ghost orchid is pollinated by the giant sphinx moth in the dead of night. This moth is the only insect with a proboscis long enough to reach down the ghost orchid's 5in-long nectar spur.

The exact locations of ghost orchids are usually kept secret for fear of poachers, who, as Susan Orlean's book *The Orchid Thief* made clear, are a real threat to their survival. But the flower's general whereabouts are common knowledge: South Florida's approximately 2000 ghost orchids are almost all in Big Cypress National Preserve and Fakahatchee Strand Preserve State Park. Of course, these parks are home to a great many other wild orchids, as is Everglades National Park.

To learn more, visit Florida's Native Orchids (www.flnativeorchids.com) and Ghost Orchid (www.ghostorchid.info).

Forests, Scrubs & Flatwoods

The forests of the mainland, such as they are, are mainly found in the Everglades, where small changes in elevation and substrate are the difference between prairie and massive 'domes' of bald cypress and towering pine trees. Cypress domes are a particular kind of swamp when a watery depression occurs in a pine flatwood.

In Florida even the plants bite: the Panhandle has the most species of carnivorous plants in the USA, the result of its nutrient-poor sandy soil.

Scrubs are found throughout Florida; they are typically old dunes with well-drained sandy soil. Scrubs often blend into sandy pine flatwoods, which typically have a sparse longleaf or slash-pine overstory, and an understory of grasses and/or saw palmetto. Saw palmetto is a vital Florida plant: its fruit is an important food for bears and deer (and a herbal medicine that's believed to help prevent cancer), it provides shelter for panthers and snakes, and its flower is an important source of honey. It's named for its sharp saw-toothed leaf stems.

Formed by the interplay of tides, coral and mangroves, the Florida Keys contain the best (and in many cases, only) examples of tropical and subtropical hardwood 'hammock,' or forest, in the continental USA. The Crane Point Museum is an excellent starting point for learning about this extremely niche ecosystem.

Mangroves & Coastal Dunes

Where not shaved smooth by sand, South Florida's coastline is often covered with a three-day stubble of mangroves. Mangroves are not a single species; the name refers to all tropical trees and shrubs that have adapted to loose wet soil, saltwater and periodic root submergence. Mangroves also feature 'live birth,' germinating their seeds while they're still attached to the parent tree. Of the more than 50 species of mangroves worldwide, only three predominate in Florida: red, black and white.

Mangroves play a vital role on the peninsula, and their destruction usually sets off a domino effect of ecological damage. Mangroves stabilize coastal land, trapping sand, silt and sediment. As this builds up, new land is created, which ironically strangles the mangroves themselves. Mangroves also mitigate the storm surge and damaging winds of hurricanes, and they anchor tidal and estuary communities, providing vital wildlife habitats.

Coastal dunes are typically home to grasses and shrubs, saw palmetto and occasionally pines and cabbage palm (or sabal palm, the Florida state tree). Sea oats, with large plumes that trap wind-blown sand, are important for stabilizing dunes, while coastal hammocks welcome the wiggly gumbo-limbo tree, whose red peeling bark has earned it the nickname of 'tourist tree' for its resemblance to sunburned visitors.

National, State & Regional Parks

About 26% of Florida's land lies in public hands, which breaks down to three national forests, 11 national parks, 28 national wildlife refuges (including the first, Pelican Island) and 160 state parks. Overall attendance is up, with more than 20 million folks visiting state parks annually. Florida's state parks have twice been voted the nation's best.

Florida's parks are easy to explore. The Florida Fish & Wildlife Commission (http://myfwc.com) manages Florida's mostly undeveloped Wildlife Management Areas (WMAs). The website is an excellent resource for wildlife-viewing, as well as boating, hunting, fishing and permits.

Florida State Parks (www.floridastateparks.org)
National Forests, Florida (www.fs.usda.gov/florida)
National Park Service (www.nps.gov)
National Wildlife Refuges, Florida (www.fws.gov/refuges/refuge locatormaps/florida.html)
Recreation.Gov (www.recreation.gov) National lands campground reservations.

Environmental Issues

Florida's environmental problems are the inevitable result of its century-long love affair with land development, population growth and tourism, and addressing them is especially urgent given Florida's uniquely diverse natural world. These complex, intertwined environmental impacts include erosion of wetlands, depletion of the aquifer, rampant pollution (particularly of waters), invasive species, endangered species and widespread habitat destruction. There is nary an acre of Florida that escapes concern.

Since the turn of the century, Florida has enacted several conservation efforts. In 2000 the state passed the *Florida Forever Act* (www.supportfloridaforever.org), a 10-year, $3 billion conservation program. Unfortunately, by 2014 its budget of $300 million per year had been slashed by more than 95%. It also passed the multibillion-dollar Comprehensive Everglades Restoration Plan (CERP; www.evergladesrestoration.gov).

Despite the political struggles, there has been some signs of progress. For instance, phosphorous levels in the Everglades have been seriously reduced, and in 2010 the state completed a purchase of 300 sq miles of Lake Okeechobee sugarcane fields from US Sugar, intending to convert them back to swamp. Along with plans to bridge 6.5 miles of the Tamiami Trail, the lake may once again water the Glades, rather than sit as a stagnant pool of contaminated algae and bacteria.

Studies have found that half the state's lakes and waterways are too polluted for fishing. Though industrial pollution has been curtailed, pollution from residential development (sewage and fertilizer runoff) more than compensates. This is distressing Florida's freshwater springs, which can turn murky with algae. Plus, as the groundwater gets pumped out to slake homeowners' thirsts, the springs are shrinking and the drying limestone honeycomb underfoot sometimes collapses, causing sinkholes that swallow cars and homes. In 2014, 15 Florida cities made a

The Florida chapter of the Nature Conservancy (www.nature.org) has been instrumental in the Florida Forever legislation. Check the web for updates and conservation issues.

ENVIRONMENT NATIONAL, STATE & REGIONAL PARKS

A KINDER, GENTLER WILDERNESS ENCOUNTER

While yesterday's swamp-buggy rides and alligator wrestling have evolved into today's glass-bottom boats and manatee encounters, the question remains: just because you *can* do something, does it mean you *should?* In Florida, everyone has an obligation to consider the best ways to experience nature without harming it in the process.

For most activities, there isn't a single right answer; specific effects are often debated. However, there *are* a few clear guidelines.

Airboats and swamp buggies While airboats have a much lighter 'footprint' than big-wheeled buggies, both are motorized (and loud) and have far larger impacts than canoes for exploring wetlands. As a rule, nonmotorized activities are the least damaging.

Dolphin encounters When encountering wild dolphins in the ocean, federal law makes it illegal to feed, pursue or touch them. Habituating any wild animal to humans can lead to the animal's death, since approaching humans often leads to conflicts and accidents (with boats). As far as attending dolphin shows and interacting (swimming) with these intelligent mammals, we don't recommend them. Dolphins never appreciate captivity.

Manatee swims When swimming near manatees, a federally protected endangered species, look but don't touch. 'Passive observation' is the standard. Harassment is a rampant problem that may lead to stricter 'no touch' legislation.

Feeding wild animals In a word, don't. Kind animals like deer and manatees may come to rely on human food (to their detriment), while feeding bears and alligators just encourages them to hunt you.

Sea-turtle nesting sites It's a federal crime to approach nesting sea turtles or hatchling runs. Most nesting beaches have warning signs and a nighttime 'lights out' policy. If you encounter turtles on the beach, keep your distance and no flash photos.

Coral-reef etiquette Never touch the coral reef. It's that simple. Coral polyps are living organisms. Touching or breaking coral creates openings for infection and disease.

'Clean Water Declaration' and began a campaign of both preventing and cleaning polluted water.

Residential development continues almost unabated. The Miami–Fort Lauderdale–West Palm Beach corridor (the USA's sixth-largest urban area) is, as developers say, 'built out.' Every day Miami and Homestead's urban (and in the case of Homestead, agricultural) footprint grows deeper into the west, on the edge of the Everglades. While conservation laws protect the national park itself, the runoff and by-products of such a huge urban area inevitably has its impact in the incredibly fragile Glades.

Then there's the coming apocalypse: rising seas due to global warming. Here, the low-lying Florida Keys are a 'canary in a coalmine' that's being watched worldwide for impacts. In another century, some quip, South Florida's coastline could be a modern-day Atlantis, with its most expensive real estate underwater.

On the subject of real estate, the Keys happen to be governed by a labyrinthine set of zoning regulations. Getting permission to build on the land that remains is an arduous process, although many Keys law firms are solely dedicated to navigating this paper trail; as such, the Keys are not immune to overdevelopment, but are also better protected than much of the rest of Florida.

Nature Guides

The Living Gulf Coast, Charles Sobczak

Priceless Florida, Ellie Whitney, D Bruce Means and Anne Rudloe

Art-Deco Architecture

Art deco embodies the essence of South Beach. This distinctive style emerged in the 1930s to celebrate the onward march into the future, with bold lines and striking iconography referencing automobiles, cruise ships and futuristic rocket ships. Architects subtly blended characteristics from Miami's unique scenery: lapping waves, palm trees and curving seashells. While today this district is well protected, the whole neighborhood would have been leveled in the 1970s if not for the few preservationists who fought to keep it intact.

Deco, Design & Dreams

The early-20th-century school of design was the aesthetic backbone of old South Beach, and the driving force of its 1980s resurrection. A sustained campaign to preserve the wonderful deco hotels of Miami Beach provided what tons of tourism brochures could never create: brand. Sun, sand and surf: a lot of cities can lay claim to them, but only Miami Beach blended them with this pastel architectural heritage.

The end of WWI in 1918 ushered in an era of increased interest in the romance and glamour of travel, which lasted well into the 1930s. There was a giddy fascination with speed and cars, ocean liners, trains and planes. Not coincidentally, the US postindustrial revolution, concerned with mass production, kicked into high gear. New materials such as aluminum, polished bronze and stainless steel were utilized in new and exciting ways. Americans began looking to the future, and they wanted to be on the cutting edge.

Meanwhile in Europe, at a 1925 Paris design fair officially called the *Exposition Internationale des Arts Décoratifs et Industriels Modernes* (and eventually abbreviated to Arts Deco), decorative arts were highlighted, but the USA had nothing to contribute. Europeans were experimenting with repeating patterns in Cubism and were influenced by ancient cultures (King Tut's tomb was discovered in 1921), and Americans had to play catch-up.

Back in the USA, a mere year later, a devastating hurricane blew through Miami Beach, leaving few buildings standing. The wealthy folks who were living here before the hurricane chose to decamp. The second blow of a one-two punch for Miami's economy was delivered by the Great Depression. But in this dark time, opportunity soon came knocking. In Miami real estate, everything was up for grabs. The clean slate of the South Florida coastline was practically begging for experimentation.

Hotel rebuilding began in Miami Beach at the rate of about 100 per year during the 1930s. Many architects had 40 to 50 buildings in production at any one time until the inception of WWII. This overlapped with a surge in middle-class tourism between 1936 and 1941, when visitors started coming for a month at a time.

The post-Depression era was an optimistic period, with hopes and dreams pinned on scientific and technological revolutions. Reverence for machines took on almost spiritual dimensions, and found its aesthetic expression in both symbolic and functional ways.

The deco district is bordered by Dade Blvd to the north, 6th St to the south, the Atlantic Ocean to the east and Lenox Ave to the west. The 1-sq-mile district feels like a small village, albeit one with freaks, geeks and the gorgeous. Which is pretty cool.

One of life's little ironies is this: deco was supposed to make its contemporary viewers contemplate tomorrow. Today it puts modern viewers in mind of yesterday.

What does all this have to do with architecture? Everything. The principles of efficiency and streamlining translated into mass-produced, modest buildings without superfluous ornamentation – at least in the Northeast USA.

Romance, Relief & Rhythms

Miami Beach, a more romantic and glamorous resort, developed what came to be known as tropical deco architecture. It organically reflected the natural world around it. For example, glass architectural blocks let bright Florida light in but kept sweltering heat out. They also served a geometric or cubist aesthetic. Floral reliefs, popular during the art nouveau period, appeared here too. Friezes on facades or etched into glass reflected native flora and fauna, such as palm trees, pelicans and flamingos. Friezes also took their cues from the uniquely American jazz movement, harmonious and lyrical. Surrounded by water, Miami Beach deco also developed a rhythmic language, with scalloped waves and fountains.

Creating a Miami Look

Whereas Northeast deco buildings had industrial, socialist overtones, the clean lines of Miami Beach architecture still made room for joyful, playful, hopeful characteristics. Forward thinking and dreaming about the future took hold. Space travel was explored through design: buildings began to loosely resemble rockets, and rooflines embodied fantasies about traveling the universe. Geometric and abstract zigzag (or ziggurat) patterns not only reflected Aztec and Egyptian cultures, but also symbolized lightning bolts of electricity. Sun rays – more imagery borrowed from an ancient culture – were employed as life-affirming elements to counter the dark days of the Depression.

Since all hotels were built on the same sized lots, South Beach architects began distinguishing themselves from their next-door neighbors through decorative finials and parapets. Neon signage also helped individualize buildings. Miami Beach deco relied on 'stepped-back' facades that disrupted the harsh, flat light and contributed to the rhythmic feel. Cantilevered 'eyebrows' jutted out above windows to protect interiors from unrelenting sun. Canopy porches gave hotel patrons a cool place to sit. To reflect the heat, buildings were originally painted white, with animated accent colors highlighting smaller elements. It was only later, during the 1980s, that interior designer Leonard Horowitz created the pastel palette that became the standard.

With the effects of the Depression lingering, ornamentation was limited to the facades; interiors were stripped down. Labor was cheap and readily available.

Miami Beach needed a large number of rooms, most of which ended up being built small. With no expectation that they would remain standing this long, most hotels were built with inexpensive concrete and mortar that had too much sand in it. Stucco exteriors prevailed, but locally quarried native keystone (an indigenous limestone) was also used. Except for the keystone, none of this would withstand the test of time with grace, which is one reason the district fell into such a state of disrepair and neglect. It's also why the district remains under a constant state of renovation.

Restoring the Deco District

South Beach's heart is its Art Deco Historic District, one of the largest in the USA on the National Register of Historic Places. In fact the area's rejuvenation and rebirth as a major tourist destination results directly from its protection as a historic place in 1979. The National Register designation prevents developers from razing significant portions of what

With more than 400 registered historic landmarks, you can follow the Beach boom phases through the district: in the 1930s 5th St to Mid-Beach was developed. Head toward 27th St for the late '30s to early '40s; then north into the '50s, the era of resorts, hotels and condominiums.

Although art deco was inspired by stripped-down modernist aesthetics, it partly rebelled against utilitarianism with fantastically embellished bas-relief and frieze work, noticeable on the exterior of many South Beach hotels.

was, in the 1980s, a crime-ridden collection of crumbling eyesores populated primarily by criminals and society's dispossessed – the elderly, the mentally ill and the destitute. It's a far cry from that now. Today hotel and apartment facades are decidedly colorful, with pastel architectural details. Depending on your perspective, the bright buildings catapult you back to the Roaring Twenties or on a wacky tour of American kitsch.

The National Register listing was fought for and pushed through by the Miami Design Preservation League (MDPL), founded by Barbara Baer Capitman in 1976. She was appalled when she heard of plans by the city of Miami to bulldoze several historic buildings in what is now the Omni Center. And she acted, forcefully.

MDPL cofounder Leonard Horowitz played a pivotal role in putting South Beach back on the map, painting the then-drab deco buildings in shocking pink, lavender and turquoise (his color palette inspired by sunrise, sunsets, the changing hues of the sea and the play of light on the landscape). When his restoration of Friedman's Pharmacy made the cover of *Progressive Architecture* in 1982, the would-be Hollywood producers of *Miami Vice* saw something they liked, and the rest is history.

One of the best things about the 1000 or so buildings in the district is their scale: most are no taller than the palm trees. And while the architecture is not uniform – you'll see Streamline Moderne, Mediterranean Revival and tropical art-deco designs – it's all quite harmonious.

Interestingly, the value of these Miami Beach deco buildings is based more on the sheer number of structures with protected status from the National Register of Historic Places. Individually, these inexpensively constructed houses would be worth far less.

Deco Daydreams

So what, you may ask, is the big deal about art deco? The term certainly gets thrown around enough in Miami. Given the way this architectural style is whispered about by hotel marketing types, you'd be forgiven for thinking art deco was the pièce de résistance: 'Well, the resort has a lovely deco facade'; 'Our boutique properties incorporate deco porches'; 'Did you notice the deco columns in our lounge?' And so on.

But to be fair, deco has been a sort of renaissance for Miami Beach. It was art deco that made these buildings unique and that caught the eye of Hollywood, which saw something romantically American in the optimism and innovation of a style that blends cubism, futurism, modernism and, most of all, a sense of movement. Beyond that was a nod to, and sometimes even reverence for, the elaborate embellishment of Old World decor. In art deco, we see the link between the lavish design aesthetic of the 19th century and the stripped-down efficiency of the 20th. Unlike a skyscraper, a deco hotel is modern yet accessible, even friendly, with its frescoed walls and shady window eyebrows.

But what's truly great about deco Miami is the example it sets. The Art Deco Historic District of South Beach, one of the hottest tourist destinations in the country, is a reminder to city fathers that preserving historic neighborhoods is not just a matter of slavish loyalty to aesthetics, but sometimes the economically practical and innovative way forward. In a city built on fast real estate, it's a bit delicious that the heart of the sexiest neighborhood is the child of preservation and smart planning.

Post-Deco, Miami Modern & Beyond

The tale of Miami architecture is defined by more than deco. As in all cities, Miami's architecture reflects the tastes and attitudes of its inhabitants, who tend to adhere to the aesthetic philosophy espoused by Miami Beach's favorite architect, Morris Lapidus: 'Too much is never enough.' The earliest examples of this homegrown over-embellishment are the

---

ART-DECO ARCHITECTURE DECO DAYDREAMS

Miami Beach cross streets are determined by building number. Two zeroes after the first number means the building is at the base of the block. So 700 Ocean Dr is at 7th St and Ocean, while 1420 Ocean Dr is at 14th St & Ocean.

Italians were the first hired to create the terrazzo floors that are so popular in Florida. They'd pour various colors of terrazzo – crushed stones, shells, marble chips or granite, mixed with concrete – into a patterned grid and then polish it. This remarkable marriage of form and function also cools the feet.

THE CONCH CASTLES OF KEY WEST

• •

Miami this, Miami that; yes, the flashy overstatement of the Magic City's architecture sure is beautiful. But what about Key West? Plenty of gorgeous historical buildings are packed into an easily walkable space and happen to be located on one of the prettiest islands in America. What are we waiting for?

Traditional Keys homes are known as 'Conch houses' for the conch shell that was used as a building material to supplement the traditionally low amounts of stone and wood; today the nickname also references Keys natives, known as Conchs. Conch houses are perhaps the finest example of Caribbean colonial architecture in the USA outside New Orleans. They're elegant, recognizably European homes, and while no two dwellings are identical, there are some commonalities. Shuttered windows, wraparound verandahs, sloped roofs and structures built on raised piers are all elements that maximized shade and airflow in an era that preceded air-conditioning.

Many Conch houses had fallen into a state of total disrepair in the early 20th century, but as in South Beach, a community of artists, gays and lesbians established themselves here, refurbished the neighborhood and saved a bit of American heritage, all the while giving Key West the distinctive aesthetic profile that adds so much to its tourism appeal. You can see plenty of Conch houses in the Key West historic district (the west end of the island); to see a particularly fine assortment in a small space, walk the four blocks along Eaton St from Eaton and William to Eaton and Whitehead.

Mediterranean-Revival mansions of Coral Gables and the Fabergé egg fantasy of the Vizcaya. These residential wedding cakes established Miami's identity as a city of fantasies and dreams, outside the boundaries of conventional tastes, where experimentation was smiled upon as long as it was done with flashiness. They also spoke to a distinct Miami attitude that is enshrined in city tastes to this day: if you've got it, flaunt it, then shove it back in their faces for a second serving.

This penchant for imaginative, decorative flair overlaid the muscular postwar hotels and condos of the 1950s, giving birth to Miami Modernism (MiMo). MiMo drew off the sleek lines and powerful presence of International Modernism, but led by Lapidus, it also eschewed austerity for grand, theatrical staging. Lapidus himself described his most famous structure, the Fontainebleau, as influenced by the most popular mass media of its time: Hollywood and cinema. The glamour Lapidus captured in his buildings would go on to define Miami's aesthetic outlook; Versace incorporated it into his clothes and Ian Schrager has decked out his hotels with this sense of fairy-tale possibility. Which makes sense: the word 'glamour' originally meant a kind of spell that causes people to see things differently from how they really are, which makes it an appropriate inspiration for the buildings of the 'Magic City.'

There are excellent deco renovations all along Miami Beach that manage to combine modern aesthetic tastes with classical deco details. But in a sense, the modern South Beach school of design is just the natural evolution of principles laid down by deco in the 1930s. Hoteliers such as Ian Schrager combine a faith in technology – in this case flat-screen TVs, Lucite 'ghost chairs' and computer-controlled lobby displays – with a general air of fantastical glamour. Conceptions of the future (a fantasy of the best the future can be), plus a deep bow to the best of historical decorative arts, still drives the design on Miami Beach. Newer hotels like 1 Hotel South Beach and the W have also expanded the architectural sense of proportion, integrating deco features into the massive proportions of MiMo (Miami Modern) style. Whereas in the past deco hotels occupied a lot on a block, the megahotels of Miami Beach's future now stretch for an entire block.

The deco movement came about in the early 20th century, when affordable travel became a reality for many. Sea journeys represented the height of luxury, and many deco buildings are decorated with nautical porthole windows.

GLOWIMAGES/GETTY IMAGES ©

Art-Deco Miami

South Beach may be known for celebrity spotting, but the area's original cachet owes less to paparazzi and more to preservation. The art-deco design movement, the architectural and aesthetic backbone of SoBe, is powerfully distinctive and finds expression in soft lines, bright pastels and the integration of neon into structural facades.

Contents

Above: Detail of a carved art-deco wall, Miami

MAISANT LUDOVIC/HEMIS.FR/GETTY IMAGES ©

1. Cardozo Hotel **2.** Lifeguard hut **3.** Essex House Hotel

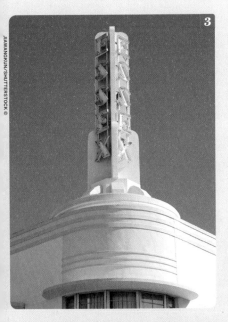

JIAWANGKUN/SHUTTERSTOCK ©

Classical Deco South Beach Structures

In the past, South Beach architects distinguished themselves through decorative finials, parapets and neon signage. Miami Beach deco relies on 'stepped-back' facades to disrupt the harsh, flat Florida light. Cantilevered 'eyebrows' jut out above windows to protect interiors from the sun.

Cardozo Hotel (p95)

This lovely building and the Carlyle Hotel were the first buildings rescued by the original Miami Beach preservation league when developers threatened to raze South Beach's deco buildings in the 1980s. With its two hubcap-like emblems on the upper facade and its sleek curves, the Cardozo has been compared to the 1937 Studebaker. Owned by Gloria Estefan.

Essex House Hotel (p107)

Porthole windows lend the feel of a grand cruise ship, while its spire looks like a rocket ship, recalling deco's roots as an aesthetic complement to modernism and industrialism. Beautiful terrazzo floors also cool the lobby.

Deco lifeguard stations on South Beach (p63)

Besides being cubist-inspired exemplars of the classical deco movement, with their sharp, pleasing geometric lines, these stations are painted in dazzling colors. Found all along the beach from 1st to 17th Sts.

Post Office (p59)

This striking building has a round facade and a lighthouse-like cupola. Above the door is the characteristic deco stripe of glass blocks. Step inside for a glimpse of geometrically laid-out post boxes (painted gold) and a fantastical ceiling with an elaborate sunlike deco light fixture orbited by stars.

Deco Elements & Embellishments

As individualized as South Beach's buildings are, they share quirks and construction strategies. Canopy porches provide cool places to sit. To reflect heat, buildings were originally painted white (and later in pastels) with accent colors highlighting smaller elements. Some hotels resemble Mesoamerican temples; others evoke cruise liners.

Room Mate Waldorf Towers (p102)

Deco guru L Murray Dixon designed the tower of this hotel to resemble a lighthouse, surely meant to shine the way home for drunken Ocean Dr revelers.

Colony Hotel

The oldest deco hotel (Map p66; 736 Ocean Dr) in Miami Beach; it was the first hotel in Miami, and perhaps America, to incorporate its sign (a zigzaggy neon wonder) as part of its overall design. Inside the lobby are excellent examples of space-age interiors, including Saturn-shaped lamps and Flash Gordon elevators.

1. Cavalier Hotel **2.** Crescent Resort **3.** Room Mate Waldorf Towers

Cavalier South Beach (p102)

This hotel makes clever allusions to nautical themes. The word 'cavalier,' which is a kind of horseman, is actually a play on 'seahorse,' examples of which are depicted in somewhat stylized forms on the facade. The tropical theme continues with palm trees, whose trunks (again as figurative designs) run down both sides of the facade.

Wolfsonian-FIU (p58)

The museum's lobby contains a phenomenally theatrical example of a 'frozen fountain.' The gold-leaf fountain, formerly gracing a movie-theater lobby, shoots vertically up and flows symmetrically downward.

Crescent Resort

Besides having one of Miami Beach's most recognizable neon facades, the Crescent's (Map p61; 1420 Ocean Dr) signage attracts the eye down into its lobby (the better to pack guests in), rather than up to its roof.

Avalon Hotel

Quirky Deco Delights

Tropical deco is mainly concerned with stimulating the imagination. Painted accents lifted from archaeology sites might make a passer-by think of travel, maybe on a cruise ship. And hey, isn't it funny that the windows resemble portholes? Almost all of the preserved buildings here still inspire this childlike sense of wonder.

Winter Haven Hotel (p108)

Outside, you'll note shade-providing 'eyebrows,' and striking geometry, with an elegant zigzag of windows creating a vertical stripe down the center of the facade. Inside, check out the wild light fixtures that evoke futuristic elements (inspired perhaps by Fritz Lang's 1927 sci-fi film *Metropolis*).

Avalon Hotel

The exterior of the Avalon (Map p66; ☏800-933-3306, 305-538-0133; www.avalon-hotel.com; 700 Ocean Dr; r $200-340; ❄️🛜) is a fantastic example of classic art-deco architecture – clean lines and old-school signage lit up by tropical-green deco, all fronted by a vintage 1950s Oldsmobile.

11th Street Diner (p113)

It doesn't get much more deco than dining in a classic Pullman train car. Many buildings on Miami Beach evoke planes, trains and automobiles – this diner is actually located in one.

Survival Guide

Directory A–Z

Accommodations

South Florida has an excellent range of accommodation options. Booking in advance for hot spots (such as Miami and Key West) is essential in high season.

Hotels You'll find simple but well-equipped accommodation as well as high-end oceanfront digs with amenities galore.

Hostels Basic dorm-style lodging, but some have bars and courtyards.

Camping There are some lovely spots in the Everglades and in the Keys, though you'll have to reserve well ahead.

B&Bs & Inns

B&Bs and inns vary from small, comfy houses with shared bathrooms (the least expensive) to romantic, antique-filled historic homes and opulent mansions with private baths (the most expensive).

➡ Accommodations focusing on upscale romance may discourage children.

➡ Inns and B&Bs often require a minimum stay of two or more days during high season, and sometimes more during major holidays and events.

➡ Advance reservations are pretty much mandatory. Always call ahead to confirm policies (regarding kids, pets, smoking etc) and bathroom arrangements.

Booking Services

Everglades National Park Camping www.nps.gov/ever/planyourvisit/camping.htm

Florida Bed & Breakfast Inns www.florida-inns.com

Florida State Parks Camping www.floridastateparks.org/stay thenight/camping.cfm

Greater Miami & the Beaches www.miamiandbeaches.com/where-to-stay

Key West Innkeepers Association www.keywestinns.com

Lonely Planet (www/lonelyplanet.com/usa/south-florida-the-keys/hotels)

Camping & Holiday Parks

Three types of campgrounds are available: undeveloped ($10 per night), public ($25) and privately owned ($30 and up). In general, Florida campgrounds are quite safe. Undeveloped campgrounds are just that, while most public campgrounds have toilets, showers and drinking water.

➡ Reserve state-park campgrounds by calling ☑800-326-3521 or visiting www.reserveamerica.com.

➡ Most privately owned campgrounds are geared to RVs (motor homes) but will also have a small section available for tent campers. Expect tons of amenities.

➡ Kampgrounds of America (www.koa.com) is a network of private campgrounds; its Kamping Kabins have air-con and kitchens. Many KOA sites offer wi-fi.

Hostels

➡ In most hostels, group dorms are mixed, though there's usually a females-only dorm room as well; alcohol is sometimes banned.

➡ Only a small percentage of South Florida hostels are affiliated with Hostelling International USA (www.hiusa.org). At these, you don't have to be a member to stay, but you will pay a slightly higher rate. You can join HI by phone, online or at most youth hostels.

➡ Florida has many independent hostels (www.hostels.com); most have comparable rates and conditions to HI hostels, and some are better.

Hotels

South Florida is rich in independent accommodation options, but in some towns, such as Homestead, chain hotels are the best (and sometimes the only) option. If you're looking to spend less than $100 a night on a room in Miami, chain hotels are a decent choice.

The calling-card of chain hotels is reliability: acceptable cleanliness, unremarkable yet inoffensive decor, and a comfortable bed. A TV, phone, air-conditioning, minirefrigerator, microwave, hair dryer and safe are standard amenities in midrange chains. A developing trend, most evident in Miami, is chain-owned hotels striving for upscale boutique-style uniqueness in decor and design. At these hotels you'll often find rooms that aren't much different to the higher-range chains, although the external amenities will probably be lacking.

High-end hotels overwhelm guests with services. You'll find plenty of boutique and specialty hotels in places like South Beach and Key West. While all large chain hotels have toll-free reservation numbers, you may find better savings by calling the hotel directly.

Chain-owned hotels include the following:

Hilton (www.hilton.com)

Holiday Inn (www.holidayinn.com)

Marriott (www.marriott.com)

Radisson (www.radisson.com)

Ritz-Carlton (www.ritzcarlton.com)

Sheraton (www.starwoodhotels.com/sheraton)

Customs Regulations

For a complete, up-to-date list of customs regulations, visit the website of US Customs & Border Protection (www.cbp.gov). Each visitor is allowed to bring into the USA duty-free 1L of liquor (if you're aged 21 years or older) and 200 cigarettes (if you're 18 or older) and up to $100 in gifts and purchases.

Electricity

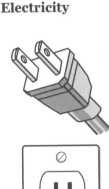

Type A
120V/60Hz

Type B
120V/60Hz

Embassies & Consulates

To find a US embassy in another country, visit the US Department of State website (www.usembassy.gov). Most foreign embassies in the USA have their main consulates in Washington, DC, but the following have representation in Miami, except Italy, which is in Coral Gables.

Brazilian Consulate (☎305-285-6200; http://miami.itamaraty.gov.br/en-us; 3150 SW 38th Ave, 1st fl; ⊗visa applications 2-3:30pm Mon-Fri)

Canadian Consulate (☎305-579-1600; www.can-am.gc.ca/miami/menu.aspx; 200 S Biscayne Blvd, Ste 1600)

French Consulate (☎305-403-4150; www.consulfrance-miami.org; 1395 Brickell Ave, Ste 1050)

German Consulate (☎305-358-0290; www.germany.info; 100 N Biscayne Blvd, Ste 2200)

Italian Consulate (☎305-374-6322; www.consmiami.esteri.it/Consolato_Miami; 4000 Ponce de Leon Blvd, Ste 590, Coral Gables; ⊗9am-12:30pm Mon-Wed & Fri, plus 3-5pm Wed)

Mexican Consulate (☎786-268-4900; http://consulmex.sre.gob.mx/miami; 1399 SW 1st Ave)

Netherlands Consulate (☑786-866-0480; www.netherlandsworldwide.nl; 701 Brickell Ave, Ste 500)

UK Consulate (☑305-400-6400; http://ukinusa.fco.gov.uk/florida; 1001 Brickell Bay Dr, Ste 2800)

Food & Drink

For more on the South Florida food scene and essential advice, check out Eat Like a Local (p38) and Tipping (p246).

Health

Florida, and the USA generally, has a high level of hygiene, so infectious diseases are not generally a significant concern for most travelers.

➡ Vaccines are not required and tap water is safe to drink.

➡ Despite Florida's plethora of intimidating wildlife, the main concerns for travelers are sunburn and mosquito bites.

➡ Ensure you have adequate health insurance in case of accidents. If you experience a major medical emergency in the Everglades, the chances are you will end up in Miami.

➡ Most of the major islands in the Keys, including Marathon, Islamorada and Key Largo, have emergency medical facilities.

Before You Go
HEALTH INSURANCE

The USA offers possibly the finest level of health care in the world. The problem is

that it can be prohibitively expensive. If you're not a US citizen, it's essential to purchase travel-health insurance if your domestic policy doesn't cover you when you're abroad.

➡ If your health insurance does not cover you for medical expenses abroad, consider obtaining supplemental health or travel insurance.

➡ Find out in advance whether your insurance plan will make payments directly to the providers or if it will reimburse you later for any overseas health expenditures. We have to stress: **a simple visit to the doctor's office can cost hundreds of dollars, and a hospital stay will cost thousands** if you aren't covered by insurance.

MEDICATIONS

➡ Bring any medications you may need in their original containers, clearly labeled.

➡ A signed, dated letter from your physician that describes all of your medical conditions and medications (including generic names) is also a good idea.

➡ Pharmacies are abundantly supplied. However, some medications that are available over the counter in other countries require a prescription in the USA.

➡ If you don't have insurance to cover the cost of prescriptions (and sometimes even if you do), these can be shockingly expensive.

WEBSITES

There is a vast wealth of travel health advice on the internet. Two good sources:

MD Travel Health (www.mdtravelhealth.com) Provides complete, updated and free travel-health recommendations for every country.

World Health Organization (www.who.int/ith) The superb book *International Travel and Health* is available free online.

Also, consult your government's travel-health website before departure, if one is available:

Australia (www.smartraveller.gov.au)

Canada (www.hc-sc.gc.ca/index-eng.php)

UK (www.fco.gov.uk/en/travel-and-living-abroad)

USA (wwwnc.cdc.gov/travel)

AVAILABILITY & COST OF HEALTH CARE

➡ If you have a medical emergency, go to the emergency room of the nearest hospital.

➡ If you need any kind of emergency assistance, such as police, ambulance or firefighters, call ☑911. This is a free call from any phone.

➡ If the problem isn't urgent, call a nearby hospital and ask for a referral to a local physician; this is usually cheaper than a trip to the emergency room.

➡ Stand-alone, for-profit urgent-care centers provide good service, but can be the most expensive option.

INFECTIOUS DISEASES

In addition to more common ailments, there are several infectious diseases to be aware of. Most are acquired by mosquito or tick bites.

Zika Miami made the news in 2016 for having an outbreak of this mosquito-borne illness. There were over 260 locally acquired cases in South Florida. Zika is of gravest concern to pregnant women, as the disease can cause microcephaly (when

---

EATING PRICE RANGES

Price indicators in reviews apply to the typical dinner main course (in Miami, you can raise this range by around $5 for each budget level):

$ less than $15

$$ $15–25

$$$ more than $25

the brain does not develop fully) and lead to serious birth defects in unborn children.

Giardiasis Also known as traveler's diarrhea. A parasitic infection of the small intestines, typically contracted by drinking feces-contaminated freshwater. Never drink untreated stream, lake or pond water. Easily treated with antibiotics.

HIV/AIDS As do all sexually transmitted diseases, HIV infection occurs in the USA. Use a condom for all sexual encounters.

Lyme Disease Though more common in the US northeast than in Florida, Lyme disease occurs here. It is transmitted by infected deer ticks, and is signaled by a bull's-eye rash at the bite and flulike symptoms. Treat promptly with antibiotics. Removing ticks within 36 hours can avoid infection.

Rabies Though rare, the rabies virus can be contracted from the bite of any infected animal; bats are most common, and their bites are not always obvious. If bitten by any animal, consult with a doctor, since rabies is fatal if untreated.

West Nile Virus Extremely rare in Florida, West Nile virus is transmitted by culex mosquitoes. Most infections are mild or asymptomatic, but serious symptoms and even death can occur. There is no treatment for West Nile virus. For the latest update on affected areas, see the US Geological Survey disease maps (http://disease maps. usgs.gov).

ENVIRONMENTAL HAZARDS

Florida's critters can be cute, but they can also bite and sting. Here are a few to watch out for:

Alligators and snakes Neither attacks humans unless startled or threatened. If you encounter them, simply back away. Florida has several venomous snakes; immediately seek treatment if bitten.

Jellyfish and stingrays Florida beaches can see both; avoid

swimming when they're present (lifeguards often post warnings). Treat stings immediately; they hurt but aren't dangerous.

Spiders Florida is home to two dangerously venomous spiders – the black widow and the brown recluse. Seek immediate treatment if bitten by any spider.

TAP WATER

Tap water is safe to drink throughout South Florida.

Insurance

It's expensive to get sick, crash a car or have things stolen from you in the USA. Make sure to have adequate coverage before arriving.

To insure yourself for items that may be stolen from your car, consult your homeowner's (or renter's) insurance policy or consider investing in travel insurance.

Worldwide travel insurance is available at www. lonelyplanet.com/travel-insurance. You can buy, extend and claim online anytime – even if you're already on the road.

Internet Access

Nearly every hotel and many restaurants and cafes offer high-speed internet access. The vast majority of places provide free wi-fi, though some pricier hotels still charge a premium for wi-fi.

You can also find wi-fi in some transportation stations in city parks, and of course at a public library (many of which also have terminals, if you lack a laptop or smartphone).

If you bring a laptop/phone from outside the USA, invest in a universal AC and plug adapter.

Legal Matters

If you are stopped by the police, there is no system for paying traffic tickets or other fines on the spot. The patrol

officer will explain your options to you; there is usually a 30-day period to pay fines by mail.

If you're arrested, you are allowed to remain silent, though never walk away from an officer.

You are entitled to have access to an attorney. The legal system presumes you're innocent until proven guilty.

All persons who are arrested have the right to make one phone call. If you don't have a lawyer or family member to help you, call your embassy or consulate. The police will give you the number on request.

LGBTQI

Miami, the Keys and Key West are out areas, where homosexuality is practiced openly year-round. Events such as the White Party and Fantasy Fest are major dates in the North American gay calendar. Smaller towns in the Everglades region are more culturally conservative, but gay travelers won't cause much of a stir. In Miami the gay scene is so integrated it can be difficult to separate it from the straight one; popular hot spots include South Beach, North Beach, and Wynwood and the Design District.

Damron (https://damron. com) Damron, an expert in LGBT travel, offers a searchable database of LGBTQI-friendly and specific travel listings. Publishes popular national guidebooks, including *Women's Traveller*, *Men's Travel Guide* and *Damron Accommodations*.

Gay Key West (www.gaykey westfl.com) Clearing house for information on LGBTQI topics in Key West.

Gay Yellow Network (www.glyp. com) City-based yellow-page listings include six Florida cities.

Miami-Dade Gay & Lesbian Chamber of Commerce (www. gogaymiami.com) Gay businesses and travel tips.

Out Traveler (www.outtraveler. com) Travel magazine specializing in gay travel.

Purple Roofs (www.purpleroofs. com) Lists queer accommodations, travel agencies and tours worldwide.

Money

Exchange foreign currency at international airports and most large banks in Miami.

There is ease and availability of ATMs. Most ATM withdrawals using out-of-state cards incur surcharges of $3 or so.

Major credit cards are widely accepted, and they are required for car rentals.

ATMs have largely negated the need for traveler's checks. However, traveler's checks in US dollars are accepted like cash at most midrange and top-end businesses (but rarely at budget places).

Taxes & Refunds

As elsewhere in the USA, tax isn't included in the posted price. You'll have to factor in an extra 7% or 8% (which varies between municipalities) when shopping, ordering food at a restaurant, purchasing concert tickets and booking tours. Groceries are exempt from this tax.

There are higher taxes for overnight lodging, with hotels charging an extra 10% to 13%.

Tipping

Tipping is *not* optional in America; only withhold tips in cases of outrageously bad service.

Restaurant servers Normal service 15%, good service 18%, great service 20%

Bartenders $1 per drink, $2 or more for complicated cocktails

Cafe baristas Some change in the jar

Taxis Tip 10-15%

Hairdressers Tip 10-15%

Airport & hotel porters $1 per bag

Hotel maids A few dollars after a few nights

Opening Hours

Unless otherwise noted standard business hours are as follows:

Banks 8:30am–4:30pm Monday to Thursday, to 5:30pm Friday; sometimes 9am–12:30pm Saturday

Bars In Miami, most bars 5pm–3am; in Miami Beach, most bars close at 5am; in Key West 5pm–4am, elsewhere 5pm–2am. In all places, some bars close earlier if business is slow.

Businesses 9am–7pm Monday to Friday

Eating Breakfast 7am–10:30am Monday to Friday; brunch 9am–2pm Saturday and Sunday; lunch 11:30am–2:30pm Monday to Friday; dinner 5pm–10pm, later Friday and Saturday

Post offices 9am–5pm Monday to Friday; sometimes 9am–noon Saturday

Shopping 10am–6pm Monday to Saturday, noon–5pm Sunday; shopping malls keep extended hours

Post

The US Postal Service (www.usps.com) is reliable and inexpensive. For 1st-class mail sent and delivered within the USA, postage rates are 49¢ for letters up to 1oz (21¢ for each additional ounce) and 34¢ for standard-size postcards. International airmail rates for postcards and letters up to 1oz are 98¢.

Public Holidays

On the following national public holidays, banks, schools and government offices (including post offices) are closed, and transportation, museums and other services operate on a Sunday schedule. Many stores, however, maintain regular business hours. Holidays falling on a weekend are usually observed the following Monday.

New Year's Day January 1

Martin Luther King Jr Day Third Monday in January

Presidents Day Third Monday in February

Memorial Day Last Monday in May

Independence Day July 4

Labor Day First Monday in September

Columbus Day Second Monday in October

Veterans Day November 11

Thanksgiving Fourth Thursday in November

Christmas Day December 25

Safe Travel

➡ Parts of Miami proper, including Little Haiti and nightlife hot spots such as Overtown (just north of Downtown), experience high crime rates. Be careful in these areas, and avoid hanging out too much in Downtown after dark.

➡ Crime is on the rise in South Beach, particularly along the carnival-like mayhem of Ocean Dr between 8th and 11th Sts.

➡ Drunk driving is a big problem all around South Florida. Be particularly vigilant when traveling late in the evening, especially on weekends.

➡ Be mindful of swimming conditions in the ocean: rip currents and jellyfish (particularly the man o' war) can sometimes be present.

Hurricanes

Florida hurricane season extends from June through November, but the peak is September and October. Relatively speaking, very few Atlantic Ocean and Gulf of Mexico storms become hurricanes, and fewer still are accurate enough to hit Florida, but the devastation they wreak when they do can be enormous. Travelers should take all hurricane alerts, warnings and evacuation orders seriously.

Hurricanes are generally sighted well in advance, allowing time to prepare. When a hurricane threatens, listen to radio and TV news reports.

Florida Division of Emergency Management (www.florida disaster.org) Hurricane preparedness.

Florida Emergency Hotline (800-342-3557) Updated storm-warning information.

Hurricane Hotline (305-468-5400)

National Weather Service (www.weather.gov)

Telephone

➡ Always dial '1' before toll-free (800, 888 etc) and domestic long-distance numbers. Some toll-free numbers only work within the US.

➡ For local directory assistance, dial 411.

➡ To make international calls from the USA, dial 011 + country code + area code + number. For international operator assistance, dial 0.

➡ To call the USA from abroad, the international country code for the USA is 1.

➡ Pay phones are a rarity even in major cities. Local calls cost 50¢.

➡ Private prepaid phone cards are available from convenience stores, supermarkets and pharmacies.

Cell Phones

Most of the USA's cell-phone systems are incompatible with the GSM 900/1800 standard used throughout Europe and Asia. Check with your service provider about using your phone in the USA.

In terms of coverage, Verizon has the most extensive network, but AT&T, Sprint and T-Mobile are decent. Cellular coverage is generally excellent, except in the Everglades and parts of rural northern Florida.

Time

South Florida is in the US eastern time zone (UTC/GMT minus four hours): noon in Miami equals 9am in San Francisco and 5pm in London. During daylight-saving time, clocks move forward one hour in March and move back one hour in November.

Toilets

You'll find public toilets at some parks and at various posts along city beaches. Outside of this, public toilets can be sparse. It's best to pop into a cafe, or if you're on the road, stop at a fuel station.

Tourist Information

There are plenty of chambers of commerce and visitor centers in the region itching to help you make the most of your trip and pass out veritable libraries of pamphlets and coupons.

To order a packet of Florida information before coming, contact Visit Florida (www.visitflorida.com).

Local Tourist Offices

MIAMI

Coconut Grove Chamber of Commerce (Map p86; 305-444-7270; www. coconutgrovechamber.com; 2701 S Bayshore Dr, Suite 300; 9am-5pm Mon-Fri)

Coral Gables Chamber of Commerce (Map p88; 305-446-1657; www.coralgableschamber. org; 224 Catalonia Ave; 9am-5pm Mon-Fri)

Downtown Miami Welcome Center (Map p72; 305-448-7488; www.downtownmiami. com; 100 NE 1st Ave; noon-5pm Mon, 10am-5pm Tue-Sat) Provides maps, brochures and tour information for the downtown area.

Greater Miami & the Beaches Convention & Visitors Bureau (Map p72; 305-539-3000; www.miamiandbeaches. com; 701 Brickell Ave, 27th fl; 8:30am-6pm Mon-Fri) Located in an oddly intimidating high-rise building.

Miami Beach Chamber of Commerce (Map p60; 786-276-2763, tourist hotline 305-674-1300; www. miamibeachguest.com; 1901 Convention Center Dr, Hall C; 10am-4pm)

THE EVERGLADES

Big Cypress Swamp Welcome Center (239-695-4758; www.nps.gov/bicy/planyour-visit/big-cypress-swamp-welcome-center.htm; 33000 Tamiami Trail E; 9am-4:30pm)

Ernest Coe Visitor Center (305-242-7700; www.nps. gov/ever; 40001 State Rd 9336;

GOVERNMENT TRAVEL ADVICE

Australia (www.smarttraveller.gov.au)

Canada (www.dfait-maeci.gc.ca)

Germany (www.auswaertiges-amt.de)

Japan (http://www.anzen.mofa.go.jp/)

New Zealand (www.safetravel.govt.nz)

UK (www.fco.gov.uk)

USA (http://travel.state.gov)

PRACTICALITIES

Newspapers South Florida has a number of major daily newspapers: *Miami Herald* (in Spanish, *El Nuevo Herald*), the *Miami New Times*, the *Key West Citizen* and the *South Dade News Leader* (www.southdadenews leader.com).

TV Florida receives all the major US TV and cable networks. Florida Smart (http://floridasmart.com/news) lists them all by region.

Weights & Measures Distances are measured in feet, yards and miles; weights in ounces, pounds and tons.

Smoking Florida bans smoking in all enclosed workplaces, including restaurants and shops, but excluding 'stand-alone' bars (that don't emphasize food) and designated hotel smoking rooms.

9am-5pm mid-Apr–mid-Dec, from 8am mid-Dec–mid-Apr)

Everglades Area Chamber of Commerce (☑239-695-3941; cnr US Hwy 41 & Hwy 29; ☺9am-4pm)

Homestead Chamber of Commerce (☑305-247-2332; www.southdadechamber.org; 455 N Flagler Ave, Homestead; ☺9am-5pm Mon-Fri)

Shark Valley Visitor Center (☑305-221-8776; www.nps. gov/ever/planyourvisit/svdirections.htm; national park entry per vehicle/bicycle/pedestrian $25/8/8; ☺9am-5pm)

THE KEYS

Islamorada Chamber of Commerce (☑305-664-4503; www. islamoradachamber.com; Mile 87 bayside; ☺9am-5pm Mon-Fri, to 4pm Sat, to 3pm Sun)

Key Largo Chamber of Commerce (☑305-451-1414, 800-822-1088; www.keylargo-chamber.org; Mile 106 bayside; ☺9am-6pm)

Key West Chamber of Commerce (Map p186;☑305-294-2587; www.keywestchamber. org; 510 Greene St; ☺9am-6pm)

Lower Keys Chamber of Commerce (☑305-872-2411; www. lowerkeyschamber.com; Mile 31 oceanside; ☺9am-5pm Mon-Fri, to 3pm Sat)

Marathon Visitors Center Chamber of Commerce

(☑305-743-5417, 800-262-7284; www.floridakeysmarathon.com; Mile 53.5 bayside; ☺9am-5pm)

Travellers with Disabilities

Because of the high number of senior residents in Florida, most public buildings are wheelchair accessible and have appropriate restroom facilities. Transportation services are generally accessible to all, and telephone companies provide relay operators for the hearing impaired. Many banks provide ATM instructions in Braille, curb ramps are common and many busy intersections have audible crossing signals.

Resources

There are a number of organizations that specialize in the needs of disabled travelers:

Access-Able Travel Source (www.access-able.com) An excellent website with many links.

Flying Wheels Travel (http://flyingwheelstravel.com)

Mobility International USA (www.miusa.org) Advises disabled travelers on mobility issues and runs an educational exchange program.

Download Lonely Planet's free Accessible Travel guide

from http://lptravel.to/AccessibleTravel.

Visas

All visitors should reconfirm entry requirements and visa guidelines before arriving. You can get visa information through www.usa.gov, but the US State Department (www.travel.state.gov) maintains the most comprehensive visa information, with lists of consulates and downloadable application forms. US Citizenship & Immigration Services (www.uscis.gov) mainly serves immigrants, not temporary visitors.

The Visa Waiver Program allows citizens of three dozen countries to enter the USA for stays of 90 days or less without first obtaining a US visa. See the ESTA website (https://esta.cbp.dhs.gov) for a current list. Under this program you must have a nonrefundable return ticket and 'e-passport' with digital chip.

Travelers entering under the Visa waiver program must register with the US government's ESTA program (https://esta.cbp.dhs.gov) at least three days before arriving; earlier is better, since if denied, travelers must get a visa. Registration is valid for two years

Visitors who don't qualify for the Visa Waiver Program need a visa. Basic requirements are a valid passport, recent photo, travel details and often proof of financial stability. Students and adult males also must fill out supplemental travel documents. The validity period for a US visitor visa depends on your home country. The length of time you'll be allowed to stay in the USA is determined by US officials at the port of entry.

To stay longer than the date stamped on your passport, visit a local USCIS (www.uscis.gov) office.

Volunteering

Volunteering can be a great way to break up a long trip, and it provides memorable opportunities to interact with locals and the land in ways you never would when just passing through. Animal sanctuaries and small parks are always on the lookout for short-term volunteer help.

Florida's state parks would not function without volunteers. Each park coordinates its own volunteers, and most also have the support of an all-volunteer 'friends' organization (officially called Citizen Support Organizations). Links and contact information are on the main state park website (www.floridastateparks.org/get-involved/volunteer).

Everglades National Park
(☑305-242-7700; www.nps.gov/ever; 40001 SR-9336, Homestead; vehicle pass $25; ⊙visitor center 9am-5pm; 🐾) Active volunteer program recruits both individuals and groups.

Florida Keys National Marine Sanctuary (☑305-809-4700; www.floridakeys.noaa.gov/volunteer_opportunities/welcome.html) Can hook folks up with a plethora of environment-focused volunteer programs across the Keys.

Miami Habitat for Humanity (www.miamihabitat.org) Does a ton of work in Florida, building homes and helping the homeless.

Shake a Leg Miami A community water-sports complex in Coconut Grove that aims to serve economically and physically disadvantaged children.

Volunteer Florida (www.volunteerflorida.org) The primary state-run organization; coordinates volunteer centers across the state. Though it's aimed at Floridians, casual visitors can find situations that match their time and interests.

Women Travellers

Women traveling by themselves or in a group should encounter no particular problems unique to Florida besides the usual drunken loutishness in Miami and Key West.

There are a number of excellent resources to help traveling women:

➡ Community website www.journeywoman.com facilitates women exchanging travel tips, with links to resources.

➡ The Canadian government (www.voyage.gc.ca) publishes the useful, free, online booklet 'Her Own Way'; look under 'Publications.' These two national advocacy groups might also be helpful:

National Organization for Women (www.now.org)

Planned Parenthood (www.plannedparenthood.org) Offers referrals to medical clinics throughout the country.

Women need to exhibit the same street smarts as any solo traveler, but they are sometimes more often the target of unwanted attention or harassment. Some women like to carry a whistle, mace or cayenne-pepper spray in case of assault. These sprays are legal to carry and use in Florida, but only in self-defense. Federal law prohibits them being carried on planes.

If you are assaulted, it may be better to call a rape-crisis hotline before calling the police (☑911); phone books have lists of local organizations, or contact the 24-hour National Sexual Assault Hotline on ☑800-656-4673 or visit www.rainn.org. Or go straight to a hospital. A rape-crisis center or hospital will advocate on behalf of survivors and can act as a link to other services, including the police, who may not be as sensitive when dealing with victims of assault.

Work

Seasonal service jobs in tourist beach towns and theme parks are common and often easy to get, if low-paying.

If you are a foreigner in the USA with a standard nonimmigrant visitors visa, you are forbidden to take paid work in the USA and will be deported if you're caught working illegally. In addition, employers are required to establish the bona fides of their employees or face fines. In particular, South Florida is notorious for large numbers of foreigners working illegally, and immigration officers are vigilant.

Resources

To work legally, foreigners need to apply for a work visa before leaving home. Student exchange visitors need a J1 visa, which the following organizations will help arrange:

➡ American Institute for Foreign Study (www.aifs.com)

➡ BUNAC (www.bunac.org)

➡ Camp America (www.campamerica.aifs.com)

➡ Council on International Educational Exchange (www.ciee.org)

➡ InterExchange (www.interexchange.org) Camp and au-pair programs

➡ International Exchange Programs (www.iep.org.au; www.iep.org.nz)

For nonstudent jobs, temporary or permanent, you need to be sponsored by a US employer (who will arrange an H-category visa). These aren't easy to obtain.

Transportation

GETTING THERE & AWAY

Nearly all international travelers come to South Florida by air, while most US travelers prefer air or car. Getting to South Florida by bus is a distant third option and by train an even more distant fourth. Miami is a major international airline hub, particularly for American Airlines, and it's the first port of call for many flights from Latin America and the Caribbean. Most flights come into Miami International Airport (MIA), although many are also directed to Fort Lauderdale–Hollywood International Airport (FLL). As it is located at the tip of the USA, Greater Miami is more of a termination of highways and rail lines, rather than a major land-transit interchange area.

Flights, cars and tours can be booked online at www.lonelyplanet.com/bookings.

Entering the Country

A passport is required for all foreign citizens. Unless eligible under the Visa Waiver Program (VWP), foreign travelers must also have a tourist visa (p248). To rent or drive a car, travelers from non-English-speaking countries should obtain an International Driving Permit before arriving.

Travelers entering under the Visa Waiver Program must register with the US government's ESTA program (https://esta.cbp.dhs.gov) at least three days before arriving; earlier is better, since if denied, travelers must get a visa. Registration is valid for two years.

Upon arriving in the USA, all foreign visitors must register with the Orwellian-sounding Office of Biometric Identity Management (OBIM), which entails having two index fingers scanned and a digital photo taken. For more information, see the Department of Homeland Security (www.dhs.gov/obim).

Air

Unless you live in or near Florida, flying to the region and then renting a car is the most time-efficient option.

Airports & Airlines

Miami International Airport (MIA; ☑305-876-7000; www.miami-airport.com; 2100 NW 42nd Ave) One of the state's busiest international airports. It serves metro Miami, the Everglades and the Keys, and is a hub for American and Delta.

Key West International Airport (EYW; ☑305-809-5200; www.eyw.com; 3491 S Roosevelt Blvd) A much quieter airport, located off S Roosevelt Blvd on the east side of the island.

Fort Lauderdale–Hollywood International Airport (FLL; ☑866-435-9355; www.broward.org/airport; 320 Terminal Dr) A viable gateway airport

CLIMATE CHANGE & TRAVEL

Every form of transport that relies on carbon-based fuel generates CO_2, the main cause of human-induced climate change. Modern travel is dependent on airplanes, which might use less fuel per kilometer per person than most cars but travel much greater distances. The altitude at which aircraft emit gases (including CO_2) and particles also contributes to their climate change impact. Many websites offer 'carbon calculators' that allow people to estimate the carbon emissions generated by their journey and, for those who wish to do so, to offset the impact of the greenhouse gases emitted with contributions to portfolios of climate-friendly initiatives throughout the world. Lonely Planet offsets the carbon footprint of all staff and author travel.

to the Florida region, located 21 miles north of Downtown Miami. Air service to Miami is frequent and direct. Flights come from all over the USA, Europe, Latin America and the Caribbean; Key West is served far less often, and often indirectly. A number of international airlines service South Florida.

Departure Tax

Departure tax is included in the price of a ticket.

Land

Bus

For bus trips, Greyhound (www.greyhound.com) is the main long-distance operator, but Megabus (https://us.megabus.com), which can transport you to Tampa and Orlando, is an increasingly viable option. Competition between the two services has helped drop the price of bus transportation. Greyhound serves Florida from most major American metropolitan areas. Greyhound also connects Miami to many major cities in Florida, but you won't be able to access smaller towns.

If you are traveling very long distances (say, across several states), bargain airfares can sometimes undercut buses. On shorter routes, renting a car can sometimes be cheaper. Nonetheless, discounted (even half-price) long-distance bus trips are often available by purchasing tickets online seven to 14 days in advance. Then, once in Florida, you can rent a car to get around. Inquire about multiday passes.

Car & Motorcycle

Driving to Florida is easy; there are no international borders or entry issues. Incorporating Florida into a larger USA road trip is very common, and having a car in Florida is often a necessity.

Sample distances and times from various points in the USA to Miami:

City	Road distance (miles)	Time (hr)
Atlanta	660	10½
Chicago	1380	23
Los Angeles	2750	44
NYC	1280	22
Washington, DC	1050	17

Train

If you're coming from the East Coast, Amtrak (www.amtrak.com) is a comfortable, affordable option for getting here. Amtrak's Silver Service (which includes Silver Meteor and Silver Star trains) runs between New York and Miami, with services that include major and small Florida towns in between. Unfortunately there is no longer any direct service to Florida from Los Angeles, New Orleans, Chicago or the Midwest. Trains from these destinations connect to the Silver Service route, but the transfer adds a day or so to your travel time.

Book tickets in advance. Children, seniors and military personnel receive discounts.

Sea

Florida is nearly completely surrounded by the ocean, and it's a major cruise-ship port. If you arrive in Miami via a cruise ship, you'll likely arrive via the **Port of Miami** (☑305-347-5515; www.miamidade.gov/portmiami), which receives around five million passengers each year. You can boat from Miami to the Keys on the **Key West Express** (☑239-463-5733; www.seakeywestexpress.com; 100 Grinnell St, Key West; adult/senior/junior/child round-trip $155/145/92/62, one way $95/95/68/31). It departs from Fort Myers Beach and Marco Island daily at 8:30am and does a 3½-hour cruise to Key West. Returning boats depart the seaport at 6pm. You'll want to show up 1½ hours before your boat departs. During winter and fall the *Express* also leaves from Marco Island.

GETTING AROUND

Air

The US airline industry is reliable and safe; and serves Florida extremely well. However, the industry's continuing financial troubles have resulted in a series of

---

BUS ROUTES

Sample one-way fares between Miami and some key US cities:

CITY	FARE ($)	TIME (HR)	DAILY
Atlanta	62-125	16-18	5-6
New Orleans	84-180	23-24	3-4
New York City	95-190	33-35	5-6
Washington, DC	95-190	27-29	5-6

TRAIN ROUTES

Sample one-way fares between Miami and some major cities:

FROM	TO	FARE ($)	TIME (HR)
Miami	New York	152-198	18-20
Miami	Orlando	46-98	5
Miami	Tampa	44-96	5

high-profile mergers: Midwest joining Frontier, Orlando-based Air Tran merging into Southwest and Continental merging with United.

In general, this has led to fewer flights, fuller airplanes, fewer perks, more fees and higher rates. Allow extra time for the USA's extensive airport security procedures.

Airlines in South Florida

Main domestic airlines operating in South Florida:

American (www.aa.com) Has a Miami hub and service to and between major Florida cities.

Delta (www.delta.com) International carrier to main Florida cities, plus flights from Miami to Orlando and Tampa.

Frontier (www.frontierairlines. com) Services Tampa, Orlando and Fort Lauderdale from Denver, Minneapolis and the Midwest.

Southwest (www.southwest. com) One of the US's leading low-cost carriers, offering free baggage and, at times, extremely low fares.

Spirit (www.spiritair.com) Florida-based discount carrier serving Florida cities from East Coast, USA, the Caribbean, and Central and South America.

United (www.united.com) International flights to Orlando and Miami; domestic flights to and between key Florida cities.

Air Passes

International travelers who plan on doing a lot of flying, both in and out of the region, might consider buying an air pass. Air passes are available only to non-US citizens, and they must be purchased in conjunction with an international ticket. Conditions and cost structures can be complicated, but all include a certain number of domestic flights (from three to 10) that must be used within 60 days. Sometimes you must plan your itinerary in advance, but sometimes dates (and even destinations) can be left open. Talk with a travel agent

to determine if an air pass would save you money based on your plans.

The two main airline alliances are the Star Alliance (www.staralliance.com) and One World (www.oneworld. com).

Bicycle

Regional bicycle touring is very popular. Flat topography, ocean breezes on the Overseas Hwy and increasing bicycle infrastructure in Miami and Miami Beach make for great itineraries. Just be wary of your surroundings, especially if you go cycling near the north of Downtown. A few blocks north of that area it is especially tense. You may want to target winter to spring; summer is unbearably hot and humid for long-distance cycling.

Renting a bicycle is easy in South Florida. Try the Everglades International Hostel if you want to cycle in the Glades. In Key West there's a plethora of options located on the main drags of Truman Ave and Simonton St; bicycle is probably the easiest way to get around flat Key West. The **Citi Bike** (☑305-532-9494; www.citibikemiami.com; 30min/1hr/2hr/4hr/1-day rental $4.50/6.50/10/18/24) bikeshare program is handy for quick jaunts. But for a fullday outing, these lumbering bikes (which don't come with locks or helmets) are not ideal. Luckily there are many traditional rental outfits in Miami and Miami Beach that offer quality bikes at competitive prices.

Some other things to keep in mind:

Helmet laws Helmets are required for anyone aged 16 and younger. Adults are not required to wear helmets, but should.

Road rules Bikes must obey road rules; ride on the right-hand side of the road, with traffic. It is legal to ride (respectfully of pedestrians) on sidewalks in Miami. Given the heavy, fast-moving

traffic on many roads (ie Biscayne Blvd), you'll want to!

Transporting your bike to Florida Bikes are considered checked luggage on airplanes, but often must be boxed and fees can be high (over $200).

Theft Bring and use a sturdy lock (U-type is best). Theft is common, especially in Miami Beach.

For more information and assistance, visit these organizations:

League of American Bicyclists (www.bikeleague.org) General advice, plus lists of local bike clubs and repair shops.

International Bicycle Fund (www.ibike.org) Advice plus a comprehensive overview of bike regulations by airline.

Better World Club (www. betterworldclub.com) Offers a bicycle roadside-assistance program.

Boat

Florida is a huge destination and departure point for cruises of all kind. The Port of Miami (www.miamidade. gov/portofmiami) likes to brag that it's the 'cruise capital of the world' with good reason: this is the largest cruise-ship port on Earth. Port Everglades (www. porteverglades.net, www. fort-lauderdale-cruises.com), near Fort Lauderdale, is also a potential gateway port to the Miami region.

For specials on other multinight and multiday cruises, see the following:

➡ www.cruise.com

➡ www.cruiseweb.com

➡ www.vacationstogo.com

➡ www.cruisesonly.com

Major cruise companies:

Carnival Cruise Lines (www. carnival.com)

Norwegian Cruise Line (www. ncl.com)

Royal Caribbean (www.royal caribbean.com)

Bus

Greyhound (www.greyhound.com) is the major carrier in and out of Miami. The main **Miami Greyhound terminal** (☑305-871-1810; 3801 NW 21st) is out by the airport. Other Greyhound stations near Miami include **North Miami terminal** (☑305-688-7277; 16000 NW 7th Ave) and the **Miami Cutler Bay terminal** (Cutler Bay; ☑305-296-9072; 10801 Caribbean Blvd). Megabus picks up from Miami International Airport.

Car & Motorcycle

Once you reach South Florida, traveling by car is the best way of getting around – it allows you to reach areas not otherwise served by public transportation.

While it's possible to avoid using a car on single-destination trips to Miami or Key West, relying on public transit is inconvenient for even limited regional touring. Motorcycles are also popular in Florida, given the flat roads and warm weather. In addition, motorized transport is practically a must to explore the Everglades. Greyhound buses run through the Keys, but you can't pull over and smell the roses by the side of the Overseas Hwy, which is 90% of the fun.

Roads are well kept and maintained.

Automobile Associations

The American Automobile Association (www.aaa.com) has reciprocal agreements with several international auto clubs (check with AAA and bring your membership card). For members, AAA offers travel insurance, tour bookings, diagnostic centers for used-car buyers and number of regional offices; it also advocates politically for the auto industry.

An ecofriendly alternative is the Better World Club (www.betterworldclub.com), which donates 1% of earnings to assist environmental cleanup, offers ecologically sensitive choices for services and advocates politically for environmental causes. Better World also has a roadside assistance program for bicycles.

In both organizations, the central member benefit is 24-hour emergency roadside assistance anywhere in the USA. Both clubs offer trip planning and free maps, travel agency services, car insurance and a range of discounts (car rentals, hotels etc).

Driver's License

Foreign visitors can legally drive in the USA for up to 12 months with their home driver's license. However, getting an International Driving Permit (IDP) is recommended; this will have more credibility with US traffic police, especially if your home license doesn't have a photo or is in a foreign language. Your automobile association at home can issue an IDP, valid for one year, for a small fee. You must carry your home license together with the IDP. To drive a motorcycle, you need either a valid US state motorcycle license or an IDP specially endorsed for motorcycles.

Rental

CAR

Car rental is very competitive. Most rental companies require that you have a major credit card, that you be at least 25 years old and that you have a valid driver's license (your home license will do but an IDP is recommended). Some national companies may rent to drivers between the ages of 21 and 24 for an additional charge. Those under 21 are usually not permitted to rent at all.

Car Rental Express (www.carrentalexpress.com) rates and compares independent agencies in US cities; it's particularly useful for searching out cheaper long-term rentals.

National car-rental companies include the following:

Alamo (www.alamo.com)

Avis (www.avis.com)

Budget (www.budget.com)

Dollar (www.dollar.com)

Enterprise (www.enterprise.com)

Hertz (www.hertz.com)

National (www.nationalcar.com)

Rent-a-Wreck (www.rentawreck.com)

Thrifty (www.thrifty.com)
Rental cars are readily available at all airport locations and many downtown city locations. With advance reservations for a small car, the daily rate with unlimited mileage can start as low as $25 a day, while typical weekly rates are $200 to $400, plus a myriad of taxes and fees. If you rent from a non-airport location, you save the exorbitant airport fees.

An alternative in Miami is Zipcar (www.zipcar.com), a car-sharing service that charges hourly/daily rental fees with free gas, insurance and limited mileage included; prepayment is required.

MOTORCYCLE

To straddle a Harley across Florida, contact EagleRider (www.eaglerider.com), which has offices in Miami. It offers a wide range of models, which start at $150 a day, plus liability insurance. Adult riders (over 21) are not required by Florida law to wear a helmet, but you should.

MOTORHOME (RV)

Forget hotels – drive your own. Touring Florida by recreational vehicle can be as low-key or as over-the-top as you wish.

After settling on the vehicle's size, consider the impact of gas prices, gas mileage, additional mileage costs, insurance and refundable deposits; these can add up quickly. Typically, RVs don't come with unlimited mileage, so estimate your mileage up front to calculate the true cost.

CruiseAmerica (www.cruiseamerica.com) The largest national RV-rental firm has offices across South Florida.

Adventures On Wheels (www.wheels9.com) Office in Miami.

Recreational Vehicle Rental Association (www.rvda.org) Good resource for RV information and advice, and helps find rental locations.

INSURANCE

➔ Insurance is legally required; if you don't have it, you risk financial ruin if there's an accident.

➔ If you already have auto insurance (even overseas), or if you buy travel insurance, make sure that the policy has adequate liability coverage for a rental car in Florida.

➔ Rental-car companies will provide liability insurance, but most charge extra. Always ask. Rental companies almost never include collision damage insurance for the vehicle. Instead, they offer optional Collision Damage Waiver (CDW) or Loss Damage Waiver (LDW), usually with an initial deductible of $100 to $500. For an extra premium, you can usually get this deductible covered.

➔ Most credit cards offer collision damage coverage for rental cars if you rent for 15 days or less and charge the total rental to your card. This is a good way to avoid paying extra fees to the rental company, but note that if there's an accident, you sometimes must pay the rental-car company first and then seek reimbursement from the credit card company. Check your credit card policy. Paying extra for some or all of this insurance increases the cost of a rental car by $10 to $30 a day.

ROAD RULES

If you're new to Florida or US roads, here are some basics:

➔ The maximum speed limit on interstates is 70mph, but that drops to 65mph and 55mph in urban areas. Pay attention to the posted signs. City street speed limits vary between 15mph and 45mph. It's 20mph in a school zone.

➔ Florida police officers are strict with speed-limit enforcement, and speeding tickets are expensive.

➔ All passengers in a car must wear seat belts; the fine for not wearing a seat belt is $30. All children under three must be in a child safety seat.

➔ As in the rest of the USA, drive on the right-hand side of the road. On highways, pass in the left-hand lane, but impatient drivers often pass wherever space allows.

➔ Unless otherwise signed, you can turn right at a red light as long as you come to a stop first. At four-way stop signs, the car that reaches the intersection first has right of way. In a tie, the car on the right has right of way.

➔ The maximum blood alcohol level while driving is 0.08%. For most people, having more than two drinks can put you over the limit.

Hitchhiking

Hitchhiking is never entirely safe in any country, and we don't recommend it. Travelers who hitch should understand that they are taking a small but serious risk. People who do choose to hitch will be safer if they go in pairs and let someone know where they are planning to go. Ask the driver where they are going rather than telling them where you want to go.

Local Transport

Bus

Miami has a reliable bus service as well as a Metromover (a monorail that operates only in downtown) and trains that provide service to

commuters. Getting between key neighborhoods (like Wynwood and South Beach) can be time-consuming on the limited bus routes operating. You'll find limited bus service in the Lower Keys; there's also a weekend bus service between Homestead and one part of the Everglades.

Taxi

Outside MIA, South Beach and the Port of Miami, where taxis buzz around like bees at a hive, you'll likely use a phone to hail a cab. Try **Metro** (☑305-888-8888), **Sunshine** (☑305-445-3333) or **Miami Yellow Cab** (☑305-400-0000) for a ride.

Taxis in Miami have flat and metered rates. You will not have to pay extra for luggage or for extra people in the cab, though you are expected to tip an additional 10% to 15%. Add about 10% to normal taxi fares (or a dollar, whichever is greater). If you have a bad experience, get the driver's chauffeur license number, name and license-plate number and contact the **Taxi Complaints Line** (☑305-375-2460).

In Key West, get a metered pink taxi from **Key West Taxis** (☑305-296-6666).

Ride Sharing

Ride sharing apps like Uber and Lyft are quite popular in Miami. Service is more limited down in the Keys.

Train

Amtrak (www.amtrak.com) trains run between a number of Florida cities. As a way to get around Florida, Amtrak offers extremely limited service, and yet for certain specific trips its trains can be very easy and inexpensive. Daily trains run between Jacksonville, Orlando and Miami, with one line branching off to Tampa. In addition, Amtrak Thruway motorcoach (or bus) service gets passengers to Daytona Beach, St Petersburg and Fort Myers.

Behind the Scenes

SEND US YOUR FEEDBACK

We love to hear from travelers – your comments keep us on our toes and help make our books better. Our well-traveled team reads every word on what you loved or loathed about this book. Although we cannot reply individually to your submissions, we always guarantee that your feedback goes straight to the appropriate authors, in time for the next edition. Each person who sends us information is thanked in the next edition – the most useful submissions are rewarded with a selection of digital PDF chapters.

Visit **lonelyplanet.com/contact** to submit your updates and suggestions or to ask for help. Our award-winning website also features inspirational travel stories, news and discussions.

Note: We may edit, reproduce and incorporate your comments in Lonely Planet products such as guidebooks, websites and digital products, so let us know if you don't want your comments reproduced or your name acknowledged. For a copy of our privacy policy visit lonelyplanet.com/privacy.

WRITER THANKS

Regis St Louis

Countless people helped along the way, and I'm grateful to national park guides, lodging hosts, restaurant servers, barkeeps and baristas who shared tips and insight throughout South Florida. Big thanks to Adam Karlin who did such an outstanding job on previous editions. I'd also like to thank Cassandra and our daughters, Magdalena and Genevieve, who made the Miami trip all the more worthwhile.

ACKNOWLEDGEMENTS

Climate map data adapted from Peel MC, Finlayson BL & McMahon TA (2007) 'Updated World Map of the Köppen-Geiger Climate Classification', Hydrology and Earth System Sciences, 11, 163344.

Cover photograph: Lifeguard tower on South Beach, Miami; Alexander Demyanenko/Shutterstock ©

THIS BOOK

This 8th edition of Lonely Planet's *Miami & the Keys* guidebook was researched and written by Regis St Louis. The previous two editions were written by Adam Karlin. This guidebook was produced by the following:

Destination Editors Trisha Ping, Lauren Keith

Product Editors Jessica Ryan, Catherine Naghten

Senior Cartographers Corey Hutchison, Alison Lyall

Book Designer Gwen Cotter

Assisting Editors Judith Bamber, Imogen Bannister, Pete Cruttenden, Melanie Dankel, Anita Isalska, Rosie Nicholson, Kristin Odijik

Cover Researcher Marika Mercer

Thanks to Ronan Abayawickrema, William Allen, Tom Heywood, Sandie Kestell, Lauren O'Connell, Ellie Simpson, Angela Tinson, Tony Wheeler

Index

MARKO MAMULA